Standing Trial

The Islamic Mediterranean

Programme Chair Robert Ilbert
Series Editor Randi Deguilhem

Published and forthcoming

1. Writing the Feminine: Women in Arab Sources
   Edited by Manuela Marín and Randi Deguilhem

2. Money, Land and Trade: An Economic History of the Muslim Mediterranean
   Edited by Nelly Hanna

3. Outside In: On the Margins of the Modern Middle East
   Edited by Eugene Rogan

4. Crafts and Craftsmen of the Middle East: Fashioning the Individual in the Muslim Mediterranean
   Edited by Suraiya Faroghi, Sadok Boubaker and Randi Deguilhem

5. Constituting Modernity: Private Property in the East and West
   Edited by Huri İslamoğlu

6. Standing Trial: Law and the Person in the Modern Middle East
   Edited by Baudouin Dupret

7. Shattering Tradition: Custom, Law and the Individual in the Muslim Mediterranean
   Edited by Walter Dostal and Wolfgang Kraus

STANDING TRIAL

Law and the Person in the Modern Middle East

Edited by

Baudouin Dupret

I.B.TAURIS
LONDON · NEW YORK

Published in 2004 by I.B.Tauris & Co Ltd
6 Salem Road, London W2 4BU
175 Fifth Avenue, New York NY 10010
Website: http://www.ibtauris.com
in association with The European Science Foundation, Strasbourg, France

ISBN 1 86064 997 1
EAN 978 1 86064 997 4

A full CIP record for this book is available from the British Library
A full CIP record for this book is available from the Library of Congress
Library of Congress catalog card: available

Typeset in Baskerville by Dexter Haven Associates Ltd, London

Contents

Contributors vii

Introduction 1
Baudouin Dupret

Part One: General Considerations on the Person and the Law

1 The Person and the Law: Contingency, Individuation and the Subject of the Law 9
Baudouin Dupret

2 The Articulation of 'I', 'We' and the 'Person': Elements for an Anthropological Approach within Western and Islamic Contexts 39
Mohamed Nachi

3 A Ghost in the Machine: Against the Use of the Notion of 'Person' in Sociology 66
Jean-Noël Ferrié

Part Two: Persons in Legal Settings

4 Justice, Law and Pain in Khedival Egypt 85
Khaled Fahmy

5 The 'Implosion' of *Sharî'a* within the Emergence of Public Normativity: The Impact on Personal Responsibility and the Impersonality of Law 116
Armando Salvatore

6 The Misbehaviour of the Possessed: On Spirits, Morality and the Person 140
Barbara Drieskens

7 The Person and Justice in a Tunisian Souq: A Reflection upon the Linkages between Justice, Impartiality and Respect for the Person 170
Mohamed Nachi

8 Intention in Action: A Pragmatic Approach to Criminal Characterisation in an Egyptian Context 196
Baudouin Dupret

Part Three: Legal Figures of the Person

9 The Notion of 'Person' between Law and Practice: A Study of the Principles of Personal Responsibility and of the Personal Nature of Punishment in Egyptian Criminal Law 233
Murielle Paradelle

10 The Regimentation of the Subject: Madness in Islamic and Modern Arab Civil Laws 264
Oussama Arabi

11 The Person and His Body: Medical Ethics and Egyptian Law 294
Baudouin Dupret

12 Can *Hisba* be 'Modernised'? The Individual and the Protection of the General Interest before Egyptian Courts 318
Nathalie Bernard-Maugiron

13 Regulating Tolerance: Protecting Egypt's Minorities 345
Maurits Berger

Index 373

Contributors

OUSSAMA ARABI is an independent scholar in Islamic law. He received a doctorate in modern logic and philosophy of language from the Sorbonne University-Paris I in 1987. His publications include: *Studies in Modern Islamic Law and Jurisprudence* (Kluwer Law International, 2001); *Early Muslim Legal Philosophy* (Center for Near Eastern Studies, UCLA, 1999); and *Wittgenstein, langage et ontologie* (Librairie Philosophique Vrin, Paris, 1982).

NATHALIE BERNARD-MAUGIRON holds a PhD in Public Law. She works on Constitutional Law, Human Rights and Personal Status Law in Egypt and in the Arab World. She also teaches law at Cairo University (French Law Section) and at the Political Science Department of the American University in Cairo. Among her recent publications: *Egypt and its Laws* (ed. with Baudouin Dupret), Kluwer Law International, The Hague-London-Boston, 2002 and *Le politique à l'épreuve du judiciaire. La justice constitutionnelle en Egypte*, Bruylant, Brussels, 2003.

MAURITS S. BERGER (LLM and MA in Arabic Studies) is a specialist in contemporary Islamic law. He has worked as a researcher in Syria and Egypt during the past eight years and as a visiting professor at several Dutch and Belgian universities. This article is part of his PhD dissertation at the University of Amsterdam on public policy in Egyptian law. Related publications are: 'Conflicts law and public policy in Egyptian family law: Islamic law through the backdoor', *American Journal for Comparative Law*, v. 50/3, summer 2002, and 'Public policy and Islamic law: the modern dhimmi in contemporary Egyptian family law', *Islamic Law and Society*, 2001 (vol. 8, no 1).

BARBARA DRIESKENS, doctor in Social and Cultural Anthropology at the Catholic University of Leuven, was research assistant at the Fund for Scientific Research-Flanders before her appointment as senior research fellow at the Institut Français du Proche-Orient (IFPO) in Beirut, Lebanon. Her doctoral research focused on the daily interactions among lower-middle-class Cairenes in relation to the invisible world and the world of *djinns.* She has authored and co-authored articles on magic, spirits, the concept of the person, and popular conciliation in the Egyptian context.

BAUDOUIN DUPRET is educated in Law and in Arabic and Islamic Sciences at the Catholic University of Leuven, Belgium, and in Middle Eastern Studies at the American University in Cairo. He received his PhD and his Habilitation à diriger des recherches in Political Sciences from the Institut d'Études Politiques in Paris. He is currently a research fellow at the French National Centre for Scientific Research (CNRS). He was based for several years at the Centre d'Études et de Documentation Économique, Juridique et Sociale (CEDEJ) in Cairo and is currently based at the Institut Français du Proche-Orient (IFPO), Damascus. He has co-edited several volumes in the field of the sociology and anthropology of law in Egypt and in the Middle East, including *Legal Pluralism in the Arab World* (together with M. Berger and L. al-Zwaini), Kluwer Law International, 1999, and *Egypt and Its Laws* (together with N. Bernard-Maugiron), Kluwer Law International, 2002. He is the author of *Au nom de quel droit. Répertoires juridiques et référence religieuse dans la société égyptienne musulmane contemporaine*, Paris, Maison des Sciences de l'Homme, 2000. His second single-authored book (forthcoming) concerns the issue of legal practices and sexual morality in the Egyptian judicial context.

KHALED FAHMY is Associate Professor of Middle Eastern Studies at New York University. He holds his PhD in Modern History from Oxford University. From 1994 to 1999 he was an assistant professor in the Department of Near Eastern Studies at Princeton University. His research interests are in discourses and practices centred on the human body. He is the author of *All the Pasha's Men: Mehmed Ali, His Army and the Making of Modern Egypt*, Cambridge, Cambridge University Press, 1997. He also contributed numerous articles in major books and journals, including 'An olfactory tale of two cities: Cairo in the nineteenth century', in Jill Edwards (ed.), *Historians in Cairo: Essays in Honor of George Scanlon*, Cairo, American University in Cairo Press, 2002; 'Prostitution in nineteenth-century Egypt', in Eugene Rogan (ed.),

Outside in: On the Margins of the Modern Middle East, London, I.B. Tauris, 2001; 'The police and the people in nineteenth-century Egypt', *Die Welt des Islams* 39, 1999; 'The anatomy of justice: Forensic medicine and criminal law in nineteenth-century Egypt', *Islamic Law and Society* 6, 1999.

JEAN-NOËL FERRIÉ holds his PhD in Political Science from the Institut d'Études Politiques d'Aix-en-Provence, France. He is currently a senior research fellow at CEDEJ. He also teaches in the Department of Political Science at Cairo University (French programme). He is also visiting professor at the Department of Political Science at Saint-Joseph University, Beirut. His research focuses on the public sphere and the democratisation process in the Middle East. He is the author of *La Religion de la vie quotidienne chez des Marocains musulmans. Règles et dilemmes*, Paris, Karthala, 2003, and *Le régime de la civilité. Public et réislamisation en Egypte*, Paris, CNRS Editions, 2004.

MOHAMED NACHI holds his PhD in Sociology from the École des Hautes Études en Sciences Sociales (EHESS), Paris. He is Professor of Sociology at the University of Liège (Department of Social Sciences) and at the University of Sfax, Tunisia (Department of Sociology). His is also a member of the Groupe de sociologie politique et morale (GSPM) at EHESS/CNRS, Paris. He mainly works in the field of the sociology of justice. Among his latest publications: 'Pour un comparatisme heuristique. Répertoires d'évaluation, identité morale et dignité de la personne', *The Tocqueville Review/La revue Tocqueville*, vol. xxiii, no 1, 2002, pp. 105–23 and *Ethique de la promesse. L'agir responsable*, Paris, Presses Universitaires Françaises (Coll. 'Philosophies'), 2003.

MURIELLE PARADELLE holds a PhD in Political Sciences. While her doctoral thesis dealt with Islamic law in the international policies of Muslim states, she currently works on legal socialisation in North Quebec Inuit communities and on international law and traditional modes of conflict resolution in Rwanda. She is a research fellow at the Research Centre in Public Law (CRDP), University of Montreal, Canada, and at the CNRS, in the team 'Urbanisation, Culture and Society'.

ARMANDO SALVATORE (PhD, European University Institute, Florence, 1994) is a Senior Research Fellow at the Institute of Social Sciences, Humboldt University, Berlin. His PhD thesis was awarded the 1994 Malcolm Kerr Dissertation Award in the Social Sciences of MESA. His primary interest lies in the analysis of the multiple links between religious, political-philosophical and legal traditions and notions of practical and public reason. Among his publications: *Islam and the Political Discourse of Modernity*, 1997, *Muslim Traditions and Modern Techniques of Power* (editor), 2001 and *Public Islam and the Common Good* (editor with Dale F. Eickelman). He is co-editor of the *Yearbook of the Sociology of Islam.*

INTRODUCTION

Baudouin Dupret

This book explores the question of the person as treated by the legal systems of various Arab countries. In a larger sense, it reflects upon dynamics which, since the beginning of the nineteenth century, cut across space, social groups and, even more, across the nation-states of a region generally referred to as Arab. It is based on the presupposition, questionable because stated but unproven, of the existence of a phenomenon of individuation which translates, in terms of law, into a tendency to focus on the legal persona. Elsewhere, one may observe that the national infrastructures of these nations is marked by a tendency towards political and legal centralisation. It is, then, the interrelatedness of the individual, society and the structural categories of social relations which is at the heart of this enterprise, and law, the code by which to state the problems.

The book is divided into three parts. Part One, *General Considerations on the Person and the Law*, is the place for general, theoretical and epistemological considerations on the person, the law and their relationships. Part Two, *Persons in Legal Settings*, addresses the various legal and quasi-legal situations in which people manifest their understanding of notions germane to that of the person. Part Three, *Legal Figures of the Person*, groups together several contributions addressing the ways in which the person is legally characterised.

Part One consists of three chapters. In Chapter 1, I explore three of the many dimensions concerning the question of the relationship between the law and the person. First, I develop the subject of the contingent nature of the individual as a social and philosophical being. Second, I examine such relations as may be established between individual, social and political dynamics. Third, I examine the nature of the individual as a subject of law. In conclusion, I examine the interest that one might have in adopting a praxiological approach to the observation of just how such a vast category of understanding evolves over the course of action, particularly legal action. In Chapter 2, Mohamed Nachi explores the articulation of the notions of 'I', 'we' and the 'person' and their significance for an investigation into the meaning of justice. Drawing on many different perspectives – liberal, communitarian and others – this essay examines how this has inherited aspects from different histories, including Muslim medieval philosophers' conceptions of the person. Jean-Noël Ferrié's contribution in Chapter 3 provides us with a critical approach to the concept of the person when used from a sociological perspective. He convincingly argues that, in this sense, the person serves as a metaphysical tool that ignores the situated character of people's interactions and bluntly duplicates their standpoint without accounting for the formal structure of their practical actions.

Part Two consists of four chapters that address various social and legal settings in which different conceptions of the person are formulated. In Chapter 4, Khaled Fahmy examines an 1863 Egyptian decree on imprisonment and puts it in the larger historical and legal Egyptian framework. The study of this decree, which replaced beating with imprisonment, gives the basis for understanding justice in Khedival Egypt, the ways in which the person was criminalised, the nature of punishment and the transformations through which it went. In Chapter 5, Armando Salvatore sketches a framework that allows one to understand some of the transformations witnessed by *sharî'a* and its connection with the relationship between the person and the law. Focusing on the last third of the nineteenth century, this chapter seeks to evaluate the nature of the relation between traditions on one hand, and modern law and modern public sphere on the other. Barbara Drieskens in Chapter 6 examines the notion of the person in a popular Egyptian context and stresses the disparity between the way that people present and negotiate the constantly shifting limits between the person and the 'other' in daily life, with its emphasis on family, reputation and divine elements, and the way that the concept of the person is constructed in the legal setting as a tool to demarcate responsibility. She also shows how, in particular cases of spirit possession and misbehaviour, both legal and local approaches are creatively combined. Mohamed Nachi's second essay, Chapter 7, illustrates how people who are engaged in an argument, a quarrel or a dispute call upon a specific argumentative register to justify the necessity of respecting the person and the individual's rights, dignity and integrity and, in so doing, attribute to the notion of the person a specific meaning.

The six chapters that compose Part Three are more directly concerned with law and the different characterisations of the person in Arab judicial settings. The first three chapters deal with criminal law. In Chapter 8, I seek to show how Egyptian public lawyers organise their activity around the establishment of one of the theoretical components of the crime, i.e. intentionality. This essay proposes a praxiological approach in which intentionality is viewed as the result of interactions integrated in the judicial institutional context which obliges the professional actors to orient themselves toward the production of a legally relevant decision. In Chapter 9, Murielle Paradelle focuses on two fundamental principles of Egyptian criminal law: the personal responsibility of the individual and the personal nature of punishment. She explores the conflicts arising from the existence of legal systems within the same society which are organised around the personal nature of criminal responsibility and sanctions. In Chapter 10, Oussama Arabi discusses one aspect of the modern institutionalisation of madness as revealed in an imperceptible change in the legal status of the mad person in contemporary Egyptian and other Arab civil law when compared with their status in classical Islamic jurisprudence. The author argues that mutations in the legal and medical institutions could not fail to affect the implementation of Islamic law, be it in terms of codification, procedure and legal evidence. In Chapter 11, I focus on the field of medical ethics where all the stakes involved in the relationship between the individual and his body are found, in the autonomy of individual will, in individual responsibility and in the freedom to dispose of oneself. Using the dispute over the notion of 'therapeutic purpose' as a starting point, I argue that the spread of the assertion of an autonomous 'self' takes place together with the shrinking of the realm where autonomous 'intimacy' is free from any legal intrusion. In Chapter 12, Nathalie Bernard-Maugiron re-situates the procedural technique of *hisba* within the broader question of the role of the individual in defence of the general interest. Drawing on Egyptian, French and US law, she reviews the different types of litigation known in Egyptian law and examines the place accorded or refused by each of them towards the protection of the general interest by individuals. In Chapter 13, Maurits Berger examines the status of non-Muslim communities within the framework of Egyptian plurality of religious family laws. Stemming from the fact that in Egypt the applicable family law is determined by one's religion, the author argues that one of the main characteristics of Egypt's personal-status legal system is the protection of the collective identity of non-Muslims.

Obviously, the many contributions to this book address the issue of the relationship between the person and the law from different and occasionally conflicting perspectives. Some of them are of a legal nature, while others are grounded in social history. However, most are sociological or anthropological although they draw from traditions which cannot always be considered as supporting each other. In this sense, this book reflects quite well the diversity of social sciences which developed various ways in dealing with social phenomena. This is not the place to discuss the merits of each perspective, and the reader will have to do his or her own shopping within the marketplace which offers contributions ranging from Habermasian sociology to the communitarian philosophy of justice, and from Elias's concept of the civilising process to praxiological studies of judicial interactions.

This publication was only possible with the help of many institutions and people. My special thanks go to Randi Deguilhem, *chargée de recherche* at the Centre National de la Recherche Scientifique (CNRS) and research fellow at the Institut de Recherche et d'Études sur le Monde Arabe et Musulman (IREMAM), Aix-en-Provence, France, for her constant support. From 1997, she was scientific co-ordinator of the European Science Foundation programme on 'The Individual and Society in the Mediterranean

Muslim World', and a participant in the seminar that gave birth to this book. She is also at its conclusion, as the general editor of the series in which this collection is published. My thanks also go to Robert Ilbert, professor at the University of Aix-Marseille I and founder/director of the Maison Méditerranéenne des Sciences de l'Homme in Aix-en-Provence, who was at the inception of this research project. Ghislaine Alleaume, director of the Centre d'Études et de Documentation Économique, Juridique et Sociale (CEDEJ), a French research centre based in Cairo, Egypt, financially and logistically supported the seminar that was held in Cairo on 7–9 November 1999. Finally, many thanks to the people who contributed very proficient translations of the papers initially written in French.

Part One

GENERAL CONSIDERATIONS ON THE PERSON AND THE LAW

CHAPTER 1

The Person and the Law: Contingency, Individuation and the Subject of the Law

Baudouin Dupret

It is the interrelatedness of the individual, society and the structural categories of social relations which is at the heart of this book; law is simply the code by which the problems are stated. The question is quite naturally multidimensional. Three dimensions shall be explored in this introductory chapter. First, I shall develop the subject of the contingent nature of the individual as a social and philosophical being. I shall then examine such relations as may be established between individual, social and political dynamics. Third, I shall examine the nature of the individual as a subject of law. Finally, I shall examine the interest that one might have in adopting a pragmatic approach to the observation of just how such a vast category of understanding evolves over the course of action, particularly legal action. In attempting to outline these various perspectives, the terms of the problem addressed by this book are stated; a solution is not attempted.

The category of the person

Marie-Thérèse Meulders-Klein makes the following observation:

> as it has been defined, the notion of the person applied to Man conceived as a unique self, autonomous and equal by rights and dignity is self-evident. However, an historical or anthropological approach reveals there is nothing to it, either in time or in space.

> The concept of the person is not an 'innate category of reason', but the result of a long process linked to the adventure of Western Man, and remains ever subject to questioning.[1]

This proposition raises a number of questions which I would like to address in this section. The first deals with the category of the person and the relation of this category to those of the individual and the self. The second question concerns the contingent nature of this category and its historical antecedence. The third question deals with the ability to free oneself socially of such categories and thus of its transposability to other sociohistorical contexts. Finally, a fourth question concerns the social markers of individuation and personalisation.

For all these questions, Mauss could conveniently serve as a point of departure[2] as it did for Carrithers, Collins and Lukes.[3]

For Mauss, it is a question of understanding how a category of the human spirit which one may presume innate may be situated historically. Reasoning from Aristotelian categories, he observes the various forms taken by the notion in time and space. Asserting from the beginning that there has never been a human being who was not conscious, not only of their body but also of spiritual and physical individuality, Mauss points out that he himself is primarily interested in the succession of forms assumed by this concept in the life of man within different societies. It is thus obvious that a large number of societies arrived at the notion of a '*persona*' or the role played by the individual in sacred theatre just as one would play a role in the family. For the Romans, however, the person becomes more than an organisational fact, more than a name or a right to assume a role and to wear a ritual mask: the person becomes a 'fundamental legal principal'. Law divides matter into *personae, res* and *actiones*, a classification which, he notes, remains the organising principle of our legal codes to this day. By this specific historic experience, law became personal, and *persona* synonymous with the true nature of the individual. Mauss states that a moral dimension was added to the legal meaning: the idea of being conscious, independent, autonomous, free and responsible. Moral conscience introduces conscience into the legal concept of rights. One must, however, look towards Christianity for the transformation of the 'moral person' into a 'metaphysical being'. Here, one finds the transition from the notion of *persona*, which is man cast in a role, to the notion of Man, which is to say, the Person. It is because the notion of the moral person has become so clear that, in our times, it is applied to all non-real persons to whom we refer as 'juristic persons': corporations, religious orders etc. Finally, the notion of the person would have become the category of 'self' through sectarian religious and reform movements concerned with individual liberty and conscience, with the right of the individual to communicate directly with God and to minister unto oneself as well as to have an internal god and, finally, through the influence of a philosophical movement for which the 'self' is the equivalent of conscience and constitutes the essential category. Fichte, in claiming that an act of conscience is an act of self, represents the culmination of this development. In this way, Mauss describes a grand evolutionary movement, which from masquerade to mask, from *persona* to a person to a name to an individual, from the individual to a metaphysical being with a moral conscience, from moral conscience to sacred being and from sacred being to an essential figure of thought and action, would culminate in this fundamental category of contemporary understanding.

Mauss makes a category of the person. From this point of view, he places himself in the tradition of Durkheim, for whom the person is a 'category of mind'. This is one of those 'essential notions which dominate our intellectual life like a "framework for understanding"' and 'which remain separate from all other knowledge both by their universality and by their necessity', which 'are independent of any particular subject' and 'constitute the point where all minds converge'.[4] He otherwise unites the notions of individual, person and self under a single concept. In Mauss's terms,[5] 'the idea of "person", the idea of "self" [is] one of the categories of the human spirit – one of these ideas which we believe innate – which is slowly conceived and developed over many centuries and much adversity'.

Confusion of these notions may seem problematic to those who, like Carrithers,[6] distinguish between traditions that place emphasis on the person as a member of a group and traditions centred on the self that portray the human being as an individual and human beings within a spiritual cosmos. From this perspective, Mauss's approach would be personalistic and would confer a moral and cognitive value upon the group. Thus, if one observes the elevation of man, it would be as a part of a whole or as a 'self' made part of a person. Carrithers demonstrates the existence of totally different historical experiences. Following the thought process of a nineteenth-century mystic, Anton Gueth, he reminds us of the extent to which German intellectual tradition is based on the individual and that individual's conscience in relation to the group, based on a morality arising from the individual and not from the group.

Let us first note that the anthropological literature makes a clear distinction between the individual as a biological organism and the person as a system of social relations, the latter being the proper study of social anthropology.[7] Two observations can then be formulated. On one hand, it would no doubt be useful to insist on the fact that Mauss, if one may consider as normative his claim that the cult of the self is pathological – assuming the self can evolve only in equilibrium with its social environment – makes no less a distinction between the person (a classification arising out of Roman law) and the self (a subsequent development arising out of religious and philosophical events). In this sense, for Mauss, the notion of self could arise as a distinct development only after that of the person. The question arises as to whether such a sequence is contingent. On the other hand, it is interesting to distinguish between the self and the person in relation to the group. From this perspective, it should be noted that law looks first to the person as a member of the group, relegating the self (which we might call 'individual conscience' or 'innermost being') to the domain of the non-legal, or that which is only to preserve integrity. This is clear from the very social nature of law, and the difficulty of extending it beyond that which can be externalised or made public. At the same time, however, and such is the interest of Mauss's evolutionism: one may observe an ever stronger legal tendency to penetrate the inner person, to question motives and one's capacity for anticipation, of the expression of one's will etc. Without doubt, the question deserves to be explored in depth, but at the very least the question is posed here.

Mauss insists on the contingent nature of the category of the person which originates in a social context. At some point, it assumes forms which may be traced and, in modern times, has developed to become 'self-evident'.[8] In other words, there exists a universal and necessary framework for thought about the person which takes different forms in different contexts. The framework developed by Mauss is, as summarised by Lukes,

> fundamental, in that it is the basis for the rest of human thought; universal in that it is to be found in all human cultures, in different forms, even if these are misshapen or diminished; necessary in that beings, like ourselves, living in some recognisable form of society, cannot escape it.[9]

On this point, Mauss adopts a line of thought generally qualified as neo-Kantian. The categories are universal while their conceptualisation is contingent. In other words, what we observe today is the conceptual development of the category of the person even though the category itself was implicit of a structuring and acting nature.[10]

Without doubt, we should make a pragmatic distinction here between the actual categorisation and the categories themselves. For the moment we are focusing on the latter and, on this point, the contingent nature of the idea of the person does not seem disputable. As noted by La Fontaine,[11] one must admit that different concepts of the person are written within a social context. From this point of view, it is perfectly possible to trace those paths which do not naturally reach their peak in the Western experience. At the same time, it is also possible to affirm the singularity of this experience and, for exact historical reasons, its tendency to go beyond its original geographic framework. If the West – and one must agree on this term – has not invented the concept of the person, it is nonetheless the source of a concept which is identifiable and specific and whose influence can be traced beyond Western boundaries.

Thus, one may recognise the existence of a framework for thought contained simply within the universal existence of a 'sense of self', of the consciousness that one may have of one's human body and of one's individuality – both spiritual and physical – but which consists above all in the fact that human thought cannot be structured without a notion of the individual in the biological sense. It can be, as it is for Taylor,[12] a structure of feelings which are specific to human nature and which combine *self-consciousness* and valorisation (or *significance*). For Mauss, it is mostly a structure of beliefs, a set of very general beliefs underlying the various forms of law, religion, customs, social and mental structure, of a series of answers to very general questions on the distinctions between human persons and other conscious agents, and on the relation between the individual and society etc. This leads Mauss, as summarised by Lukes, to the description of the various situations:

> Among the Pueblo, the person is seen as 'absorbed in his clan', yet already detached from it in ceremonial; among the Romans, 'persons' are both ritually linked to society and their ancestors and the bearers of rights, and, with the Stoics, come to acquire 'a sense of being conscious, independent, autonomous, free and responsible' (a consciousness which then entered the law); with Christianity and modern secular philosophy, 'the revolution in mentalities is accomplished' so that we are both social beings and bearers of 'metaphysical and moral value', indeed sacred beings.[13]

From this perspective, to say that the person is a fundamental category is to assert the relation between thought and social structure, but it is also to encourage the interpretation of a culture's implicit and explicit ideas such as the translation of fundamental ideas and deeply rooted structures. These ideas or theories can be explicit, as is the case for specialists who devote their time to developing them. Thus, Carrithers describes Buddhism as 'a decisive step in human thought about humans in relation to their mental and physical individuality'.[14] These ideas or theories can be implicit and consist in underlying postulates. Here one finds, for example, the contribution of La Fontaine who, in his comparison of four non-Western societies, makes the connection between indigenous psychologies and sociopolitical contexts.[15]

Mauss's outline definitely gives an impression of evolutionism that culminates in a modern world where the person has become

> A sacred being, the possessor of metaphysical and moral value and of moral consciousness – the bearer of rights and responsibilities, the source of autonomous motivation and rational decision, valuing privacy and capable of self-development.[16]

This point of view, positively evaluating this evolution, thus once again normative, is definitely disputable. It has, in fact, many opponents. Following Lukes,[17] one notes that for Foucault the individual in his modern version is an artificially built unit associated with the language of ethics and law; one may also note that for Musil the individual no longer has a clearly defined and historically understandable identity, and is no longer the unifying focus of experience and a *locus* of personal responsibility. The fact remains that evolutionism, as opposed to determinism, does not constitute in itself one of the deadly sins of sociology.[18] Furthermore, and for simple practical reasons, it is impossible to undertake research without recognising the necessity of certain common categories, even if those are historical. The reference to the idea of 'person' is one such category. From this point of view, reconciling concepts to objects with the effectiveness in the formulation of ideas, there exists a way of individualistic thinking that is characteristic of our contemporary societies which focuses on will, choice, evaluation and calculation: here, the individual thinks and acts – one might say 'thinks of oneself' and 'acts of oneself' – as an autonomous agent in relation to others who are no less autonomous.[19] Research is not spared this constraint.

Whether we like it or not, whether such an evolution is to be considered desirable, one must notice the impossibility of escaping from the modern notion of person, of individual and of self when one undertakes the study of the various forms of display. These concepts permanently affect our way of accounting for other ways of thinking. Once this is established, however, one may identify a number of markers of this modern thought and bring to light some of the characteristics of this distinctive process of modern thinking.

As examples one can use, among many others related to such markers, a few recurring notions from Kantian and Freudian arguments such as autonomy, freedom, will, conscience and motive. Will, defined as the 'capacity to freely determine whether or not to act' constitutes, with autonomy, one of the cornerstones of philosophy and modern epistemology. For Kant, the subject has become a causal principle of a certain force called action or intentional process. This suggests that the subject represents a fundamental element, irreducible to any other element, transcendent or immanent. In other words, the subject, the Kantian '*cogito*', is an autonomous element attributing a certain objectivity to the objects. The objects as such only become knowable in relation to the subject which precisely gives them a certain meaning, a meaning which is never definite in itself, but which is always the expression of the *intentionality* of the subject's actions and interactions.[20] Freedom is also classically associated with the will:

> the human being can only judge what is appropriate through the use of a faculty called 'will'; whereas the idea of will assumes the existence of other faculties by means of which it operates, especially freedom. We speak of freedom as the faculty by which will can express itself.[21]

The legal principle of the autonomy of will, the very basis of contract law, probably best expresses the importance of this philosophical concept in law. In Gounot's words,

> the individual is to be found at the foundation of the social and legal edifice, which is to say 'free will'. Freedom makes of the human being its own and only master; it makes him infinitely respectable and sacred; it raises him to the dignity of an end in itself. Law is nothing other than this initial and sovereign liberty which belongs to all men. From free will everything comes; to free will everything returns.[22]

Will, autonomy, freedom and intentionality are thus the very foundations of the philosophical system of modern law, and one immediately sees all the implications of this concept related to a subject acting freely and autonomously in terms of responsibility, imputation, premeditation, decision or judgement, all notions which are readily evident on the simple reading of the civil and penal codes.

The process of individuation: the person, the society and the state

We shall now integrate the category of the person in broader dynamics, associating the individual to society and power. Norbert Elias's writings are used as a basis for this chapter inasmuch as we deal explicitly with the development of the mental and socially established state structures. Following our effort to define the nature, both contingent and universal, of the person as a category of thought, we establish the close relationship between its development and the emergence of a very specific process of political formation, the nation-state.[23]

Elias proposes a now-classical model, in which the phenomenon of monopolisation – otherwise synonymous with centralisation, which characterises the emergence of the contemporary state – induces a progressive differentiation of functions and, subsequently, an increasing interdependence. One of the most attractive features of this thesis is the ability to associate interdependence with self-restraint, to show the extent to which, within a dynamics of relations restrained by a framework of complex interaction, the tendency is to elaborate codes of conduct to establish them as distinct signs, to progressively spread them, to share them and, finally, to internalise them – an ambiguous term, incidentally – in the socialising process experienced by all individuals in society. These codes of conduct, these ethical codes are thus the result of increasing self-restraint which, for its part, expresses a distinct individuation. Individuality, interdependence and self-restraint are not so apparently opposed as their reciprocal condition: 'the division and the differentiation of the mental functions of the human being expressed in the word "individuality" are only made possible when the individual grows within a group of individuals, in a society'.[24] The individualisation, the cumbersome assertion of an individual conscience, the subsequent control of emotional reactions – all attitudes towards oneself and others – seem evident and natural and yet express 'a very distinct historical imprint of the individual'. The 'individualised' individual, with an overdeveloped 'self-conscience', is the individual forced by the society's constitution to adopt 'a very high degree of restraint', to master his or her impulses and to submit to a code of ethics.

> In a word, this 'self-conscience' refers to a structure of interiority which develops during well-defined phases of the civilising process. It is characterised by a clear differentiation and by a marked conflict between social constraints and proscriptions acquired and transformed into inner constraints, and the instincts and tendencies proper to the individual, untamed but contained.[25]

We would like to highlight some of the issues raised by Elias's thesis which are of particular interest to the problems addressed in this book; first, the correlation between changes in power structure and changes in individual and social behaviour; second, the connection between interdependence and self-constraint; finally, the relationship between the monopolisation of violence, state formation and legalisation of behaviour.

Several authors, first among whom Duerr, take exception to the idea of a progressive model in which, whatever may be the vicissitudes of evolution, society passes from impulsive behaviour to self-restraint. Using an impressive collection of examples and counter-examples, Duerr claims to prove that 'the civilising process' is a myth obscuring the fact that, 'in all probability in the last forty thousand years there have been neither wild nor primitive peoples, neither uncivilised nor unnatural peoples'.[26] Even if the theoretical demonstration seems superficial, the accumulated empirical evidence forces the question. Examining the question of modesty, Duerr asserts that rules governing the subject are an integral part of social relations.

For our part, we follow the analysis of Burguière, for whom, if one agrees with this supposition, one must at the same time note that these rules must be contextualised. The identity of uses through time and space does not, in any way, indicate a lack of change in the surrounding emotional and moral climates. In other words, concepts of the body may be universal concepts. However, one must, in any case, consider the extreme plasticity and variability with which identical conceptual and gestural models assume different forms and evolutionary paths in different societies. The question then becomes one of knowing how the same constituent uses of the body by the human species fit into each culture and how they structure society, given that culture is above all an act of memory, of selection, of internalisation and of repression to the point of oblivion. The issue is to explore the means by which the individual appropriates the basic categories of self-perception and the perception of others to build his or her own system of regulation of interpersonal relations. On this subject, Elias's contribution is useful to the extent that it simultaneously explains the transformation of society and the person and seeks to account for the changes in scale in systems of power and social control.[27]

The main interest in Elias's thesis is the connection that he makes between changes in the structure of power and changes in individual and collective behaviour, what A. Dumont calls 'the mechanism of social capillarity'.[28] Not only is individuality made possible 'when the individual grows among a group of individuals, in a society',[29] but one must also admit that states are social organisations whose formation is a social process as well[30] and that, as such, their evolution is closely combined. Mental structures and state structures are so closely related that we must completely rethink the classical dichotomy between individual and society. In this process, we observe the establishment of new configurations which characterise both an era in its historical specificity and a society in its continuity.

In that sense, evaluating the importance of the 'I' can only be done in a contextual, relational and evolutionary manner, evaluating a social configuration in which the individual inserts him or herself, a situation of interdependence which is both empirical and dynamic.[31] In Elias's words,

> the control of nature, social control and individual control are chained in a sort of circle; they form a functional trilogy whose vision can be used as a fundamental model for the observation of human problems; none of these elements can develop without the others; the measure and form of one depends on the measure and form of the others and if any of the three collapses the others will eventually follow.[32]

Another important question raised by Elias's writings is the relation between specialisation, interdependence and self-restraint among individuals. Within the purview of this book, the question is no doubt relevant in order to understand the phenomenon of modern state formation, of the development of law, of the appearance of a new socio-professional category and of the legalisation of morals. Returning to Elias:

> From the origin of Western history to this day, we observe an ever increasing differentiation of social function under the growing pressure of competition. With this differentiation comes a continuous increase in functions and men, upon which each individual is entirely dependent, whether he accomplishes the most simple and ordinary tasks or the most complicated and unusual tasks. Thus, the behaviour of an increasing number of persons must be co-ordinated and interdependent acts must be organised more strictly and precisely so that each isolated act fulfils its social function. The individual has to differentiate, to control, assert and regulate his movements [...] Whether conscious or unconscious,

> the course of behaviour in relation to increasingly differentiated regulation of the mental apparatus is determined by a greater social differentiation, by a division of function and by the lengthening chains of interdependence into which each movement, each expression of the isolated man is directly or indirectly integrated.[33]

The unconscious aspect of self-restraint may appear particularly questionable. This said, it can be understood as a phenomenon of privatisation of norms under the effect of pressure which leads to action in anticipation of the behaviour of others and of future situations. In a context of permanent social restructuring, new categories are regarded as different and this applies to a lengthening of the chain of interdependence linking the individuals. These new social positions pose 'problems of type classification, and consequently of action'[34] and lead to the reinforcement of the individuation of control.

Elias's writings are also interesting in that they associate the monopolisation of violence and state centralisation with the internalisation of affects and legislative intrusion. The theory of a state monopoly on violence is old. It has been recognised by schools often radically opposed in their views, but which recognise the idea that giving up the diffuse and private exercise of violence to benefit the exclusive exercise of the state characterises the transition from the state of nature to the state of law (Hobbes, Locke), the idea that sovereignty belongs to the representatives of the state, which delegates its ability to give orders to the law-maker (Bentham), or the idea that the state is the sum of institutions of one group dominating the other and that law is the legal recognition of this inequality (Gumplowicz). Finally, one should recall that according to Weber law proceeds from a human authority that is especially established to guarantee the validity of an order by its capacity to enforce respect or punish its violation.[35]

Elias goes further in linking the state monopoly on violence to the internalisation of affects. He does not describe a decrease in violence, but a change in its modes of expression: the intensification of the legitimate violence of the state-at-war is a response to the intensification of the control of violence and of the rules of peace.[36] To the compartmentalisation of violence is thus added its restrictive definition and a policy of concentration 'concerned with separating controlled use from a slide towards loss of control', 'attentively watching all points from which this shift could occur' and insisting 'on all the techniques which make it possible to recover self-control'.[37] Here we can bring up Elias's studies about sports and also more contemporary debates on the use of drugs, the consumption of tobacco and alcohol, the relationship with nature, the politically correct etc.

The association of the monopolisation of violence with the internalisation of the affects makes it possible to summarise

> a whole set of processes which contain violence within specific limits, which establish its legitimate origins which specify its condition of use, which mandate accepted enforcers to carry it out and which regulate the reactions of a population deprived of the right to exercise any form of violence.[38]

I would be personally inclined to say that the affects are never, as such, internalised; that, on the contrary, they are always revealed, made public and externalised, and that their mode of externalisation is modified. It is thus the role of sociology to describe how this externalisation occurs, in order also to show its changes.

The subject of law

This section opens discussion about the recourse to the lexicon of the person through law. It is, in fact, obvious that the legal context has appropriated a whole series of concepts whose organisation if not formulation itself originates in Kantian philosophy. As Meulders-Klein notes,

> contrary to the statement that, in order to recognise the existence of the legal person law must draw on nature and biology, the notion of person, as a subject of law, far from being natural, is a cultural notion, and one of many forms of representation of the human being, dependent upon the condition of specific social structures, and independent of the universal aspect of the biological and psychological attributes of man.[39]

The biography of the category of the person is partly legal, as underscored by Rorty:

> our idea of person comes from two sources; the first is theater, the dramatis personae of the stage; the other is law. An actor wears masks, literally personae, through which the sound and the different

> roles come ... so the person stands behind his role, chooses them and is judged on his choices and on his capacity to stage his personae within a global structure which is the unfolding of his drama. The idea of the person is the idea of a unified center of choice and action, that unity to which the legal and theological responsibility relates. After making a choice the person acts and thus is legally and morally responsible. It is in the idea of action that are gathered the legal and theatrical sources of the concept of the person.[40]

Further, Rorty shows that:

> it is only when the legal system gives up the notions of clan and family responsibility and that the individuals are considered as primary agents, that the class of persons coincides with the class of biological human beings. In principle, and often in law, this coincidence is not necessarily obvious. A given human being, while recognised as being an individual, can also be considered as having a whole series of personae, each one a distinct and unified agent, a locus of responsibility for a wide scale of choice and action.[41]

Now, in terms of law, the concept of individual is dissociated from the concept of the person and the latter is not characterised by his identity to a biological human being, but by his quality as a subject of law and obligation. To refer to Locke, 'the term "person" is a "court term" [a *forensic* term]; this means that treating an individual as a person, is to consider him responsible for his acts before a court of law or of ethics, literally or figuratively – or even to some, before a court of divine judgement'.[42] At the same time, we should not fail to note that everyday language does not make a natural distinction between the individual and the person, but only a difference of degree, the person somehow being endowed with greater moral value. The individual has indeed been given, since the time of William of Ockham, the power to make laws. The individual has become the subject of law which is to say the beneficiary 'of a power recognised by positive law'. As L. Dumont notes, legal nominalism, positivism and subjectivism expressed in such views signal the birth of the individual in philosophy and in law:

> When there is no longer anything ontologically real beyond a particular being, when the notion of 'law' relates, not to a natural and social order, but to a particular human being, this particular human being becomes an individual in the modern sense of the term.[43]

The philosophy of the autonomous subject and legal individualism undoubtedly proceeds from the same movement which ensures a central position for the person. Does that mean that the moral subject in philosophy and the subject of law in law are one and the same? To answer affirmatively would amount, no doubt, to an oversight of the autonomy proper to the legal argument and to its performative quality. Must we, on the contrary, claim that law is completely impervious and that its subject is then nothing more than a mere semantic artefact? This would also be excessive. The very fact that law is thoroughly influenced by the ideology of the individual cannot be totally foreign to the sociohistorical establishment or modern legal activity, while we must recognise the force of the constitution of its system. We are now at the core of a tangle of questions; this volume specifically addresses two of them. The first one concerns legal theories of the person that are presented in the light of the differentiation between law and ethics. The second deals with the legal conception of related notions and particularly with those of liberty, will, responsibility and intentionality (which goes back partly to previously developed arguments).

Here, we specifically address the question posed by Ricœur, 'who is the subject of law?', as well as considering the answers that the legal doctrine can give. The study of this debate, which will most certainly continue that of the distinction between law and morals, has the advantage of revealing both the social and historical establishment of legal concepts and their ability to form an autonomous argument.

In his book *Le Juste*, Ricœur devotes a chapter to demonstrating that the legal question of the subject of law (who is the subject of law?) also relates back to a moral question (who is the subject worthy of esteem and respect?) which, in turn, relates back to an anthropological question (what fundamental features make the self worthy of esteem and respect?).[44] The question of 'who' calls for identification, from where comes the notion of 'able subject'. Posing this question is a matter of ascribing to someone an action or a part of an action. The attribution of the authorship of an act is fundamental in any imputation of rights and duties: it is the very heart of the notion of capacity. Capacity, however, assumes the ability to distinguish between the good and the bad, between the permitted and the forbidden. A subject of accusation results from reflective application: 'The subject of imputation is the result of the reflective application of "good" and "obligatory" predicates to the agents themselves'.[45] Inasmuch as we are capable subjects, we can evaluate and judge our own actions.

To be effective, this aptitude for self-esteem and self-respect requires the mediation of another, both personal (in relation to 'you') and institutional (in relation to 'they'). This is where, according to Ricœur, the transition from capable subject to subject of law occurs: 'Indeed, only the relation to a third party, placed in the background of the relation to the you, provides a basis for the institutional mediation required by the constitution of a real subject of law, in other words, of a citizen'.[46] One must master the relation to the 'you' to be able to recognise the other as equal in rights and duties, but one must also master the relation to the third party to be able to integrate a community of 'speakers of a same natural language who do not know one another and are only related through the recognition of common rules which distinguish one language from the other'.[47] One then observes the outgrowth of the interpersonal relationship and the transition to the institutional relationship and to the social link, which is well characterised by the use of the personal pronoun 'each' so characteristic of modern legal language.

To summarise, we shall say that Ricœur places the subject of law in a threefold relationship: to 'me' (individualism), to 'you' (interactionism) and to 'they' (institutionalism), which we may otherwise call the three poles of a non-metaphysical thought of the person.

What could the legal doctrine respond to this philosophical expression of the subject of law? According to Rommel, three main legal theories on the subject in law can be identified which propose a *continuum* of visions from the idea of a free and responsible person to that of an operational fiction breaking away from the biological and the social.[48] Classical doctrine considers the subject of law as a pre-legal reality. This is in Hegel's line of thought, a philosopher for whom the subject of law is 'the fullness of the human person in all its value, its dignity and its freedom'.[49] 'Every human being is a person', say Aubry and Rau, and 'every being capable of possessing rights and of submitting to obligations is a person', which implies then, that every human being is capable of possessing rights and duties.

By analogy to the individuality of the physical person which is a work of nature, the concept of physical person was created, and 'is only based on a legal abstraction'.[50] There is, then, a direct link between man and the legal person; law confers the latter quality to a being who already possessed it in a latent state. For Aarnio, 'in the domain of law, the human being forms an important ontological category. He forms the category of subject of law.'[51] On this basis, the subject of law is the holder of subjective rights, which is to say of legally protected interests.

Hans Kelsen's doctrine makes of the subject of law, a construct of the science of law, which has no bearing in natural reality: 'The physical person, in the sense of law, is not a man, but the personified entity of legal norms which impose legal obligations and confer rights to a sole and unique individual'.[52] Subjective law is then reduced to objective law to the extent that the person is nothing more than 'the personification of a system of legal norms' and to the extent that rights and obligations of the person are reduced to the legal norm 'which punishes a certain behaviour of an individual and which subordinates the execution of the sanction to an appropriate legal action'.[53]

The third doctrine radically dissociates man from the subject of law. Rommel refers to Althusser, for whom the reference to natural man serves to present law as a natural and evident activity, although it is nothing more than subjection. In *Les Mots et les choses*, Foucault, for his part, qualifies law as 'semantic artefact'.[54] Finally, for Teubner, the semantically artefactual nature of human actors constitutes one of the three main theses of the theory of an autopoeisis of law.[55] If, as he says, 'social institutions like law make the cognition of the individual a social matter', these same institutions 'independently of the psychic process of their members' conceive of and create 'independent worlds of meaning', 'completely independent of the constructs of the legal world' whose mental constructs only function as 'disturbances'. If law, as a social process, 'immediately and permanently confronts man', these, in fact, constitute little more than 'semantical artefacts' that are both indispensable to and the fabrication of legal communication. Contrary to Kelsen, the systemic theory affirms the central nature originating with the subject of law, but legal subjectivity is constituted only of legal figures named and created by law:

> It is at the cost of neglect of the legally constituted nature of the subject of law and of its avatars that the traditional doctrine gave law the appearance of a rooted place in life, of a *Sitz im Leben*. The advent of the subject of law and of its functioning in the effectuation of law proves that law has no *Sitz im Leben*. The subject of law as articulated by law does not exist in life, and human behaviour which makes up the content of rights and duties is nothing more than a legally created nomenclature for relations between the subject of law and the object of law, or to another subject of law (legal intersubjectivity), a relation named and simultaneously created by law with another legal concept.[56]

As for legal practice, it concentrates on the realisation of one of these figures through procedures that aim at its certification or at its falsification. Put simply, 'the physical or moral subject of law is not a pre-existing entity, but the original concept of law which makes possible all other legal concepts'.[57]

The ultimate question, then, is who is the subject of law? We cite the two extremes of the answer, that of legal dogmatics, which considers law in systemic terms as totally impervious to that which is outside of it, and that of philosophical anthropology, which seeks to place the law at the centre of the quest for justice. For the latter, 'the subject is taken as the counterpart of law, its recipient, and not as the support or beneficiary (individual or collective) of positive rights'[58] – the opposite of the dogmatic position that considers the subject as the condition, the means and the object of law.[59] The question of the identity of the subject, essential for Ricœur, is irrelevant for Rommel, who considers the subject as a simple abstraction necessary to the functioning of the legal proposition.

On the question of capacity, these two views are complete opposites; the view of philosophical anthropology is that 'the capacity of a human agent to designate himself as the author of his acts supposes that he is able to act intentionally, which is to say, by premeditation, and his capacity to initiate efficient changes in the course of things',[60] whereas the view of dogmatic systemics is that the legal fiction of intention allows law to act 'as if' man and the subject of law were synonymous, while only the act performed through the language of law is a legal act. This same capacity, which is a means of action for the philosopher (mastery of the rules of language, of self in the promise of agreement, of narration etc.) and an 'inevitable connection to any legal recognition',[61] is, in the opposite view, conditioned only by the enunciation of a legal proposition, 'which is to say, any proposition relating to a legal state of things (in law there is no other) and thus creating a legal rule'.[62]

There may be ways, not of reconciling but of repositioning these theses, which would make it possible to position each argument at different levels of legal activity. It is, in fact, not obvious that the two antagonistic points of view apply to the same object: the law. We would rather lean towards the idea of different perspectives (philosophy and dogmatics) applying to different objects (law as a legal issue and law as a product of speech). Legal dogmatics, however, does not exhaust the question of law. It is only an aspect of it, no doubt important, but just as certainly partial. Then if it is dogmatically true that the fact only exists in law through its legal qualification, it is no less true that, cognitively and sociologically, this transition from fact of life to legal fact occurs *a posteriori* in the course of the judge's interpretation and never *a priori* in an operation where law would 'dictate' what is the fact of law. In the same way, if a judge reads the law dogmatically, then cognitively and sociologically he can only construe the law in terms of law. From this point of view, it would be very useful to mention the thesis of Lenoble and Ost on the 'mytho-logical' shift of legal rationality; their work dismantles the mechanics of perpetuating a logician's ideal in modern legal dogmatics.[63] To say that law (and not only legal dogmatics) has no *Sitz im Leben* amounts to erasing the action which leads to the production of law as an institutional fact (cf. *supra*) for the benefit of systemic metaphysics. Many contemporary debates, however, tend to prove that the legal community (which does not consist only of dogmatists) gives a human substrate to the subject of law and gives a legal character to corporations and associations which operate by an analogy 'which does not question the strict superposition of the human being and the subject of law, namely the *analogatum princeps*'.[64] The fact remains, however, that the human being whose legal activity is identified with the subject of law is not a simple biological being, but a certain conception and implementation of this biological being.

Individualism is, no doubt, at the core of modern law. Furthermore, legal individualism carries with it a specific conception of a series of notions related to that of the person as liberty, will, capacity, responsibility and intentionality.

Following Waline, to take only one example, we first note the extent to which 'the Declaration of the Rights of Man (and of the citizen of 1789) is individualistic in its principle and evidently individualistic in its content'.[65] This individualism embodies multiple paths: political, philosophical, legal, literary and economic. We shall note the emphasis placed on the free development of the personality, the priority given to the individual over society, the exclusion of any interference between the individual and the national community, and the consecration of the right of property. From a legal point of view, this is expressed by the constitution of the individual as 'purpose of law and of all social institutions', as the unique holder of liberties. This exaggerated individualism, even if partially diminished later on, remains one of the fundamental characteristics of modern law and leaves a significant mark on the modern legal conception of the person. That person is declared free, and from that individual freedom of man comes his ability to create law.[66] In Gounot's words, 'law is nothing but this initial and sovereign freedom which belongs to all men'.[67] A series of ideas follow, among them, the idea of fault and responsibility for fault. In criminal cases, the theory of free will has been widely questioned where subjective situations are distinct from objective situations and, in cases of industrial accidents, where the no-fault responsibility is recognised, or in other cases where responsibility is founded on presumption.[68] The fact remains that these distinctions originate in the model of the conscious individual gifted with will, acting intentionally, capable and thus susceptible to the consequences of his or her acts.

The theory of the autonomy of will originates in the nineteenth century under the influence of Kantian philosophy. It claims that the restraining force of private legal acts originates primarily in the will of the authors of the acts. This theory clearly rests upon the philosophical conception of human beings as master of their acts and, consequently, determines situations in which the acts of individuals escape their will (for example, the theory of lack of consent). In the same way, there is a distinction between an agent contracting to accomplish legal acts and the same agent contracting to accomplish simple material acts. The will to contract implies the deliberate intention to obligate oneself, while the violation of a contractual agreement does not imply the intention to engage one's responsibility, but has this responsibility as a consequence.[69] If the original theory of the autonomy of will knows more and more limitations, we shall simply note that it remains a cornerstone in systems of civil law. So, the intention of the parties in contracting is fundamental in the law of obligations as well as in matters of civil responsibility. In criminal matters, the will of the author of an act determines its qualification, and one must look to the evidence of the author's will and not merely to the material facts surrounding the act committed.[70] And if, as in the law of responsibility, intentionality changes, it is not in the sense of its disappearance, but in the sense of its unlimited extension where the author of each act must keep in mind the infinite chain of the empirical consequences of his act.

Responsibility is a concept whose legal formulation is linked to liberal political philosophy, and the civil code is one of its principal means of expression. Its appearance in the legal field is an obvious product of the Kantian philosophy of causality and imputation, in which each must consider themselves as the unique and ultimate starting point of what happens to them. The field of responsibility is certainly a field where law and philosophy are closely intertwined. The notion of fault constitutes the junction between the two. We shall note the immanently moral nature of the latter. The theory of responsibility has considerably evolved, particularly in the twentieth century, and not only has been replaced in certain fields by a principle of solidarity and resulted in other fields in its disintegration (with the notion of risk in labour law, for example), but also determines the transition from a philosophy of individual fault to a philosophy of collective reparations. We speak of a crisis of responsibility 'with as a starting point a shift in the emphasis previously placed on the presumed author of the damage and nowadays preferably placed on the victim who is in a position to demand reparations for damages',[71] with the transition 'from an individual handling of the fault to the socialised handling of risk'.[72] We shall note again with Ricœur the enormous paradox of a 'society only concerned with solidarity in the interest of willingly reinforcing a philosophy of risk' and 'the vindictive search for the guilty which amounts to the recrimination of the identified author of the damages',[73] but of outrageous damages exceeding in a huge way the predictive abilities of the presumed guilty (as, for example, the contaminated blood scandal). Be that as it may, it is important to notice that this extension in space and this lengthening in time of the legal philosophy of responsibility does not work in the sense of a 'dis-individuation', but in the sense of a reinforcement of the ability to predict and of interdependence that Elias precisely links to individuation. It is no longer only a matter of imputation of fault, but also initially of the demand for caution and precaution, and is approaching a sense of responsibility for the potential effects of each person's acts.

Towards a pragmatic study of the person in context and in action

This introduction is aimed essentially at exposing a certain number of theses, debates and postulates which the chapters in this book explain by using the example of the legal experience of Arab societies; this is why the question was deliberately dealt with in a general way.

We can therefore address the question of the person as a category of the law of various Arab countries on multiple levels. The perspective inspired by the sociology of Mauss is a study of the historical and social dynamics which led the emergence of this category, this 'biographical' process describing in the end its present contents. In Elias's approach, the very principle of individuation growing in our societies lies in the association of the processes of differentiation, interdependence and self-restraint. However, in Luhmann's systemic manner, the emphasis is on the personality as the semantic artefact through which law gives a being, physical or abstract, or even a thing, the capacity to accomplish legal acts.

Finally, there is another pragmatic possibility, where the category of the person is not dissociated from its use, which is necessarily local, contextual and contingent. This, however, supposes the substitution of a praxiological approach that considers law and the legal person only in its practice to a sociology of great explanatory schemes.

As Watson points out, the notion of person and of 'self' tends to be hypostatised.[74] This affirmation of an autonomous or quasi-autonomous self, however, is contingent, as we have previously seen. Moerman thus shows that the Thai cultural context does not tend to reify a 'self' who would be an agent thinking, planning, acting from within, any more than it tends to consider interactional events as the product of the action of multiple autonomous or quasi-autonomous selves.[75]

In this respect, the theorisations of the persons alleged by the people, ordinary people or professionals of philosophy, do not necessarily constitute the model for 'their actual practical, pre-theoretical use of their ordinary mental concepts and predicates'.[76] In other words, the notion of a singular and integrated 'self' constitutes not an obscure and unexplained analytical resource, but the subject in itself of empirical investigation, the objective being then 'to analyse the methodic practical use of whatever conception of self is employed by a collectivity'.[77] The person, the 'me', the 'self', are not essences,[78] but the constant interactional product of public 'linguistic' resources displayed culturally, which is to say contextually, in a methodical manner. It is in and through conversation and other systems of language exchange (among them law) that character features – motivation, intention and rationality – or mental states – joy, fear, depression, suicidal intentions, hostility etc. – are attributed to the person.

> These imputations and ascriptions are, without exception, invoked on particular interactional occasions in order to make sense – culturally standardised, utterly practical sense – of a given action which is part of the conversation or is described within it, (or both). The 'nature and attributes of the self' are always methodically identified, defined, formulated and contested through action and interaction, i.e. they are constituted in the public domain and operate entirely as public, transparent phenomena.[79]

It is now no longer a question of trying to identify the great social and historical dynamics, but of undertaking what Coulter (1992) calls 'a praxiological understanding of the "mental"'.[80]

Notes

1 Meulders-Klein, 1993, p. 436.
2 Mauss, 1950.
3 Carrithers, Collins and Lukes, 1985.
4 Durkheim, 1912, pp. 9, 13.
5 Mauss, 1950, p. 333.
6 Carrithers, 1985.
7 La Fontaine, 1985, p. 125.
8 Mauss, 1950, p. 334.
9 Lukes, 1985, p. 284.
10 Collins, 1985.
11 La Fontaine, 1985, p. 138.
12 Taylor, 1985.
13 Lukes, 1985, p. 287.
14 Carrithers, 1985, p. 253.
15 La Fontaine, 1985.
16 Lukes, 1985, p. 294.
17 Lukes, 1985, pp. 294–95.
18 Elias notes that evolution, however intelligible, defies deliberate planning. Elias's evolutionism claims to be radically critical of the teleological reconstruction that is proper to the philosophy of history and which, for him, is nothing more than metaphysics (Garrigou and Lacroix, 1997, p. 24). For Elias, evolution stems from an order which is both immanent change and void of any finality. It is a 'progressive structure for which we can elaborate a model in which the succession, at first sight purely of facts and events, is organised in a comprehensible sequence' (Colliot-Thélène, 1997, p. 68). The question remains concerning the coherence of the elaboration of such a type of model.
19 Lukes, 1985, p. 298.
20 Stockinger, 1993, p. 48.
21 Pufendorf, as cited in Arnaud, 1993, p. 345.
22 Gounot, 1912, p. 27.
23 It is important to note that my reading of Elias is radically generous. What I mean by this is that the criticism of his evolutionism, his determinism, his psychologism and even his metaphysics of nature and of human nature are generally well-founded (on this subject, see Ferrié, 2001). I believe, however, that Elias suggests a certain number of paths which, though he is far from following them, are nonetheless fertile, especially concerning the relations between 'small' (everyday life) and 'great' (power) things. It is the path

followed by Schütz, Berger and Luckmann and by ethnomethodology (on this subject, see Dupret, 'Forced Interaction: intersubjectivity, institutions and history', 2001).

24 Elias, 1991, p. 59.
25 Ibid., p. 65.
26 Duerr, 1998, p. 4.
27 Burguière, 1998.
28 As quoted by Burguière, 1997, p. 165.
29 Elias, 1991, p. 59.
30 Ibid., p. 268.
31 Henry, 1997, 203.
32 Elias, 1991, pp. 189–90. On this point, we can legitimately think that Louis Dumont agrees with Elias when, on the subject of the philosophy of Herder, he demonstrates that his theory of cultures is a 'national alternative' to the individualistic ideology and system of modern values (Dumont, 1983, p. 139). In other words, Dumont recognises the idea that a change in the prevailing structure and in its ideological representation has led to the transformation of the ways of thinking and acting.
33 Elias, 1975, pp. 185–86.
34 Courty, 1997, pp. 167–68.
35 Weber, 1971, p. 33.
36 Defrance, 1997, p. 294.
37 Defrance, 1997, p. 296.
38 Defrance, 1997, p. 297. On this particular point, law must play a fundamental role and, in conclusion, we may underscore the extension of the field of regulations carried out by the legal process of codification. The fruit of this monopolistic and centralised element of power, the code is a system of rules put in writing to reinforce their imperativeness notwithstanding the question of their effectiveness. In that, it is different from the textbook on ethics which, because of its need to prescribe common practice, reflects instead on a loosening of restraint whose element of control moves away from the individual and opens a space for withdrawal (Burguière, 1998, p. xxiii). Hence, the paradox of the norm which, when legal, increases the external control upon the individual and which, when ethical, increases his or her personal autonomy. The simultaneous reinforcement of these two phenomena can, in any case, appear specific to modern society where the monopoly of the legal system and the relegation of ethics to the 'private sphere' go together.
39 Meulders-Klein, 1993, p. 437.
40 Rorty, 1976, p. 309.

41 Ibid.
42 Locke, 1968, II, XXVII, § 26.
43 Dumont, 1983, p. 88.
44 Ricœur, 1995.
45 Ricœur, 1995, p. 32.
46 Ricœur, 1995, p. 34.
47 Ricœur, 1995, p. 35.
48 Rommel, 1999.
49 Rommel, 1999, p. 63.
50 Aubry and Rau, 1936, I, p. 305.
51 Aarnio, 1987, p. 28.
52 Rommel, 1999, p. 62.
53 Rommel, 1999, p. 63, who quotes Kelsen, 1962.
54 Foucault, 1966.
55 Teubner, 1992.
56 Rommel, 1999, p. 67.
57 Rommel, 1999, p. 68.
58 Ganty, 1999, p. 38.
59 Rommel, 1999, pp. 69–70.
60 Ganty, 1999, p. 41.
61 Ricœur, 1995, pp. 34–35.
62 Rommel, 1999, p. 74.
63 Lenoble and Ost, 1980.
64 Dijon, 1999, p. 53.
65 Waline, 1945, p. 376.
66 Savatier, 1959, § 356.
67 Gounot, 1912, p. 27.
68 Arnaud, 1993, p. 346.
69 Rigaux, 1993, pp. 648, 649.
70 We shall note that the classical theory of Islamic law (*fiqh*) considers that the voluntary nature of homicide can only be established objectively with the proof that the instrument used to kill constitutes a weapon in itself (cf. Peters, 1990).
71 Ricœur, 1995, p. 58.
72 Engel, 1993.
73 Ricœur, 1995, p. 59.
74 Watson, 1998.
75 Moerman, 1987.
76 Coulter, 1992, p. 249.
77 Watson, 1998, p. 212.
78 'Even though, for Mead, the origins and anchorage of the self are social and even though the self reflects the social process, it

is a cognitive phenomenon, an inner dramatisation of the external process. In Mead's work, there is an essentialism (Mead, indeed, writes of the "essence of self": Strauss, 1964, p. 228) and a parallel reification of the self/interaction boundary. Mead certainly does not fully transcend the "internal-external" or "self-interaction" distinction upon which a conception of such a boundary is based. The distinction is only mitigated, not abolished, by treating the self as the indwelling of the social process' (Watson, 1998, p. 214).

79 Watson, 1998, pp. 214–15.

80 Coulter, 1992.

Bibliography

Aarnio, A., *The Rational as Reasonable*, Dordrecht, Reidel-Kluwer, 1987.

Arnaud, A.J., 'Liberté', in A.J. Arnaud et al. (ed.), *Dictionnaire encyclopédique de théorie et de sociologie du droit*, 2e ed., Paris, Libraire Générale de Droit et de Jurisprudence, 1993, pp. 345–46.

Aubry, C. and C. Rau, *Cours de droit civil français*, Paris, Marchal and Billart, 1936.

Boltanski, L. and L. Thévenot, *De la justification. Les économies de la grandeur*, Paris, Gallimard, 1991.

Burguière, A., 'Processus de civilisation et processus national chez Norbert Elias', in A. Garrigou and B. Lacroix (eds), *Norbert Elias, la politique et l'histoire*, Paris, La Découverte, 1997, pp. 145–65.

– 'Entre sociologie et anthropologie: La civilisation des mœurs en procès', preface in H.P. Duerr, *Nudité et pudeur. Le mythe du processus de civilisation*, Paris, Éd. de la Maison des Sciences de l'Homme, 1998, pp. ix–xxi.

Carrithers, M., 'An alternative social history of the self', in M. Carrithers, S. Collins and S. Lukes (eds), *The Category of the Person. Anthropology, Philosophy, History*, Cambridge, Cambridge University Press, 1985, pp. 234–56.

Carrithers, M., S. Collins and S. Lukes (eds), *The Category of the Person. Anthropology, Philosophy, History*, Cambridge, Cambridge University Press, 1985.

Chartier, R., 'Formation sociale et économie psychique: la société de cour dans le procès de civilisation', preface in N. Elias, *La société de cour*, Paris, Flammarion, 1985, pp. i–xxviii.

Chazel, F., 'Emile Durkheim et l'élaboration d'un "programme de recherche" en sociologie du droit', in F. Chazel and J. Commaille (eds), *Normes juridiques et régulation sociale*, Paris, Libraire Générale de Droit et de Jurisprudence, 1991, pp. 27–38.

Collins, S., 'Categories, concepts or predicaments? Remarks on Mauss's use of philosophical terminology', in M. Carrithers, S. Collins and S. Lukes (eds), *The Category of the Person. Anthropology, Philosophy, History*, Cambridge, Cambridge University Press, 1985, pp. 46–82.

Colliot-Thélène, C., 'Le concept de rationalisation: de Max Weber à Norbert Elias', in A. Garrigou and B. Lacroix (eds), *Norbert Elias, la politique et l'histoire*, Paris, La Découverte, 1997, pp. 52–74.

Coulter, J., 'Cognition: "cognition" in an ethnomethodological mode', in G. Button (ed.), *Ethnomethodology and the Human Sciences*, Cambridge, Cambridge University Press, 1991, pp. 176–95.

– 'Bilmes on internal states: A critical commentary', *Journal for the Theory of Social Behaviour*, 22/3, 1992, pp. 239–52.

Courty, G., 'Norbert Elias et la construction des groupes sociaux: de l'économie psychique à l'art de se regrouper', in A. Garrigou and B. Lacroix (eds), *Norbert Elias, la politique et l'histoire*, Paris, La Découverte, 1997, pp. 166–91.

Defrance, J., 'Le goût de la violence', in A. Garrigou and B. Lacroix (eds), *Norbert Elias, la politique et l'histoire*, Paris, La Découverte, 1997, pp. 290–301.

Dijon, X., 'Le sujet de Ricœur: côté droit', in F.X. Druet and E. Ganty (eds), *Rendre justice au droit. En lisant Le Juste de Paul Ricœur*, Namur, University Press of Namur, 1999, pp. 51–57.

Duerr, H.P., *Nudité et pudeur. Le mythe du processus de civilisation*, Paris, Ed. de la Maison des Sciences de l'Homme, 1998.

Dupret, B., 'Intersubjectivity, Institutions and History: Remarks on Interaction and Constraint' (in Arabic), *Mutûn 'asriyya fî'l-'ulûm al-ijtimâ'iyya*, 2, 2001, pp. 44–52.

Dumont, L., *Essais sur l'individualisme. Une perspective anthropologique sur l'idéologie moderne*, Paris, Seuil, 1983.

Durkheim, E., *Les formes élémentaires de la vie religieuse*, Paris, Alcan, 1912.

– 'De la détermination du fait moral', *Sociologie et philosophie*, Paris, Alcan, 1924, pp. 49–116.

– *La division du travail social*, Paris, Alcan, 7e ed., 1960 (1893).

Elias, N., *La civilisation des moeurs*, Paris, Calmann-Lévy, 1973.

– *La dynamique de l'Occident*, Paris, Calmann-Lévy, 1975.

– *La société des individus*, Paris, Fayard, 1991.

Engel, L., 'Vers une nouvelle approche de la responsabilité. Le droit français face à la dérive américaine', *Esprit*, June 1993, pp. 13–27.

Ferrié, J.-N., 'The Thoughtless Interaction' (in Arabic), *Mutûn 'asriyya fî'l-'ulûm al-ijtimâ'iyya*, 2, 2001, pp. 53–58.

Foucault, M., *Les Mots et les choses*, Paris, Gallimard, 1966.

Ganty, E., 'Du sujet de droit au sujet du droit: attestation et reconnaissance', in F.X. Druet and E. Ganty (eds), *Rendre justice au droit. En lisant Le Juste de Paul Ricœur*, Namur, University Press of Namur, 1999, pp. 37–49.

Garrigou, A. and B. Lacroix, 'Norbert Elias: le travail d'une œuvre', in A. Garrigou and B. Lacroix (eds), *Norbert Elias, la politique et l'histoire*, Paris, La Découverte, 1997, pp. 7–27.

Gounot, E., *Le principe de l'autonomie de la volonté en Droit privé. Contribution à l'étude critique de l'individualisme juridique*, Paris, 1912.

Henry, C., 'Eléments pour une théorie de l'individuation. Quand le domestique Mozart se prenait pour un libre artiste', in A. Garrigou and B. Lacroix (eds), *Norbert Elias, la politique et l'histoire*, Paris, La Découverte, 1997, pp. 192–212.

Isambert, F.A., 'Durkheim et la sociologie des normes', in F. Chazel and J. Commaille (eds), *Normes juridiques et régulation sociale*, Paris, Libraire Générale de Droit et de Jurisprudence, 1991, pp. 51–64.

Jackson, B.S., *Law, Fact and Narrative Coherence*, Liverpool, Deborah Charles Publications, 1988.

– *Making Sense in Law. Linguistic, Psychological and Semiotic Perspectives*, Liverpool, Deborah Charles Publications, 1995.

– 'Towards a semiotic model of professional practice, with some narrative reflections on the criminal process', *International Journal of the Legal Profession*, 1/1, 1994, pp. 55–79.

Kelsen, H., *Théorie pure du droit*, Paris, Dalloz (trans. Reine Rechtslehre, Vienna, Deuticke), 1962 (1934).

La Fontaine, J.S., 'Person and individual: Some anthropological reflections', in M. Carrithers, S. Collins and S. Lukes (eds), *The Category of the Person. Anthropology, Philosophy, History*, Cambridge, Cambridge University Press, 1985, pp. 123–40.

Lenoble, J. and F. Ost, *Droit, mythe et raison. Essai sur la dérive mythologique de la rationalité juridique*, Bruxelles, Publications of the Saint-Louis University Faculties, 1980.

Locke, J., *An Essay Concerning Human Understanding*, London, Dent, 1968.

Lukes, S., 'Conclusion', in M. Carrithers, S. Collins and S. Lukes (eds), *The Category of the Person. Anthropology, Philosophy, History*, Cambridge, Cambridge University Press, 1985, pp. 282–301.

Mauss, M., 'Une catégorie de l'esprit humain: la notion de personne, celle de "moi"', *Sociologie et anthropologie*, Paris, Presses Universitaires de France (extract from *Journal of the Royal Anthropological Institute*, vol. lxviii, 1938), 1950, pp. 333–61.

Meulders-Klein, M.T., 'Personne', in A.J. Arnaud et al. (eds), *Dictionnaire encyclopédique de théorie et de sociologie du droit*, 2e ed., Paris, Libraire Générale de Droit et de Jurisprudence, 1993, pp. 435–38.

Moerman, M., *Talking Culture*, Cambridge, Cambridge University Press, 1987.

Montefiore, A., 'Identité morale', in M. Canto-Sperber (ed.), *Dictionnaire d'éthique et de philosophie morale*, Paris, Presses Universitaires de France, 1996, pp. 691–97.

Peters, R., 'Murder on the Nile: Homicide trials in 19th century Egyptian shari'a courts'. *Die Welt des Islams*, 30, 1990, pp. 95–115.

Ricœur, P., *Le Juste*, Paris, Esprit, 1995.

Rigaux, F., 'Volonté', in A.J. Arnaud et al. (eds), *Dictionnaire encyclopédique de théorie et de sociologie du droit*, 2e ed., Paris Libraire Générale de Droit et de Jurisprudence, 1993, pp. 647–49.

Rommel, G., 'La nature du sujet en droit', in F.-X. Druet and E. Ganty (eds), *Rendre justice au droit. En lisant Le Juste de Paul Ricœur*, Namur, University Press of Namur, 1999, pp. 59–74.

Rorty, A., *The Identities of Persons*, Berkeley, University of California Press, 1976.

Savatier, R., *Les métamorphoses économiques et sociales du droit privé d'aujourd'hui. Approfondissement d'un droit renouvelé*, Paris, 1959.

Searle, J.R., *The Construction of Social Reality*, London, Penguin Books, 1995.

Stockinger, P., 'Autonomie', in A.J. Arnaud et al. (eds), *Dictionnaire encyclopédique de théorie et de sociologie du droit*, 2e ed., Paris, Libraire Générale de Droit et de Jurisprudence, 1993, pp. 47–49.

Strauss, A.L., *Mead on Social Psychology*, Chicago IL, University of Chicago Press, 1964.

Taylor, C., 'The person', in M. Carrithers, S. Collins and S. Lukes (eds), *The Category of the Person. Anthropology, Philosophy, History*, Cambridge, Cambridge University Press, 1985, pp. 258–63.

Teubner, G., 'Pour une épistémologie constructiviste du droit', *Annales Economies, Sociétés, Civilisations*, 6, 1992, pp. 1149–1169.

Veyne, P., *Les Grecs ont-ils cru à leurs mythes? Essai sur l'imagination constituante*, Paris, Seuil, 1983.

Waline, M., *L'individualisme et le droit*, Paris, Domat Monchrestien, 1945.

Watson, R., 'Ethnomethodology, Consciousness and Self', *Journal of Consciousness Studies*, 5(2), 1998, pp. 202–23.

Weber, M., *Economie et société*, Paris, Plon, 1971.

CHAPTER 2

The Articulation of 'I', 'We' and the 'Person': Elements for an Anthropological Approach within Western and Islamic Contexts

Mohamed Nachi

In order to understand the 'meaning of justice', it is necessary to examine both individual aspects – as related to a specific individual – and collective aspects – as related to a community. Therefore, the categories of 'I', 'we' and the 'person' are at the heart of our investigations into justice.[1] The question first calls for a determination of the appropriate status of the two fundamental categories of 'I' and 'we'. How can one define them? Is it through the *autonomy* of the 'I' and its freedom to act according to moral principles (the 'determining I' of Kant). Or is it through the dominance or primacy of the 'we' within which the 'I' belongs and has its roots? How are these categories linked to the idea of the person? These questions are important because they present one with significant epistemological implications as well as decisive ethical issues.[2]

This chapter examines these implications and issues evolving from numerous differing and even opposing concepts: those of the 'liberals' (Rawls, in particular) and the communitarians, but also those of other authors, among whom one notes Schapp, Mead and Ricœur. The debate fuelled by each author leads to a clarification of the critical roles played by the 'I' and the 'we' in a determination of the basic meaning of justice. The status of 'I', 'we' and the 'person' cannot be grasped without a precise study of certain related ideas, such as *me*, *self* and *subject*. 'We', as it is used here, always assumes the existence of a group of individuals; one could say an aggregate of 'I,' sharing common experiences, concerns, values and a certain togetherness. For its part, the 'I', as Etzioni says, needs the 'we' in order to exist. To have conflict-free cohabitation between individuals or co-subjects, there must be agreement on certain rules, norms and conventions that are equally shared. All this is preliminary to the existence of a social or community link and leads to what Wittgenstein calls a 'life form' (*Lebensform*). Furthermore, it should be clear that the relationship between the 'I' and the 'we' is never established definitively. On the contrary, it is in a constant state of evolution and must be regularly redefined in order to respond to the needs of a situation or action. In this way, it can be considered as a *process.*

For a deeper analysis of these different concepts and to show their *articulation* with each other and with the notion of 'person', I refer to the works of both Western Christian and Muslim authors. The choice of these works is based on their theoretical contributions and on the renewed look that they provide into the question of the person.

Even though this question has been the subject of multiple classical research efforts in social psychology, sociology and anthropology, I believe that it deserves a closer re-examination, tapping into recent discoveries in social science and philosophy.[3] By introducing a renewed discussion of the categories of 'I', 'me', 'self' and the 'person' as inspired by contemporary moral philosophy as well as current historical and anthropological research, I hope to generate a more detailed and satisfactory analysis of the *articulation* between these different fundamental categories.

I propose, therefore, to adopt a diachronic and *genealogical* perspective derived from the contributions of numerous disciplines. One of the goals of this study is to define the parameters of the idea of 'person' within an Islamic context. This includes examining how in the West it has inherited aspects from a long history, and how in the classical Islamic context it benefits from a specific status that precedes or predetermines the one attributed by modern Western society.

The liberal versus communitarian debate and the question of the subject

Authors called communitarian have usefully formulated the most definitive criticism of the fundamentally epistemological presuppositions contained in the 'liberal' interpretation of the question of this subject. This interpretation is considered too global, too abstract and, in some ways, incompatible with the concrete reality of the human person. Looking at the well-known critique formulated by Arendt regarding the concept of human rights and transposing that onto Rawls's concept of this same subject, one can say there is 'an obvious paradox, because of the reference to an 'abstract human being' that does not seem to exist anywhere'.[4]

So one has, in effect, both this hypothetical 'abstract human being' and its underlying values of universality, axiological neutrality and individualism that are criticised and rejected in whole by most of the communitarian authors. The best illustration of these authors' position is the 'metaphor of habitation' that Walzer uses to sum up his opposition to the idea of a subject without belonging or attachment.[5] This metaphor aims to reject any concept of the 'me' as an abstract entity that claims to transcend casual facts and escape from any cultural or historical determination. It is not possible, according to Walzer, to make an abstraction of these determinations or to ignore attachments.

The communitarian criticisms take on several forms and are concerned as much with the presuppositions of liberalism as a philosophical and political theory as with Rawls's fundamental assertions concerning the 'justice as equity' theory. Among these, one must consider what are called the 'three priorities' at the heart of Rawls's demonstration, that to some degree make up the epistemological assumptions of his moral anthropology. These priorities can be summarised as follows: the priority of right versus good; the priority of the self versus ends; the priority of individual rights versus societal rights. I am limiting myself to the second priority, being the most important in this study, since the others have already been examined.[6]

For certain liberals, a single satisfactory concept of the common good is as illusory as the concept of an end (*telos*) that arises from a consensus or an adhesion to something by all members of society, because, according to them, it is impossible to choose the 'best possible good life' or the best common good for a community to the extent that no unanimous agreement is conceivable without falling into authoritarianism. This is why 'liberals' challenge the idea of the priority of good over right. Referring to Kant, they affirm that only the 'autonomy of will', meaning the freedom of the subject to act in conformity with moral principles, can be considered as a 'supreme good'. In this sense Rawls, following Kant, maintains that 'the concept of justice is independent from the concept of good and precedes it', and that the self always precedes its ends. As de Benoist notes:

> This priority of the self over its ends means that I am never defined by my engagements or my attachments, but, on the contrary, I can at all times distance myself from them in order to freely determine my choices which is only possible if the individual is positioned as a separate being.[7]

Instead of considering the basis of the 'me' as intrinsically composing its identity, liberals see it as being without social bearings, without history. The communitarians do not in any way share this view of the self 'out of context' and reject the idea of a society that defines itself as a simple juxtaposition of individuals. Thus, by showing the *limits* of what he calls 'deontological liberalism', based on Kantian tradition, Sandel reveals the inadequacies of the Rawlsian concept of the subject and the self. The priority of the subject over its ends, he writes, means that I am never defined by my possessions, but always capable of stepping back to assess them, then to revise them.[8]

Sandel adds:

> For a subject as presented by Rawls, the ultimate moral question is not: 'Who am I?' for the answer to this question is considered a given, but rather: 'What goals am I going to select?' Therein is the question that leads to the idea of will. It seems, therefore, that the subject according to Rawls possesses an impoverished epistemological me, poorly-equipped conceptually to engage in the sort of self-reflection that can transcend a simple attention to preferences and desires in order to see and be able to re-describe the subject encompassing them.[9]

This concept of the self is not *realistic,* for it gives pre-eminence to the intrinsic qualities of the individual to the detriment of the relationships that the individual has with the 'fundamental structure of society' (Rawls) in which he or she is an active participant. Such a concept sets forth the thesis of a pre-existing and independent composition of subjectivity, thereby demanding the *priority of the self over its ends.* In other words, this concept assumes that the constituting elements of a person have priority over the values and ends that an individual may pursue, and that identity is determined independently of any membership of a community, of any tradition within which it is rooted.

This concept of a subject stripped of all exterior influence, of an 'unencumbered self' and of an individual promoted to the rank of abstract autonomous entity is, according to Sandel, inconsistent. For Sandel, the individual, as conceived by Rawls, 'is stripped of all his contingent attributes, acquires a supra-empirical status essentially without attachments defined in advance and then given to his ends, a pure action figure with possessions, ultimately impoverished'.[10]

In addition, Sandel reveals a contradiction in the way that Rawls makes use of a singular and similar concept of the subject in order to justify two different but essential aspects of two 'principles of justice': an *intra-subjective* aspect and an *inter-subjective* aspect.[11] The 'veil of ignorance', whose major function is to allow members to choose these principles, justifies, in the final analysis, the '"principle of equal freedom" only to the extent that it places members *on an equal footing*'.

For Sandel, the 'principle of difference' requires a different and necessarily broader conceptualisation of the subject. A concept in which the primary concern would be to justify individuals' altruistic preoccupations guarantees, in a sense, a certain social solidarity. Sandel shows that such a principle assumes a high degree of solidarity among its participants. Yet this solidarity is shown to be totally lacking in the abstract definition of a subject without history, stripped of all connection with its past and with the social world whose members are defined as mutually indifferent. In addition, this definition appears as demeaning and, finally, as incompatible with the social and altruistic vocation of the 'principle of difference'. Sandel adds:

> Without a broader concept of the possessing subject, as the Rawlsian idea of common good also demands, there would not be a compelling reason why these goods should be offered for communal

> social ends rather than to serve individual ends. On the other hand, absent any enlarged idea of the possessing subject, to look at 'my' faculties and talents as simply instruments for a greater social end, is to use me as a means to ends that are pursued by others, and therefore to violate a central Kantian and Rawlsian moral commandment.[12]

Therefore, the idea of an 'unencumbered self', the idea of a deontological liberal subject unaware of its ends and its belongings is undermined both by the criticism that Sandel has put forth and by the contradiction that Sandel has succeeded in revealing. Therefore, this idea must, according to Sandel, give way to a *constitutive concept of subjectivity* that portrays the identity of the 'me', of the subject and of the person as the product of a combination of history, culture and, even, chance. It is a question of a self in the context of all its social attributes. Far from preceding its ends, the self is unavoidably *composed* of them, including the values, which form the base and give meaning to the community to which it belongs. The self is always embedded and located in a sociohistorical context. It is these different sociohistorical religious aspects that contribute to the formation and the development of the identity of the self. On this subject, Sandel writes: 'To imagine a person incapable of constitutive attachments does not lead to the concept of an ideally free and rational agent, but rather to the concept of a person totally stripped of character and moral depth'.[13] In order that the 'principle of difference' does not use certain persons as a means to the ends of others, according to Sandel, it is necessary that the subject be located within a 'we' rather than a 'self'. Such circumstances assume the existence of individuals who share a strong sense of community.[14]

The belonging of 'I' to a 'we' thus becomes a primary condition, one that is thereby necessary for any definition of the person to the extent that it constitutes the basis for the formation of identity and individual personality. As a result, justice can no longer benefit from the priority standing that Rawls and the liberals accord it, since it is circumscribed within a community. The common good of this community creates limits for justice and can, henceforth, be considered as preceding it. Sandel claims, in the tradition of Aristotle, that the common good of a community has priority, putting justice in second place.

The individual as an autonomous subject is, as has been seen, at the centre of Rawls' theory of justice. Individual rights demand, therefore, absolute priority and are guaranteed in an intangible manner. As Rawls writes: 'Each person has an inviolability based on justice that, even in the name of the well-being of the whole of society, can not be transgressed'.[15]

The priority status of individual rights is, according to Rawls, the logical consequence of the two other priorities. Once the communitarians and Sandel demonstrated the inconsistency of the first two priorities, it follows that this third priority, which is a logical consequence of them, evaporates *de facto.*

The thesis of the primacy of the rights of the individual over those of society is not valid according to communitarians to the extent that it appears to be excessive. According to communitarians, the reasoning for the cult of the individual is put forward to the detriment of other more significant virtues for the individual. These virtues contribute to the formation of individual identity and allow a thinking-subject to give meaning to his or her actions. This explains why the idea of virtue holds an important place in the communitarian concept of justice.

Ultimately, we find ourselves looking at two opposing concepts, both of which err by too much rigidity: one focusing on the idea of autonomy, the other accentuating the idea of belonging. In order to avoid the logical difficulties of one or the other, it makes sense to view the connections between the 'I', the 'we' and the 'person' in terms of articulation.

The development of a paradigm articulating the 'I', the 'we' and the 'person'

The categories of 'I', 'we' and the 'self', and their articulation

In this research, I am interested in all aspects relating to 'I', 'we' and 'self', especially the specific clues that allow one to explore the question of the 'person' and the theoretical preconceptions that help understand the relation between these different fundamental categories. This implies, as Etzioni states, the development of a 'new paradigm' that articulates the whole.[16]

By giving priority to the *dialogic situation* and, more precisely, to ordinary narration found in daily life, my approach to the meaning of justice has, as one of its foundations, the relationship of 'I' and 'we'. Through this relationship and the narrative configuration that it expresses, one finds personal judgements and individual or collective attitudes that exist in the social world. Through the 'I' and the 'we' and the fundamental relationship which usually unites them, but which also sometimes separates them, one finds meanings that people assign to justice and injustice, to that which is praiseworthy or blameable. In giving voice to the 'I' through speech and in a narrative mode, one gets closer to the 'we', revealing its impact on the 'I'; one can thereby examine their internal connections and entanglements. For, no doubt, the 'I' is as important for the 'we' as the 'we' is for the 'I'.

The 'I' and the 'we' have in common their participation as integral members in the development of a social link at the heart of which are combined individual and collective histories, the destiny of each and the destiny of all. It is not a question of a juxtaposition of the 'I' and the 'we', nor a super-positioning of the two simply because of their continual overlapping and intermingling. Just as there are personal histories, seen as narrative configurations of a speaking or telling 'I', there are collective histories that reflect the communal life of the 'we'. But, these stories are not without strong interconnections and articulations. It is in this sense that stories or recitations ('affairs' that are explained later on in this chapter), albeit of an individual origin, allow access to the collective/anthropological dimension. In explaining the status and the role of spoken narrative, allowing for an anthropological approach, Balandier writes:

> The objective is to access, from within, a reality that goes beyond the narrator and gives him form. It is a question of grasping the social experience, the subject in his activities, the manner in which he negotiates social conditions that are specific to him.[17]

Therefore, while telling a story, the 'narrating I' lets us know about a person's feeling of belonging to stories shared with others or being 'entangled in stories' according to the formula of Schapp.[18]

Throughout our investigation, narrative configurations are considered, ordinary slice-of-life stories, examining that which implies the collective, the entanglement – in short, the 'we'.

Some may reproach me for making the 'I' depend on the 'we' and, by doing so, giving dominance to a kind of methodological holism. On the other hand, others could consider that my approach renders the 'we' just as an adjunct to the 'I', implying the pre-eminence of methodological individualism. To both, I respond that, in my point of view, these are articulations and contact points for grounding and making connections between the 'I' and the 'we', between individual and collective, and worthy of our attention.

Why, henceforth, do I start with the 'I' and why do I not try to start with the 'we'? The reason is, above all, epistemological. It is a fact that one cannot grasp the 'we' unless one returns to its materialisation in a 'universal history' that is not within the scope of this work. Outside this 'universal history', it would be difficult to get to the 'we'. What remains, therefore, is the trail of the 'I', that is to say the narrative activity or the story in order to try to reach the 'we'. Ordinary stories of daily life can guide one on this path. They can help one uncover some of the specific and primordial traits that characterise belonging to the 'we'.

Whether these traits are insufficient or sometimes more or less simplistic is not too bothersome, since the 'we' is not taken to be something that it is not – i.e. a homogeneous monolithic entity – and we do not fall into caricature, thereby, neglecting the most significant traits. These traits constitute bridges between the 'I' and the 'we'. Thanks to them, the 'I' can reach the 'we' with bearings to fix its belonging and to define its identity. For 'the "I" needs the "we" in order to exist'.[19] As Schapp repeats, 'belonging, this internal belonging to the unique "We", to the community that encompasses everything, is grasped in new twists and turns'.[20] It is now appropriate to explore these traits or styles while *articulating* the 'I' in relation to the 'we' in order to expand the anthropological basis for our approach and especially to arrive at a global reflection concerning the sense of justice.

We have attempted to do this through the analysis of stories from lives of ordinary people, recognising the constant risk of falling into one of two excesses: to restrict the analysis to the point of cutting the 'I' off from its bearings – an 'I' stripped of all belonging – or, to enlarge it to the point of drowning or dissolving it, which would result in the loss of its 'soul' or its 'substance'. It would be interesting to pursue this reflection as

Schapp does, for example, in order to discover the internal process which creates the relationship between the 'I' and the 'we' and to show how 'the I and the We are integrated in a universal story, how the singularity of the I is abolished in the We, how the we becomes a community we'.[21] It would also be interesting to demonstrate the philosophical and even the ontological interplays between 'I' and 'we' as, for example, Schrader does.[22]

But investigating this in a closer way would take one further into the subject, which is neither the intention nor the ambition of this study. What I now propose is to clearly approach the question of 'I' by correlating it to the question of the 'me', the 'self' and the 'we' in order to arrive finally at the question of the 'person'. I will do this by leaning on the analyses which Mead and Schapp have devoted to these ideas. I will keep in mind, as Ricœur has remarked, that the 'I' has 'this strange property of sometimes meaning *whoever* is speaking (who, by speaking, designates himself or herself) and sometimes meaning the single *me*, that who I am myself'.[23] This is what Ricœur calls the 'amphibology of the "I"'.

Narration and entwining of the 'I' and the 'we' according to Schapp

My study, as I have said, aims to get closer to and understand the sense of justice via stories of everyday life and, therefore, via narration. Narration has as its basis the fact that human beings are entwined in stories just as things are. This is the very provocative thesis defended by Schapp, on whom I will now focus.

Schapp's thinking deals with narrative phenomena in general, and stories in a larger sense, both considered from a phenomenological point of view and treated according to Heidegger's concept of historiality. The philosophical stakes of Schapp's concept are essential for such an approach to history or stories, but it would be long and useless for me to dwell on them. What is important here are the analyses that he devotes to the study of the rapport between the 'we' and the 'me'. I am going to try to grasp this relationship by following the path traced by the author. His plan is to seek the 'We which corresponds to the me, entwined in stories'.[24]

In the relationship between 'me' and 'we', it seems that the 'we' occupies a primary place in the sense that it is the We, which corresponds to the entwined me. For, as Schapp observes, 'The me entwined in stories wears itself out by virtue of being entwined in stories'.[25] It is true that, at a linguistic level, the 'we' is one personal pronoun among others. In Schapp's view, the fundamental pronoun seems to be the 'me' to the extent that the me 'can apply to each person, to each man who appears in stories'. But, Schapp adds quickly, 'if we take our manner of speaking as the foundation, each person can refer to a different entwined me'.[26]

The linguistic investigation proves to be inadequate in the sense that it does not allow one to reach the 'me' entwined in stories. It is true that the starting point or, as Schapp calls it, the 'original point of reference' is the 'speaking me' that 'alone makes possible the jump toward the we'.[27] But, one must never lose sight of the idea that the 'me' is always contained within a 'we'. In addition: 'each We in a story has as its point of departure a me that is understood as part of the We'.[28] Furthermore, because it includes different individual segments, the 'we' can take on varying depths: it can be superficial as well as profound. It is only through individual stories relative to a 'me' that one can approach the 'we' and grasp the relationship that unites them. Schapp writes:

> Just as we first meet the me, entwined within stories, in individual stories, and we then meet the We, albeit an incomplete We, a We on the horizon, this We comes to meet us as if it were complete, graspable, in universal history or in universal stories. It is the We to which we belong.[29]

By introducing the idea of 'self', one can define the relationship between the 'I' and the 'we'.

The 'I', the 'self' and the 'we' as clarified by the works of Mead and Ricœur

These categories hold a central place in the philosophy, psychology and sociology of Mead. Even though some of his assumptions that are sometimes derived from a behavioural perspective are not shared here, I believe that his analysis of the ideas that concern this research is enlightening. One of the contributions of Mead's thinking is his tendency to consider the genesis and development of social groups or of society as deriving from the formation of the 'self', beginning with the internalisation of models of social attitudes and roles by the 'self'. For Mead, 'it is the self as such that allows for a specifically human society'.[30] Society is made up, therefore, of an aggregate of 'self'. However, Mead attributes predominance to the social, the collective, making it a *sine qua non* condition for the emergence of the 'self'. In the manner of Durkheim, he sets forth the pre-eminence of the collective conscience in relation to that of the individual:

> Human society as we know it could not exist, if there were not minds and self. [...] In other words, the human social process in which men are engaged had to be present before the existence within man of the mind and of the self so that, thanks to this process, a mind and a self might develop within him.[31]

Mead's sociological theory in its entirety.[32] Instead, elements from his analysis can be directly useful to us in building an understanding of our initial categories. It is important, however, to know that for Mead, the fundamental principle of human social organisation is that of 'meaningful communication', with the undeniable characteristic of creating a social process with situations for interaction. It is communication that, by establishing significant relationships between self and others, makes possible the emergence of the multiple self and creates lasting co-operation among them. Regarding this, the author writes:

> The principle that I have considered as fundamental in human social organisation is the communication that implies participation with others. This demands that the other appears in the self, that the self identifies with the other, and that one becomes conscious of the self because of the other.[33]

I find such affirmations at the heart of Taylor's analysis. For him, 'one is only a self in the midst of other selves'. A 'me' only exists inside of what he calls 'speaking networks'. The author observes that 'one can not be a me by oneself. I am only a me in relation to certain speakers.'[34]

But what must be the definition for the ideas of 'self' and of 'others' in Mead's point of view? And how can his analysis help me better express my approach to the person? The strength of his analysis is found in an operative distinction between the basic categories that concern me, between the 'I', the 'me' and the 'other'. Taking a closer look, it can be seen that according to Mead, the self can only evolve from a well-constructed society by its rapport with others. In one sense, 'other' corresponds to a 'we' integrating the self, that which Mead calls 'generalised others'.[35] As Daval observes Mead calls the 'other' the organisation of attitudes of those who are engaged in the same social process; the individual creates itself by internalising the other.[36]

The unified self or the unity of 'self' can only be realised through the process of being integrated into a society and internalising social attitudes, which allows the self to belong to a 'generalised other'. However, this self, as whole as it might be, does not 'correspond' simply to internalised social attitudes, nor is it made up of a single homogeneous instance. In this case, Mead insists on the fact that one must distinguish two essential elements in the self: the 'me' and the 'I'. He does not establish any hierarchy between them. But for Mead, the 'I' is not a 'me' and cannot become one. 'The "I" is the action of the individual as distinct from the social situation assumed by his own conduct.' The 'me' presents itself thanks to the adoption of the attitudes of others. By adopting these attitudes, we have introduced the 'me' and we react to it as an 'I'.[37] In general terms, one could say that the 'me' is the expression of the social dimension of self while the 'I' is the expression of the individual dimension with its most intimate attitudes and behaviours and its most personal temperament. Mead writes: 'The "I" is the reaction of the organism to the attitudes of others, the "me" is the organised ensemble of the attitudes of others that one assumes oneself'. The attitudes of others make up the organised 'me' to which one reacts as 'I'.[38] Commenting on the analyses of Mead, Daval puts forth elements that clarify his proposal and, at the same time, portray the nature and the basis of his distinction. For Mead, the 'I' and the 'me' are, in effect, starting points to define the way that one acts as influenced by attitudes of society represented within 'us' as 'me'; at the same time there is a bit of individual initiative in any act, and this is what makes up the 'I'.

Daval concludes:

> It is clear that, through this distinction between the me and the I, G.H. Mead wishes to preserve individual freedom. He insists, indeed, on the fact that reacting to a situation the I is always unpredictable and uncertain, while, on the contrary, the me is involved in the social attitudes that the individual assumes.[39]

In Mead's perspective, the concepts of 'I' and of 'me' therefore take on a strong epistemological status and, in a certain way, respond to a requirement of a philosophical order. Also, the concept of 'self' takes a new shape, marking both the conscience and the person of the individual. The interaction of the 'me' and of the self forms the basis for the formation of the personality and for the determination of the 'content of the mind'. Underscoring the central place of the self, Ricœur has us notice that 'the term self exists to put us on guard against the reduction to a me centred on itself'[40] and, one might add, to put us on guard against all forms of solipsism.[41] This shift also allows us to avoid the 'auto-foundational assumption' of the 'I'.

One must remember that Mead does not create a wide distinction between, on one side, the 'self' and, on the other, the 'I' and the 'me'. For him, it is less a question of two distinct elements than of a 'frame' within which social experience plays a dominant role. Only social action can allow access inside this frame and to the relationship that connects the 'self' to the 'I' and the 'me'. Daval underscores this aspect of Mead's thinking when he writes:

> The three ideas of self, I and me can only be understood within the framework of the social process of experience. [...] The 'I' and the 'me' can only be understood within the frame of social action. An 'I' that expresses itself completely outside the norms of his social group would be an individual exhibiting psychological problems and would, in no case, be a man advancing human society and the group to which he belongs.[42]

From all of this springs simultaneously the role of the 'I' and the 'we' in the determination of action and in the formation and execution of judgement, meaning, finally, in the affirmation of a 'practical subject', a 'subject of moral imputation', as Ricœur would say.

The dualism of 'I' and 'we' along with the dualism of 'I' and 'me' can take on complex forms as in paradoxical relationships, notably when one looks at the category of 'person'. In order to avoid eventual logical difficulties, Ricœur prefers to return to the use of the word 'self'. As Descombes observes, 'Ricœur especially emphasises the distance which separates self and I'.[43] For Ricœur, in fact, 'to say my self is not the same as to say *I*. The "*I*" is put forth or is put aside. The self is involved reflectively in the operations wherein analysis precedes the return toward itself.'[44] Thus evolves Ricœur's project of constructing a *hermeneutique du self*,[45] a hermeneutic 'characterised by the indirect status of the position of the self'.[46] It is from the 'centrality of the self' that Ricœur determines the idea of person, showing the necessity of having thought processes that define and confer upon that person an appropriate empirical description. For Ricœur, one can not 'go far in the determination of the concept of person without bringing into the discussion, at some point, the power of auto-designation which makes the person not only an example of a unique type, but a self'.[47] This brings us to a clarification of the articulations of the three main ideas.

On the articulations of 'I', 'we' and the 'person'

I have just shown how the 'I' becomes the 'we' and vice versa, by making a correlation between 'the I lived and anchored, and a slice of world history'.[48] Such an approach allows the *inscription* of the 'I' in a relationship that brings in the 'other', or rather, 'others'. Thus, the 'I' who has since become 'self' requires social attributes that make the self more a 'person' than a simple 'me'. And it is here that the unique category of 'person' appears and demands our attention.

If one considers that our examination of the traits common to these diverse ideas have provided access to different writings on what makes up the identity of the human person, one can now add that the idea of 'person' will allow us to articulate these writings in order to have a coherent vision of the whole. In this sense, the person corresponds to an integral being in a social setting with the particularity of having a specific capacity to act as well as having rights and responsibilities.

Thus, it is at the crossroads of these different writings and by attributing a certain primacy to the idea of a 'moral person' with privileged status and required 'competence', one can grasp the sense of justice in all its complexity and in an articulation of certain 'ethical dimensions', thereby placing it at the heart of a judicial and moral anthropology.[49] It is the axiological dimension at the core of the idea of 'person' that makes both possible and necessary the existence of moral imperative: the respect and the dignity of the person.[50]

Variation on the category of 'person' in a Western context

One of the characteristics of the idea of 'person' in the Western context is that it is 'heir to a long tradition' and that, moreover, 'the word is today still charged with meanings acquired over the course of time and that the great upheavals in Western culture did not sweep everything away, but on the contrary, have often left traces'.[51] This is the thesis defended by Ladrière in a most enlightening study which I add to my analysis. However, in a way that is different from Ladrière, our intention is not to discuss ancient or medieval origins of this idea nor to bring up certain great historical moments, but to clarify these implications as they relate to the 'meaning of justice'. At any rate, for the clarity of my proposal, it is appropriate to expose different writings on the idea of 'person' and to emphasise their philosophical and anthropological contributions.

An approach to 'person' can be viewed in at least three different ways: judicial, theological and linguistic. In each of these ways, the idea of 'person' requires its own meaning and reveals itself marked by its own history and by the controversies that have contributed to its shape and parameters.[52]

Thanks to the contribution of the Roman jurists, the judicial aspect is no doubt the first that provides a definition of the idea of 'person'. Roman law established the affirmation of the person as a functionally judicial category with a completely autonomous status. It is true that the person continued to pursue learning and their own amplification through numerous stages in order to reach the present with more maturity and consistency and to become a specifically modern category. However, in spite of these transformations and the challenges of his evolution, one can consider the person's genesis and original affirmation as being the most significant for determining this person's meaning. Mauss underscores the importance of what the Romans brought to this defining process in that even though they did not invent the word and the institution, 'it was at least they who assigned the primitive meaning that we have adopted'. On this, Mauss writes:

> The person is more that a fact of organisation, more than a name or the right to a personage and a ritual mask; it is a fundamental fact of the law. In law, the jurists say: there are only personae, res and actiones: this principle still governs the separations in our codes.[53]

This *summa divisio* between persons, things and actions continues today to be at the basis of any reflection on the law (individual responsibility law, penal law etc.). At risk in all this is, most notably, the fundamental question of the judicial status of belongings and persons as well as that of qualification. It is not up to us to set out the different aspects of this question.[54]

I prefer to focus, even briefly, on another equally fundamental dimension that consists of considering the person as a 'moral fact'. This dimension concerns law as much as it does ethics to the extent that, as Mauss observes, 'to a judicial sense, one adds a moral sense, a sense of being aware, independent, autonomous, free, responsible'.[55] This change in the meaning of the idea of person was, according to Mauss, introduced via the voluntary moral of the Stoics. One thus injected 'moral conscience' into the judicial concept of the person. From a purely judicial perspective, I now come to the person who is considered as a 'moral fact', a meaning that assumes the existence of a conscious moral person and implies the intervention of the 'consciousness of self'. In brief, one moves to the meaning of the 'awareness of good and evil'.

But, as decisive as it may be, this change in the genesis and development of the idea of person remains inadequate and of limited value since it lacks an essential theological-philosophical foundation – an ontological dimension. Mauss notes clearly: 'The idea of person is still missing a reliable metaphysical basis. This foundation comes out of Christianity.'[56] Christian theology brought about decisive progress.

It was, in fact, the Christian theologians and, most particularly, St Thomas Aquinas who defined the ontological dimension of the person.[57] Ladrière brings our attention to the double limitations that impede efforts toward reflection and deeper understanding due to the substantialist nature of ontology and also to the fact that it only functions within a theology. Henceforth, he observes, 'the idea of person passes through the mysteries of theology'. He then adds:

> The idea of person, tied to a questioning about God, is increasingly linked to a questioning about man. But, this incontestable process of secularisation must not mask the paradoxical reality that confronts us: the idea of person that will end by saying that man's most human characteristics historically pass through a process that only concerns the Christian God.[58]

The idea of person has emerged reinforced and confirmed. It is during this period that it acquired a complete consistency in an irreversible and irrevocable way. It is finally during this period that evolved the 'passage of the idea of *persona, homme revetu d'un état,* to the simple notion of man, of human person.[59]

Unfortunately, I cannot prolong my investigation here in order to consider the upheavals that this notion of person must have dealt with in the coming of modern times in what has been called the 'philosophy of the subject' (Descartes, Kant, Hegel etc.).[60] Let it simply be said that it must have undergone a profound new mutation, adding to it another essential dimension: the primacy of subjectivity. This is the beginning of the person as subject.[61]

From all this comes the thought that the idea of person is heir to numerous traditions and the product of a long history, that it is essentially historical. That is why Mauss insisted on establishing its social history as a 'category of the human mind'. It is now appropriate for me to take a brief look at how this 'category' is situated within the framework of Islamic thought.

What is the status of the person in Islamic thought?

What about the Islamic tradition? All the authors discussed so far hardly even mention it. Does this mean that Islamic thought did not concern itself with this essential idea? Far from it. It is obvious to all that Muslim authors, whether *fuqahâ* (judicial counsellors), *mutakallimûn* (theologians) or *falâsifa* (philosophers), have certainly developed a profound study on the status of the person within an Islamic context. However, the frame of reference for the different approaches can appear to some as inadequate or outdated in the sense that it has remained an output of the mysteries of speculative theology. That, at least, is the point which Arkoun raises and from which he proposes to rethink the question of the person. He writes:

> On the Islamic side, the theme of the person is highly present in various tendencies of Islamic thought. One cannot, however, be satisfied with the religious, ethical, judicial and philosophical frameworks passed down via speculative Islamic thought. One must carve a critical reflection out of the new conditions that have evolved in Muslim societies since the 1950s.[62]

In my opinion, this speculative approach to the person must serve as a point of reference or, as Mauss says, a 'metaphysical basis' for reflection. This metaphysical basis of the idea of 'person', missing from Roman and Greek moral traditions, is found clearly in and, in certain ways, is an outgrowth of Islamic tradition. This undeniably presents an inestimable gain.[63] On the other hand, what is still lacking here is the freeing of the idea of 'person' from this initial frame and the fitting of it into a sociohistorical and anthropological perspective – an attempt numerous authors from St Thomas to Mauss have made in the Western context.

The choice of a classical author or tendency of thought as a point of reference in the development of a new approach implies, of course, epistemological and theoretic positions. In any case, it is from this perspective that I have had to call upon *Mu'tazilism* and *Ash'arism* in order to shed light on the debate concerning the idea of justice that endured in the classical era. It is necessary to proceed in the same way to uncover the status of the person.

In effect, classical thought, particularly the *falsafa* in its speculations on 'the mind' (*rûh*), 'the soul' (*nafs*), 'essence' (*dhât*), the

'I' or 'me' (*anâ*) etc. can without doubt contribute to the basis of an approach to the person in this historical context. As Arnaldez observes, there already exists 'in the tradition of thought inspired by the Koran, all the elements of an original doctrine of the person'.[64] For Arnaldez, one already finds in an author such as Fakhr al-Din al-Razi a philosophy of personal pronouns and the premises of a doctrine of the person beneath an intermingling of existential and essential languages. One also sees in Razi's writing 'traits that precede in this word (*shakhs*) the modern idea of person'.[65]

Although of great importance, the contribution of Razi does not advance those of Avicenna or Ghazali and remains, in certain respects, trapped in a 'mystical ontology'. It seems, in fact, that Avicenna is the philosopher who went the furthest in this perspective. His thinking on this point is often rightly presented as having foreshadowed the preoccupations of modern authors, preceding in some ways relevant concepts laid down by Descartes and Kant.

In discussing the work of Taylor on the 'sources of self', Brague reproaches him for limiting himself to the exploration of the modern idea of 'self' without taking into account the pivotal names and concepts which preceded him, going back to the Middle Ages. The contribution of these concepts is, in fact, totally lacking in the analysis of Taylor. Brague affirms that 'we can not be clear on modernity unless we are clear on that which is pre-modern'.[66] In this respect, it is clear to Brague that 'the ancient and medieval equivalent of the *self* is the soul (*psukhe, amina, nafs, nefesh*); its Christian equivalent is the person (*prosopari, persona*)'.[67]

Taking into account the conditions for the formation of the concept of 'self' and its passage into modernity, it is precisely in Brague's view of 'historic continuity' that one can inscribe the contribution of Avicenna, whose primary concern is precisely the passage of the idea of soul to that of 'I'. In this way, he is the predecessor of Descartes and, in a sense, the founder of the modern concept of the subject. The concept of soul, central for the entire Middle Ages, shows itself henceforth, according to Brague, richer than that of the self, a concept dear to Taylor. The work of Avicenna on the transition between the idea of soul and the idea of 'me' is undeniably one of the most revealing and significant. In a well-known epistle, Avicenna clearly defines the soul as follows: 'what is meant by "soul" is all that one evokes while saying: "me" (*anâ*)'.[68] Brague reminds us that '[Avicenna] is probably the first to provide in the 11th century a central concept, relevant to the soul, on the idea of self-awareness'.[69] Arnaldez develops the same idea and does not hesitate to speak of an 'Avicennian precedent of the Cartesian Cogito'.[70] Elsewhere, he writes:

> One must go back to the strange passage in Kitab al-Nafs, in the Shifa, where one can discern a sort of Avicennian *cogito* and elsewhere in order to put forth that permanence of a reality which cannot be simply reduced to the body, Avicenna leans on the experience of I and of his identity throughout diverse stages of existence.[71]

It is therefore obvious that, at the heart of classical Islamic thought, one finds the necessary elements to establish a basis for current thinking on the idea of the person. I have just illustrated this by briefly evoking the work of Avicenna.[72] There are surely other works that sustain and affirm such a perspective. However, that is only the starting point and, consequently, the essential remains to be done. Indeed, one cannot simply be satisfied with the reactivation of a philosophical tradition, as promising as it may be. What remains is to know how to grasp it and extract from it in order to reach an understanding of the present situation.

The question thus posed obliges us to adopt a sufficiently critical attitude *vis-à-vis* classical thought and heritage. From this point of view, there are many contemporary authors who extol such an attitude and call for the reworking of Islamic thought. What interests me here is the fact there are several attempts, certainly still embryonic, which tackle the question of the subject, the individual or the person.

For example, based on a reflection of the subject and individuality in Islam, Benslama puts forth the following question: 'Is it possible to lay down the bases of an idea of the subject in Islam that takes into account both the ancient and the modern approach in its critical (deconstructive), analytic and constructive aims?'[73]

The same questioning, stirred up by other concerns, is found throughout the project of applied Islamic study inscribed by

Arkoun. In order to introduce the study of the person, he has formulated three questions:[74] how does the problem of the person appear as an undeniable reality in contemporary Muslim societies? Which intellectual equipment and which scientific and cultural resources are used in contemporary Islamic thinking to find answers that are new and respect both positive traditional teachings and the unavoidable imperatives of modern times? And, how does one place the 'Islamic' answer to the problem of the person among the concepts and concrete attitudes imposed by modern scientific thought?[75]

The questioning on the subject and individuality advanced by Benslama and that of Arkoun concerning the person coincide on at least one fundamental point: the need to join together the contribution of classical thinking with that of contemporary thinking in order to present a new approach to the subject or to the person in an Islamic context. Arkoun underscores the importance of the anthropological approach in the study of the status of the person. In addition he believes that 'one cannot identify the status and the functions of the person present or past, without beginning with a sociology of Islamic law'.[76]

Here, one is at the heart of the author's reflection and present preoccupations. Clearly, the basic crux of this kind of sociology is to examine the status of the person in contrasting sociohistorical contexts. Such a study necessitates a profound discussion on both the past and present significance of the polysemic concept of *haqq* (truth-reality-right). How must one understand the distinction that one often makes between *huqûq* Allah (God's law) and *huqûq al-insân* (rights of the person). For, as seen, the idea of 'subjective rights' (*huqûq*) raises the question of the 'subject' and, in a more general way, that of the 'person'. These rights touch directly on the question of what is called 'personal status' (*al-ahwâl al-shakhsiyya*).[77]

A broad subject, indeed. But my contribution seeks, at most, to put down markers for an epistemological approach to these fundamental categories that are found at the heart of all moral and judicial anthropology. This has been the focus of my study.[78]

Notes

1 These questions are further developed in Nachi, 1998a.
2 This work is a revised and extended version of a paper given at the colloquium: 'Legal Personality: What Kind of Modernity for Law in Arab Societies', CEDEJ, Cairo, November 1999. The translation of certain terms and pronouns in this text gave rise to some specific difficulties. The choice has been made here to translate '*moi*' into 'me', '*soi*' into 'self', '*nous*' into 'we', even if the English terms do not perfectly correspond to the French sense. I gratefully acknowledge the contribution of Elvyne Léonard for his commentary and suggestions on the translation.
3 Carrithers, Collins and Lukes, 1985.
4 Arendt, 1982, p. 271.
5 Walzer, 1990, pp. 25–26.
6 Nachi, 1996, pp. 402–407.
7 de Benoist, 1994, p. 9.
8 Sandel, 1984, p. 9.
9 Sandel, 1984, p. 153.
10 Sandel, 1982, p. 94.
11 Sosoe, 1988, p. 83.
12 Sandel, 1982, p. 141.
13 Sandel, 1984, p. 91.
14 Sandel, 1984, p. 80.
15 Rawls, 1987, p. 30.
16 Etzioni, 1994.
17 Balandier, 1983, p. 8.
18 Schapp, 1992.
19 Etzioni, 1994.
20 Schapp, 1992, p. 234.
21 Schapp, 1992, p. 235.
22 Schrader, 1981.
23 Ricœur, 1987, p. 62.
24 Schapp, 1992, p. 221.
25 Ibid.
26 Schapp, 1992, p. 222.
27 Schapp, 1992, p. 223.
28 Ibid.
29 Schapp, 1992, p. 230.
30 Mead, 1963, p. 204.
31 Mead, 1963, p. 193.
32 For a concise presentation of his theory, see Daval, 1997.

33 Mead, 1963, p. 215.
34 Taylor, 1998, p. 57.
35 Mead, 1963, p. 131.
36 Daval, 1997, p. 294.
37 Mead, 1963, p. 148.
38 Mead, 1963, p. 149.
39 Daval, 1997, p. 296.
40 Ricœur, 1990b, p. 117.
41 Petit, 1996.
42 Daval, 1997, p. 299.
43 Descombes, 1991, p. 550.
44 Ricœur, 1990a, p. 30.
45 Hermeneutic of self: the title that Ricœur gives to his own project, which is to lay out a practical philosophy within which a central place is given to the subject of action and passion ('acting and suffering man'). The hermeneutic sets forth a subject, but it does so indirectly by passing through the facts of language, action, narration, law, legitimate institutions and ethics: Descombes, 1991, p. 546.
46 Ricœur, 1990a, p. 28.
47 Ricœur, 1990a, p. 45.
48 Ricœur.
49 Williams, 1994.
50 It is the meaning of Lucien Sève's proposal 'For a common definition of the person'. He writes: 'In its ethical sense, the only one in which the word is not replaceable with any other, the person is the value-form equally assigned to any individual in his belonging to the human race': Sève, 1994, p. 82.
51 Ladrière, 1991, pp. 29–30.
52 For more detail on the specificity of the idea of person in each of these recordings, see Jacob, 1989, p. 220.
53 Mauss, 1983, p. 351.
54 For a presentation of several aspects of what is involved in qualification, see Nachi, 1998a, pp. 565–69.
55 Mauss, 1983, p. 355.
56 Mauss, 1983, p. 356.
57 The definition that dominated the Middle Ages and that continues to be cited is from Boèce (sixth century): the person is 'an individual substance with a rational nature', Ladrière, 1991, p. 33.
58 Ladrière, 1991, p. 32.
59 Mauss, 1983, p. 357.

60 See Ladrière's study that consecrates concise developments to this period, shedding light on the contribution of these different philosophers: Ladrière, 1991.
61 One can refer to the introduction to this work in which Dupret underscores this evolution, notably using the outline developed by Elias.
62 Arkoun, 1989, p. 144.
63 For an approach that demonstrates the parallels between the status of the idea of person in the three monotheological religions, see Waardenburg, 1989.
64 Arnaldez, 1972a, p. 72.
65 Arnaldez, 1972a.
66 Brague, 1998, p. 222.
67 Brague, 1998, p. 222.
68 Michot, 1984, p. 485.
69 Brague, 1998, p. 221.
70 Arnaldez, 1972b.
71 Arnaldez, 1972b, p. 96.
72 For additional information see Pinès, 1954.
73 Benslama, 1994, p. 49.
74 Arkoun, 1989, p. 143.
75 Ibid.
76 Arkoun, 1989, p. 146.
77 Ben Achour, 1992, p. 171.
78 In a subsequent chapter, I study a specific case in order to provide an empirical basis for this theoretical concept.

Bibliography

Arendt, H., *L'impérialisme*, Paris, Fayard, 1982.

Arkoun, M., *Ouvertures sur l'islam*, Paris, J. Grancher, 1989.

Arnaldez, R., 'Le moi divin et le moi humain d'après le commentaire coranique de Fakhr al-Dîn al-Râzî', *Studia Islamica,* XXXVI, 1972a, pp. 71–97.

– 'Un précédent avicennien du Cogito Cartésien?', *Annales Islamologiques,* XI, 1972b.

Balandier, G., 'Introduction', in F. Ferrarotti, *Histoire et histoires de vie: la méthode biographique dans les sciences sociales*, Paris, Méridien Klincksck, 1983, pp. 5–13.

Ben Achour, Y., *Politique, religion et droit dans le Monde Arabe,* Tunis, CERES Productions, 1992.

Benslama, F., 'L'individualité en Islam', *Cahiers Interlignes* 8–9, automne 1994, pp. 49–63.

Brague, R., 'Le problème de l'homme moderne', in G. Laforest and P. de Lara (eds), *Charles Taylor et l'interprétation de l'identité moderne*, Paris, Cerf, 1998, pp. 217–29.

Carrithers, M., S. Collins and S. Lukes (eds), *The Category of the Person: Anthropology, Philosophy, History*, Cambridge, Cambridge University Press, 1985.

Daval, R., 'Société humaine et communication significative selon George Herbert Mead', *Revue philosophique*, 3, 1997, pp. 285–304.

de Benoist, A., 'Communautariens vs libéraux', *Krisis*, 16 June 1994, pp. 2–29.

Descombes, V., 'Le pouvoir d'être soi', *Critique*, 1991, pp. 529–30.

Etzioni, A., 'Le paradigme du "Je" et du "Nous"', *Krisis*, 16 June 1994, pp. 55–61.

Jacob, A., 'L'éthique comme anthropologique: conscience, sujet, personne aujourd'hui', in A. Jacob (ed.), *Encyclopédie philosophique universelle (I), l'univers philosophique*, Paris, Presses Universitaires de France, 1989, pp. 213–23.

Ladrière, P., 'La notion de personne, héritière d'une longue tradition', in S. Novaes (ed.), *Biomédécine et devenir de la personne*, Paris, Seuil, 1991, pp. 27–85.

Mauss, M., 'Une catégorie de l'esprit humain: la notion de personne, celle de "moi"', *Sociologie et anthropologie*, Paris, Presses Universitaires de France, 1983, pp. 331–62.

Mead, G. H., *L'esprit, le self et la société*, Paris, Presses Universitaires de France, 1963.

Michot, J., 'L'épître sur la connaissance de l'âme rationnelle et ses états attribuée à Avicenne. Présentation et essai de traduction', *La Revue philosophique de Louvain*, 82, November 1984, pp. 479–99.

Nachi, M. 'Le juste entre l'universel et le contextuel. Le débat anglo-saxon contemporain et son apport pour une approche socio-anthropologique du sens ordinaire de la justice dans un pays de tradition arabo-islamique', *Social Science Information/Information sur les sciences sociales*, XXXV (2), 1996, pp. 389–425.

– 'Le juste entre formalisme et substantialisme', *Information sur les sciences sociales*, 37/4, 1998a, pp. 565–69.

– 'Le sens de la justice. Étude comparative des formes de jugement et de justification en Tunisie et en France', unpublished PhD thesis, Paris, EHESS, 1998b.

Petit, J-L., *Solipsisme et intersubjectivité*, Paris, Cerf, 1996.

Pinès, S., 'La conception de la conscience de soi chez Avicenne et chez Abu'l-Barakât al-Baghdâdi', *Archives d'histoire doctrinale et littéraire du Moyen Age,* XXI, 1954, pp. 21–98.

Rawls, J., *Théorie de la justice,* Paris, Seuil, 1987.

Ricœur, P., 'Individu et identité personnelle', in P. Veyne et al., *Sur l'individu, colloque de Royaumont,* Paris, Seuil, 1987, pp. 54–72.

– *Soi-même comme un autre,* Paris, Seuil, 1990a.

– 'Approches de la personne', *Esprit,* 160, March–April, 1990b, pp. 115–30.

Sandel, M., *Liberalism and the Limits of Justice,* Cambridge University Press, 1982.

– *Liberatism and Its Critics,* Oxford, Basil Blackwell, 1984.

Schapp, W., *Empêchés dans des histoires,* Paris, Cerf, 1992.

Schrader, G., 'The "I" and "We": Reflexion on the Kantian Cogito', *Revue internationale de philosophie,* 136–37, (2–3), 1981, pp. 358–82.

Sève, L., *Pour une critique de la raison bioéthique,* Paris, Odile Jacob, 1994.

Sosoe, L., 'Individu ou communauté: la nouvelle critique du libéralisme politique', *Archives de philosophie du droit,* XXXIII, 1988, pp. 77–89.

Taylor, C., *Les sources du Moi,* Paris, Seuil, 1998.

Waardenburg, J., 'La personne en deçà et au-delà de l'islam', *Arabica,* 36/2, 1989, pp. 143–62.

Walzer, M., *Critique et sens commun,* Paris, La Découverte, 1990.

Williams, B., 'Personne, caractère et morale', in B. Williams (ed.), *La fortune morale: Moralité et autres essais,* Paris, Presses Universitaires de France, 1994, pp. 227–51.

CHAPTER 3

A Ghost in the Machine: Against the Use of the Notion of 'Person' in Sociology

Jean-Noël Ferrié

This chapter argues that the notion of 'person' is flawed and inappropriate for the field of sociological analysis. While this attempt may not convince the habitual users of this notion, I hope that it will at least highlight the problems inherent to the use of the resources of metaphysics in pragmatic analysis. In fact, it is my contention that the notion of 'person' tends to assume, in the background of action, the existence of an indescribable source of individual agency ensuring the maintenance of the acting entity through the diversity of that entity's interactions in the course of daily life. I hold that such an authority simply does not exist, since analysis of the courses of action and the adjustments between actors – which, together, essentially make up the main object of sociological inquiry – does not allow a claim to more than the existence of a series of events (reasonably) attributable to a same entity. In other words, statements using the notion of 'person' in the sense just described are entirely void of any meaning.

The notion of 'person' that I am referring to emerged – at least, in the use I am questioning here – as an alternative to the notions of 'actor', 'individual' or 'agent' in a number of French publications in pragmatic sociology, all revolving around the idea of 'justification'.[1] This notion provides a 'being' suitable to the idea that actors would essentially act in a co-ordinated fashion and would use 'judgement' in order to adjust to one another. Unquestionably, the ideas of 'judgement' and 'justification' imply (at least, if we wish to use them appropriately) a reference to 'orders of scale' irreducible to 'persons', that is, an extension of the ontology in use. One must describe these 'orders' as well as require that one conceive of a more dense and complex cognitive agency of acting that is suitable to these new capabilities.

The following argument is in three parts. First, I state my point of view. Second, I discuss a case study at considerable length which has a particular perspective on 'sexual morals' (a phrase that, moreover, is meaningless) and which very often leads to reference to the 'person' and its metamorphoses. This case study is not examined according to the precepts of ethnomethodological analysis to which I refer since the debate already draws upon enough factual arguments so as not to require additional ones. Thus, the instance that I cover only serves as an example which clarifies a number of points made in the first part of this argument. Third, I conclude by explaining exactly why the person is a 'void'.

My perspective on the issue

I can see Peter get up, go to the window and then go back and sit down without asking myself the question as to whether it is the same Peter who is doing these actions. In a similar vein, if I learn that Peter is leading a double life, that is if he has both a wife and a mistress, I will not doubt that it is the same Peter who has a wife and a mistress. For this, I do not need to know that Peter is a 'person' but merely to know that Peter is Peter. But, if I come to blame Peter because he has a mistress (or because my wife is his mistress), I thereby assume the existence within Peter of something other than the deed that prompts my condemnation. I need to think that Peter is different enough from his actions so that these may be judged, regardless of the circumstances and cognitive capabilities involved in their realisation. No doubt, the notion of 'person' or of something similar that will indicate the permanence of the self's intentionality irrespective of the flow of circumstances is then necessary, but only in a sense that does not allow its use in a 'top-down' fashion. In pragmatic terms, I need to conceive of Peter as a morally stable entity in order to blame him. This requirement does not imply that the person exists outside the pragmatic context of his involvement.

Indeed, let us suppose that Peter decides to 'pick up' a woman. He will have to deploy a number of skills such as, for example, recognising (or not recognising) the interest that he can prompt on her part. We can assume that the way she is, how she walks and looks (at people), her clothes and the place where she strolls (if she is strolling) will all make up indications of her approachability. But Peter can be wrong in reading as signs of approachability details that imply no such thing for the woman, or in taking as proofs of unapproachability other details that also do not imply anything as such. Every time, his taking into account of a detail will imply a normative typification such as: 'a woman behaving this way can only.' We can assume a similar attitude on the part of the woman. These different attitudes thus stem from a morality of cognition, in the ethnomethodological sense of the word, but do not imply using the notion of 'person'.

What is relevant here is somehow the 'type': the expression of something. Peter does not need to think that the woman he is trying to attract is a 'person' in order to try to approach her nor to momentarily become intimate with her. Yet, perhaps he will have to consider her as a 'person' if he has a longer-term relationship in mind. In this sense, the 'person' becomes a convention required by some actors' aims. I deny his being a reality external to these aims. The result of this denial is that we cannot lend any value (except, possibly, of a literary nature) to the moral description that is made of an actor. Indeed, such a portrait implies the existence of a self that is separate from courses of action, whereas sociology has no means of confirming the presence of this self without venturing into metaphysical abstraction. On the opposite side of the question, all that we know is what takes place in the course of the action itself. Surely we often assume that people with whom we interact exist as 'persons', but that is merely an actor's view, a requirement of everyday life that does not allow abstraction and that is the search for constituent features of the person regardless of the interactive situation in which we are involved.

In fact, conceiving the person as an entity separate from courses of action is an operation typical of a certain trend in moral philosophy. The assumption of uniqueness of the cognitive agency of acting that presupposes such an ontological bias leads us to think either that all actions ascribable to an entity are morally coherent as a whole (and if not, that the entity is faulty), or that the entity dwells in the tension, indeed the pain of choices always unsatisfying since the chosen option does not deny the relevance of the solution left out. In both cases, the 'truth' or 'truthfulness' of the being always lies in the background of his deeds. If the first possibility wrongfully appears as pragmatic in the sense that we do not necessarily choose the best thing possible or that a choice made is not necessarily the best, the second possibility does not accurately describe what people do – they can decide to do one thing instead of another without seeing the thing left out as bad and without regretting having left it out. Of course, they can later think that they were wrong, that is they can change their preferences according to a new situation. But, this does not reflect any ambivalence on the part of the actor when the choice was made, nor does it indicate that they view most of the circumstances of their daily life as dramatic involvement of their moral identity.[2]

In fact, I hold that by veering us away from the practical conditions of action and, particularly, from the expression of preferences, the notion of 'person' wrongfully leads us to the idea that an actor's identity, the fact of being someone rather than, for example, a regrettable series of accidents, implies some form of internal substance. It is such a substance that enables moral judgement of actions, both blame and praise; it is, if you like, the human counterpart of the realism of values and that is why I mentioned that the conception of 'person' is inseparable from moral philosophy and, more particularly, from moral realism.

We know, in fact, that moral realism contends that values are true in a pre-predicative way.[3] At the same time, a proponent of moral realism is (of course) unable to consider values other than in the form of a rule for action. Values pre-exist action, of course (always according to moral realism), but do not exist apart from it; they are thus liable to be spoiled by the fundamental relativism of acting (as even a moral realist knows that we may also act under the weight of the moment). It is thus important that we conceive of a cognitive agency of acting which is able to preserve the supremacy of values in the ordering of action itself by somehow separating two mechanisms, the one that runs the immanent intentional activities (evaluation of a situation, for example) and the one managing the transcendental intentional activities (such as trying to 'pick up' a strolling woman). In this sense, the notion of 'person' involves something similar to a dual conception of the mind.

While the users of such a notion are usually interested in philosophy, they fail to draw the consequences of this implication (or simply fail to take it into account). One cannot simultaneously hold such a view and claim to be a pragmatist, since moral realism sees the cause for action (or for lack thereof) as lying in interiority. In fact, when I act, it is me who is acting, but while I am able to act owing to a number of capabilities found inside me, the conditions for action are not within me. In other words, acting is, in the strong sense of the term, inseparable from the circumstances of action, that is, these are part of the cognitive agency of acting. To put it in terms of the philosophy of the mind, the circumstances of action are not data grasped by the mind; they make up part of the mind. This stance that consists in not separating morals from action by separating the mechanisms is usually rejected by 'moral realists' in philosophy and by those using the notion of 'person' in sociology. Regardless of the problem of finding a common root to both groups, we can still identify a common concern: that of bringing substance to morals. The means used for this is the same (it is, by the way, common to all those who seek the same aim): to found morals transcendentally with regard to action.

I now come to my main contention: the transcendental founding of morals as regards action made 'pragmatically correct' through notions such as the 'person' is self-invalidating in the sense that the 'person' is built from the outside according to a pragmatic process involving common-sense categories or specialised ones. To put it differently, proponents of the transcendence of interiority with regard to the course of action do not construct this transcendence on the basis (and strictly on the basis) of the typical procedures of the exteriority of the courses of action (to which they allege to bring depth or a particular substance). In the literal sense of the term, the 'person' and that person's world are thus merely an illusion, a narrative, that is the result of a situated action that comes down to describing a virtual world and making public such a description.

This illusion may be regarded as a conventional requirement by reinstating it in the course of exchanges between actors or as a reality in and of itself, that is not as a virtual world but rather as the very world of these actors. In my view, such a treatment can easily lead to confusion between pragmatic analysis and hermeneutics.[4] It then becomes relevant to *interpret* the behaviour (or absence of behaviour) of actors according to their interiority and even to comment on the latter's structure in a way that if (for the moment) it escapes culturalism we still do not inquire about how the 'values' and 'words' of a 'culture' shape the individual. This does not happen as regards fundamental anthropology; indeed, we do ask how the shared humanity of actors shapes their actions. This involves, more or less clearly, placing oneself in an ontological perspective in the sense of a questioning on the 'to be' of the 'being' that implies bringing down the features of the being into the causality of action. Generally speaking, the process comes down to explaining the actions less according to the situation than to the fundamental predispositions of the actor. Indeed, we may attempt to return (successfully at first) to a pragmatic questioning by seeking to thereby explain involvement in situations, that is by considering the situations as perspectives for action and by limiting their capacity to explain this action. But in the end this scenario does not appear very different from the previous one. Actually, it is probably only a sophisticated version of it.

In fact, both cases entail projecting oneself into the circumstances, thus bringing us back to a dual conception of the mind, while the pragmatic perspective can only allow us to say that we are *in* the circumstances (as 'water in water').[5] The idea of projection can hardly be supported without assuming the existence of a causality of action inherent to human nature, something like a 'tension towards' that indicates the direct or indirect influence of personalism – or the presence of a similar type of concern. Yet, I do not suggest (and this point must be emphasised) that we cannot go back to inquiring about the predispositions of the actor and therefore about the mechanism of these predispositions. But, on the other hand, I do claim that this cannot be done in a valid way by reinstating the dualism of a machinery that would handle the immanent intentional activities and of another that would manage the transcendental intentional activities; of one where permanence lies or, if you prefer, the durability of the actor's moral identity and of another that manages action *per se*, that is, the scattering in circumstances.[6] In other words, the use of the notion of 'person' to describe human agency in full entails going back to a *problématique* of predispositions (which, in itself, is not a problem and indeed, seems to prove necessary), and introduces a dual conception of the cognitive agency of acting and two levels. This seems arguable, and is the point with which this author disagrees.

On the contrary, the actor is *in* his body, *in* his language and *in* his life form in an inextricable way. This does not allow conceiving actions that would make up the *surface* or the reflection of an actor's interiority. To put it differently, a claim supporting that the person would exist as a real subjective entity and any related claim are meaningless in that they are metaphysical assertions which are themselves void of any sense. That is, they technically support claims which are no doubt required in ordinary exchanges. One must, indeed, view the actor in an entirety so as to be able to praise or blame that actor, to engage in a relation with him or her but this must be done on the sole basis of the pragmatic requirements inherent to these exchanges. To make it into a theory that is external to these exchanges (and overhanging them) stems at least from 'a pathology of understanding struggling with language'.

A case study

This case study is drawn from an Egyptian news item: the dismantling of a prostitution network.[7] An apparently respectable widow, a mother, always decently dressed, actually turned out to be a pimp who sought naive young girls and, under threat, forced them to prostitute themselves; she even filmed their frolics in order to blackmail them. For reasons that may be left out here,[8] the issue of morals and sexual respectability forms an intrinsic part of Egyptian identity when Egyptians are asked to define it.[9] The press stigmatised the behaviour of this woman as a 'person', that is, not as the 'pimp-who-did-this-when-she-did-it' but as the 'the-person-who-did-this'; in other words, as if her past were also part of her present. Without the notion of 'person', such an accusation is difficult to make. The same holds from a legal perspective: if we do not accept the continuity that this notion entails, it is impossible to hold someone responsible once the reprehensible act has already been committed. To punish someone at one particular time indeed requires that they be the same entity as that which at another time committed the deed for which they will be punished. Therefore the notion of 'person' makes it possible to link an actor to a past action. It also allows one to identify what they should not have done, for which it seems justified to blame them. Thus, the pimp is blamed for having pushed naive young girls into prostitution.

Prostitution is an activity that is quite generally regarded as immoral, since it involves giving sexual favours for money. The idea that there can be good reasons to do it only comes up if the reasons mentioned pertain, in one way or another, to constraint. Thus, 'to mix business with pleasure' will never be considered a good reason to prostitute oneself, while the same attitude will appear as acceptable with regard to other activities. A moral person is not supposed to indulge in mercenary debauchery. Without getting into details, let us note that condemning prostitution implies having a general and abstract opinion on what one can or cannot make of oneself with others (whereas the opposite may be considered). However, this opinion – as general and abstract as it may be – must be appropriate to human beings or to what we believe they are. The 'person', in the vague sense of 'human person', thus comes as the necessary support to such an appropriation.[10] It is also the support of a basic psychological theory allowing determination, within specific individuals, at the motivating forces behind action, intention and evaluation without having to describe them at length. In fact, if in order to lay the blame for an act on someone, we had to go through all the causes and effects, to go back from the senses to the neuronic chain and from there to the 'ideas' and 'feelings' – in short, if we were able to do what we are unable, because, from the start we disagree on the proper ontology to use[11] – it would become impossible to find anybody responsible since this series of causes and effects, already impossible to isolate and describe in theory, would also have to be retrospectively validated for every pending case. When we blame someone for indulging in prostitution, we need a notion such as that of 'person' in order that this blame be 'operational'. It is, in some way, a pragmatic necessity.

This notion is also required, in the case just presented, to transform prostitutes into mere victims of a pimp while still condemning prostitution. One must only show that they were forced to do so, that is, that they did not intend to act that way. The account of the pressures they faced suggests that a 'human person' cannot coolly agree to sell their body to someone else. The fact that these naive and unfortunate young girls were forced into doing such an act implies pain since in order to perform such an act they had to go against something intolerable inside themselves. This idea re-establishes something that may be described, in literary terms, as the duality of body and mind (indeed soul) or, in philosophical terms, as the duality of a machinery running immanent intentional activities and another managing transcendental intentional activities. Of course, this is not exactly what people do when they sympathise with the victims in their grief. They simply express an obvious moral feeling. But what is relevant to actors who, in fact, do not have to describe their activities in technical terms in order to find a theoretical coherence in them, is no longer so when it comes to describing what the actors have actually done. They have really done something at some point in time even though we are unable to grasp that specific something, not because it is vague, but rather since we were unable to grasp it.

The blame and suffering described is neither the actors' point of view nor anything that informs us about what the actors did, thought or felt. It is simply an account given by actors external to the events which they recount. This account points towards an end.[12] In this sense, it lies upon a dramatic psychology, that is specifically upon a stylised psychology.[13] To put it differently, this indicates to us the discourse that can be held about prostitution at a certain moment and in a specific context. It also tells us what to do pragmatically in order to lay the blame on someone and to condemn a deed from the perspective of 'shared humanity' which is, when all is said and done, the only way possible to blame someone. Quite obviously the notion of 'person' is useful in these situations, but there is no reason to believe that it also applies to what people do when they do not intend to judge the behaviour of others. Thus, those who wrote on the case stigmatised the particular fact that the pimp seemed a totally respectable person – a widow and a mother – while she actually was not. There is no reason to think that this 'appearance' was not also a part of herself at a certain point in time.

While we cannot be sure of it (yet it is not wrong *a priori*), the pimp may have also had moral principles, a conventional view on how to rear her children and a religious practice. In this sense, her respectability may have been perfectly real in situations where it was shown. In order to doubt it in a consequential way, we must start from the idea that all actions ascribable to an actor must be coherent as a whole and that if they are not, some of them are dishonest or attributable to *akrasis* (lack of will). But this doubt cannot be so unless we consider the idea that actions stem from a unified entity that is external to the course of action, that is, from a 'person'. Without this notion of 'person', it cannot be viewed as impossible to be simultaneously respectable and to commit moral abominations.

The question raised here is this: can a social scientist justifiably use this notion in order to make people's behaviour understandable while it usually serves to (over)simplify such behaviour? I believe that the answer is no, except if social scientists also seek to produce a narrative, that is, to give their own view on the world and, more precisely, to expound their own teleology.

Let us go back to the beginning of the naive young girls' career as prostitutes. The newspapers' version of it is one of pure and simple coercion. This account of the facts is totally understandable when seen from the circumstances of ordinary life, in which one must stigmatise a conduct to show that we share the standard view on good and evil, in short, that we are respectable 'persons'. But on the other hand, this idea of pure and simple coercion presents a problem from the technical point of view of sociology. It brings a conception of action as something set once and for all. But on the contrary, action is submitted to an infinite number of contingencies as it follows its course.[14] It is, as ethnomethodology has pointed out, indexed, that is it is dependent on the setting. From this standpoint, the way that an actor describes what he or she is doing (or what he or she did or plans to do) is closely related to the dynamics of the situation and of the actor's place within this set-up. My point is not to defend a relativist stance, a type of sophisticated 'people-always-act-in-their-own-interests', but to recall that there is no such thing as a viewpoint that is external to the situation because such a viewpoint can only be that of God, and that the absence of such a standpoint does not prevent actors from agreeing to act in a situation. If a young girl is forced to prostitute herself, it is doubtful that getting into such a situation has not resulted from a previous course of action. For the same reasons, it is also questionable that she would always judge her situation in the same way as other people. Likewise, we have seen that the pimp could also be a 'respectable woman',[15] that is, she could also see herself as such according to the courses of action.

This description does not pose sociological problems. Indeed, it actually avoids a common type of denial of experience which consists in not taking into account all of the acts and attitudes of an actor during a course of action or according to the main identity under which he or she appears to us. All professional acts of a prostitute cannot be brought down to the obligation under which the prostitute is alleged to be, otherwise this is equal to saying that these acts exist regardless of the situations of which they are part. For example, we can admit such a possibility with regard to the workday of a bus driver, who fulfils a task that compels him or her to gestures and to a specific position. But at the same time, throughout the driver's shift and while keeping to the route, he or she can stop, schedule, assume different attitudes and perform actions related or unrelated to this work, such as chat with a passenger, use a mobile phone, smile because it is a nice day outside. These types of secant actions are the very 'stuff', it may be said, of the professional life of a bus driver. If we transpose this 'materiality' to a prostitute, it comes down to saying that while the prostitute is careful to use his or her body appropriately in order to satisfy his or her clients, he or she can also appreciate the conversation of some of them, enjoy talking with her colleagues or find pleasure in the actual frolics. But referring to these minor events does not exactly have the same implications as referring to the enjoyable (or annoying) events in a bus driver's workday. To recall events that are enjoyable or simply similar to those in the everyday life of 'respectable' members of society implies a 'trivialisation' of the activity of prostitutes, these also being depicted as carrying on an ordinary activity. Yet a large portion of public discourse on sexuality in Egypt and in other Muslim societies as well as in 'Western' ones, albeit to a lesser degree, makes it something unusual which must not be trivialised. In such contexts, to present prostitution as a normal activity, that is simply as an ordinary activity[16] could raise two objections, both of them 'moralising' (even though the second objection may not appear as such at first). In the first case the analyst is criticised for presenting debauchery without stigmatising it and, in the other for presenting it as something (that could possibly be) trivial, whereas it implies a form of suffering that (of course) should be stigmatised but mostly restored as the very experience of the actors.

From this perspective, the indifference[17] almost inherent to the radical indexicality of description would underdetermine the common assessments that do not rest on full devices but on (over)simplifications. This blame, worded as an epistemological critique, is usually aimed at ethnomethodology, as the latter claims the necessary indifference of the analyst.[18] But it is out of place: we can, in fact, be methodologically indifferent to the position of actors (and we can even be so from a deontological viewpoint) without thereby bringing down the analysis of their actions to make sense of the way that they order their lives and, more commonly, their way of life.[19] We can include their ethical preferences in the analysis as long as they express them conspicuously or prompt a conversation. As such, the ethical torments (supposing an ethical torment is not necessarily indicated in technical terms) of the prostitutes can certainly appear in their conversations[20] or in a number of courses of action of which they are part. In this sense, the moral indifference of the social scientist does not imply the moral indifference of the actors of whom the scientist is talking. For the social scientist to leave a position of indifference in the sense used by the critics referred to, that scientist would not have to limit him or her self to noting the sequence of moral stances that he or she comes across during an inquiry, but to also consider that one of these is a key element in accounting for the situation and identity of the actors.[21]

This choice is external to the course of action which does hold any interpretative key. Just how then does the social scientist make this choice? From his or her own environment as an ordinary person, that is from a possible judgement on the type of ongoing action based on 'normal' assessments available in everyday life. If we bring these common assessments into the analysis of people's actions, we are actually allowing ourselves to take an overhanging stance (that is the idea that we know better than they about what they are doing) based, in fact, on the common perspective justified by technical concerns.[22] In other words, to consider the fate of the prostitutes in the case mentioned[23] from the angle of their suffering does not describe the situation of these same prostitutes, but rather reveals the situated standpoint of the (so-called) commentator. The notion of 'person', if the commentator allows himself to use this notion so as to describe their lot, thus serves to root this standpoint in the make-up of the entity in question in order to give the impression that the former proceeded from the latter (and, no doubt, believing this is so). But in the face of the suffering and humiliation of others, just as we are faced with many other less dramatic feelings, we, as social scientists, find ourselves in the situation of Jacques the Fatalist faced with the suffering of a woman in labour: we believe what she shows without being able to feel it and without being able to carry on with the description. This is not to say that we do not know what she is going through and that she is bearing things that we cannot know. Rather, it means (radically speaking) that we cannot know if there is something more than what she is showing. As a 'member', this is enough for us to feel sorry for her (which will comfort the fine-natured); as an 'analyst', this must suffice in order to describe the situation in which she finds herself.

Conclusion: the person as a 'void'

The notion of 'person' is thus, in each of its uses, a means of giving a moral identity to the actors, independent of the courses of action of which they are part in order to be able to assess what they did and what they are. In everyday life in which, as Gibbard notes, we spend our time commenting on the actions of others[24] as in a number of professional activities, it is thus useful (and, in fact, practical) to be able to see others not only as humans but also as 'persons'. On the other hand, the use of this term by social scientists poses a clear epistemological problem or, more to the point, two problems.

The first has to do with the fact that these social scientists bring common-sense views into the explanation of actions in order to grasp their meaning. Thus, they force from the outside an order into the courses of action which they analyse. They stand above them (paradoxically) from an ordinary standpoint,[25] using a sort of compassionate irony where (unfortunately) the ordinary actor's need to judge merges with the analyst's duty to explain. In doing so, they obscure the motivating forces behind action since the behaviour of *x* becomes explainable by the feelings of *z* regarding the behaviour of *x* (or by the biases of *z* concerning the actual order of preferences of *x*). The second problem is the following: while ordinary actors use a notion without feeling the need to establish it in theory, social scientists feel the need to draw up the theory of the person, that is, to give an autonomous existence to a notion merely serving, in the common use, to say something about something and, besides that, void of 'thickness'. Just like the anthropologists who used to speak for hours on end about the 'totem' or the *mana*, they confuse an operation or an operator with an entity, thereby, without any good reason, making the ontology of social sciences more complex.[26]

Notes

1 The founding work is Boltanski and Thévenot's *De la justification*, 1991.
2 I believe that a similar point is made in Williams (1994). This also suggests dropping the classic views on the weakness of the will or considering the ideal choice: the one not burdened by *akrasis* as a retrospective illusion.
3 E.g. Ogien, 1999.
4 But, as Sharrock and Coulter, 2001, mention, the task of sociology is not to interpret. In other words, there is no sociological hermeneutics that is sociologically significant and there is not any room for hermeneutics in sociology, nor for a Heideggerian perspective.
5 Moureau-Bondy, 1991.
6 Descombes, 1994.
7 Ferrié and Radi, 2000.
8 Ferrié, 2001.
9 See Ferrié, 1998. This definition is not related to Islam; it is also common to Copts (Radi, 1998) and this is why we may label it as 'Egyptian'.

10 I use the word 'person' instead in the sense of an entity postulated for pragmatic ends which does not significantly change according to the languages used to refer to it, somewhat like a car which can be referred to in Arabic or in Finnish but is always still a car. I believe that the idea that things significantly change according to words stems from the hermeneutic error I mentioned earlier. From this perspective, an inquiry into the names for 'person' in Arabic would be irrelevant. This is why I do not use vernacular terms; if ordinary uses of language do not require a hermeneutical approach, then this means that the words of a language do not carry anything indescribable in another language. On this specific issue see Putnam, 1981.

11 Descombes, 1994.

12 Such as the piecing together of a crime during police questioning or during a trial: see, for example, Komter, 2001; Matoesian, 1997.

13 As Bernard Williams has pointed out, it is also the case of characters in Greek tragedies. Their psychology and the way that they engage in courses of action are proportionate to the author's dramatic intent: Williams, 1997.

14 Suchman, 1987.

15 For example, a transsexual such as Agnes could be a woman just by behaving like one: see Garfinkel, 1967.

16 From a 'moralising' standpoint, this account is deeply shocking in the sense that a behaviour considered as abnormal (that is, running against conventional norms) is hardly ever seen as rational (Gibbard, 1998); on the other hand, a conduct presented as ordinary is very likely to be perceived as normal: Ferrié, 1998.

17 We may speak of indifference, in the primary sense of the word, since the component elements of a course of action are not ranked (or, which comes to the same, compared to one another).

18 Dodier, 2001; Paperman, 2001.

19 Contrary to Patricia Paperman's criticisms: 'Ethnomethodology views its task, in this case, as grasping the emergence of the moral characterizations of situations, by making what it [ethnomethodology] calls "moral diversity" into a natural feature of the understanding of order. It thus takes an overhanging stance with regard to common intuition for which moral diversity is not only a "token" of common situations, but also a token of divergence and conflict surrounding the circumstances, on what makes up the reality of the world to be dealt with in common. The ethnomethodological definition of social order is restrictive in the sense that it excludes evaluation. [...] The sense of order that this analysis restores makes

the ability of the members to morally assess and judge this order an unessential, contingent element.' Paperman, 2001, p. 357.

20 Here used in the sense of conversation analysis: see, for example, Heritage, 1984.

21 In assessing the course of action, the social scientist indeed behaves like an actor but inevitably – contrary to Paperman's view – takes a top-down perspective, since he or she claims to render the meaning of what is at play in it regardless of the change in the position of the actors, that is, asserting his or her own determination in relation to the objective order of preferences of an actor. This can involve stating that the latter is humiliated even though unaware of it. This viewpoint is arguable (the beginning of a discussion is found in Margalit, 1999).

22 As opposed to what Paperman claims (see note 21). Ethnomethodology does not seek to replicate the actors' point of view (in which case, we would not see the use of this paraphrase); rather it aims at making sense of the formal structure of practical action (following Garfinkel and Sacks, 1986). Thus, the goal is not to interpret what the actors feel but to describe what they do from a formal standpoint, that is to bring meaning to the external mechanics of action.

23 Because talking about an entity (whether human or an object) in general makes no sense since entities only exist in a situation.

24 Gibbard, 1998.

25 It is a fact that ethnomethodology has criticised such an 'ironic' stance: see, for example, Watson, 1998.

26 Lévi-Strauss, 1958, p. 1972.

Bibliography

Boltanski, L. and L. Thévenot, *De la justification. Les économies de la grandeur*, Paris, Gallimard, 1991.

Descombes, V., *La Denrée mentale*, Paris, Minuit, 1994.

Dodier, N., 'Une éthique radicale de l'indexicalité', in M. de Fornel, A. Ogien and L. Quéré (eds), *L'ethnométhodologie. Une sociologie radicale*, Paris, La Découverte, 2001.

Ferrié, J.N., 'Figures de la morale en Egypte. Typifications, conventions et "publicité"', in J. Dakhlia (ed.), *Urbanité arabe. Hommage à Bernard Lepetit*, Paris/Arles, Sindbad, Actes Sud, 1998, pp. 113–46.

Ferrié, J.N., 'L'identité morale de l'Egypte, ou de la relation entre l'histoire sociale des typifications identitaires et des pratiques qui les utilisent', *Hermès*, 30, 2001, pp. 73–83.

Ferrié, J.N. and S. Radi, 'Consensus national et identité morale: le sida comme analyseur de la société égyptienne', *Maghreb-Machrek*, 167, 2000, pp. 32–7.

Garfinkel, H., *Studies in Ethnomethodology*, Cambridge, Polity Press, 1967.

Garfinkel, H. and H. Sacks, 'On formal structures of practical actions', in H. Garfinkel (ed.), *Ethnomethodological Studies of Work*, London/New York, Routledge & Kegan Paul, 1986, pp. 160–193.

Gibbard, A., *Sagesse des choix, justesse des sentiments*, Paris, Presses Universitaires de France, 1998.

Heritage, J., *Garfinkel and Ethnomethodology*, Cambridge, Polity Press, 1984.

Komter, M., 'La construction de la preuve dans un interrogatoire de police', *Droit et Société*, 48, 2001, pp. 367–93.

Lévi-Strauss, C., *Anthropologie structurale*, Paris, Plon, 1958.

Margalit, A., *La Société descente*, Paris, Climats, 1999.

Matoesian, G., '"I'm sorry we had to meet under these circumstances": Verbal Artistry (and Wizardry) in the Kennedy Smith Rape Trial', in M. Travers and J.F. Manzo (ed.), *Law in Action: Ethnomethodological and Conversation Analytic Approaches to Law*, Aldershot, Dartmouth/Ashgate, 1997, pp. 137–82.

Moureau-Bondy, C., *Rift 1*, London, Water Press, 1991.

Ogien, R., *Le réalisme moral*, Paris, Presses Universitaires de France, 1999.

Paperman, P., 'Indifférence, neutralité, engagement', in M. de Fornel, A. Ogien and L. Quéré (eds), *L'ethnométhodologie. Une sociologie radicale*, Paris, La Découverte, 2001, pp. 345–60.

Putnam, H., *Raison, vérité et histoire*, Paris, Presses Universitaires de France, 1981.

Radi, S., 'L'image de l'Occident chez les prêcheurs musulmans et coptes au Caire, aujourd'hui', *Egypte/Monde arabe*, 30–1, 1998, pp. 159–71.

Sharrock, W. and J. Coulter, 'Réflexions sur le raisonnement', in M. de Fornel, A. Ogien and L. Quéré (eds), *L'ethnométhodologie. Une sociologie radicale*, Paris, La Découverte, 2001, pp. 75–97.

Suchman, L., *Plans and Situated Actions*, Cambridge, Cambridge University Press, 1987.

Watson, R., 'Ethnomethodology, Consciousness and Self', *Journal of Consciousness Studies*, 5/2, 1998, pp. 202–23.

Williams, B., *La Fortune morale*, Paris, Presses Universitaires de France, 1994.

Williams, B., *La Honte et la nécessité*, Paris, Presses Universitaires de France, 1997.

Part Two

PERSONS IN LEGAL SETTINGS

CHAPTER 4

Justice, Law and Pain in Khedival Egypt

Khaled Fahmy

In the early 1860s, while touring the streets of Cairo, a British traveller lamented that tourists in those days were no longer likely to see convicted thieves having their hands chopped off according to 'the ancient law of Islamism'. While this kind of corporal punishment must have had some deterring effect, he opined, its eventual banning must have been due to the realisation that it pushed offenders into destitution since it necessarily 'incapacitated the criminal from gaining his bread'. As a result, the preferred punishment for theft was to 'send thieves to work, chained, in the arsenal'. No sooner had Mehmed Ali (reigned 1805–48) and his authorities decided on this preferred punishment for theft, he added, than they fell into another problem: since political offences were met with the same kind of punishment, namely hard labour, potential thieves scarcely held it ignominious and Mehmed Ali therefore determined that the thieves should henceforth be marked on the hand with the word '*harami*' (robber) or at least with the initial of the word. There were, however, other punishments: 'for during my residence in Cairo thieves...were paraded about Cairo with their hands and heads in a wooden frame reminding me of the designs of Chinese punishments'.[1]

Paton was not the only European travel writer to comment on the regime of punishment applied in Egypt. This was, in fact, a typical theme that European travellers sensationally dwelt upon to describe a legal system that they saw as unjust and arbitrary. It was not strange for Paton, therefore, to allow his mind to wander from Egypt to China, for both belonged to what was known in Europe as the despotic Orient.

While some features of Paton's description of public punishment in the nineteenth-century Egyptian legal system are borne out by the archival record, the reason for starting with his sensational account is not to show how perceptive or accurate he was. Rather, it is to point out the polemical nature of much of the writing on the history of Egyptian law in the nineteenth century both by British contemporary observers and by much of the subsequent Egyptian nationalist historiography.

After the British occupation of 1882, according to this polemical account, colonial administrators set out to reform the legal system that they saw as primarily responsible for the chaos and corruption that prompted the Europeans to interfere in Egyptian affairs. Lord Cromer (the British Consul-General from 1883 to 1907 and *de facto* ruler of the country), for example, could only judge the Egyptian legal system before the advent of the British as lacking in some essential features that he deemed to be characteristic of English law. Specifically, he judged the conflation of the judiciary with the executive as such a repellent feature of the whole system of government and justice that he could easily dismiss it as despotic and inhumane. Priding himself for abolishing the 'three Cs', *corvée*, corruption, and *courbash* (that is, the whip), he considered the legal reform that he instituted to have been one of the most significant achievements of his administration, and to have been due to the fact that 'the Anglo-Saxon race have [*sic*] broad shoulders'.[2] With regard to the 'customary' use of the *courbash*, this, he insisted, had been abolished by a circular of a fellow British administrator which 'constitute[d] a landmark in the administrative history of Egypt... having dealt a decisive blow to the system of government by flogging'.[3]

Similarly and in an uncanny way, numerous Egyptian observers in the 1890s and early 1900s (most notably, Ahmad Fathî Zaghlûl and Azîz Khankî)[4] and the majority of subsequent Egyptian legal historians (most significantly, Abd al-Rahmân al-Rafi'î and Latîfa Sâlim)[5] dismissed the legal system before the creation of the Mixed Courts in 1876[6] as despotic and inefficient. Specifically highlighted in the writings of these scholars are the following features of the legal system in the Khedival period:[7] the lack of clear distinctions between the judiciary and the executive, the absence of any clear notion of procedural law and its differentiation from substantive law, the denial of litigants of the right not only of legal counsel but also of appearing in front of the legal tribunal reviewing their case. As shown below, what was a complex and highly elaborate legal system was, therefore, suddenly dismissed as a system essentially characterised by a series of lacks and absences. Mostly by implicitly arguing that contemporary European legal systems were superior to the Ottoman or Egyptian ones, these absences suddenly become manifest. The only conspicuous presence uniformly noted is that of torture, a presence soon reduced, however, to another set of absences, in this case the absence of equality, justice and due process.

This study challenges these Eurocentric assumptions that inform much of the writing on the history of the Egyptian legal system prior to the British occupation of 1882 and specifically prior to the establishment of the Mixed Courts. It relies on material drawn from legal and administrative bodies established in Egypt from the late 1840s called *majâlis siyâsiyya*, bodies which adjudicated criminal, administrative and civil cases and whose correspondence, judgements and verdicts are housed in the Egyptian National Archives. Specifically, offered below is a study of a highly significant, but little-known decree that was passed in 1862 (exactly when Paton was visiting Egypt) known unambiguously as the Decree of Replacing Flogging by Imprisonment (*Lâ'ihat tabdîl al-darb bi'l-habs*).[8] By putting this decree within the larger history of criminal legislation in Egypt and by checking how the decree was implemented, this study attempts to understand the role that flogging and other forms of physical punishment played in the Egyptian legal system in the nineteenth century, and to speculate on what might have prompted this decisive move to ban flogging. On a more general level, the study elaborates upon the notions of justice and the connection between justice and the law in Khedival Egypt.

Possible explanations of the abolishment of torture in Egypt

Passed a good twenty years prior to Cromer's inauguration of his much celebrated legal reform, the Decree of Replacing Flogging by Imprisonment has passed largely unnoticed by Egyptian legal historians and, therefore, there is very little analysis in the literature on what might have prompted the authorities to pass it. Scholars studying other parts of the world, however, have attributed a remarkably contemporaneous move to abolish corporal punishment to the spread of Enlightenment ideas from Western Europe. Historians studying Russia, for example, have argued that what lay behind the passing of an 1863 decree abolishing torture in Russia were the developing ideas of justice, equality and liberal humanism as expounded by such thinkers as Beccaria, Locke and Montesquieu.[9] Whereas the political system does not seem to have been affected, it was argued that new subversive ideas could not be prevented from crossing borders and affecting increasing numbers of influential members of society. Gradually these ideas spread to the rest of the body politic and eventually a change in the law was effected. Indeed, the role that principles of the Enlightenment played in Russia is emphatically stressed: 'The men behind Russia's 1863 reform were well-educated, city-dwelling bureaucrats and reformers who found physical punishment barbarous and anachronistic'.[10]

In Egypt, whereas the 1862 decree has escaped the attention of most legal historians, the entire process of legal reform is usually attributed to the impact of the 'West'. As in the Ottoman Empire where the reform movement known as the Tanzimat has traditionally been interpreted as the result of Western influence that prompted state officials to introduce what were seen as urgently needed legal reforms,[11] the contemporaneous process of legal reform in Egypt is similarly seen to have been Western-inspired.[12] Ahmad Fathî Zaghlûl, for example, whose work occupies canonical importance in the historiography of modern Egyptian law, considers Europe to have been an important influence in shaping the course of nineteenth-century legal reform.[13] Farhat Ziadeh, another prominent historian of Egyptian legal history, moreover, starts his analysis of legal reform in the nineteenth century by declaring that '...there was very little in the Islamic background of Egypt that was conducive to the rise of constitutionality or the rule of law'.[14]

Given this stagnation, change could only come from without: 'The reform that was a complete innovation and set the pattern for later reforms by Mehmed Ali and his successors in the field of judicial organization was the establishment by the French in 1799 of a commercial court, Mahkâmat al-Qadya.'[15] Recent scholarship (mostly by Rudolph Peters) on the history of Egyptian law in the nineteenth century, however, has shown that whatever European influence there might have been 'remained a matter of form and not of content'.[16] In the absence of any historical evidence, e.g. the deliberations of judicial councils, that explicitly ties the decree to European-inspired legal principles, therefore, it seems reasonable to assert that the ideas of the Enlightenment were in no way responsible for the abolition of torture in Egypt as stipulated by the 1862 decree.

What other reasons could there have been for passing this decree? Was the move to ban torture part of a universal movement that saw it as an affront to humanity? Can one argue that the decree belonged to a transcultural trend that signalled the appearance of a new sensitivity to pain, a sensitivity that might have prompted similar movements to abolish torture at around the same time in such diverse places as Russia and the British Army in colonial India?[17]

In a brilliant essay, Talal Asad questions the ease by which the 'progressivist story' has attempted to explain why the infliction of physical pain was banned from one after the other of Western European legal systems two centuries ago. According to this story, torture suddenly appeared scandalous because its 'intolerable cruelty emerged more clearly...[as] the pain inflicted in judicial torture was declared to be *gratuitous*'.[18] But why did torture appear so suddenly to be a scandalous practice? Why was torture not seen as inhumane before Voltaire and Beccaria? Asad argues that for Enlightenment thinkers the problem was not with physical punishment as such, but rather with the quantification of pain. It was the incommensurability of pain that forced Enlightenment thinkers to regard torture as inhumane, because it was difficult to compare it and to deduce that it affected people equally. Torture was thus seen as ill-suited to upholding principles of justice.

Taking his cue from Foucault, Asad adds that prison, by contrast, was seen as more egalitarian because it was based on a philosophical tradition that regarded freedom to be the natural condition.

> Penal reformers reasoned that since the desire for liberty was implanted equally in every individual, depriving individuals of their liberty must be a way of striking at them equally...No form of punishment accorded so precisely with our essential humanity, therefore, as imprisonment did...By a reductive operation, the idea of a calculus has facilitated the comparative judgement of what would otherwise remain incommensurable qualities.[19]

In a similar vein and in an earlier ground-breaking study on which, in fact, Asad partly relies, John Langbein argues that the abolition of judicial torture in Europe in the seventeenth century had little connection to Enlightenment thought (the 'fairy tale' explanation, as he calls it).[20] Torture was abolished after confession had lost its centrality as the prime means of establishing legal proof. This, in turn, was prompted by the gradual emergence of a new system of proof in the seventeenth century which allowed for free judicial evaluation of criminal evidence and which made redundant the reliance on confession. The increasing reliance on circumstantial evidence and the theoretical arguments that allowed it to replace the traditional means of establishing legal proof according to Roman canon law, namely confession and two eyewitnesses, amounted to nothing less than a revolution in legal thought. What is noteworthy about Langbein's periodisation is his placing this shift before and not after the emergence of such Enlightenment thinkers as Voltaire and Beccaria, who had supposedly embarrassed European legislators into abolishing torture. In other words, it was after the cumbersome and lengthy procedure of legal torture had become redundant that Enlightenment thinkers stepped into the scene, theorising a process that had already taken place and condemning it as inhuman, excessive etc.

If the 'fairy tale' explanation of the abolition of physical pain both as punishment and as judicial torture seems to be as unsuitable in European legal development, can one use Asad's and Langbein's arguments to explain the passing of the 1862 decree in Egypt? If, in other words, one finds little evidence that the spread of Enlightenment ideas about the integrity of the human body was behind that decree, can one argue that what prompted it was the gradual realisation that, due to the incommensurability of pain, torture was seen as an unjust punishment, and/or the gradual replacement of judicial torture with other means of establishing legal proof? To answer this question, one has to look closely at the specific roles that physical pain played in the Egyptian legal system and to trace how these roles developed over time, giving rise to a new meaning of legal truth, new techniques of punishment, a new connection between law and justice, and, finally, a new conception of justice itself.

The place of physical pain in the Egyptian legal system in the Khedival period

Pain, confession and the question of legal proof

Physical pain played a crucial role in the criminal system that developed in Egypt during Mehmed Ali's long reign and that of his successors. While describing the general characteristics of this system falls outside the parameters of this study, suffice it to note some of its features which are relevant for our purposes here. The most important of these features is that, contrary to common belief, this legal system cannot be seen as a step towards the inevitable secularisation of the legal system and the relegation of *sharî'a* to a marginal position within the burgeoning (allegedly Western-inspired) legal system. This may have been true of the heartland of the Ottoman Empire in the nineteenth century, where the historiography of the process of legal reform usually stresses the Western influences that inaugurated the Tanzimat Reforms and that culminated in the adoption of Western-inspired codes nearly a century later. In Egypt, both the process of legislation in the field of criminal law and the administration of justice in legal courts, by contrast, were guided by an unmistakable deference to *sharî'a*. The idea was to complement *sharî'a* institutions and practices and not to supplant or to circumvent them. An example of this doubling of *sharî'a* with what was called *siyâsa* (state-enacted laws, on the one hand, and the execution of justice in judicial-administrative bodies, the *majâlis*, on the other) could be seen in how murder cases were investigated and adjudicated. Explaining how *sharî'a* was coupled with *siyâsa* in adjudicating criminal cases is necessary to identify the exact role played by physical pain in this complex legal system.[21]

While *sharî'a* courts (*mahâkim*) were competent in viewing murder cases (*qatl*), the new judicial councils (*majâlis*) were also entrusted with simultaneously investigating the same cases. Moreover, these *majâlis* themselves included a *muftî* among its members and the murder case at hand was tried in his presence. By reviewing numerous murder cases adjudicated by these *majâlis*, it becomes clear that the main role of the *sharî'a* judge (*qâdî*) in his court was to establish whether a given case of violent death was the result of human action or was beyond anyone's control (*bi'l-qadâ' wa'l-qadar*). If the former was the case, then the *qâdî* had to further establish whether death was a result of a wilful intentional act by the defendant, i.e. murder (*qatl 'amd*), thus requiring capital punishment (*qisâs*) or manslaughter, in which case blood-money (*diyya*) would be required to be paid by the defendant or his family to the family of the deceased.

These duties of the *qâdî* were, of course, typical *sharî'a* duties that had not deviated from traditional duties as elaborated in classical *fiqh* manuals. What was novel, however, was how these duties were coupled with new *siyâsa* procedures. For one thing, as mentioned above, *qâdî*s now ruled not only in their own *mahâkim*, but *muftîs* also served in the newly founded administrative-judicial councils (*majâlis siyâsiyya*). For another thing, the *qâdî*'s final sentence, especially if it was capital punishment, had to be reviewed by what can be described as a supreme court, Majlis al-Ahkâm (al-Jam'iyya al-Haqqâniyya before 1849) whose verdict, in turn, had to be approved by the Khedive. Finally, as a further example of how *sharî'a* and *siyâsa* worked in tandem, the Khedive could not pass a death sentence on anyone except if that person had earlier been found guilty of murder in a *qâdî* court.

To pass a capital-punishment sentence (*qisâs*), the *qâdî* was circumscribed by stringent procedures of establishing legal proof as stipulated by *fiqh* manuals. For these manuals, as in Roman canon law, required either confession by the defendant (*iqrâr*) or the testimony of two male witnesses (or one male witness and two female witnesses). In theory, it was the duty of the plaintiff to supply the witnesses and/or induce the defendant to give a confession. In case the plaintiff could not substantiate his or her case against the defendant, the *qâdî* would ask the defendant to swear an oath of innocence. If he or she gave the oath, then it was necessary for the plaintiff to come up with better evidence.

In practice, this coupling of *sharî'a* with *siyâsa* had very serious repercussions not only on how the *sharî'a* side of the criminal system functioned, but also on how new procedures of establishing legal truth developed and how the use of physical pain became one of these procedures. The first discernible result of this coupling of *sharî'a* with *siyâsa* was the attempt of the *siyâsa* councils to get around the stringent procedural rules of *sharî'a* in order to convict a defendant against whom there was overwhelming circumstantial evidence, but who could still not receive a *sharî'a* conviction because the evidence presented did not meet *sharî'a* standards. One way to do so was to critically engage with the *fiqh* manuals in order to give a wider definition of a certain act that would make it punishable under *sharî'a* rules.

A good example of this crucial development is a discussion that was held among the *muftîs* of Majlis al-Ahkâm in 1858 ten years after its foundation. The discussion was triggered by the concern that Majlis al-Ahkâm's members had about murder cases that were systematically dismissed as manslaughter and could not be regarded as murder cases because the murder weapon used was the *nabbût*, a thick wooden stick that men in the Egyptian countryside, and in Upper Egypt in particular, were in the habit of carrying. The question revolved around whether or not to view the *nabbût* as physically embodying criminal intent, the argument being that death resulting from the use of a *nabbût* did not necessarily warrant a capital punishment, since it could be argued that the perpetrator did not use it with the intention to kill, but only to inflict an injury. According to traditional Hanafî doctrine, predominant in Egypt in the nineteenth century, only a weapon that could be seen as embodying the intent to kill, such as a cutting knife, could be considered 'homicidal'. Accordingly, after it was proven in a *sharî'a* manner (i.e. after confession or witness testimony) that such a weapon had been used, its user would be sentenced to capital punishment since the *qâdî* could assume, given the very nature of the weapon, that the condition of the intention to kill had been satisfied. The problem for the members of Majlis al-Ahkâm was that Abû Hanîfa, the founder of the Hanafî doctrine, did not agree that wooden sticks embodied intention to kill. After checking their files, and after reviewing many *sharî'a* court cases in which the *nabbût* was used, the members of Majlis al-Ahkâm became concerned that people were resorting to the *nabbût* to kill their opponents (especially in disputes over land) because they knew that they could get away with murder and receive only a *diyya* and not a *qisâs* sentence from the *qâdî.*

A general meeting of all *muftî*s working in Majlis al-Ahkâm was convened to discuss the matter. After some lengthy deliberations, the *muftî*s decided that, even though Abû Hanîfa had rejected the *nabbût* as a homicidal weapon, his two companions, Abu Musa and Muhammad b. al-Hassan, as well as the three other *imams* Mâlik, al-Shâfi'î and Ibn Hanbal, all accepted the argument that stressed that the *nabbût* embodied homicidal intentions in the same way as a knife. Henceforth, Majlis al-Ahkâm ruled that any case involving the use of a *nabbût* would be treated as murder and not only a manslaughter case and that the user of the *nabbût*, once it had been established according to *sharî'a* methods of establishing proof that he or she had used it, could be sentenced to death.[22]

This discussion about whether or not to consider the *nabbût* as a homicidal weapon shows the degree to which the new *siyâsa* councils attempted to confront the serious problem of rural crime, i.e. not by dismissing or side-stepping *sharî'a*, but by critically engaging with some of its principles. If these deliberations show how much Majlis al-Ahkâm was, in effect, successful in expanding the *sharî'a* definition of murder, getting around the *sharî'a*'s stringent procedural rules proved to be more tricky. As briefly noted above, *sharî'a* is very explicit about the way that legal proof is established in a *qâdî* court. There are very detailed criteria for accepting the testimony of witnesses and the confession of the defendant, and while circumstantial evidence was not completely ruled out, *sharî'a* clearly favoured these two methods of establishing proof: witnesses' testimony and the defendant's confession. In practice, therefore, many cases were summarily dismissed by the *qâdî* for lack of *sharî'a* proof (i.e. testimony or confession) even though there was overwhelming evidence of wrongdoing.

The authorities' response to this particular problem was to stipulate that such acts would still be punishable – if not in a *qâdî* court then by a *siyâsa* council. Article 11 of Section One of the main penal code, al-Qânûn al-Sultânî of 1852, stipulated, for example, that:

> Murder acts that should have received capital punishment [*qisâs*] but in which a blood-money [*diyya*] verdict was issued [due, among other reasons, to not meeting sharî'a criteria of establishing legal proof]...will be punishable by imprisonment for a period that ranges from five to fifteen years...[23]

Publication of this article meant that some acts would receive a severe punishment even though the evidence gathered for conviction did not meet *sharî'a* standards and thus opened the way for legal authorities to pursue their own investigation, using their own methods of establishing proof, methods that would not be admitted in a *qâdî* court.

The main method of establishing proof according to *siyâsa* was for the newly founded police force to act as a public prosecutor, an institution unknown in *sharî'a*.[24] Called the *zabtiyya* in urban centres and the *mudîriyya* in the provinces, the police acted more as an inquisitorial than investigative body in their investigation of crime. By arraigning, questioning and examining suspects, the police were intent on securing a confession from a defendant, even if the means to extract it would not stand up in a *qâdî* court. Realising that such confessions would be inadmissible in a *sharî'a* court, the police were still content that they would be accepted in a *siyâsa* council.

One technique employed by the police was to apply physical pain to force the suspect to give a confession. For example, we read a typical report in the records of the province of al-Minûfiyya in the Delta, in which the governor complained to one of his superiors that suspects arraigned in a recent theft case had not confessed to their crime in spite of repeated beatings:

> We had lashed them with the whip numerous times until the flesh had fallen off their legs [*hattâ tanâthar lahm arjulihim*]. One of the suspects, a sentry [*ghafîr*], was forced to stand up for 48 hours until his feet got swollen. But, they did not confess and alleged that they had been accused unjustly [*mazlûmîn*].[25]

It has to be stressed, therefore, that torture as a means of extracting evidence from suspects was, up to the 1850s, not something that the authorities tried to hide. The notion that torture was resorted to by the police in a secret manner 'partly because inflicting pain on a prisoner to extract information...is "uncivilised" and therefore illegal'[26] belongs to another, later period. As shown below and as attested to by the contemporary popular saying: 'You get nothing by serving the Turks [i.e. the ruling elite] except beating [*âkhir khidmat al-ghuzz 'alqa*]',[27] the practice of torture while in police custody was commonly known and understood both by state officials and the people. Nor was it even a 'public secret' whose efficacy lay precisely in being both secretly performed and widely recognised.[28] Torture (*'adhâb*) was, rather, a legal procedure to which the police resorted in order to secure confession, which was still considered the prime method of establishing proof. Even though such confessions would be dismissed in a *sharî'a* court, the fact that they were admitted in *siyâsa* councils and the fact that these councils themselves were considered complementary and not contrary to *sharî'a* allowed the police to rely on torture as a matter of course and for that policy to be accepted as legal.

The legal aspect of torture in police custody, notwithstanding, it was not without its problems. For one thing, as shown by the case mentioned above, torture did not guarantee confession and, oftentimes, suspects did not break down nor give the legally required confession. In other cases, moreover, torture resulted in 'wrong' confessions. An 1855 theft case from Cairo clearly illustrates this shortcoming of the use by the police of physical pain to secure a confession. An Abyssinian woman accused her female servant and five male neighbours of stealing jewellery from her house in her absence. The police quickly moved in to investigate the case, arrested the suspects and 'applied pressure on them' (*bi'l-tadyîq 'alayhim*). The suspects then confessed to the theft. Their houses were searched and some jewellery was indeed found there. When the experts (in this case, jewellers from the Cairo gold market) were summoned to testify as to the nature of the 'exhibits', they ascertained that this was, in fact, stolen jewellery, but that it had been stolen from another house whose owner had earlier reported the theft. On interrogating the suspects again, they all withdrew their earlier confessions insisting that they had given them under duress. The *siyâsa* tribunal accepted this argument and had the suspects released 'since it had transpired that their confessions were the result of the beating they had received'.[29]

Claiming that earlier confessions were 'faulty' since they had been given under duress was occasionally resorted to by defendants, but this was not always accepted by the councils. This, for example, was the argument used by a certain Hanafî Muhammad who was accused in March 1853 of killing a Syrian Christian man called Khawâja Ibrâhîm. After being caught red-handed by the neighbours robbing Khawâja Ibrâhîm's house, Hanafî was escorted to the village head and eventually to the provincial headquarters, where he confessed to having killed Khawâja Ibrâhîm earlier in a nearby village using a double-barrelled rifle and having thrown his body in the Nile. Hanafî repeated his confession when he was interrogated by the *qâdî* of the provincial town, Ashmûn. However, he later retracted his confession, claiming that he had given it 'out of fear of beating and imprisonment' (*khawfan min al-darb wa'l-habs*) and claimed that the provincial governor, Ma'jûn Bey, was the one who threatened him with torture and had thereby extracted that confession from him. The investigating authorities, however, did not believe this later denial and reasoned that even though

> he had claimed that his confession was due to beating, this claim was not substantiated and it is obvious that he resorted to this [denial] in order to escape conviction [*bi-qasd takhlîsihi min al-mujâzâ*] ...He is heretofore sentenced to hard labour in al-Qal'a al-Sa'îdiyya for life.[30]

It is significant to note that even though Hanafî could not substantiate his claim of having been tortured while in police custody, the use of physical pain itself was not in question in this case. Indeed, and as has been pointed out before, torture was, strictly speaking, legal and was not something that the authorities were embarrassingly trying to hide. However, what was being increasingly questioned was its efficacy of securing a reliable confession. For, as shown above, whereas the use of physical pain by the police sometimes failed to force suspects to give a confession, by the mid-1850s, it was discovered that its use was, to wit, too successful, for it occasionally produced wrong confessions.

A more reliable means of establishing legal proof had to be found, one that would save the authorities from the ambiguities that confessions based on torture necessarily entailed. Forensic medicine fulfilled these needs, offering the authorities a secure, reliable and 'scientific' means to establish legal proof, one that effectively supplanted confession as 'the master of all proofs'. While the history of how forensic medicine came to occupy such a prominent place in the Egyptian legal system is beyond the confines of this study,[31] it is important to point out a couple of features that are pertinent to our discussion here. The first is that by the early 1850s the burgeoning Egyptian medical establishment had managed to produce a nationwide network of male and female forensic doctors who staffed the different police stations in urban and provincial centres.[32] These forensic doctors were appointed to police stations in cities and in provincial headquarters in the countryside and they were required to investigate cases of serious injury as well as all cases of death occurring in their respective quarters or provinces. The reports that they wrote after such investigations give a fascinating insight into a neglected aspect of medical and legal history. The very rich police records of Cairo and Alexandria, as well as those of the various *majâlis siyâsiyya* culminating in Majlis al-Ahkâm, are replete with cases in which the report of the forensic doctor proved crucial in reaching a final verdict.

Most importantly, forensic-medicine reports were very often relied upon to convict a defendant in front of a *siyâsa* council after a *sharî'a* court had not convicted. There are numerous cases of this sort, records of which are kept in the Egyptian National Archives, that clearly illustrate this crucial role played by forensic medicine. Given that we have already briefly reviewed the discussion about the *nabbût*, what follows, as an example, is a murder case that involved the *nabbût* and in which the report of the coroner proved crucial in convicting the defendants. The case involved two brothers, Alî and Khamîs Abâza, who on 17 June 1864 went to steal some cotton from the field of Muhammad Bideiwî on the fringe of their village in Gharbiyya province in the Delta. Two of the landlord's sons, Ali and Dissoûkî, were present during the robberies and once they saw the two thieves, they beat Khamîs with *nabbûts*, until he fell unconscious. The following day, Khamîs died. When his family brought a charge of homicide to the regional *sharî'a* court, Mahkâmat Tanta, the presiding judge, asked the plaintiffs to produce their evidence. Since they could not produce any witnesses for the beating and since the defendants denied the charges, the case was dismissed for failing to produce the evidence stipulated by the *sharî'a*. However, the local police, acting as public prosecutor, brought murder charges against the defendants in the local *siyâsa* council, Majlis Tanta. The police had earlier conducted their investigations from which it was ascertained that both defendants were present at the scene of the crime. Most crucially, the police presented a forensic report which specified the cause of death: 'the dislocation and breaking of the first and second neck vertebrae which was due to an external reason such as falling or beating'. The Majlis was satisfied with its *siyâsa* evidence and found the defendants guilty of murder. They were sentenced to five years in prison according to Article 11 of Section One of al-Qânûn al-Sultânî mentioned above.[33]

By reading the records of many criminal cases (especially murder cases) that were reviewed by both *sharî'a* courts and *siyâsa* councils from the late 1850s and early 1860s, it becomes clear that the police were increasingly relying on reports written by forensic doctors to establish legal proof. This was happening just when doubts were being raised about relying on witness testimony or a defendant's confession. While *sharî'a* courts had to abide by their own methods of establishing legal proof, the new *siyâsa* councils were increasingly accepting circumstantial evidence supplied by the police, the most important of which was forensic medicine. Eventually, confession lost its centrality as the prime method of establishing legal proof and the report of the forensic doctor came to occupy an increasingly central position in criminal investigation.

Pain, deterrence and loss of freedom

Besides being a tool in establishing legal proof, physical pain played another role in the legal system of Khedival Egypt, that of public punishment. Indeed, the very public performance of beating, specifically flogging, was essential for physical pain, *'adhâb*, to fulfil this function. Relying partly on the *sharî'a* principle of *ta'zîr* (i.e. unspecified physical penalties that are left to the discretion of the *qâdî*) and partly on older Ottoman criminal legislation, but primarily on an ongoing process of local legislation,[34] the Egyptian criminal system – as it had evolved from the late 1820s until the late 1860s – reserved a prominent place for beating, specifically, flogging and caning.[35] For example, out of 17 articles mentioned in Mehmed Ali's first criminal code of September 1829, six articles stipulated lashing with the *kirbâç* (*kurbâj* in Arabic), the whip.[36] Similarly, Qânûn al-Filâha, which was passed a few months later and which dealt with offences relating to damages to public property as well as to misconduct of government employees, stipulated the use of the *kirbâç* in 31 of its 55 articles.[37] In addition, al-Qânûn al-Sultânî of 1852, which functioned as the main criminal code until the British takeover of 1882, stipulated lashing anywhere between 3 and 99 lashes for a wide range of offences.[38]

The different legal councils that adjudicated criminal cases in the 1850s, 1860s and 1870s (*al-majâlis al-siyâsiyya*) made a point of referring to specific articles of this latter code when passing their verdicts. For example, when in October 1855, the Jewish moneylender Rahmîn Nassîm was charged with violating market regulations and sentenced to receive 30 lashes, this was in accordance with Article 19 of Section Three of al-Qânûn al-Sultânî which stipulated a range of lashes from 3 to 99 lashes for such offences.[39]

This and other examples of legally stipulated punishment by flogging belonged to a larger regime of what Foucault called 'spectacular power'.[40] In such a regime, the spectacles of the gallows and public whipping were essential for punishment to fulfil its roles of retribution and deterrence. There are many incidents from the early to the middle years of Mehmed Ali's reign (the 1810s and the 1820s) that illustrate this heavy reliance on public punishment to deter onlookers and to achieve retribution.

For example, al-Jabartî, the well-known chronicler of the early years of the Pasha's reign, famously reports how Cairo's market inspector (*muhtasib*) was given a free rein to punish many market offences in the most severe and spectacular manner: currency counterfeiters were hanged from one of the old gates of medieval Cairo with coins clipped to their noses; butchers caught cheating in weighing meat had their noses slit with pieces of meat hanging from them and *kunâfa* merchants caught cheating in weight and prices were forced to sit on their hot pans while they were still on fire.[41] After conscription had been introduced to Upper Egypt in the early 1820s and after it had become known that many mothers and wives were assisting their men in maiming their bodies to escape the draft, Mehmed Ali ordered these women to be hanged at village entrances 'as example to others'.[42] Furthermore, when in 1824 a huge rebellion broke out in Upper Egypt against the Pasha's authority, Mehmed Ali ordered the elderly and disabled villagers who partook in the rebellion to also be hanged at village entrances as a reminder to others of the fate awaiting them in case they joined the rebellion.[43]

There was nothing new or unique in this frequent reliance on spectacular punishment for retribution and deterrence. In *sharî'a*, both *ta'zîr* and *hudûd* punishments rely heavily on public execution to yield their main purpose, namely deterring onlookers. Public spectacular punishment was also an integral part of the legal system in Mamluk Egypt[44] and under Ottoman law, numerous examples of corporal punishment (amputation of body parts, impaling, branding) and capital punishment were often performed publicly.[45] In this respect, the different criminal legal codes passed in Egypt in the first half of the nineteenth century, including al-Qânûn al-Sultânî, were a continuation of an age-old politico-legal tradition that relied on the public performance of physical punishment to instil the idea of the expendability of the body of the criminal in the minds of onlookers and the huge gap that separated it from the body of the sovereign. Public torture was therefore seen as essential for the sovereign to reconstitute his momentarily injured sovereignty. It does so

> by manifesting [that sovereignty] at its most spectacular...[O]ver and above the crime that has placed the sovereign in contempt [public punishment] deploys before all eyes an invincible force. Its aim is not to establish balance [as much] as to bring into play, as its extreme point, the dissymmetry between the subject who has dared to violate the law and the all-powerful sovereign who displays his strength.[46]

However, there are some significant novel features about the numerous criminal codes of the late 1820s to the early1850s and the place occupied by public physical punishment in them that are absent from earlier legal traditions. As Rudolph Peters's pioneering scholarship has shown,[47] unlike previous criminal codes which simply defined some acts as illegal and hence deserving of punishment, these new laws not only specified the kind of punishment that should be meted out, but also attempted to quantify it. It was no longer sufficient, for example, to say that those who violated market regulations were to be punished in the unqualified manner that Mehmed Ali's market inspector enjoyed inflicting on his victims as mentioned above. Rather, a new precise taxonomy of pain was introduced which attempted to link punishment (in this case, the number of lashes) to the seriousness of the offence, to the physical constitution of the offender (a point that will be dealt with in more details below), to whether this was the first or a repeat offence,[48] and (as elaborated below) to the social standing of the offender.

Another novel feature of how physical punishment was stipulated in these laws was the increasing reliance on imprisonment to buttress the deterring effect of flogging. The different Egyptian criminal codes passed in the first half of the nineteenth century often coupled flogging with imprisonment to enhance the deterring effect that the punishment was hoped to have. A decree passed in February 1830, for example, as a supplement to Mehmed Ali's first criminal legislation, stipulated that acts of market irregularities were mostly to be punished by flogging. However, repeat offenders, in addition to having the initial number of lashes increased, were to be sentenced to incarceration for periods believed to be commensurate with the number of times they had repeated the offence.[49]

The third novel feature of how physical punishment featured in these new criminal codes was the attention paid to the social class of the offenders in determining punishment. The fact that punishment was often 'tailored' to fit with the offender's social status was, in itself, not new or unique to these nineteenth-century Egyptian laws. According to classical Islamic law, the judge, in using his discretionary power to pass sentences on convicted criminals (*ta'zîr*), had to take the social standing of the defendant into account.

> The underlying idea was in order to achieve the desired result, namely deterring the culprit from repeating the offence, the punitive measure should fit his status: for high ranking offenders

> and '*ulamâ*', the mere disclosure of their deeds or leading them to the door of the court was generally sufficient, whereas the lower classes had to be restrained by all possible means, including imprisonment and beating.[50]

Nor was taking the social standing of the offender into consideration unique to *sharî'a*. The Russian aristocracy, for example, was privileged for much of the eighteenth and nineteenth centuries by being exempt from punishment by the knout, a privilege that, together with exemption from conscription and paying poll tax, helped constitute the distinctions between the 'high' and the 'low' in Russian society.[51] As a further example, the British Army in India decided against punishing sepoys by lashing and preferred dishonourable discharge for them, the idea being that dismissal would be seen (in an allegedly caste-ridden society) as directly affecting the sepoy's self-esteem and sense of honour. Corporal punishment was seen as suitable only for soldiers as it was believed that they had nothing but their bodies, their loss of freedom and their poverty, precluding the possibility of imprisonment or fines acting as suitable punishment.[52]

If the idea of making allowance for the social position of the defendant when passing a verdict on him or her was not new, what was new in these nineteenth-century Egyptian laws was the types of people whom the new laws considered worthy of this legal privilege. For, in addition to the '*ulamâ*', the *sâdât kirâm* (the descendants of the Prophet [the *sayyids*] and the descendants of 'Alî),[53] the 1852 Criminal Law (al-Qânûn al-Sultânî) also adds 'notables' (*wujûh al-nâss*) and high-ranking civil servants (*ashâb al-rutab*).[54] The addition of these new social groups to the 'traditional' groups of people who were punished preferentially was not only a function of the 'ruling class's *perception* of social distance *vis-à-vis* other groups in Egyptian society' as argued by Peters,[55] rather, it was an indication of how these new laws now functioned as important tools of social engineering. In other words, the law was not only reflecting a social distance that its drafters perceived as natural barriers separating different classes, but was a means of bringing about this distance in the first place.[56] While members of the clergy or descendants of the Prophet or of 'Alî were traditionally thought to be entitled to be spared the ignominy of public torture, the new criminal law now added the state's civil servants and members of the ruling household to this list of privileged legal persons.[57]

There was another more significant change in the manner upon which punishment was decided in these new laws. By comparing al-Qânûn al-Sultânî to Mehmed Ali's first criminal legislation of 1829 or to Qânûn al-Muntakhabât (Code of Selected Enactments of 1830–44),[58] one clearly sees that the number of repeat offences had become an important criterion in deciding on the punishment meted out; it was arguably the prior record more than the severity of the crime or the social standing of the defendant that was crucial in deciding on punishment. For example, Article 5 of Section Two stipulates this for drunkards and gamblers:

> If they perform their offence once and twice and if they are not deterred [by previous punishment] from following their whims and insist on their offence, then they should be exiled or sent to prison chained [in shackles] until they repent.[59]

Article 11 of Section Three, furthermore, stipulates that

> he who has stolen three times, been punished and has not been deterred, then it should be understood...that he is not rectifiable [*ghayr qâbil li'l-istiqâma*] and is incapable of proper behaviour. Accordingly, he should be exiled and estranged to the Sudan.[60]

As a further example, Article 19 of Section Three, dealing with market offences, stipulates that those who cheat in prices or weights should be beaten between 3 to 79 times on the first offence. On the second offence, their punishment is to be increased by being imprisoned because imprisonment would entail 'closing down their shops and losing their means of subsistence'. If they persist and repeat the offence a third time, 'they should pay any debts that they might have incurred and then be sent back to their villages in order not to be counted as merchants'.[61]

Increasingly, then, it was the 'criminal' who was being punished and not the crime that he or she had committed. Indeed, as Foucault has noted with regard to eighteenth-century French criminal codes, the 'criminal' appears as a result of the specific legislation and of the state's ability to keep prior records of its 'criminals'. It followed that punishment would henceforth not have retribution or deterrence as its aim, but rather rehabilitation and reform. For if the crime ceased to be seen only as a violation of social norms and hence to be punished by taking into account the extenuating circumstances surrounding it, including the social standing of the offender, and if, instead, it appeared as a transgression of state law by deviant subjects, then punishment should reflect this change in the meaning of crime. From now on, punishment would be directed not to the body of the offender to restore the *status quo ante* or to cow the spectators into submitting to the will of the sovereign, but to the mind of the criminal with the intention of reforming him or her and redeeming his or her soul.

If by reading the texts of various criminal laws passed in the first half of the nineteenth century one can detect a change in the meaning and purpose of punishment, the same shift can also be detected by following how these laws were implemented and by studying how punishment was executed. As mentioned above, the problem of administering a 'just measure of pain' practically meant how to quantify pain. It was this commensurability of pain that was behind the need to specify the exact number of lashes in the law that different crimes deserved. It was not certain, for example, that the same offence would receive the same punishment when executed in different places and by different people. For even if the law now specified a given number of lashes per offence, there was no way to standardise the severity of the blows throughout the realm so that the amount of the ensuing pain would be commensurate and comparable. In addition, it proved difficult to ensure that no excessive beating took place. Reports were being received that the local governors who were responsible for carrying out the legally stipulated punishments were exceeding the maximum number of lashes and/or canes. This prompted Sa'id Pasha to write to his Minister of the Interior, warning him that 'beating in excess of the limit stipulated by law [for each offence] is something that is contrary to Our wish', adding that under no circumstance should beating exceed 200 lashes 'and, in this case, a physician should be present during the execution of the punishment'.[62]

The same stipulation, that a physician should be present during the execution of the public beating, is repeated in the records of some of the court martials. In the absence of effective control over the officials who executed the physical punishment, be they local governors (for civilian matters) or high-ranking officers (in the military), there was a fear that excessive beating might lead to death or incapacitation, resulting, in the case of soldiers, in discharge from service 'and, in this case, the government [*al-mîrî*] would have lost the said soldier's services'.[63] This abhorrence of waste (rather than concern for the humanity of the culprits) was another reason behind the occasional replacement by Majlis al-Ahkâm of beating verdicts issued by lower courts and their replacement with imprisonment sentences.[64]

Besides the above-mentioned problems attending the process of executing punishment, namely the difficulty of quantifying and standardising pain and the fear that excessive beating might lead to physical permanent injury and/or death, the authorities were also concerned about the ambivalent impact that public beating had on the spectators. Although we lack the minutes of any meeting that might have been convened to discuss such a problem, there are numerous criminal cases which refer to examples of local disturbances breaking out as a result of what must have been perceived as excessive and 'unjust' beating. One such case occurred in Cairo in 1858 when a prominent official beat a slave to death, prompting a minor mutiny in the household in which this slave worked. The details are interesting enough to warrant going through them in some detail.

The case took place in the estate of Ilhâmî Pasha who was the son of 'Abbas Pasha, the previous ruler, and who was the great nephew of Sa'id Pasha, the current ruler. It involved the *nâzir* (supervisor) of the stables of the estate, a certain 'Umar Bey Wasfî. On a regular inspection tour of the stables, 'Umar Bey noticed that a slave, Sultan by name, had gone missing. When Sultan reappeared after a couple of days which he had spent in nearby Cairo, 'Umar Bey decided to beat him with the intention of disciplining him (*bi-qasd al-ta'dîb*) and to make an example of him in front of others. After ordering a number of fellow slaves to beat Sultan with the whip and after they had got tired of doing so due to the excessive number of lashes, 'Umar Bey decided to take matters in his own hands and he proceeded to beat Sultan himself, who had been stripped naked and who was then bleeding heavily from his back and his buttocks. To make matters worse, 'Umar Bey ordered Sultan's legs to be shackled in iron chains and had molten lead poured on the shackles. When the beating (which one of the slaves subsequently claimed had reached around 1500 lashes) had stopped, Sultan was deprived of any water or food. As a result of this barbaric punishment, Sultan died the following day. Horrified and fearing for their own lives and instead of being cowed into politely following 'Umar Bey's orders, the slaves fled in droves to the nearby police station where they gave detailed testimonies incriminating 'Umar Bey.[65]

Admittedly, this case is not about disturbances breaking out following the execution of a court sentence. Nevertheless, given the fact that up to that time there was no distinction between the executive and the judiciary, and since the incident took place in a palace belonging to a very central figure of the ruling family, one can assume that the punishment, severe as it was, was thought of as legal and not extra-legal. This is, in fact, what 'Umar Bey claimed in the police station when he was summoned for interrogation. He also insisted that such severe punishments were needed to discipline disobedient slaves, otherwise there was a danger that their insubordination would spread. The Cairo police commissioner, who handled the case personally, saw things differently. His report to Sa'id Pasha suggests that he accepted the slaves' testimony against 'Umar Bey and recommended that the Bey be punished since it was clear that he took the law into his own hands and thus 'attacked the dignity of the state and... violated its sanctity [*dayya' hurmat al-hukûma wa-hataka hurmatahâ*]'. Apparently convinced of the police commissioner's arguments, Sa'id Pasha personally ordered the Bey to be exiled and never to return to 'these lands'.[66] Nevertheless, of interest in this case for our purposes is the vivid and graphic illustration of incidents which were supposed to be deterring intimidating spectacles, but which occasionally turned into occasions for insubordination and minor rebellions. This and other similar cases provided further impetus for the need to replace corporal punishment.

As seen with the reliance on forensic medicine which made beating redundant as a means of establishing legal proof, an alternative had to be found to replace beating in its role as legal punishment. This is what Egyptian prisons provided from the late 1840s, namely a reliable, safe alternative to beating as a means of punishing offenders. But for prisons to play this new reforming role and to cease to be seen as places of exile to which people were sent never to be seen again, prisons had to be turned into more hygienic places. This must have been the main reason for the marked attention paid to health conditions in prisons and jails all over Egypt from the 1850s onwards. Indeed, by the time that the 1862 decree had been passed, health conditions of Egyptian prisons had already improved significantly.[67]

It thus appears that the 1862 decree abolishing public beating and replacing it with imprisonment as the preferred regime of punishment fits in nicely with the Foucauldian analysis of the rise of the prison. Accordingly, the decree would belong to a larger trend that could be detected in other parts of the world (for example, in India and Russia as well as in Western Europe), a trend that signalled the appearance of the modern nation-state which both saw the 'population' as the object of its care and used it as a means of securing its own power.[68]

Conclusion

To recapitulate, torture played a number of specific roles in the Egyptian legal system prior to 1862. The first role played by torture was a means of extracting confession from the defendant during interrogation. The numerous police registers clearly show that the police activity could best be described as inquisitorial rather than investigative, with the police commissioner acting both as investigator and public prosecutor. As stated above, there was nothing new in the way the Egyptian police went about fulfilling this function. As with the legal systems of many countries in early modern Europe where Roman canon law required either confession or the testimony of two eyewitnesses to pass a conviction, the Egyptian legal system, which relied partly on *sharî'a,* similarly depended heavily on confession or eyewitnesses to establish legal proof. Consequently, torture while in police custody was an integral part of the functioning of the police in its roles both as investigator and public prosecutor. The second role was as 'spectacular' punishment, the intention being to deter the spectators rather than reform the offender. In this respect, public punishment that was directed at the body of the offender was neither unique nor novel: older legal systems both in the Ottoman Empire and elsewhere in the world had frequent recourse to the 'spectacle of the gallows' as an effective means to express what Foucault calls 'sovereign power'.

Third, legally stipulated public beating was an effective means of bringing about class and social distinctions. The numerous criminal laws passed in Egypt in the first half of the nineteenth century continued an age-old tradition (also noticeable in other parts of the world) in which law was used as a tool of social engineering to bring about distinctions among different social groups. Lastly, public flogging was an important means often resorted to by provincial governors and high-ranking officials to perform important demands of the state that placed a heavy burden on the population, chief among which were conscription, *corvée* and tax-collection. It is important to note that, in this respect, public beating performed by these high-ranking administrators was, strictly speaking, legal. In the absence of the principle of separation of powers, the use of the whip or the cane by local administrators and provincial governors was a legal means of implementing state policy. However, starting from the first criminal code that Mehmed Ali passed in 1829, one can discern a trend of limiting the power of the provincial administrators. In fact, most of the earliest criminal codes passed from the 1820s to the 1840s could be read as a manner in which provincial administrators were increasingly being reined in: severe punishments were prescribed to the recalcitrant among them and more and more guidelines were passed that increasingly limited their wide discretionary powers. The 1862 decree abolishing torture was the final step in this long process of reining in the provincial administrators: by replacing beating with imprisonment, the authorities, now acting more as a central government than a ruling household, took the important function of punishing law-breakers away from provincial administrators, who were (rightly) suspected of abusing this right, and entrusted it to salaried officials of the prison system.

The 1862 banning of physical pain from the legal system was triggered, therefore, not by any spread of Enlightenment ideas from Europe or the sudden spread of a new sensitivity to the inhumane nature of flogging as legal punishment, but to developments in the legal and political system within Egypt. With the increasing use of forensic medicine, the police and the *siyâsa* councils found a reliable means of investigating cases, one which could replace the defendant's confession and the eyewitness testimony as means of establishing legal proof. At the same time, the gradual improvement of the health conditions of prisons meant that prisons could offer themselves as practical alternatives to flogging to deter criminals effectively. Prisons could thus avert the 'excess of meaning' inherent in the spectacles of public punishment that often ended in rowdy, uncontrollable affairs. Finally, by bypassing numerous criminal codes that ostensibly dealt with rural crime but which, on closer inspection, can be seen to have been aimed at reining in the provincial governors, the 1862 decree was the last step of turning the provincial governors into salaried bureaucrats.

Notes

1 Paton, 1863, pp. 263–64.
2 Cromer, 1908, II, p. 521.
3 Cromer, 1908, II, p. 402.
4 Zaghlûl, 1900; Khankî, p. 1.
5 al-Rafi'î, 1987, p. 261; Sâlim, 1991, pp. 13–18.
6 For the Mixed Courts see the classic study of Brinton, 1930; see also Hoyle, 1986; Brown, 1993; Cannon, 1988.
7 By Khedival, I mean the period that stretched from the reign of Mehmed Ali, known in Egypt as, among other things, the Khedive, until the reign of Ismâ'il Pasha, who in 1865 had succeeded in extracting the right from the Ottoman sultan to the exclusive use of the title of 'Khedive'.
8 A version of the decree is found in *Dâr al-Wathâ'iq al-Qawmiyya* (The Egyptian National Archives), hereafter DWQ, Muhâfazat Misr, L (Lâm) 8/20/1 (old no 1108), Order no 3, pp. 71–73, on 11 Sha'bân 1278/11 February 1862.
9 Adams, 1986.
10 Adams, 1986, p. 71.
11 For a very telling example of this line of simplistic reasoning that takes Europe to be the origin of all Ottoman reforms, see Lewis, 1953, who argues that ideas of liberty, equality and fraternity percolated across Europe until they reached Ottoman lands, where they started as a trickle that soon grew into a river, then a flood. They eventually 'struck root in the [alien soil] of Islam' and eventually bore 'sweet and bitter fruit'; pp. 106, 124–25.
12 Sometimes, this Western influence is seen to have been mediated via the Ottomans. For example, see Baer, 1963, who argues that

despite the fact that 'Egypt preceded Turkey, especially with regard to criminal law' (p. 29), the introduction of the main criminal law, that of 1852, should be seen to have been a result of the attempt of the Ottoman government to impose its laws in Egypt. Given that the original 1850 Ottoman Criminal Law was itself European-inspired, the argument thus links Egyptian legislation to European influences and not to local developments.

13 Zaghlûl, 1900, pp. 172, 179, 182–83; see also Sâlim, 1991.

14 Ziadeh, 1968, p. vii.

15 Ziadeh, 1968, p. 10.

16 Peters, 1996, p. 13.

17 For the abolition of corporal punishment in the British Army in colonial India see Peers, 1995.

18 Asad, 1998, p. 291 (original emphasis).

19 Asad, 1998, p. 292.

20 Langbein, 1977.

21 For a summary of how the *qâdî* courts adjudicated murder cases, see Peters, 1990.

22 DWQ, Majlis al-Ahkâm, S (Sîn) 7/10/2, p. 32, ruling dated 13 Safar 1275/22 September 1858.

23 As quoted in Zaghlûl, 1900, Appendix, p. 159.

24 For the role of the police in nineteenth-century Egypt, see Fahmy, 1999b.

25 DWQ, Mudîriyyat al-Minûfiyya, L (Lâm) 6/1/1, Sâdir (outgoing letters), 24 Shawwâl 1260/6 November 1844, p. 209. Also see ibid., letter dated 6 Dhû al-Qa'da 1260/17 November 1844, where deprivation of sleep and chaining in iron shackles are added as further examples of *'adhâb*. I thank Rudolph Peters for bringing this case to my attention.

26 Asad, 1998, p. 289.

27 Baqlî, 1987, p. 13.

28 Rao, 2001.

29 DWQ, Muhâfazat Misr, L (Lâm) 1/20/1 (old no 794), case no 8, pp. 7–9, on 13 Safar 1272/25 October 1855.

30 DWQ, Muhâfazat Misr, L (Lâm) 1/20/1 (old no 794), case no 26, pp. 28–30, 22 Rabî' II 1272/1 January 1856. The reason why the accused did not receive capital punishment in spite of confessing to having killed the deceased intentionally was because the plaintiff could not establish his relationship to the deceased using *sharî'a* rules, another procedural detail that frequently mitigated *hudûd* punishments. Al-Qal'a al-Sa'îdiyya was a fortification that Sa'id Pasha (reigned 1854–63) built in 1855 at the apex of the Delta. It

was heavily armed and put under the directorship of a French officer by the name of Motté; see Sirhank, 1894, II, p. 268.

31 For an account of the role played by forensic medicine in the legal system see Fahmy, 1999a.

32 On the forensic roles played by female doctors, *hakîmas*, see Fahmy, 1998.

33 DWQ, Majlis al-Ahkâm, S (Sîn) 7/10/25 (old no 629), case no 57, pp. 60–61, 17 Jumâda I 1281/18 October 1864.

34 See the work of Rudolph Peters, which stresses local influences in shaping the development of the Egyptian criminal system in the nineteenth century: especially 1999a and 1999b.

35 Peters, 1996; Peters, 1999a, pp. 169ff.

36 Peters, 1999a, pp. 184–188.

37 Jallâd, 1894–1895, III, pp. 351–378.

38 See, for example, Article 2 of Section Two (for infamy [*hatk al-'ird*]), Article 5 of Section Two (for gambling), Article 7 of Section Two (for public quarrels with no use of lethal weapons) and Article 19 of Section Three (for market irregularities): text in Zaghlûl, 1900, Appendix, pp. 156–77.

39 DWQ: Muhâfazat Misr, L (Lâm) 1/20/1 (old no 794), case no 5, pp. 3–4, 3 Safar 1272/15 October 1855. Specifically, Nassim's crime was that he bought jewellery without asking for a guarantee (*dâmin*) from the seller and that the jewellery turned out to have been stolen by a slave woman from her Jewish master, Ishâq Hayîm.

40 Foucault, 1979.

41 Jabartî, 1880, IV, pp. 277–79. Kunâfa is a favourite Ramadân pastry.

42 DWQ; Ma'iyya Saniyya, Turkî, S (Sîn) 1/48/3, letter no 325, 7 Rajab 1243/24 January 1828.

43 Fahmy, 1997, p. 130.

44 el-Leithy, 1997; Espéronnier, 1997.

45 Heyd, 1976, pp. 262–65.

46 Foucault, 1979, pp. 48–49.

47 Peters, 1999a, pp. 167–72.

48 Peters, 1999a, p. 170.

49 Peters, 1999a, pp. 170–71, note 28.

50 Peters, 1999a, p. 177.

51 Schrader, 1997.

52 Peers, 1995.

53 Shaykhzâda, 1301/1884, quoted in Peters, 1999a, pp. 177, note 46.

54 Article 2 of Section Two of al-Qânûn al-Sultânî: text in Zaghlûl, 1900, Appendix, p. 161.

55 Peters, 1999a, p. 178.

56 For similar cases of law as a tool of social engineering see Schrader, 1997; Peers, 1995.
57 This use of the law to bring about the differences between rulers and ruled also had strong ethnic connotations for members of the ruling elite were *ipso facto* Turkish-speaking while the masses were *evlad-i Arab*, literally, sons of Arabs, i.e. Arabic-speaking. For an analysis of how this distinction was visible in Mehmed Ali's army and how Turkish-speaking soldiers were mostly spared the ignominy of public flogging see Fahmy, 1997, p. 138.
58 Text in Jallâd, 1894–95, pp. 351–78 and in Zaghlûl, 1900, Appendix, pp. 100–55.
59 Text in Zaghlûl, 1900, Appendix, pp. 161–62.
60 Text in Zaghlûl, 1900, Appendix, p. 165.
61 Text in Zaghlûl, 1900, Appendix, pp. 166–67.
62 DWQ, Dîwân Dâkhiliyya, Daftar qayd al-awâmir al-karîma, Register no 1310, Order no 80, p. 25, 9 Ramadân 1274/23 April 1858.
63 For example DWQ, Dîwân Jihâdiyya, Register no 2538, case no 27, pp. 46–49, 9 Safar 1294/23 February 1877.
64 See, for example, DWQ, Majlis al-Ahkâm, S (Sîn) 7/10/1, case no 107, p. 48, 20 Dhû al-Hijja 1274/1 August 1858, where a lower-court verdict of 79 lashes was replaced with a prison sentence of 30 days for a servant who stole clothes valued at 1600 piastres.
65 DWQ: Majlis al-Ahkâm, Reg. S (Sîn) 7/10/3 (old no 665), pp. 54–56, 22 Rabî' II 1275/30 November 1858. For a fuller analysis of this case see Fahmy, 1999b, pp. 31–35.
66 DWQ, Ma'iyya Saniyya, 'Arabî, Register no 1891, al-Awâmir al-'aliyya al-sâdira li'l-dawâwin wa'l-aqâlim (microfilm no 25), Order no 12, p. 85, on 28 Sha'bân 1275/2 April 1859.
67 Fahmy, 2000; see also Peters, forthcoming.
68 Foucault, 1976.

Bibliography

Adams, Bruce F., 'Progress of an idea: The mitigation of corporal punishment in Russia to 1863', *The Maryland Historian*, 17, 1986, pp. 57–74.

Asad, Talal, 'On torture, or cruel, inhuman, and degrading treatment', in Arthur Kleinman, Veena Das and Margaret Lock (eds), *Social Suffering*, Delhi, Oxford University Press, 1998, pp. 285–308.

Baer, Gabriel, 'Tanzimat in Egypt – The penal code', *Bulletin of the School of Oriental and African Studies*, 26, 1963, pp. 29–49.

Baqlî, Muhammad Qandîl al-, *al-Amthâl al-sha'biyya (Popular Proverbs)*, Cairo, General Egyptian Book Organization, 1987.

Brinton, Jasper Y., *The Mixed Courts of Egypt*, New Haven CT, Yale University Press, 1930.

Brown, Nathan J., 'The precarious life and slow death of the Mixed Courts of Egypt', *International Journal of Middle East Studies*, 25, 1993, pp. 33–52.

Cannon, Byron, *Politics of Law and the Courts in Nineteenth-Century Egypt*, Salt Lake City, UT, University of Utah Press, 1988.

Cromer, Lord, *Modern Egypt*, London, Macmillan, 1908.

el-Leithy, Tamer, 'Public punishment in Mamluk society', M.Phil. thesis, Cambridge University, 1997.

Espéronnier, M., 'La mort violent à l'époque mamlouke: le crime et la châtiment', *Der Islam*, 74, 1997, pp. 137–55.

Fahmy, Khaled, *All the Pasha's Men: Mehmed Ali, His Army and the Making of Modern Egypt*, Cambridge, Cambridge University Press, 1997.

– 'Women, medicine and power in nineteenth century Egypt', in Lila Abu-Lughod, ed., *Remaking Women: Feminism and Modernity in the Middle East*, Princeton, Princeton University Press, 1998, pp. 35–72.

– 'The anatomy of justice: Forensic medicine and criminal law in nineteenth-century Egypt', *Islamic Law and Society*, 6, 1999a, pp. 224–71.

– 'The police and the people in nineteenth-century Egypt', *Die Welt des Islams*, 39, 1999b, pp. 1–38.

– 'Medical conditions in Egyptian prisons in the nineteenth century', in Robin Ostle (ed.), *Marginal Voices in Literature and Society: Individual and Society in the Mediterranean Muslim World*, Aix-en-Provence, Paul Roubaud, 2000, pp. 135–53.

Foucault, Michel, 'Politics of health in the eighteenth century', in Colin Gordon (ed.), *Power/Knowledge: Selected Interviews & Other Selected Writings, 1972–1977*, New York, Pantheon, 1980, pp. 166–82 (originally published as 'La politique de la santé au XVIIIe siècle', in Michel Foucault, Blandine Barret-Kriegel, Anne Thalamy, François Beguin and Bruno Fortier (eds), *Les Machines à Guérir [aux origins de l'hôpital moderne]*, Paris, Institut de L'Environnement, 1976).

– *Discipline and Punish: the Birth of the Prison* (trans. Alan Sheridan), New York, Vintage, 1979.

Heyd, Uriel, *Studies in Old Ottoman Criminal Law*, Oxford, Oxford University Press, 1976.

Hoyle, Mark S.W., 'The Mixed Courts of Egypt, 1875–1885', *Arab Law Quarterly*, 1, 1986, pp. 436–51.

Jabartî, 'Abd al-Rahmân al-, *'Ajâ'ib al-âthâr fi'l-tarâjim wa-l'akhbâr*, Cairo, Bûlâq, 1880.

Jallâd, Fîlîb, *Qâmûs al-idâra wa'l-qadâ' (Dictionary of Administration and the Judiciary)*, Alexandria, al-Bukhariyya, 1894–95.

Khankî, Azîz, *al-Tashrî' wa'l-qadâ' qabl inshâ' al-mahâkim al-ahliyya (Legislation and the Judiciary Before the Establishment of the National Courts)*, Cairo, n.p., n.d.
Langbein, John, *Torture and the Law of Proof: Europe and England in the Ancien Régime*, Chicago IL, University of Chicago Press, 1977.
Lewis, Bernard, 'The Impact of the French Revolution on Turkey', *Journal of Modern History*, 1, 1953, pp. 105–25.
Paton, A., *History of the Egyptian Revolution*, London, Trubner, 1863.
Peers, Douglas M., 'Sepoys, soldiers and the lash: race, caste and army discipline in India, 1820–50', *Journal of Imperial and Commonwealth History*, 23, 1995, pp. 211–47.
Peters, Rudolph, 'Murder on the Nile: Homicide trials in 19th century Egyptian *sharî'a* courts', *Die Welt des Islams*, 30, 1990, pp. 98–116.
– 'The Origins of pre-1883 Egyptian Criminal Legislation', paper presented to the 1996 annual MESA meeting, Providence (Rhode Island), 21–24 November 1996.
– '"For his correction and as a deterrent example for others": Mehmed 'Alî's first criminal legislation (1829–1830)', *Islamic Law and Society*, 6, 1999a, pp. 164–92.
– 'Administrators and magistrates: The development of a secular judiciary in Egypt, 1842–1871', *Die Welt des Islams*, 39, 1999b, pp. 378–97.
– 'Controlled suffering: mortality and living conditions in nineteenth-century Egyptian prisons', *International Journal of Middle Eastern Studies*, forthcoming.
Rafi'î, 'Abd al-Rahmân al-, *'Asr Ismâ'îl* (*Ismâ'il's Reign*), Cairo, Dar al-Mâ'arif, 1987.
Rao, Anupama, 'Problems of violence, States of terror: Torture in colonial India', *Interventions: The International Journal of Post-Colonial Studies*, 3, 2001, pp. 186–205.
Sâlim, Latîfa, *Târîkh al-qadâ' al-Misrî al-hadîth (History of the Modern Egyptian Judiciary)*, Cairo, General Egyptian Book Organization, 1991.
Schrader, Abby M, 'Containing the spectacle of punishment: The Russian autocracy and the abolition of the knout, 1817–1845', *Slavic Review*, 4, 1997, pp. 613–44.
Shaykhzâda, *Majma' al-anhûr fî sharh multaq al-abhûr*, Istanbul, n.p., 1301/1884.
Sirhank, Ismâ'îl, *Haqâ'iq al-akhbar 'an duwal al-biha (True Narrations About Maritime Nations)*, Bûlâq, al-Matba'a al-amîriyya, 1894.
Zaghlûl, Ahmad Fathî, *al-Muhâmâh* (*Advocacy*), Cairo, n.p., 1900.
Ziadeh, Farhat, *Lawyers, the Rule of Law and Liberalism in Modern Egypt*, Stanford, Hoover Institution, 1968.

CHAPTER 5

The 'Implosion' of *Sharî'a* within the Emergence of Public Normativity: The Impact on Personal Responsibility and the Impersonality of Law

Armando Salvatore

Traditions and normativity

In this study, I would like to sketch an interpretative framework for some specific transformations within Islamic traditions which pivoted on a reformulation of *sharî'a*, or its 'implosion', as I will attempt to show. This process configured a conceptual and partly institutional network impacting notions of disciplinary normativity (based on 'governmentality'), impersonality and procedurality of norms, and personhood and personal responsibility: a triad that is presupposed in any modern notion of legal personality. I will relate this process of transformation to a particularly intense stage of legal reform and public argument in Egypt, the last third of the nineteenth century, which saw the emergence of the media infrastructure, the intellectual personnel and the state-legal pre-conditions for what is called a modern public sphere.[1] During this period, the long march of legal positivism which obfuscated the impact of traditions upon norms was just beginning. This is why the study of this historical juncture offers us a privileged observatory for evaluating the relation between traditions on one hand, and modern law and modern public sphere on the other.

The focus of this study is on a concept that has drawn close to the centre of Islamic discursive traditions, to God and His *shar'*, i.e. legislating will. This is the concept of *sharî'a* which is, nonetheless, not a central Qur'anic keyword and not even one with which the first generations of Muslim leaders and scholars after the revelation were concerned, not even at the stages – later reached through the work of the four classic schools – when they engaged in a systematic effort to build up the edifice of Islamic jurisprudence (*fiqh*). However, *sharî'a* is a notion that has acquired momentum through the later growth and consolidation of Islamic traditions – notably at a more specifically philosophical and theological level[2] – and has finally attained a discursively prominent place precisely in the period and in the context with which we deal here.[3]

My methodological approach supports a sociological perspective on tradition, suitable to assess how social transformations – including the rise of the modern printing press – have contributed to redesigning the conceptual centre and peripheries of the discursive traditions of Islam.[4] This, however, is entirely different from issuing verdicts on the tenor of Islamicity versus non-Islamicity of this or that notion that we find in the public discourse of Muslim reformers, as well as on the degree and quality of normativity that are attached to diverse categories. The need for a distinction between an Islamic and a non-Islamic character of discourses and concepts arose at a later historical juncture in the development of the Egyptian public sphere (notably the 1920s and 1930s). The distinction was not the concern of the actors involved in the transformation described here. The discussion of *sharî'a* and the parallel reform of the legal systems did not produce, at the stage examined here, any major public dispute on 'opting in' or 'out' of Islam and its normative sources, in spite of the fact that the issue of the 'defence of Islam' (thus, a certain reification of the notion itself of Islam) from foreign penetration was clearly a public issue at the time.[5] It was nonetheless during the waning nineteenth century, when a sharp opposition between Islam and secularism was not on the agenda, that a crucial formative transformation in the understandings of *sharî'a*, and in the above-mentioned, tyriadic conceptual cluster was initiated.

One side of the civilising process: Reform of civilising traditions and emergence of the accountable person

As evidenced by Dupret in the introductory chapter to this volume, the notions of person in Arab societies do not necessarily reflect the discourse of positive law and the category of legal personality. It is probably appropriate not to approach the question in terms of a mismatch, but through investigating the complex relationship between reformed Islamic legal traditions (including the apparatus of notions through which they are reformed) and the discourse centred on the subject of rights and legal personality. This is much more than a legal discourse, but the discourse itself of modern liberalism, subjective autonomy and the 'rule of law'.

There is a common Platonic-Aristotelian root to the category of the person, both in the three main Western religious-civilising traditions based on Abrahamic monotheism (Judaism, Christianity and Islam) and within modern liberalism, though the latter understands itself as having emerged after a fierce battle against the Aristotelian-Thomist ideas of cosmic and social order. However, it is true that within different Western civilisations, we observe distinct articulations of the notion of the person as well as – as stressed by Dupret – a major bifurcation between those traditions laying an emphasis on the person within the community, such as Aristotelianism, and those stressing the individual self within a spiritual cosmos, such as Stoicism.[6]

The only way not to overestimate either common traits or differences between the two types of tradition cannot merely consist of accurately weighing the characteristics of both. We should also assess how they are linked and in tension with each other historically and genealogically. In this sense, the moments of prevalence of the latter tradition that provide the entry point into liberal modernity are related to situations of fragility, collapse or conscious contest with the cosmic and moral order shaped by the Aristotelian tradition. Stoicism was a response to the erosion of the bases of ancient republican citizenship both in Greece and in the Roman Empire, and an attempt to bypass their institutional axis represented by membership in the community and the cultivation of the virtues required by ancient citizenship. The device for bypassing this institutional and moral core was the quite-singular virtue of an immediate, direct tuning of the self into cosmic order. As Dupret also observes, 'heterodox' religious movements within all three Western monotheistic civilisations have taken up the task of re-establishing such a direct link between the faithful's consciousness and God's will, thereby delegitimising the mediation of authorised religious specialists.[7] In particular, in medieval Europe, the Franciscan theological vanguards (from Saint Bonaventura to Ockham) have acted as the spearheads of criticism of the Thomist order, exactly at the high time of the latter's influence during the thirteenth century,[8] and have decisively contributed to legitimise the Stoic-Augustinian idea – later relaunched by Luther and other reformers – of the centrality of the faithful's consciousness, along with his will, due to be directly tuned into God's will.

If we opt for a socio-anthropological and not a philosophical approach, we should be aware that there is nothing intrinsically 'superior' to this second tradition – unless we refer it to a process of gradual inculcation or acquisition of models of self-control, or what Elias refers to as the 'civilising process'.[9] At the same time, if we stay on the sociological side, we should not dismiss, at the outset, the long-term civilising potential of the first tradition in contexts of modernity. That is its capacity to create order along the axis linking the self to the community and make the community prosper, as well as enabling the latter to educate its members into practising the virtues that are conducive to *eudaimonia*. This sociological balance can only be kept if we assess and measure modernity – sociologically – in terms of social differentiation and specialisation (or, more generally, of *Vergesellschaftung*), as well as in terms of the related configuration of the self apt to act in the resulting multiplicity of social fields, in other words, if we do not indulge in the exercise of seeing modernity wherever we believe we meet intrinsically superior forms of self and community.

Put differently, there is no contradiction between seeing the free and responsible person as a product of social emancipation from the 'chains of traditions' and seeing in it a technical-operative fiction allowing for the mechanisms of imputation and ascription of intentional actions necessary for a modern legal system to function. The latter interpretation is sociologically interesting as elucidating the mechanism for the production of order within a differentiated social field ('modern law'), whose specialised function consists in adjudicating cases in which rights are violated or obligations foregone. The former claim is sociologically relevant as the necessary formula for legitimising the mechanisms of ascription along with the related process of disciplining the person into the moral skills. These skills are less and less formulated as virtues or virtuous practices – a typically traditional concept – and increasingly as competencies and habitus. These skills are also requisite for the technical-operative fiction to effectively function. What is new here is that while the notion of the person was for both types of tradition illustrated above a construction essential for justifying the cosmic and moral order, modern liberalism rendered the category of the person quite strictly functional for justifying the political order of the modern state at its passage from absolutism to the rule of law.[10] In this sense, the legal notion of the person pinpoints and legitimises those traits of the personality demanded of modern subjects in the process of increasing internalisation of affection constraints highlighted by Elias' theory of the civilising process that is strictly tied to the rise of modern (first absolutist) states.[11]

How does this discussion fit the historically and sociologically specific topic dealt with here? Though committed to the revitalisation of Islamic traditions, Muslim reformers valued all modern instruments of state-legal regulation, including modern courts and modern codes, which definitively became a reality of Egyptian legal and public life in the last quarter of the nineteenth century.[12] The problem of the dilemmas faced and solutions devised by the reformers cannot, however, be formulated in terms of their allegedly 'modernist' approach of squeezing Islamic traditions into modern institutions and leaving behind what was considered unsuitable. Reformers did, in fact, dismiss several methods and institutions of Islamic traditions in the educational and legal fields, but they basically wanted to redress and render operative again (*islâh*, improperly translated as 'reform') – and not discard – the theological and conceptual apparatus of these traditions.

In the discourse of Muslim reformers, *sharî'a*, although not overwhelmingly used as a keyword, acquired a more central and complex position as a normative notion within the discursive traditions of Islam than in the era preceding the formation of a modern state and a modern public sphere. This centrality and complexity were reflected in the ways that the normativity of Islam was simultaneously reconstructed on a plurality of levels which happened to be classified (from the vintage point of the modern legal system) as non-legal ('moral'), semi-legal (such as the realm of *fatwâs*, i.e. answers to legal questions formulated by a *mustaftî* who can be any Muslim with a personal concern for the question asked) or legal in a fully fledged, positive sense. These levels, however, from the viewpoint of Islamic normativity, were still strictly related to each other under the umbrella of *sharî'a*. The main difference to the more weakly formulated *sharî'a* of the period prior to the reform was that in the reform era, the congruity of Islamic normativity in holding together these various levels had to be discursively justified in face of the accelerating process of social differentiation, especially as regards the formation of a legal system increasingly taken over by the state and positivised. While firmly considering law as a vehicle of social normativity, Islamic reformers' views on the conceptual and institutional cluster covered by the notion of *sharî'a* impacted the metalegal dyad personality-impersonality.

Let us roughly summarise what we see as the main discursive approach of Islamic reformers. Through their lectures and lessons, as well as through their direct and indirect involvement with the organs of the modern printing press, the reformers emphasised the importance of moral 'refinement' (*tahdhib*), to be acquired through appropriate 'guidance' (*irshâd*). A correct moral disposition was considered necessary for the proper exercise of knowledge. Discussions of the dangers of ignorance in its many forms occupied a prominent place not only in the discourse of Islamic reform, but also in the general press of the time. These discussions also contained a stress on an explicitly defined civilisational dimension as revealed by the wide use of the term *tamaddun*, reflecting the virtues of the urban educated population as opposed to the 'ignorance' of the rural uneducated *fallâhîn* ('peasants').

This was no pure discourse, since clubs and associations of various kinds, including charitable ones, attempted implementing the discourses of moral reform to the advantage of all members of the community, including peasants, through inculcating dispositions that would help Egyptians (and Muslims in general) to reverse the 'decline' of their society.[13] Clearly, the civilising discourse, though recompacting general moral norms, created avenues of intervention within discrete fields of social activity and sustained their sectorial rationalisation. The discourse legitimised and provided the apparatus for the diffusion of a civilising process in the making that was parallel to the rationalisation of the state-bound steering capacities as well as of the economic, mainly agricultural, production.

It is in the context of the acceleration of this civilising process – which is probably too limiting to conceive of in strictly Eliasian terms – that the normativity of public moral discourse acquired new functions. The novelty of this modern normativity as opposed to the regulating capacities of civilising traditions is in a singular mechanism of anticipation of due behaviour. Parallel to the discourse on *tamaddun*, *âdâb* (a traditional term close to the Greek *paideia* and to the Latin *disciplina*) acquired new and multiple significations and usages, ending up delimiting a moral field that defined morality and its rules in terms of the skills of the subjects to anticipate the consequences of their behaviour.[14] At the same time, however, this mechanism of anticipation needed a *telos*, for anticipation cannot be regulated by a mere utilitarian calculating reason, as the one demanded by the sectorial rationalities of social fields.

This teleological orientation that animates public intellectuals in general, and Muslim reformers in particular, in their attempts to address the general public, consists of tuning into a superior, non-sectorial, normative reason building the moral substratum of modern subjectivity. This capacity is to be achieved through the acquisition of adequate knowledge and education. Seldom does this plea result in a mere moralising discourse; it is more often sustained by a view of objective social relations or interdependencies resulting from the way that the educated subjects are expected to enter into relationships with each other. A relational analysis of how morality is produced does not exclude a teleological orientation that is, in turn, generated in the process of intervening upon traditions. This modern morality is put into operation through the capacity itself of the subjects to anticipate the consequences of their action, by which we can see the hub of what Foucault called 'governmentality', defined as a genuinely modern form of power that functions by shaping self-regulating autonomous subjects. Governmentality, produced in the process of modern state-formation, requires the philosophical fiction of autonomous agency and the juridical fiction of legal personality.

The other side of the civilising process: modern state-formation and the rise of a normative public sphere

Elias's notion of the civilising process has the merit of using the increasing interdependence entailed by *Vergesellschaftung* and the self-constraint that goes along with it to explain the formation of codes of conduct and their simultaneous use as signs of distinction. Individualisation and the shaping of civilised selves respond to the necessity of building up competencies to act within different social fields. In other words, the self-consciousness of 'inwardness' is a product of the cumulative necessities of self-control due both to the increasing functional specialisation and to competition within the various socially functional fields. This cumulative process is the measure of 'rationalisation', in that rationality is measured by exactly the capacity to constrain oneself according to the demands of increasing specialisation and interdependence. The process is reflected in the differentiation and control of outer gestures according to the specificity of circumstances, but also in tune with a homogenisation of rules of general public conduct. The result is a permanent tension and unstable balance between specialisation of competencies and generalisation of duties and rights.

Elias has been criticised for not specifying with enough clarity the relation between two fundamental components of the civilising process: the monopolisation of force through the state and functional differentiation. Suffice it here to remark that the idea of a 'general interest' and of 'society' itself as an organic body would be unthinkable outside of the process of modern state-formation and, furthermore, that at the stage of the formation of public sphere largely autonomous from the will of the ruler, the discursive processing of functional differentiation through public intellectuals has often been slow and reticent. We are interested here in the specific case of Muslim reformers meeting the formation of an increasingly differentiated legal system, resting on the philosophical fiction of autonomous agency and the juridical fiction of legal personality.

In the classic scheme – reflected in the history and ideology of civil law – the centralised monopoliser of force issues a systematised corpus of rules based on notions of personal autonomy and the legitimacy and binding force of these rules is, in turn, based on the fiction of a contractually grounded consensus over delegating this force to its monopoliser that, in turn, guarantees the preservation of personal autonomy. The transformation of *sharî'a* and its impact on the dyad personality/impersonality (through the prism of the emerging modern normativity as moral competence to anticipate behaviour) should be analysed in these terms. Islamic reformers did support codification and the civilising logic immanent in it as nurturing both their projects and their social power of public educators, i.e. of educators of the emerging public.

This process unfolded in Egypt from the beginning of the nineteenth century on, within the context of the massive efforts of state-formation and centralisation undertaken by Muhammad 'Ali, directly affecting the standardisation of personal identity and its functionalisation in relation to the rationalisation of the state and the economy. This 'belated' (if compared to Western European models) process of state-building created a gap in the long term elaboration of discursive-institutional solutions by the scholarly carriers of the civilising tradition. It also gave a sense of urgency to the efforts of the reformers when, 'after the state', a public sphere, a largely new terrain of communicative power for the educational-civilising ('modernist') projects, was formed. A modern public sphere rests on the infrastructure, the personnel, the audiences and the market of modern media; first of all of the printing press, as centred on newspapers and periodicals.

Within Egyptian society of the 1870s and 1880s, while momentous reforms of the legal system were being implemented, the emerging public sphere provided the concrete institutional and discursive platform for the formulation of normative claims affecting both the improvement-redressment (*islâh*) of the selves as well as of society. These normative claims were finalised to fill the gaps between the traditionally given four levels of regulation and disciplining (state-emanated, i.e. positive law, *qânûn*; the human interpretation of Islamic law, *fiqh*; *sharî'a* as the manifestation of God's legislating will, *shar'*; *âdâb* as the etiquette of social intercourse) through building a unitary field of public morality.

The enterprise of building up and justifying a moral field as distinct from theology, law and aesthetics is central to the formative phase of modernity within Protestant- (or Jansenist-) dominated Northwestern European societies,[15] but the impetus of delimiting a field of public morality can be seen as well in other societies at the intersection of the formation of a modern public sphere and a modern legal system, both occurring in the wake of modern state-formation. This was the case of Egyptian society in the period under examination here. It is important to distinguish the structural affinity of the process in Western centres and in Egypt as well as in other Muslim societies from all due differences: that for Muslim reformers, the transcendence-bound character of the discourse of *sharî'a* was not completely absorbed into the field of morality, yet it imploded into a normative kernel that could permanently feed the rules and mechanisms of public morality.

The point here is that the crucial link between technologies of domination and technologies of the self, highlighted both by the Eliasian notion of 'civilising process' and by the Foucauldian concept of 'governmentality', have to be mediated by intellectual technologies of communication. Here, the specificity of the integrative mode of the public sphere is at stake. Here, also, civilising traditions are able to keep their thread, to hold together the chain of transmission of traditional knowledge. This happens at the cost of a deal with the initiators of the structural and institutional transformations within state-building, which affects the traditionally sensitive fields of law and education. More than that, this happens through the creation of new fields of undifferentiated general social power (i.e. distinct from the specialised fields of social action); the major such field is the public sphere.

The implosion of *sharî'a* into a disciplining metanorm of the public sphere

Sharî'a, as it crystallised during the classic era of *islâh* in the late nineteenth century, should be understood as a metaphysical term of reference, a 'terministic screen'[16] holding together a series of other notions more concretely linked to institutional solutions, as shall be seen. In this sense, its theological underpinning is fragile and increasingly taken for granted (and, therefore, of marginal importance for our discussion). This new *sharî'a* concerns us for its capacity to influence normative discourse in the public sphere and its chances and alleys of institutionalisation through notions claiming a central place within Islamic traditions.[17]

Therefore we are called to question views of a '*sharî'a* society' perpetuating itself through subsequent phases of social differentiation well into the era of nation-states. The definition itself of *sharî'a* as a conceptual tool defining an entity-like normative system has been slow and gradual, and not inbuilt within any particular legal-cultural repertoire residing either in Scripture or in the historic experience of the proto-community (the *umma*) of Muhammad, His companions and the first rightly guided caliphs.

The process of the 'implosion' of *sharî'a* took place in the field of tension between the differentiation of an autonomous legal system in Egypt and the undifferentiating, normative discourse of *islâh*. Implosion of *sharî'a* is meant here as the transformation of its understanding, mainly mediated by Islamic reformers' discourse, away from the softly co-ordinated, yet positive, systemic and institutional – albeit limited by the profane regulation of *qânûn* – efficacy of divine law based on *fiqh* doctrines and institutions[18] of the epoch prior to modern state-building, to its pretended authentic normative and civilising kernel. This imploded *sharî'a* impinged both on a definition of the subject and on a view of objective social relations or interdependencies.

In other words, the implosion of *sharî'a* reflects the process of its redefinition that turns back the historical crystallisation of the institutions and efficacy of Islamic law and returns law to its fictive kernel, i.e. to a claimed permanent source of normative disciplining and anticipation of behaviour demanded to the faithful. Since the mechanism of anticipation that characterises this kind of normativity as governmentality is strictly related to modern state-formation and the subsequent emergence of the public sphere (or to the wider civilising process), the implosion of *sharî'a* is a process that can only be explained by taking account of the compound of modern technologies of domination, of the self and of communication. Muslim reformers did not like regional local differences in the enactment of Islamic law, and disliked the classic division into four schools: the making of a 'kernel' was very much due to the intent to define a unitary (and 'authentic') source of normativity. What was earlier factual and procedural (the co-ordination of *fiqh*) as well as minimalistically theological (God's will as a source) became normative, or rather, the source and term of reference of all normative claims – therefore, one major source of metanorm. It was in this context that the talk about *sharî'a* as a normative system first became intelligible to everyone in the public arena and, over time, popular.

This kernel-like understanding of *sharî'a* was reformulated not merely under the pressure of an identitarian syndrome or an obsession with authenticity in face of colonial encroachment, but according to the new rules of the public sphere and, in particular, of the necessary search for a metanorm, i.e. a norm of norms, linking up the subjective requirements to perform good with an objectified vision of collective welfare.[19] Thus we at the same time see a principled irreducibility of the imploded *sharî'a* to modern positive law and its logic and fundaments, and an affinity with it as to the required mechanisms of normative anticipation that also impacts on the notions of legal personality and impersonality of law.

The implosion of *sharî'a* provided a normative ground for accepting, even promoting, the positivisation and codification of law and the legitimisation itself of a civil-law approach based on the notion of responsible persons voluntarily entering contractual relations. This was not completely different from what Locke did centuries earlier. The main difference was that Locke's work had a foundational import for liberal legal and political theory whereas the Muslim reformers confronted a ready-made civil-law rationality. Therefore, all that they could do was to proceed on a normative reshaping and reduction of *sharî'a* and influence codification in a way that they themselves considered coherent with the normative imploded kernel of *sharî'a* as opposed to the casuistic rationality of *fiqh*.

A good example of this process of furthering the dyad personality-impersonality through the normative implosion of *sharî'a* is the already-mentioned discourse on the refinement and education of the Egyptian peasants whose 'ignorance' threatened – according to the discourse – to impair all progress within social and legal relationships. If the peasants stayed so ignorant and unrefined that they were regularly cheated both by state officials and by moneylenders, i.e. if they remained incapable of knowing and implementing their *huqûq* (provisionally translated here as 'rights'), there would be no moral cohesion and no legal security for the whole *watan* (provisionally translated here as 'nation'). The peasant, and every other member of the community, was in dire need of *tamaddun*, i.e. the acquiring of moral skills for participating in civic life by the training of virtues and the practice of good morals sustained by – within an Islamic context – the primacy of *sharî'a*. *Tamaddun* – that reformers did not consider a civilisational monopoly of Islam – is nothing else than the civilising process normally associated with the constraints of life in an urban and modern context, with mastering its diverse stimuli and meeting the variety of social responsibilities implied by modern life.

The concept of *huqûq* comes really close here to that of legitimate rights as based on personal interest, as when 'Abdallah al-Nadim wrote that 'we know our *huqûq* through just laws that conform to our *sharî'a* and *qawâ'id* (principles), and with this we preserve much of our money, real estate, and land'.[20] However, *huqûq* are not naturally known by the subject, but are apprehended through the knowledge of law, conforming to divine *sharî'a*. In this perspective of a quite explicit discourse of governmentality, the concept of rights appears to take root.

Sâhib al-haqq (the 'subject of rights', a notion which is not new to Islamic legal traditions) would define here a 'soft' legal personality, linking up the pursuit of interests, the welfare of the 'nation' (*watan*) and the teleology of a *sharî'a*-governed social world. The civil code along with the 'French-style' rights that, at the end of the nineteenth century, became part of the Egyptian legal system, did not provide by default a ready-made metanorm resting on a prefabricated view of the responsible person as the one stemming from the views of the Scottish and French Enlightenment, but rather a disciplining and mobilising instrument of governmentality with a tendentially culture-neutral and civilisationally universal power validated by the necessities of nation-state building. The enduring – though not dramatic – gulf between 'rights' and *huqûq* did not contradict the search for a more encompassing metanorm of social intercourse and intersubjective justice which reformers rooted in the imploded *sharî'a*.

One might well be tempted to see in this understanding of *sharî'a* a mere paying of lip-service to an Islamic source of normativity (i.e. a mere identitarian syndrome, an Islamisation of a culture-neutral modern normativity) or the definition of an empty space or, at best, a fragile screen of natural law upon which to project all kinds of non-Islamic reforms.[21] However, the view of *sharî'a* was consciously elaborated upon in the new situation determined by the tension – alongside the need of co-ordination – between the two sides of the civilising process illustrated here: state-*cum*-subject-building on one hand, and intellectual governance of the fundaments of political legitimacy as well as definition of the 'general interest' and 'society' on the other. The view of a 'weak' *sharî'a* might have resulted from a methodological short-cut that is sociologically unacceptable: from the analysis of *sharî'a* as an isolated keyword of discourse. Instead of such a kind of weak content analysis, I have opted for the tentative exploration of a whole discursive-institutional cluster situated in the field of tension between both sides of the civilising process.

New discursive clusters and the limits to their institutionalisation

I am going to refer to three partly institution-based approaches – legitimised within a reconstructed *sharî'a* framework – regarding the production of norms on which Muslim reformers insisted with particular emphasis within the context of the emergence of a modern public sphere: *ijtihâd*, *hisba/ihtisâb* and *iftâ'*. The first two notions are immediately linked to the dyad personality-impersonality. Firstly, the double emphasis of reformers on a new understanding of the procedural notions of *ijtihâd* ('free reasoning in looking for legal solutions') can be seen as a generalised legal-normative competence of method of a reconstituted

Muslim subjectivity. Secondly, the communicative-disciplining notion of *hisba/ihtisâb* (the canonical injunction of 'enjoining good and prohibiting evil') can be seen as the interpersonal rule linking mature Muslim subjects with each other, thereby defining the criteria of the impersonality of rulings by reference to a kernel-like view of personhood and of moral-legal duties towards a generalised 'other'. Both categories were known to Islamic juridical traditions, but have been condensed and proceduralised by the *islâh* school into disciplines of the citizen. The novel understandings of these two notions, whose complex conceptual and institutional life within Islamic traditions cannot be recapitulated here,[22] are rooted in the formation of a modern public sphere and its modes of discourse. I will add some observations on the transformations of the institution of *iftâ'* (the delivering by legal scholars, *muftîs*, of *fatwâs*) which re-articulate both the new canons of personhood and the relationship between general moral-legal competencies of Muslim subjects and those with scholarly credentials.

Ijtihâd was propagated by reformers no longer as a technical-juridical skill of excellence or a device for updating the legal system,[23] but as a method to regulate and encourage the participation of all Muslims in discussions of issues of common interest to foster a moral and discursive discipline for addressing such questions, and to establish a new view of lawfulness and consensus of communication in the public sphere. *Ijtihâd* was expanded from a classic method for articulating the normativity of scriptural sources through the independent reasoning of scholars of exceptional insight and leadership into a discipline of rational-critical debate in the public sphere to be practised in such a way as to establish the legislating authority of reason bound only by the Qur'an and, subordinately, by the *Sunna*.

Rashid Rîda', who inherited, updated and radicalised the project of the *islâh* of Muhammad 'Abduh (mainly via their common project, the journal *al-Manâr*), went so far as to affirm that each Muslim should be a *mujtahid* – a practitioner of *ijtihâd*.[24] As Skovgaard-Petersen has put it, according to reformers, *ijtihâd* was not merely permitted, but was in a sense obligatory,[25] thereby constituting an essential part of the social and public personality of the Muslim. The rupture with traditional views of *ijtihâd* was strictly related to the new requirements of the public sphere, yet the traditional rooting of the 'new' *ijtihâd* should not be underestimated. Even traditionally, *ijtihâd* was a sort of meta-procedure rooted in the capacity of excellent spirits: without *ijtihâd*, there would be no authoritative meta-instance for controlling the extent to which the acts of Muslims could be considered acceptable to God, hence lawful.[26]

Along with *ijtihâd*, many reformers saw a major axis of the new press and of the new public sphere in the *hisba/ihtisâb*. Targeting the moral behaviour of people in public through the exemplary observance and admonishment of the fellow believer was the new 'essentialist' understanding of the Muslim canonical injunction. Reformers liked to pivot their claims on this injunction because it provided a clear and general standard fitting a procedural and disciplining kind of normativity more than one of actual casuistic prescriptions. Major reformers, including Rîda',[27] explicitly considered the *hisba/ihtisâb* the main rationale of press activity.

Going one step further, interest in *fatwâs* by the reformers experienced a revival in the context of the formation of a modern public sphere and of the emergence of the new *ijtihâd*, altering the scope and function of these 'legal opinions', thus depersonalising the link between the *mustaftî* and the *muftî*. Some reformers were tempted to collapse the Islamic notion of legal personality resulting from *iftâ'* into the state's legal system, a project that played into the hands of the state efforts at unifying and centralising the legal system. 'Abduh wanted to give the power to enforce *sharî'a* to the state *muftî*ship in the form of non-appealable judgements. The grounding of *dar al-iftâ'* presided by a 'state *muftî*' in 1895 fell short of integrating the system of *iftâ'* into the state-legal system and was more modestly an attempt towards establishing a symbolic centrality of state-blessed Islamic institutions. Equipped with a growing apparatus for collecting queries and issuing *fatwâs*, *dâr al-iftâ'* soon entered in competition with other Islamically authorised agents endowed with the faculty to issue *fatwâs* and capable of reaching significant sections of the public via every kind of new media available.

Especially after this attempt to integrate the *iftâ'* into the state-centred legal and judicial system failed, reformers worked on redefining *iftâ'* according to their view of *ijtihâd*. Once again, the most daring and consequent among them was Rîda' who maintained that the last instance for enforcing *al-maslaha* or *al-maslaha al-'âmma* (the traditional category of 'general interest' strictly tied to *hisba/ihtisâb*) should be *fatwâs* unbound by the state-centred legal system. He asserted that as far as state *ulama* were not able to do so, *maslaha* should be applied through *fatwâs.*[28] He supported the view of institutionalising *iftâ'* within the public, but not immediately state-bound realm of the exercise of *ijtihâd*; this step contributed to imparting a strong procedural dimension to the imploded *sharî'a* .[29] He was very active in implementing this programme of linking *hisba/ihtisâb*, *ijtihâd* and *iftâ'* in his main editorial project of *al-Manâr*, a journal that still enjoys the fame of the most successful medium of *islâh* in the public sphere, right after the earlier and short-lived *al-Urwa al-wuthqa'* of al-Afghani and 'Abduh. From the end of the nineteenth century until today, *iftâ'* has proved more successful via a 'soft institutionalisation', i.e. within social loci and media largely autonomous from the state-centred legal system:[30] think of famous Egyptian scholars like al-Qaradawi, Kishk and al-Sha'rawi, whose *fatwâs* collections have been bestsellers – not only in Egypt – during the last quarter of the twentieth century.[31]

The revival of *fatwâs* as a popular genre affecting legal and moral practice and their work of incorporation into Islam's normativity in the life of a modernising, though vastly heterogeneous, Muslim majority society restates the original reformers' idea of the *iftâ'* as combining the capacity to act legally for the sake of one's own interest (mediated by *ijtihâd*) and one's empowering to act for the sake of the community (whose main entry point is the *hisba/ihtisâb*). We might dare to add that the rediscovery of interest in *fatwâs* by the reformers led to an alteration of the scope and function of *iftâ'* and rendered the link between *mustaftî* and *muftî* more and more impersonal: due to the imperative itself of publicity, an increasing number of *fatwâs* published in the press were issued in the absence of a real *mustaftî*'s query, but through fictive ones formulated by the *muftîs* themselves according to what they deemed could attract the interest of a wider public.

One, two or indefinite normative orders?

Within the framework of the implosion of *sharî'a*, *ijtihâd* was redefined as the generalised legal-normative competence of every Muslim to recognise a social problem and approach a solution. *Ihtisâb* was reformulated as the interpersonal rule linking mature Muslim subjects not only with each other on an interpersonal level, but also with a generalised other. *Iftâ'*, on the other hand, acquired the function of a channel of transmission between the general normative competencies of Muslim subjects and those with scholarly credentials to which Muslims turn if their own *ijtihâd* does not suffice.

The institution of method (*ijtihâd*), the institution of primary binary instruction (*ihtisâb*) and the law-interpreting and law-activating institution (*iftâ'*) were collapsed by the *islâh* into the notion of an imploded *sharî'a* operating within the public sphere and, in this way, were invested with a public-normative meaning superordinate to their immediate legal significance. Through their contribution to the implosion of *sharî'a* at this public-normative level, the elaboration of all three institutions intervened in the redefinition of concepts of personhood, impersonality and procedural rationality that still define the border territory between *sharî'a* and positive law on the issue of legal personality. *Sharî'a* thus defined has provided a soft and flexible background to the notion of legal personality either by constituting an 'environmental noise' for the operation of the legal system proper or by educating Muslim citizens into forms of personhood that conform to the impersonality of rule and are able to ease up their access to the higher formalisation of legal personality within the system of positive law.

In either case, the impact of the imploded *sharî'a* on the legal system is impossible to predict according to a theoretical formula (such as the one that categorically excludes that the legal system might 'need' to draw moral norms from a noisy environment). Relocating research at this juncture on the dilemmas faced by legal actors might be highly beneficial. The imploded *sharî'a*, without being a Trojan horse of 'modernity' in the camp of 'tradition' finalised to the long term, selective incorporation of all 'usable' (and acceptable for the state and, especially, the judiciary) references of Islamic law into positive law, has created a major channel for the resolution of (or, at least, for treating) the permanent tension between the notion of legal personality and the theological foundations of the normativity of *sharî'a*. As stressed by Dupret in the introductory chapter, this relation between a positive and a metaphysical dimension of norms is not exclusive to Arab Muslim majority societies, but also characterises Western ones, since it is embedded in the tension itself between norm and law.

Now we come to the more specific issue of the relationship between the *sharî'a*-related normative order centred on *iftâ'* and the legal-constitutional order in principle bound to *sharî'a* after the constitutional amendment of 1981 that stipulates that *sharî'a* is the main source of state legislation. Is it the same *sharî'a*? Our guess is that in the consciousness of most Muslim citizens it is indeed the same *sharî'a*, and this might be identified in many instances with the imploded *sharî'a* defined by the reformers of the period between the 1870s and 1920s, most of which enjoyed an undisputed scholarly reputation within contemporary 'liberal', as well as 'fundamentalist', 'clerical' and 'lay', interpreters of Islamic traditions. Belonging to the group of the earliest heroes of the Egyptian public sphere, the enduring impact of their formulation of key-notions of the Islamic discourse cannot be overestimated.

Therefore, it would be too simplistic to describe the present situation either as a competition between two distinct normative orders or as the process of collapsing the autonomous and traditional *sharî'a*-based order into the state-centred system, notably through the jurisprudence of the Supreme Constitutional Court and its interpretation of *ijtihâd*, or, inversely – and this could be the intent of the 'Islamic lawyers' operating exclusively within the field of positive law – through colonising the state legal system through divine law. What I see here is not a dualistic normative and legal landscape, but mechanisms of translation between different levels of formalisation of norms legitimised by different institutions or authorities. Within these mechanisms, the same imploded view of *sharî'a* plays a role in authorising mechanisms of disputation and adjudication with varying degrees of formalisation as well as of exposure to the procedures of law enforcement through state instances.

One might see in this phenomenon an interpenetration between normative orders, but I would object that as far as the same imploded view of *sharî'a* operates at all levels, there are no distinct normative orders establishing, maintaining and selectively opening up their boundaries to interpenetration. There might only be distinct legal actors contingently drawing borders for their own sake and, in the process, referring back to the notion of *sharî'a*. At the same time, the implosion of *sharî'a* into a kernel-like notion of order does not mean that it is the hub of one specific normative order. Rather, in the process of consolidation of a specialised legal system, the normative potential of reformed Islamic traditions is neither fully integrated into the systemic logic of modern law nor fully impaired from impinging upon the system of constitutional and positive law.

Notes

1 Farag, 2001; Gasper, 2001; Salvatore, 2000.
2 See Smith, 1965.
3 See Smith, 1962.
4 For this notion, see Asad, 1986.
5 al-Kûmî, 1992, pp. 67–85; Smith, 1962.
6 See also MacIntyre, 1984, pp. 168–70.
7 See Eisenstadt, 1986.
8 Santoro, 2003 (1999).
9 It is not the purpose of this study to delve into the complexities of Elias's theory of the civilising process (Elias, 1976), its strength and weakness and the surrounding debates (for a balanced assessment: see Ludwig-Mayerhofer, 1998). I am merely suggesting here the importance of devoting enough attention to the one side of the civilising process represented by the discursive traditions rooted in religious civilisations that unfold a regulating-disciplining power. This is a plea for situating civilising processes within the concrete social and historical formations where political and cultural elites (and 'public intellectuals', a general category into which the Muslim reformers mentioned here fit well) define and implement distinctive notions of civilisation. These configurations were characterised not only by class cleavages, but also by complex mechanisms of cultural distinction and normative recomposition between elites and 'society' or 'the general public' (that the reformers often termed *al-sawad al-a'zham*). The latter mechanisms have been the object of particular attention by Elias. However, right at the beginning

of the first volume of his main work on the civilising process, he also attempts a historically situated analysis of those distinctive notions of civilisation that pivot the discourse of cultural elites within different national settings by comparing Germany with France.

10 Santoro, 2003 (1999).
11 See Dupret's introductory chapter.
12 See Salvatore, 2000.
13 Gasper, 1999.
14 Farag, 2001.
15 MacIntyre, 1984, pp. 38–39.
16 The notion of 'terministic screen' was introduced by Kenneth Burke to designate all concepts that are necessarily used as final arguments; all such concepts, also in profane speech, are at least implicit 'God-terms', i.e. they are virtual theological concepts in that they prevent further questioning: Sakaranaho, 2000.
17 Salvatore, 1997, pp. 41–61.
18 The identification of or the claim of coherence between *fiqh* and *sharî'a* was, however, never unproblematic among Muslim scholars.
19 The issue of the reformers' *sharî'a* as a contribution to metanorm is dealt with by the author in more detail in two other publications: Salvatore, 1998; Salvatore, 2000.
20 The examples and quote are from Gasper, 1999.
21 See Kerr, 1966.
22 *Ijtihâd* has been the object of much scholarly attention for quite a long time (see Hallaq, 1984), while *hisba*, being an even hotter issue in some contemporary Muslim societies (both in legal cases and in public disputes), including Egypt, is attracting a growing amount of research efforts (see Dupret and Ferrié, 2001; also worth mentioning is the work in progress of Hussein Agrama, Dyala Hamzah and Jörn Thielmann).
23 Johansen, 1993, pp. 29–30.
24 Rîda', 1988, pp. 115–16.
25 Skovgaard-Petersen, 1997, pp. 65–79.
26 Moreover, *ijtihâd* was also a prerogative of the rulers of some pre-modern or proto-modern states (such as the first Saudi state based on Wahhabi doctrines) to intervene in the law for the sake of public interest or public order.
27 Skovgaard-Petersen, 1997, pp. 69–71.
28 Layish, 1978, pp. 276–77.
29 Ridâ', 1988, p. 268.
30 See Masud, Messick and Powers, 1996.

31 Commenting on the work of the thirteenth century scholar al-Qarafi, Jackson has stressed that a *fatwâ* as such is not merely a non-binding advisory legal opinion, but 'a direct endowment of a legal right that empowers a person to act, independent of any authorisation or intervention by the state': Jackson, 1993, p. 122. This legal activation performed by *iftâ'* configures a sort of legal personality directly tied to God's *shar'* and therefore is a legal personality that we can certainly define as 'Islamic'. In this sense, a *fatwâ* is an 'opinion' only from the viewpoint of state's law. Jackson tries to characterise the *fatwâ* as rooted in the authority of the Prophet, but his definition is probably anachronistic if referred to the *iftâ'* of the period prior to modern state-building since the sort of sharp definition of the state's legal authority as autonomous and, therefore, its looking at *fatwâs* as mere opinions is a modern product. The anachronism of the interesting definition of the *iftâ'* provided by Jackson adds to the one that unhistorically projects back reform-bent views of *sharî'a* to a pristine normative perfection of the Islamic community. We know, for example, that in early Islamic times, the *iftâ'* slowly began to differentiate itself from *hadîths* (the canonical certified sources reporting sayings and deeds of the Prophet) and was thereby defined as a source of rulings separate from the authority (originally of the Prophet) that issued it. The passage from being a mechanism for issuing legal rulings to one bestowing the faculty to act legally upon the *mustaftî* might have taken a lot of centuries and is probably not yet complete (and never will be?). However, there is enough evidence that *iftâ'* played a central role in the legal imagination of the Islamic reformers, exactly for configuring a legal authority and a mechanism of empowerment to act on a legal level independently of the mechanism of political domination.

Bibliography

Asad, T., *The Idea of an Anthropology of Islam*, Washington D.C., Georgetown University, Center for Contemporary Arab Studies, 1986.

Dupret, B., and J.N. Ferrié, 'The Inner Self and Public Order', in A. Salvatore (ed.), *Muslim Traditions and Modern Techniques of Power, Yearbook of the Sociology of Islam 3*, Hamburg, Lit Verlag, New Brunswick NJ and London, Transaction Publishers, 2001, pp. 141–62.

Eisenstadt, S.N., 'Introduction: The Axial Age Breakthroughs – Their Characteristics and Origins', in S.N. Eisenstadt (ed.), *The Origins and Diversity of Axial Age Civilizations*, Albany NY, State University of New York Press, 1986, pp. 1–25.

Elias, N., *Über den Prozess der Zivilisation*, Frankfurt, Suhrkamp, I and II, 1976 (first printing 1939).

Farag, I., 'Private Lives, Public Affairs. The Uses of Adab', in A. Salvatore (ed.), *Muslim Traditions and Modern Techniques of Power, Yearbook of the Sociology of Islam 3*, Hamburg, Lit Verlag, New Brunswick NJ and London, Transaction Publishers, 2001, pp. 93-120.

Gasper, M., 'Citifying and Civilizing: Islamic Modernism, the Egyptian Press and the Peasants Question in late 19th Century Egypt', paper presented at the workshop Multiple Modernities: Between Nation-Building and Muslim Traditions, European University Institute, Florence, 4 October 1999.

– 'Abdallah al-Nadim, Islamic reform, and "Ignorant" Peasants: State-building in Egypt?', in A. Salvatore (ed.), *Muslim Traditions and Modern Techniques of Power, Yearbook of the Sociology of Islam 3*, Hamburg, Lit Verlag; New Brunswick NJ and London, Transaction Publishers, 2001, pp. 75–92.

Hallaq, W.B., 'Was the Gate of *Ijtihâd* Closed?', *International Journal of Middle East Studies*, 16, 1984, pp. 3–41.

Höfert, A. and A. Salvatore, 'Introduction. Beyond the clash of civilisations: The transcultural politics between Europe and Islam', in A. Höfert and A. Salvatore (eds), *Between Europe and Islam: Shaping Modernity in a Transcultural Space*, Brussels/Berlin/Oxford, Presses Interuniversitaires Européennes/Peter Lang, pp. 13–35.

Jackson, S., 'From Prophetic Action to Constitutional Theory: A Novel Chapter in Medieval Muslim Jurisprudence', *International Journal of Middle East Studies*, 25, 1993, pp. 71–90.

Johansen, B., 'Legal Literature and the Problem of Change: the Case of Land Rent', in C. Mallat (ed.), *Islam and Public Law: Classical and Contemporary Studies*, London, Graham & Trotman, 1993, pp. 29–47.

Kerr, M., *Islamic Reform. The Political and Legal Theories of Muhammad Abduh and Rashid Rida*, Berkeley CA, University of California Press, 1966.

Kûmî, 'A. al-, *al-Sahâfa al-islâmiyya fî Misr fî'l-qarn al-tâsi' 'ashar*, al-Mansûra, Dâr al-wafâ' li'l-taba'a wa'l-nashr wa'l-tawzî, 1992.

Layish, A., 'The contribution of the modernists to the secularization of Islamic law', *Middle Eastern Studies*, 14, 1978, pp. 263–77.

Ludwig-Mayerhofer, W., 'Disziplin oder Distinktion? Zur Interpretation der Theorie des Zivilisationsprozesses von Norbert Elias', *Kölner Zeitschrift für Soziologie und Sozialpsychologie*, 50, 1998, pp. 217–37.

MacIntyre, A., *After Virtue. A Study in Moral Theory*, Notre Dame IN, University of Notre Dame Press, 1984 (first printing 1981).

Masud, K.M., B. Messick and D. Powers, *Islamic Legal Interpretation: Muftîs and their Fatwâs*, Cambridge MA, Harvard University Press, 1996.

Ridâ', R.M., *al-Khilâfa aw al-imâma al-'uzmâ*, Cairo, al-Zahra' li'l-a'lâm al-'arabî, 1988 (first printing 1922).

Sakaranaho, T., 'The Rhetoric of Normative and Cultural Islam', paper presented at the workshop on 'Islam and Public Space', Cairo, CEDEJ, 26 May 2000.

Salvatore, A., *Islam and the Political Discourse of Modernity*, Reading, Ithaca Press, 1997.

– 'La *sharî'a* moderne en quête de droit: Raison transcendante, méta-norme publique et système juridique', *Droit et Société*, special section: *Une sociologie non culturaliste de la norme en contexte arabe*, Baudouin Dupret (ed.), no 29, 1998, pp. 293–316.

– 'The Islamic Reform Project in the Emerging Public Sphere: The (Meta)normative Redefinition of *sharî'a*', A. Höfert and A. Salvatore (eds), *Between Europe and Islam: Shaping Modernity in a Transcultural Space*, Brussels/Berlin/Oxford, Presses Interuniversitaires Européennes/Peter Lang, 2000, pp. 89–108.

Santoro, E., *Autonomy, Freedom and Rights: A Critique of Liberal Subjectivity*, Dordrecht, Kluwer, 2003 (1999).

Skovgaard-Petersen, J., *Defining Islam for the Egyptian State*, Leiden, Brill, 1997.

Smith, W.C., 'The Historical Development in Islam of the Concept of Islam as an Historical Development', B. Lewis and P.M. Holt, (eds), *Historians of the Middle East*, London, Oxford University Press, 1962, pp. 484–502.

– 'The concept of *sharî'a* among some *mutakallimun*', in G. Makdisi, ed., *Arabic and Islamic Studies in Honor of Hamilton A.R. Gibb*, Cambridge MA, Harvard University Press, 1965, pp. 581–602.

CHAPTER 6

The Misbehaviour of the Possessed: On Spirits, Morality and the Person

Barbara Drieskens

The concept of the person in a popular Egyptian context appears to be quite different from the legal person in state law. There is a disparity between the way that people present and negotiate the constantly shifting limits between the person and the 'other' in daily life and the way that the concept of the person is constructed in the legal setting as a tool to demarcate responsibility. The ideas about personhood in daily life are (quite) different from our Western individualised concept, and always include a wider context of family, reputation and divine elements. What a person 'is' is never neatly defined, and is only implicitly revealed in daily praxis with all its contradictions and inconsistencies.

In particular cases of spirit possession and misbehaviour, both legal and local approaches are creatively combined. Sceptical neighbours use psychological arguments against someone who is possessed in order to hold him or her responsible for his or her misbehaviour and, on the other hand, a judge uses the vagueness of popular ideas about spirits and personhood to convict a possessed healer for murder while avoiding contradicting the Qur'anic truth that spirits exist.

From an anthropological perspective, I will try to account for the ever-shifting diversity in morality, discourse and practice related to the concept of the person. This diversity is one of the main characteristics of the suburban lifestyle, but it is veiled by a rigid ideology. Starting from the concrete issue of spirit possession and misbehaviour, I will try to draw a sketch of the multiple practices and discourses concerning personhood and its interaction with ideology. Implicated in spirit possession is the question of the borders of the person: where does the human being end and the spirit begin? Since the spirit controls the actions and words of the possessed, moral responsibility is also at stake. The answer to the question 'spirit and human, are they as one or are they two persons?' will immediately determine if the possessed is to be held responsible for behaviour ascribed to the spirit or not.

In the context of a court, the answer to this question has to be firm and unambiguous, but outside this particular context, the approaches are diverse and inconsistent. If people are eager to condemn somebody for his or her behaviour, then they will present possession as a mere invention or a strange psychological state, reducing human and spirit to one category (one person); these same people under other circumstances might consult a diviner to find out the supernatural causes of headaches, sleeplessness and bad luck, following the same lines of reasoning as those underlying spirit possession.

I have been doing fieldwork since September 1998 on spirit possession in Cairo, an enormous city with a very dense population. To the outsider, it might look like any modern city with a concentric structure including administrative and commercial centres, but apart from these apparent functional centres, Cairo is a patchwork. There are many small communities of people living in the same building, the same alley and the same street: small patches of streets and people which form the main life-space for most Cairenes.

I have chosen not to restrict my fieldwork to one neighbourhood, dealing with it as if it were a village[1] and confining myself to a concentric logic; rather, I have been following the relations traced by local networks that span different neighbourhoods,[2] connecting people through family ties, marriage, work, savings communities etc. The inhabitants of Cairo with whom I am working belong more or less to what one might call the lower-middle class. Men and women – if they work – are mostly functionaries in the government or in the recently privatised enterprises. They live on low wages and baksheesh and the support of more well-off family members. It is a very diverse group: some have university degrees while others hardly have any diploma; most of them, however, know how to read and write. Because of the diversity within the group that is also reflected in every family,[3] and the geographical dispersion, it becomes difficult to find a common denominator by which to refer to these people: they are more like a pack of people than a defined group.

I started my fieldwork in Imbâba, an area of suburban Cairo, but was soon confronted with the way that the suburbs invaded the rural districts as well as with the infiltration of the suburban logic in the urban. Farming land at the edges of the city is constantly being converted into built-up areas, rural houses become overgrown with apartment buildings and the rural is swallowed up within the logic of the suburbs, which divides space to the limit of liveability: can people go further than sharing 12 square metres with two adults and six children?

The suburbs present a creative blend of rural and urban lifestyle, with many people living in small spaces, with goats on roofs, chickens on balconies, a mud-brick oven for sun-risen bread, pigeon-breeding etc. This suburban lifestyle infiltrates right through the city centre, where the enormous increase in population has made it necessary to divide apartments and subdivide rooms and which has spread families over different neighbourhoods. This is the suburban logic of cutting-up: scattering space and groups of people into tiny fragments with vague borders, overthrowing clear-cut segmented structures of what is historically a strict, hierarchical and stratified society. Rural economies invade back streets, roofs and balconies of what once used to be bourgeois districts. People still try to distinguish themselves from the class below them, but 'class' has become an empty concept where a plumber earns more than a doctor. Because of the general spreading of the suburban logic, all positioning becomes relative and values multiply: consumption, education, Westernisation, Islamisation etc. The suburban structure and logic are like rank weeds infiltrating the whole city and surrounding lands and, in this sense, suburban Cairo becomes another topological layer of the city not defined by geography. Therefore, when I speak here of suburban people, it refers not only to those living at the edge of town, but also to all those who are subject to suburban logic, whether they live in the centre of Cairo or in Imbâba.

The 'logic' of spirit possession

A blessed sheikh appeared in Gizeh who was healing wealthy ladies from all kinds of afflictions, until one of them died while he was treating her for epilepsy. Apparently he had beaten her to death. A journalist from *al-Ahrâm* newspaper visited the healer to find out what had happened. The sheikh claimed to be in contact with *djinns* and that he treats women for *mass al-shaytân* (being touched by the devil). He asserted that the woman who died was possessed by four spirits and was killed by one of those *djinns*.[4]

This woman's death is not an isolated case. Just one week earlier, *al-Ahrâm* published an article about a retired functionary whom the court had sentenced to 25 years' imprisonment for the murder of his neighbour. He convinced her that an evil spirit (*rûh*: plural *arwâh*)[5] possessed her and that she and her children were in danger because of this. He took her to his son's flat in one of the desert cities to treat her through praying over her body. The woman was strangled and beaten to death. Her neighbour declared that the spirit choked the woman when leaving her body and then took possession of him and used his body to kill the woman.[6]

Possession and exorcism

Beliefs in spirits and practices concerning spirit possession are widespread in Egypt, especially – but certainly not only – among the lower classes in Cairo and in the countryside.[7] These beliefs are sustained by the Qur'an but have a pre-Islamic origin and are also shared by the Coptic minority in Egypt, as is shown in the second case, where both the accused and victim were Copts.[8] In the local quarters of Cairo, spirit possession is a current affliction that mostly, but not exclusively affects women. It affects the mental and physical health of human beings and their social relations. The symptoms of possession are usually diverse and vague and include complaints of sleeplessness, tiredness, lack of appetite, pains in the back and limbs, headaches and dreams.

This suffering is attributed to the malicious action of different kinds of spirits, mostly *djinns*. The diagnosis of spirit possession is not established prior to consulting all kinds of doctors and healers and trying different kinds of treatments; only when there is not any improvement in the patient's situation and no satisfactory explanation for the suffering, the plausibility of spirit possession increases.[9] The patient and his or her family then visit a specialist in spirit possession to confirm their presumption.

A city like Cairo, with at least 16 million inhabitants, houses all kind of healers, swindlers and amateurs. Some of them are deeply religious people healing only with the text of the Qur'an, others became healers through an initiating illness and learned how to deal with so-called spiritual illnesses (*amrâd rûhâniyya*) through restoring their own health. There are healers who claim to have assistants in the world of the spirits and others who have just read some books on witchcraft and healing that can be found at any bookseller in the street. The business of healing can be very remunerative and partly due to this fact, many crooks and amateurs are also found in this business. Usually people claim that the real sheikh does not ask for money, considering the healing capacity as a gift from God and helps the afflicted for free, receiving a gift only if his treatment is successful.

The causes of possession can be very diverse. According to its internal logic,[10] possession can be the result of the malign action of a neighbour or enemy who consulted a specialist to harm the victim through witchcraft and magic. Witchcraft harms through the mediation of spirits and it can be at the origin of spirit possession. A more common reason of possession however, is carelessness towards the *djinns* that are wandering around everywhere, especially in wet and dirty places like the bathroom or wasteland: in Cairo, this includes ruins or buildings in construction. If a woman accidentally spills boiling water on the floor or a man throws a rock away they can hurt a spirit, who will then be looking for revenge. Spirits can be particularly harmful when a person is already weakened, which can occur through ritual pollution such as not mentioning the name of Allah as often as one is supposed to do or because of sleeping when one is upset. Most of the time, the cause is a combination of these factors: 'My husband hit me on my head, I slept crying and woke up in the middle of the night and went to the bathroom. Since this time I don't feel well any more...'[11]

One of the healers whom I have met is the imam of a mosque in the citadel quarter in Cairo. After the Friday prayer, people from the neighbourhood come to consult him for all kinds of problems and afflictions. He gives advice and treats spiritual illnesses free of charge, only using the text of the Qur'an. He explains the causes of spirit possession as follows:

> Every person has a sphere around him or her, like a field of force. But with almost everybody this sphere has flaws, especially when someone is not strong in his or her beliefs. When someone shocks a person these cracks widen and when this happens in the proximity of a spirit, he[12] can take advantage of this moment of weakness and can slip inside the human body. The spirit can occupy different places in the body: in the stomach he causes lack of appetite, in the heart he causes sadness, but a spirit can also cause renal failure for instance if he sits in the kidneys. In cases of spirit possession biomedical treatment produces no results and so sometimes we succeed in healing those physical diseases only through following the Islamic prescriptions of prayer, purity and dress and an intensive use of the Koranic word.[13]

Some healers even claim that spirit possession can be at the origin of cancer and other incurable diseases. 'Miraculous' cures of so-called 'biomedical' diseases seldom occur and the symptoms are mostly vague and coincide with what we usually put down to psychosomatic complaints. The Egyptian government is taking severe action against those traditional healers claiming to heal 'physical' diseases like cancer or diabetes. In the autumn of 1999, the story of Sheikha Nadia even reached the headlines of the television news. Her reputation got out of proportion and hundreds of people from far away came to see her, desperately looking for a miraculous cure. Too much money was involved and the sheikha ended up in prison.[14]

The terminology that the inhabitants of Cairo use to refer to spirit possession is varied, and they often prefer vague references because they believe that even the articulation of the word is enough to make the spirits present themselves. That is the reason that, in street talk, people carefully say: '*andu wâhid* ('he has one [a *djinn*]'). More openly, the afflicted refers to her situation as: '*anâ mazûr*' ('I'm visited'). Only the sheikh has the heart to pronounce the verdict openly: *lamsa 'ardiyya* (touched by one of the earth), *lams al-shaytân* (touched by the devil) or, when the case is more serious, *labs*, where the spirits actually possess or 'wear' their victims.

When all other treatment has failed and the diagnosis of spirit possession is confirmed, there are two courses of action. The afflicted has to choose between exorcism, ridding the victim of the spirit, or reconciliation between the possessed and the spirit. Ideally, this choice is non-existent because reconciliation is not accepted: most people regard it as weakness to give in to the spirits and placate them; consequently exorcism is regarded as the only valid option. Particularly, in both male and public discourse, any other course of action will be ruled out as '...against Islam...beliefs of ignorant persons...ways to make money out of the poor'.

Exorcism, however, is a dangerous operation. The spirits are considered to be very strong and difficult to control. Anyone who gets involved with spirits must know what he or she is doing, because it is one thing to call up the spirits, but it is even more important to know how to dismiss them. Many stories tell of inexperienced people experimenting with *djinns*: as soon as the spirit appears, they get scared and have doubts, and in these moments of weakness the *djinn* paralyses the tongue so that the human cannot utter the words to subdue him. Many young men and women, so it is said, lose their speech and their reason in this way, but exorcism is most dangerous for the one possessed.

Treating a possessed person starts by forcing the spirit to manifest his presence by the reading of powerful Qur'anic verses. The spirit shows him or her self through entrancement of the afflicted (see below), then the sheikh asks him or her to identify him or herself and the *djinn* talks through the mouth of the possessed. This moment is a key element in the validation of the diagnosis: only when the spirit manifests himself as a being, independent from the human, is possession confirmed. As soon as the spirit mentions his name and his religion,[15] the sheikh starts to convince him to leave the body and if reasonable arguments are not enough, he threatens him with burning and beating. Spirits can be harmed through texts alone, but some sheikhs actually hit the patient in order to hurt the spirit. When the *djinn* finally agrees to leave the body, the most dangerous part of the exorcism begins: healers assert that the spirit has to leave the human body, preferably through the big toe of the patient, because if he leaves through the head, for example, serious injury or even death can follow.

Another danger is that a spirit can easily possess any other living creature that is nearby when leaving a body, or that it only temporarily leaves to take possession again as soon as the sheikh is not around, whereupon his revenge is fierce: pain and sorrow and strange accidents will turn the life of the afflicted one into hell.[16] Therefore, when a healer argues that a patient's death during exorcism is due to the spirits, this sounds entirely reasonable and even realistic following their logic of spirit possession and exorcism.

Humans, spirits and those possessed

In order to understand the nature of the spirits, we have to mention something first about human nature. The nature of mankind in suburban conceptions is a very complex matter; I am confining myself here to those aspects that are relevant to this research. It should also be noted that this information is deducted from the stories, sayings and reactions of the lower-middle-class inhabitants of suburban Cairo, and that their concepts of the human person are not unified nor elaborate (nor are they logical) and they also contain many contradictions. Therefore, it is inevitable that this outline is a rough sketch.

Human beings are seen as composite creatures, composed of both material and non-material components. Neither aspect is necessarily simple and no strict distinction is made between the material and the non-material. The main components of a human being are not univocally distinguished from each other: *qalb*, *'aql*, *nafs* and *rûh* can each indicate a specific aspect of a person, as well as the person in his or her totality and, in the last sense, they can also be considered as synonyms. *Qalb* is the bodily organ of the heart as well as the seat of emotions and the capacity of deeper insight. *'Aql* can be translated as reason: it is the faculty of knowing. In the Egyptian context, reason and emotion are not seen as opposites. Therefore, when a person makes a moral mistake, it is not because that person's desires prevail over his or her reason, but because of a general confusion: not knowing right from wrong. Knowing the right way (*al-sirât al-mustaqîm*) is not an innate capacity or an acquired ability, it has to be constantly reinforced through religious teachings and preaching and the good example of others, enforced by social control. *Nafs* is the self or the human soul, while *rûh* is the divine soul. However, in a more bodily sense, *rûh* also means the 'vital spirits' in the blood.

Rûh, or more often the plural, *arwâh*, is also used to indicate the spirits. These spirits are quite confusingly presented as if they were only souls, but the more common term is *djinn*. The world of the *djinns* is very similar to ours. They have schools and hospitals, cars and food, they marry and have children. There are Muslims, Christians, Jews and non-believers among them, and the latter can be especially very vicious. Their world is not separated from ours but situated amongst us, invisible to our eyes: only very young children, fools and diviners can see them.

The difference between human and spiritual beings does not lie in the material and the non-material. It is a difference in materiality: human beings are made of clay while spiritual beings such as angels and *djinns* are respectively made of light and fire. Spirits are considered to have a body that functions like the human body: they eat and drink and get ill; they have doctors and medicines. The difference between them and us is mainly one of intensity and speed: *djinns* are insubstantial and transient, they can fly through the air or walk through a wall, they are much faster than humans and live a lot longer.[17]

One of the main characteristics of the *djinns* is that they do not accept any authority except under pressure and that they are amoral. They are not evil as such and, in this sense, differ from the devil, *al-shaytân*,[18] but they do not make any distinction between good and evil. Their behaviour is unpredictable and their wishes and demands are always changing. Their origin is often connected to Iblîs,[19] the only one of the spirit beings who refused to kneel before Adam when God ordered him to do so.

When a human being is possessed by a spirit, people say that there is only one tangible and visible body but two souls (*rûh*). The principle of spirit possession is that, in certain situations, the 'other' takes over: the human being loses control over his or her body and enters into a state of complete possession where the spirit has all the power. This is what happens when a trance is induced during the healing treatment, but apparently it can also happen when the spirit uses the human body to commit a crime – at least, if we believe the healer who was accused of murder. According to Islamic tradition, a person can only be considered responsible for his or her mistakes when he or she is *'âqil* (from the word *'âql*, 'reason'), that is in full possession of his or her faculties and capable of rational conduct, because only the *'âqil* can make the distinction between good and evil.[20] The question concerning spirit possession is the following: can a human being be considered *'âqil* in these temporary states of complete possession?

Many Cairenes would say that persons are not *'âqil* when completely possessed by the *djinn* as they have no control over their actions and no longer distinguish between good and evil, between admissible or inadmissible behaviour. In this logic of possession, the arguments of the healers sound very reasonable. We have seen that there is a great danger inherent in exorcism for those who are present, that the patient risks losing his or her life if the *djinn* leaves the body in an uncontrolled way, and that any living creature in the vicinity of the patient runs the risk of being possessed by this *djinn*, now thirsty for revenge. So it seems possible that this is what happened in the case of the man trying to heal his neighbour. He was not an expert, he became frightened during the operation and when he sensed that he was not able to cope with the situation the spirit exploited his weakness and took possession of his body, using him for his revenge. Following the same argument, we have to assume that the healer from Gizeh was not much of an expert either; he was not capable of guiding the spirit out of the woman's body in the correct way so as to safeguard the patient.

However, these cases are judged in court, where another logic prevails. Here, instead of the suburban juxtaposition of different opinions, we find a hierarchical model determined by the centrist power of the state with its monopoly over violence. The first healer is still waiting for the verdict of the court; the second 'murderer' was sentenced to 25 years of imprisonment. The reason given in this judgement is that even if the devil can harm a person in his or her body, he cannot take hold of the person's soul (*rûh*) because there exists no authority over the soul of a human except Allah (*lâ sultân 'alâ rûh al-insân illâ Allâhi*).[21]

It seems remarkable, at least from our Western point of view, that the judge is not denying the existence of spirits and the reality of spirit possession. On the other hand, this should not surprise us in the Egyptian context, since the existence of *djinns* is established in the Qur'an[22] and anyone doubting this fact could be considered to be an unbeliever. When the judge argues that the spirit has no authority over the soul, the judge is presuming that a *djinn* cannot urge a person to commit a crime unless the person agrees with him. In this way, the judge conceives of a narrative of *djinns* compatible with the judicial context. *Djinns* are not denied recognition, but rather are turned into powerless beings unable to control human action. The judge is denying one of the distinguishing features of spirit possession, namely the complete lack of control that the human has over his or her words and deeds in well-defined, clear-cut timings. In short periods of complete possession, the spirit sways the human reason and self-control. By denying this force and giving his own interpretation, the judge applies the suburban principle that many contradictory narratives of *djinns* coexist and that anybody can conceive of their own as long as Qur'anic truth and empirical reality are respected.

In the narrative of the judge, spirits are domesticated, they lose their power and specificity and are reduced to one category of evil inspiration that is common to all human beings. In this argument, the judge negates one of the basic principles of spirit possession, namely the absolute exteriority of evil and the 'otherness' of the spirit. Human and spirit are conceived of as one person, while in suburban logic it is quite fundamental that the illness or impairment is not a part of the afflicted: suffering finds its origin in the 'other', the spirit, which has his own personality and his own reasons to 'wear' (*labs*) the human being.

In his judgement, the judge identifies the spirit with *al-shaytân*, the devil, and reduces the packs of multiple spirits to one single and abstract category of evil, personified in the devil. This reasoning simplifies the case. If the argument of spirit possession is turned simply into 'inspiration by the devil', the argumentation is easy: no Muslim or Christian in Cairo would disagree that all human mistakes are inspired by the devil and that the devil has no authority over the human soul. In this way, this case is no different from any other case of murder: every person has a free will and it is his or her choice to refuse or to give in to the devil. It is this free will together with the capacity to distinguish between good and bad (*'aql*) that makes someone a moral person.[23] In the logic of spirit possession, there exists an essential difference between inspiration or temptation by the devil and possession by *djinns*. The possessed loses his or her free will through the constraints of a spiritual being, but the judge is not willing to conceive of spirits as an external constraint to human free will, considering possession as a normal psychological state (temptation by the devil), and thus cannot take limited liability into account.

Against convention

The story of Soheir

> The mother in law of my sister was a terrible woman. My sister was afraid of her but I was not. One day we had a fight over my sister's furniture, it is very bad for me to get angry and excited because 'the one on me' does not want me to be upset. I got into such a state that I do not remember a thing of what I've said and what I've done. They told me later that I insulted the old lady really badly and when she shouted back and refused to give in, I took my baby, Hussein, he was only three months old then, and I threw him out of the window. Luckily he had only a few scratches as the flat was on the second floor and he fell into the tree underneath the window.[24]

At this time, Soheir was living in a local area in Imbâba and regularly organised elaborate *zâr*-rituals to appease the spirits that possessed her. The fact that she insulted an older woman and even threw her baby out of the window had, according to her, no further effect on her life and did not affect her reputation as a decent woman and good mother since, after all, everybody knew that she was possessed by *djinns* and nobody could blame her for this. She said that she had suffered enough already because of them. Later I heard other people talking about her, saying that she was never really possessed and that she used to organise *zâr* only in order to make money and that she used the spirits as a pretext for her wild behaviour and lack of self-control.

During my fieldwork, I heard many similar stories, but most of them were less extreme. There exist even more diversified ideas about the spirit world and the way that humans and spirits live together especially amongst elder women and even sometimes among men in the local alleys of the city. People believe there are *'afrît* who appear only at the end of the night who enjoy scaring people but do not harm them. The *zâr* or *asyâd* are a special kind of *djinn* that are particularly fierce and strong and that never leave the human body once they take hold; this affliction is even considered to be hereditary. *Makhâwî* are inseparable and invisible companions to mankind; some people say they are like the *qarîn*, the double that we all have, but the stories about *makhâwî* are more sexually loaded: they are partners and lovers. There are *djinns* in the river, bewitched men living in the water and other *djinns* living below the surface of the earth. Many fascinating stories are told about these creatures, often with contradictory details. There is no such a thing as a unified, logical and systematic classification of spirit beings.

The spirit as a companion

In the stories of the elder Cairene women and men, spirits appear to be more like companions and allies. Although they are always unpredictable and dangerous to a certain degree, they are not enemies that have to be driven out of the body with threats, beating or burning. If you know how to treat them well, they provide protection and companionship. The *qarîn* is the most striking example of such a spirit. Most Egyptians believe that every human being is accompanied by a *qarîn* from birth until death. Their descriptions of these *qarîn* are much more diverse and contradictory than those of the *djinns*. As with all matters, the ultimate reference for knowledge concerning the invisible world is the Qur'an, but although *qarîn* are mentioned a few times in the Holy Book, the information on them is limited and not very clear.[25]

The *qarîn* has a double origin in Egypt. The Islamic concept is identified with the representation that the ancient Egyptians had of persons and their doubles.[26] We can see bas-reliefs on the wall of the temple of Luxor representing the god of creation,

Khnum, modelling the Pharaoh out of clay. On the potter's wheel, we can see not only one small person in clay but two: it is the Pharaoh Amenhotep and his double. In the first place, the persistence of pharaonic practices and concepts, especially in the life-world of local Egyptian women, is real[27] and these ancient representations probably lie at the basis of the idea that the *qarîn* is made out of clay like us and lives below the surface of the earth, mirroring our actions. The *qarîn* is often referred to as *ukht min taht al-'ard* (sister from under the earth).

Second, some consider this double more like a kind of *djinn* living amongst us, made out of fire and invisible to most of us, but accompanying us in everything that we do and everywhere we go. This idea can be traced back to the pre-Islamic Arabian understanding of the word *qarîn* and, as such, the term is mentioned quite a few times in the Qur'an. *Qarîn* in old Arabia was also the *djinn* who accompanied a poet and brought the poet's verses; this use has been transferred in Islam to the angel who was with the Prophet and who brought him his revelations. The double inspires his brother or sister in many different ways; this inspiration is an important aspect in the context of this research and we will demonstrate the compulsivity of this inspiration in cases of spirit possession. The first commentators on the Qur'an spoke of two angels accompanying a person and inspiring him or her in his choices: one who tempts that person into evil and the other who induces him or her to do good,[28] and it is in this moral sense that the word is used by some Egyptian people with a more specific interest in religious matters.

There is also no agreement from the different sources on the sex of the *qarîn*. Some say that every woman has a spirit brother as a reversed double, others say she has a sister mirroring her in all her actions, marrying when she marries and giving birth when she gives birth. The sexual connotation in many of the stories about humans and their double is evident. In suburban Cairo, people are well aware of the bad influence of a jealous *qarîn*. Sometimes the relation between a human and his or her double is so intimate that the *qarîn* would not permit him or her to marry or to have contact with his or her spouse. When a *qarîn* is unsatisfied with the behaviour of its human counterpart, it can harm him or her through nightmares, headaches, or loss of weight and energy. There is also the question of whether the spirit is an integral part of the person or if it is to be considered as alien, a different and separate being, a person in itself. The case of the *qarîn* is particularly interesting in this perspective, because it seems to occupy an intermediate position. The *qarîn* is the other self: somewhere between the idea of the person and the spirit as separate entities and the idea of the spirit as an integral part of the person.

It should be noted that the affliction caused by an unsatisfied *qarîn* has exactly the same symptoms as possession by a *djinn*, but pain and suffering are not the only consequences of the spirit's discontent accounted for by the local inhabitants. Causing suffering is only one way through which the spirit shows his dissent with human behaviour and, in certain circumstances, he might take hold of the whole of a person and make him or her lose control over his or her words and deeds. Here, too, the distinction between *djinn* and *qarîn* is unclear; some will say that this loss of control is a distinguishing feature of spirit possession and has nothing to do with the person's double, while others contradict this. In general, though, people agree that these are states of complete possession when the spirit takes over. It is in such cases that a man hits his wife and destroys the household goods or that a woman is capable of throwing her baby out of the window, unable to remember anything afterwards. However, most of the time the damage or injury is smaller and the effect of the spirit on the human is seen only in his or her unconventional or asocial behaviour.

It is important to mention that the influences of spirit possession are not merely negative: many of the possessed admit that they do not want to get rid of their spirits, that they have a special bond with their *djinn* and their presence provides consolation and protection. Because of the spirits, they are more independent from other people, never afraid to be lonely.

Sakaya divorced her husband three times, although they liked each other. Her spirit just could not stand a man around. Some people find it strange that even after 15 years, she never remarried, and they gossip. Sakaya says that it is all because of the spirits and that she does not need a man. She is never really alone or afraid.[29]

The doubles and spirits can push the human with whom they are in dissent into different courses of action: from homosexuality to obsessive ritual pureness, from dancing in the street to violence and destruction. It should be noted that this 'loss of control' by the afflicted is only a temporary phenomenon, limited in time and space, caused by a specific impetus. Certain situations function like a trigger, starting off complete possession. These situations are different for every afflicted person: some react violently to certain music, but for others, strong emotions of sadness, anger or fear can be the cause of inducing this state in which the spirit masters the human.

Take the case of Mona: Mona married when she was not yet sixteen years old. After a few months of marriage she became pregnant. One night she stayed home alone, and was sleeping when a strange woman entered her house and ordered her to leave. At first Mona could not believe her ears, but men came in and confirmed that this stranger was now married to her husband and that Mona was divorced. It was already late at night when she found herself in the street on her way back to her parents' house with only the clothes that she was wearing and the baby still growing in her womb. She stumbled in a dark alley, and since this time has been possessed. Now she has remarried and is a mother of six children, but every time she hears the drums in the street, she can not stop herself. The spirit forces her to dance. When this happens, people laugh and cheer at her, but on other occasions nobody mentions it and nobody dares to treat her badly for it.[30]

Uniting human and spirit

One of the main differences between this concept of spirits and the concept leading to a request for exorcism is shown in the way that the affliction is 'healed'. Patients always follow the general pattern of home treatment with herbs and incense, a visit to the doctor in the hospital, a visit to a specialist and sometimes even a psychologist and, finally, the consulting of a diviner. The first main difference lies in the choice of the diviner. People can go to a sheikh in a mosque or a man with strong beliefs, but there are also the diviners who work through an assistant in the spirit world. These men or women are often distrusted, because someone who knows how to manipulate spirits for good can also use their power to cause evil and practise witchcraft in order to harm people. A common method used by these diviners is that they put a cloth belonging to the patient (*attâr*) under their pillow at night. The spirit then appears in their dreams, giving them his diagnosis and pointing out the origin and reason for the suffering and the way to cure the patient.

A diagnosis of spirit possession is recognised as legitimate when there is severe suffering by the afflicted, coupled with a failure of all other forms of healing and the diagnosis of at least one authorised diviner. The validation of the diagnosis of spirit possession is very important for the sick person and his or her family. As the example of Soheir shows, there is often discussion about the validity of the diagnosis, and proof has to be abundant and witnessed by everybody. If both the symptoms and the authority of the diviner are not strong enough, this can have serious consequences for the reputation and the respect that the patient and his or her family have in the neighbourhood. The afflicted will, in this case, be held responsible both for not performing his or her duties and for his or her unconventional behaviour.

What makes some people doubt the reality of possession are the secondary gains to be made, particularly through the organisation of large healing rituals. In the first place, there is the prestige of a large group of people mobilised for the sake of the sick person. Secondly, there are the beautiful clothes and sometimes even jewellery demanded by the spirits and, thirdly, there exists a system of gifts, *nuqta*, that means that the organising family often makes money on *zâr* instead of only paying out. Every woman participating in a *zâr* ritual volunteers with a small amount of money. According to the principle of reciprocity, gifts are later returned on similar occasions,[31] preferably worth just a bit more than the received amount to enhance prestige.

These healing rituals do not aim at exorcising the spirits or at curing the afflicted from suffering for the rest of his or her life, but rather they aim at a reconciliation between humans and spirits so they can live together in peace. The Egyptian term for reconciliation is *sulh,* and this name is often used to indicate these rituals, although others speak of *zafâra* or *zâr*. This appeasement of the spirits is a thorn in the eye of many Islamic purists, who consider it unacceptable that the human gives in to the spirit, especially because reconciliation includes sacrifice. In *sulh*, an animal is slaughtered to satisfy the spirit while the Islamic doctrine stipulates very clearly that sacrifice can only be performed in the name of God.

When I first came to Cairo, I intended to focus my fieldwork on *zâr*, the elaborate rituals of reconciliation that can last up to seven days. In my inquiries about *zâr*, informants would always state that it had disappeared, that people used to do it a long time ago, but that nowadays everybody knew better. In line with Islamic reformism, they would say that reconciliation is not the appropriate way to deal with the spirits, they should be exorcised by a respectable sheikh. At first I suspected that this was only part of a discourse, but it is true that *zâr* is not performed any more in all its glory in a city like Cairo. In rural areas, *zâr* is still much more prevalent than in the capital where schooling, modernisation and Islamic reformism have all had an important influence on the decline of *zâr*. In addition, the increasing levels of poverty make it almost impossible for the lower classes of Cairo to organise these big and costly rituals.[32] Even the term, *zâr*, is not used any more to refer to rituals of reconciliation. Cairene men and women prefer the terms *zafâra* or *sulh* to refer to the new but still comparable treatments of spirit possession, because *zâr* practitioners and rituals have gained a bad reputation via the propaganda of newspapers and television and religious pressure.

Scattered rituals

The new suburban rituals usually do not last longer than one afternoon and they can easily take place without the knowledge of too many people. What traditionally was united in one elaborate ritual has now been scattered over different therapeutic actions.[33] The core of the reconciliation is of course still there, the sacrifice of an animal to the spirit who has made his demands known in the dreams of the diviner: a red chicken, two white rabbits or a black goat, for example. The blood of the sacrificed animal is spread over the clothes and head of the patient in order to satisfy the spirit and the meat is taken by the diviner. In the dialect of Cairo, the blood and intestines of the sacrificial animal is indicated by the term *zafâra*, which means dirt or a bad smell and which also indicates the ritual itself. The blood placates the spirit; people also use it to make prints of hands on the clothes of the possessed and on the walls. This is a very common practice in Cairo, not only in possession rituals, but also with any ritual slaughtering. These bloody signs of the hand with the five fingers, *khammas*, can be seen on almost every building in town and its main function is to keep away the harmful effects of envy: *hasad*, the evil eye.

Sometimes, the sacrificial element is combined with drumming and singing, through which the spirit's presence is assured, inducing a trance-like state in the afflicted. The dancing and singing is now mostly performed independently of the sacrifice by semi-professional musicians in specific places, usually in a tent or a private house near the shrine of a saint. Whilst in the old tradition the diviner and ritual specialist used to take care in accompanying the new *zâr*-adept during the first trance experience, this role is now played by one of the musicians. Every time the musicians successfully convince a spirit to manifest himself in the dance they receive some extra money, and when they succeed in inducing a trance, their fee is doubled. In public discourse, men will mostly affirm that spirit possession is a women's problem, but, in reality, exorcism as well as reconciliation is performed by both men and women. The dancing, on the other hand, is women's business, and any man who shows himself dancing and being in a trance in *zâr* is considered to be homosexual.

Spirit possession is often a case of multiple spirits possessing one patient, and each of these spirits has to be satisfied. Every spirit has a name and his own characteristics, and each song is dedicated to a particular spirit. In the old days, in the elaborated rituals, the patient changed clothes for every different spirit that manifested himself through his or her body in the dance. Famous spirits are the Moroccan spirit and the Coptic priest, the General and the little girl, Rukush. The rhythm and tune of the songs suit the character of the spirit and each one dances in a particular way. In the present rituals, it is often obvious whether a woman is just following her intuition and copying what he or she sees or if he or she is one who has been properly initiated by a specialist. The latter's dancing is much more controlled and varies much more for each spirit. The person usually belongs to the older generation and she masters his or her possession much better, not falling down as easily in a wild trance or kicking and passing away like the younger and inexperienced ones do.

Older people tell of huge rituals with plenty of food: whisky for the Christian priest, cigarettes for the General and sweets with milk for Rukush. Food prescriptions are still an important element in the therapy and form a part of the daily living with the spirits. Some of the possessed can never eat pickled fish (*fasîkh*) and others drink milk or smoke a cigarette whenever they have dreams or other symptoms of the spirit's discontent. Another way to appease the spirit is by putting a burning candle in a pot of yoghurt next to the bed or by visiting holy places like the shrines of Sayyeda Zeinab, al-Hussein and Sayyeda Aisha. The many forms of spirit placation are scattered in the daily lives of the afflicted. As if suburban life not only divides families over different neighbourhoods and spreads rural economies over different roofs and balconies, it also divides ritual time over different days inconspicuously mingled in with the *bricolage* of surviving, on the edge of poverty, on the border between illness and health.

Practical moralities

The difference between exorcism and reconciliation can be seen as the difference between discourse and practice where discourse formulates exorcism as the only acceptable way to deal with spirit possession and reconciliation is often considered much more effective and practical; however, putting it this way is an over-simplification. Exorcism is practised, even successfully, by the most renowned and respected healers. On the other hand, reconciliation is not considered to be unacceptable by everyone, not even in public discourse: usually, people will state that exorcism better conforms to ideology and reconciliation is not equally as good, but also that the sick have to search for healing wherever they can even if this carries them far away from social and religious norms.

The difference between both sorts of treatments can be presented as a difference between male and female options. Men will hesitate longer before they opt for rituals of reconciliation, which are generally considered to be women's business. Exorcism is almost always performed by male healers and often takes place in the mosque which can be considered a male space, while reconciliation rituals are often performed by female specialists and diagnosed by female diviners. However, it seems more accurate to focus on the general difference in suburban Cairo between ideology as dogmatic and unified ('Allah is one') and the multiplicity of human reality. From the point of view of ideology, exorcism and reconciliation are strictly divided and even opposite, as are male and female, religion and superstition, but (even) behind this mask of unequivocal distinctions, there exists a multiplicity where everything is mingled and embedded in a *bricolage* of searching for a pragmatic solution. In this optic, 'the best solution' is to find healing without too much effort, for little cost, minimising risks and without entering into an open conflict with ideology.

Spirit possession always implies, in some way, 'losing control'. In exorcism, the losing of consciousness is induced by the reading of Qur'anic verses and burning incense. It is a kind of trance in which the healer is in control calling upon the spirit to take over the body and tongue of the human being and, in this way, communicating with the 'other', convincing him to leave the human body. In dancing rituals, a trance is induced by drumming, music and personified songs, each calling down a different spirit. When the song appeals to the spirit that possesses one of the participants, his or her hands start to tremble and shoulders to shake. He or she can not resist the impulse of the spirit and has to give in to his will, forcing him or her to stand up and dance: the *djinns* dance through the bodies of the afflicted. When a spirit is not satisfied with the behaviour of his victim, he makes them fall to the ground kicking and shaking and he expresses his desires through their mouth.

As already mentioned, the spirit takes hold of the human not only when called upon, but also in other situations: full possession can be caused by excitement, anger, fear and sorrow outside of the ritual context. The spirit announces his presence through convulsions, excessive perspiration and rolling of the eyes. Onlookers testify that a person becomes different, 'other', as soon as the spirit is present. He or she does not act 'as usual', talking with another voice and acting differently towards those present: 'It is the spirit that speaks and the spirit that acts through the body of the possessed.' Afterwards, the afflicted person calms down and is left in a state of exhaustion and oblivion.

This uncontrolled trance only arises when a spirit is seriously disturbed by the behaviour of the possessed person or by actions of persons in the surroundings. Frequently a third person is the cause of the spirit's manifestation and often the anger of the spirit corresponds with the discontent of the afflicted. So, it would appear that the induction of a trance is not entirely unrelated to the will of the possessed and, in this sense, the argument of the judge (*lâ sultân 'alâ rûh al-insân illâ Allâh*) agrees with the experience of the more sceptical Egyptians: there is no authority over the human soul and giving in to the spirits is a matter of choice. How far the possessed really has control over the onset of trance is difficult to tell. There can be little doubt that, in the moments of full possession, a person has no control over his or her actions and that the inconvenience for the possessed of what happens in the trance and the resultant oblivion means that it cannot easily be faked, but as already mentioned, the secondary gains are not insubstantial. Even after the disappearance of the large rituals, possession still provides an excuse for excursions, unconventional behaviour and attention-seeking, but the suffering and the reality of physical pain make it difficult to dispose of possession as mere invention and amusement.

In the Egyptian community in the suburbs of Cairo, but also in scientific literature, we can distinguish three general attitudes towards spirit possession. The very sceptical one considers the spirits only as a fantasy, something people invented; it regards spirit possession as an excuse invented by women refusing to fulfil their duties, a pretext for excursions to the shrines of saints and a way to attract the attention of family members who are mobilised in the search for healing.[34] Only in recent times has a new critical perspective found acceptance, mostly among the more educated and scholarly citizens of Cairo. A number of foreign authors have published studies, some time ago now, in which spirit possession was inserted into the Western category of psychosomatic illness and healing rituals were considered as a psychotherapy.[35] It is this interpretation that has been adopted by some Egyptian psychologists and, through them, this has been published in the local press and broadcast on television. The third point of view can be considered as the insider's point of view: the logic of the healers and the patients for whom the reality of the spirit is beyond all doubt. The spirit is the 'other': another person with a name, a character and a history just like any human person, but made out of fire instead of clay. The spirit is not the evil inside the self but is an ambivalent creature, sometimes good, sometimes evil, difficult to control and unpredictable. Healing, therefore, does not focus on the self but aims at re-establishing the right distance between the human and the spirit or trying to create a balanced relationship between the human and the spirit that is satisfactory for both.

All three perspectives are not strictly segmented across different categories of people. Therefore, in the same way that a person might shift from exorcism to reconciliation in discourse as well as in effective choice, another person may share all these perspectives, depending on to whom he or she is talking, in which environment he or she is found and what his or her role is in any given situation, be it patient, counsellor, healer or judge.

As Dupret shows in his introductory text, the notion of 'person' is closely linked with responsibility and morality, certainly in a judicial context. To talk about the concept of the person in the context of spirit possession, we should first look at the meaning of responsibility and morality in the daily praxis of conflict solving in suburban Cairo. Making a mistake or breaking a rule – such as the transgressions of moral and social order occurring under the influence of spirit possession – can have two different kinds of social repercussions. On one hand, damages have to be repaired: the offender has to apologise and costs have to be refunded – nevertheless, reparations do not necessarily entail any moral implications. A second consequence of misbehaviour can be that the offender loses his or her good reputation. This is, by far, the worst thing that can happen in the local alleys where everybody knows everything about everybody else.

Egyptians use the word *karâma*: literally it means generosity and, in the suburban context, it means self-respect and the respect others have for you. *Al-karâma fûq kul shay'* (*karâma* before anything else) is a popular expression among Cairenes. Losing *karâma* means losing social identity, it means a bad reputation and the exclusion of a person from the dense network of social relationships. Losing one's reputation can happen independently from a person's intentions and actions. In the case of rape, for example, a girl loses her *karâma* through the irremediable loss of her purity: she is to blame for this loss even if the rape is not linked to any of her own intentions or actions.

In court people speak of offences, guilt and punishment; in suburban Cairo they speak of misbehaviour, indemnification and reputation. In the local context, words such as 'guilt' and 'responsibility' acquire another meaning. Egyptians believe that every creature will have to account for his or her choices on Judgement Day, but in the here and now, every person has to take care of his or her *karâma*, avoiding even the slightest presumption of misbehaviour because rumours and gossip can harm his or her 'respect' just as much as actual wrongdoing. Guilt and responsibility are, in the daily suburban context, always related to a third person who observes and comments.

Introducing spirit possession as an excuse for one's actions can save a reputation, as we saw in the earlier example: the woman insulting her elder and throwing her baby out of the window did not lose her *karâma*. She is still considered to be a decent woman and a good mother, at least by those who subscribe to the diagnosis of possession. On the other hand, however, this excuse can damage one's reputation in the eyes of others: some will consider the possessed as somebody who deals with superstition or witches and who wastes his or her money on swindlers and, worst of all, they can designate the afflicted as 'not a good Muslim'.

When spirit possession is simply used as an excuse for someone's unconventional behaviour, it does not guarantee a spotless reputation. Besides, possession does not discharge a person from his or her duty to repair what has been broken: even the possessed have to pay the costs they have incurred and apologise for the insults they have uttered. This responsibility, however, does not involve the offender in a really personal way. Refunding and apologising is not high on the scale of humiliation, certainly not as high as can be when spirit possession is not the reason for the unconventional behaviour. It is as if the reparations for mistakes are done in the name of another person:

a child or a fool for whom the possessed carries responsibility. In many ways, a spirit is like a child or a fool – outside of the moral order and not accountable for his or her actions. As already mentioned, spirits are amoral. They are not evil as such but make no distinction between good and bad; they are like children and fools: lacking the capacity of distinction, *tamyîz*, and, as such, cannot be held responsible for their deeds.

The principle of having a double: two persons, one in spirit and one in human guise, is certainly not a way of refusing responsibility and, in extreme situations, such as where the victim dies, no Egyptian would consider those healers innocent. Healing is a skill that demands a lot of self-control and esoteric knowledge. So, when a person is not qualified enough to perform this task, he or she deliberately endangers not only him or herself but also the patient. As soon as a healer feels that he or she cannot master the *djinn*, the healer has to quit as quickly and as safely as possible, but even then it can be too late and thus anybody dealing with spirits should consider these risks before starting. In the case of the retired functionary treating his neighbour for spirit possession and killing her, if the judge had paid heed to the rules of spirit possession and followed its logic then he would have come to the same judgement, but on other grounds. In suburban logic, a healer in those circumstances loses all credibility as a healer and as a person and he will have to pay for this mistake.

In a big city like Cairo, with all the modernisation and flow of information, a number of different mechanisms are operating that really result only in one thing: the annihilation of the otherness of the spirit. First, we notice how the judge identifies *djinns* with the devil. This identification reduces the ambivalent and multiple pack of personified spirits to a single category of evil. Second, we see how the reality of possession is often denied and the afflicted is considered to be a person who is merely swayed by her or his emotions and/or that the affliction is that of some psychological disorder. Finally, *zâr* has been recycled and reduced to psychotherapy. Each of these three mechanisms can be considered as a way of internalising guilt and responsibility: they are mechanisms to reduce the multiplicity of man and spirits to one moral person, and each of these mechanisms denies the principle of multiplication (human being and multiple spirits) that is characteristic for the suburban logic of spirit possession where – as already explained – the spirit is a person in himself.

Conclusion

Spirit possession always entails some ambivalence: when human and spirit are too close, there is always a risk of chaos (trance) and a lack of clarity about responsibility. Exorcism tries to end this condition by establishing a sufficient distance between human and spirit. Reconciliation, on the other hand, allows for indistinctness and ambivalence and, in this way, leaves space for otherness and for the unexpected. This is a space for inspiration: not only for unconventional behaviour and playfulness, but maybe also in some sense for beauty: many old stories recount the inspiration that poets and musicians, philosophers and singers have had through the interference of *djinns.*[36] Through the doubling of the person in human-person and spirit-person, spirit possession offers a possibility for experimentation, a chance to put things into a different perspective outside of the constraints of morality. In a limited but fairly accepted way, the logic of spirit possession offers a space for unconventional behaviour and creativity.

Spirit possession is considered to be an affliction of the poor and uneducated of Cairo, but when it intrudes in rational and public discourse, the deep roots of these ancient beliefs, the tangibility of the suffering and the authority of its sources mean that even a judge in a criminal court cannot dispose of spirit possession as a mere invention or a psychological disorder and must search for arguments to reduce spirit and human to one judicial category: the legal person.

Notes

1 Practical problems also influenced this choice: the gossip and jealousy made it impossible to have equally profound relationships with competing neighbours.

2 I am working with families in Imbâba, Bashtîl, Shubra al-Khayma, al-Zilzâl, Dâr al-Salâm, Bâb al-Lûk and 'Abdîn.

3 Different members of one family often choose very different lifestyles, making different choices: university or working, holding on to traditional values or Westernisation.

4 'The gifted ones', *al-Ahrâm*, 23 October 1999.

5 In this article, the journalist wrote about *rûh*, another name for a spirit or *djinn*. The word *rûh* is a more general term which means soul or divine soul. Both human beings and spirits have a *rûh*.

6 'Retired functionary convinces his neighbour that she is possessed and kills her', *al-Ahrâm*, 20 October 1999.

7 Many Egyptians like to present things as if spirit possession only happens among the poor and uneducated. Newspaper articles contradict this view and account for possession rituals in luxury apartments in the Westernised neighbourhoods of Cairo.

8 Of course, some differences exist between Muslims and Copts concerning status and the characteristics of spirits, but these are not essential in the practices related to possession.

9 People are reluctant to accept the idea of spirit possession because possession only occurs with persons who are not very strong in their beliefs. To be possessed always implies, somehow, that one is not a good Muslim.

10 Social anthropologists, on the other hand, explain possession by referring to social, economic and psychological factors. Saunders, 1977; Morsy, 1993; Kennedy 1978, considering the local aetiology as merely symbolic.

11 Interview, 'Izbat al-Sa'îda, 7 January 1999.

12 A *djinn* can be male or female (*djinniya*). To avoid too many unwieldy references to the use of 'he or she', I will simply refer here to a *djinn* as a male subject.

13 The Qur'anic word has to be heard in the first place, but the written word is also burned with incense, is dissolved in water to drink or to bathe in and can be carried in a small pocket on the body. Through hearing, smelling, touching, tasting and seeing, the word is incorporated in the body of the afflicted. Interview, Sûq al-Silâh, 17 November 1998.

14 'Sheikha Nadia arrested', *Ahbâr al-Hawâdith*, 25 September 1999, pp. 27–29.
15 If the *djinn* turns out to be a Christian, the healer often refers the patient to a priest to be treated with texts from the Gospel. Many Coptic priests are renowned as healers and many of their patients are Muslims.
16 One of the possessed persons complained, for example, that the spirit hurts him by repeatedly spilling boiling water on him when he is making tea.
17 Cf. the story of Aladdin, in which the *djinns* are so fast that they build a wonderful palace in one night. In Egypt, *djinns* survive from the Pharaonic period, guarding their treasures and their secrets.
18 However, evil *djinns* are often called *shayâtîn* (devils) and some persons identify all *djinns* with the devil, such as, for example, in the second contribution in this volume referring to the court case.
19 The approach of Abdelsalam (1994, p. 86), who considers Iblîs as the only *djinn* or angel with a sense of humour, is interesting: his amorality lies in his laughter.
20 In the legal context, the term *tamyîz* refers to this faculty of distinction: Dupret, 2003.
21 The judge referred here to Jewish, Christian and Muslim sources to sustain his argument.
22 Qur'an, sura XLVI, verses 29–32.
23 Mauss ascribes this meaning of personhood to the influence of sectarian and reformist movements in Western Christianity. In Islamic philosophy, this notion of the moral person can already be found in the works of Fakhr al-Dîn al-Râzi and is more developed in the eleventh century by Ibn Sînâ: see Nachi, chapter 2 in the present volume.
24 Interview, 'Abdîn, 5 June 1999.
25 Qur'an, sura IV, verse 37; sura XXXVII, verse 50; sura XLI, verses 24–25; sura XLIII, verses 35 and 37; sura L, verses 22, 26–27.
26 Daressy, 1893, p. 69.
27 Ejchenrand, 1987.
28 Macdonald, 1978, p. 643.
29 Interview, Imbâba, 8 October 1998.
30 Interview, Imbâba, 27 November 1998.
31 This system of *nuqta* applies as well to marriage, birth and circumcision, and connects people in networks over different neighbourhoods and between different families.
32 Even if the system of *nuqta* means that the organising family can make money on a *zâr*, the organisation of these rituals still demands a considerable amount of money to be invested.

33 The secondary gains of the ritual are reduced through this division and, therefore, the ritual gains some legitimacy and respectability.
34 Even in the approach of Morsy (1993) and Saunders (1977), one sees this scepticism.
35 Cf. Crapanzano (1973) on the Hamadsha in Morocco. He states that they are using procedures that are considered to be important in Western therapies such as, for example, group support, participation of the patient, suggestibility, catharsis and others. Kennedy (1978) applies this approach to the *zâr* cult.
36 Bounfour, 1999, pp. 35–41.

Bibliography

Abdelsalam, S., 'L'Hôte divin: Etymologie du mot Zar', *Nouvelle Revue d'Ethnopsychiatrie*, 24, 1994, pp. 73–90.

Ahbâr al-Hawâdith, 25 September 1999.

Al-Ahrâm, 20, 23 October 1999.

Bounfour, A., 'Voix, image, lettre en Islam', *Revue d'Esthétique*, 35, 1999, pp. 25–64.

Crapanzano, V., *The Hamadsha: A Study in Moroccan Ethnopsychiatry*, Berkeley CA, University of California Press, 1973.

Daressy, G., *Notice explicative des ruines du Temple de Louxor*, Cairo, Imprimerie Nationale, 1893.

Dupret, B., 'The person in an Egyptian judicial context: An ethnomethodological analysis of courtroom proceedings', *International Journal for the Semiotics of Law*, 16, no 1, 2003.

Ejchenrand, J., 'Isis contre Iblis : une mémoire féminine rituelle du sacré et du profane', *Nouvelle Revue d'Ethnopsychiatrie*, 7, 1987, pp. 149–62.

Kennedy, J., *Nubian Ceremonial Life: Studies in Islamic Syncretism and Cultural Change*, Cairo, American University Press, 1978.

Macdonald, D.B., 'Karîn', *Encyclopaedia of Islam*, 2nd edition IV, Leiden, Brill, 1978, pp. 643–44.

Morsy, S.A., *Gender, Sickness and Healing in Rural Egypt: Ethnography in Historical Context*, Boulder CO/San Francisco CA/Oxford, Westview Press, 1993.

Saunders, L.W., 'Variants in Zar Experience in an Egyptian Village', in V. Crapanzano and Garrison V. (eds), *Case Studies in Spirit Possession*, New York/London/Sydney/Toronto, John Wiley and Sons, 1977, pp. 177–91.

Interviews

'Abdîn, 5 June 1999
Imbâba, 8 October 1998; 27 November 1998
Izbat al-Sa'îda, 7 January 1999
Sûq al-Silâh, 17 November 1998

CHAPTER 7

The Person and Justice in a Tunisian Souq: A Reflection upon the Linkages between Justice, Impartiality and Respect for the Person

Mohamed Nachi

> Was not our introduction to law signalled by the outcry: 'It's not fair!?' Such is the cry of indignation whose discernment, as measured by the yardstick of our hesitancy as adults summoned to make positive determinations on questions of fairness, is sometimes staggering.[1]

In Chapter 2 of this volume, I tried to highlight the importance of the relation between the 'I', the 'we' and the 'person'. A fact which emerged from that study is that the 'person' is a fundamental axiological category which supposes the unity and entirety of other categories: it is the exact constituent of the 'I', the 'me' and the 'self'; it is individuality proper to the subject. As such, it is a whole and supposes no fundamental opposition between the various categories. Consequently, social and moral life is based essentially on respect for the human person and on the integrity of moral identity.[2] Roughly, the person can be considered as 'a capacity to be a holder of rights and obligations'.

In continuing this idea, I propose illustrating certain aspects by concrete elements drawn from a case study. Indeed, through the analysis of a conflict within a Tunisian souq, one sees how, in everyday life, this notion plays an essential part both in the speech and action of the social players.

Let me first specify that this contribution does not claim to be a global analysis, nor does it draw general conclusions; my aim is much more modest. Among other things, my contribution relates neither to the analysis of legal texts nor to the discussion of the status of the person in such or such a code of the statute of the person. It aims instead at showing, through an occurrence of ordinary life, how people engaged in an argument, a quarrel or a dispute call upon a specific argumentative register to justify the necessity of respecting the person and the individual's rights, dignity and integrity. In so doing, social players attribute a specific meaning to the notion of 'person', which we may bring forward and study. In the process of argument and in the forms of justification, what is the place of the notion of 'person'?

It would be well to recall that this approach will focus less on the study of legal texts than on the narrative or argumentative figures implying specific outcomes or embodying the meaning of justice. What is more, judgements referring to law or, more generally, to the legal system are not those that one finds most frequently: in view of the problem arising from this incident, a tendency for moral or conventional principles that prevail over recourse to specific standards of a legal nature becomes apparent.

A myriad of notions, each having a direct link to the category of the person, are outlined through the forms of justification on which a judgement is based. Among these notions, one can mention respect, integrity, impartiality, loyalty etc. They are moral notions strongly *articulated* with a common sense of justice for everyone. Such confirms our global approach of the anthropological foundation of fairness whose main objective is to establish linkages between this sense of justice and what I have designated as 'fundamental ethical dimensions'. I have shown various connections with specific dimensions such as friendship and duty or the 'extra-rogatory'.[3] I intend to continue this investigation by investigating certain as yet unexplored aspects and by introducing other axiological categories to a study of the sense of fairness.

The example studied here, while contextually rich, cannot be studied regrettably in all its detail. I therefore focus on certain aspects to the detriment of others. In addition, I should note that this study does not pretend to be an in-depth or a definitive study, but rather an attempt to outline various notions which are sufficiently complex so as to deserve individual treatment.

Given this system of ideas, I thus pay special attention to the marks of respect (or disrespect) for oneself, for the person and for the other. Our subject also relates to the question of impartiality in connection with the sense of justice which I characterise as an 'acceptance of the person'. All these questions are addressed in part three of our study. In anticipation of that discussion, I devote part two to the analysis of the forms of judgement and justifications which I was able to collect in connection with this incident.

Presentation of the story and of the method used

The body of empirical data forming the basis of the analysis is twofold. On one hand, there is a detailed recital of a sequence of events as recounted by a Tunisian. On the other hand, there are the results of a survey administered to Tunisian and French respondents, as well as materials collected as a result of discussions and conversations of people reacting to the story's events.[4]

In the story, Kamel, the narrator, is the manager of a cafe and enjoys an undeniable local notoriety. He is in his forties. Ridha, one of the two protagonists, is about fifty-five years old. He has always been in the business. Prior to developing an interest in the trade of orange blossoms, he was mostly involved with livestock trade (mostly cattle). He is not an important businessman, but he has a respectable capital base. As for the 'foreign' (who comes from outside the village) buyer, the other protagonist, who is also the person at the origin of the incident, there is not much to say about him except that he is between thirty-five and forty years old.

Kamel relates the events of an incident which occurred in a local market of Cap Bon. In the late afternoon, the fellahs arrive in the souq to trade their day's harvest of painstakingly gathered orange blossoms. The buyers are generally people of the village although outside merchants sometimes come to the market to replenish their supplies. As a native of the village, Ridha has established his control of the souq and has an interest in the various trades whether by controlling prices, thwarting the competition or other means – even violence. Therefore, when a foreign merchant comes to the souq to buy orange blossoms, Ridha inflates the bidding and then uses his influence with the *hâbat* (the public weighmaster who calculates invoices) to lower the producer's price. In order to do so, he does not hesitate to advance his *nisba*, i.e. the fact that he is a native of the village (*ould bled*) and that he should, as such, be privileged and enjoy certain advantages over other merchants. The foreign buyer however, is not intimidated. He condemns Ridha's unfair manoeuvring as well as the weighmaster's partiality and demands either restitution of the goods or payment of the last negotiated price. Given Ridha's refusal and arrogance, the story ends in a dispute.This is the story, as told by Kamel:

> Orange blossoms (*zahir*) sell well at this time, so much the better for fellahs because picking them is arduous work. Fellahs suffer enormously and spend an incredibly long time collecting these two or three *waznât* [literally, weighings; a *wazna* = 4kg]. Every day in the late afternoon, they bring back what they were able to harvest during the day to sell at the souq. Most of the buyers are locals [natives of the village] though, from time to time, other consumers and even 'foreign' buyers come and 'shake' the rhythm of the souq with their purchases. This is particularly true in periods of shortage [*mush sâba*] when one may see *barrânia* [strangers to the village] buyers enter the market and 'disrupt' the local trade [at which time, Kamel adds, as is often the case following the use of this term, *mâ barrâni kân al-shaytân* (literally, 'only the devil is a foreigner')].

Speaking of local trade, everyone has noticed, though none dares speak of it, that for the past two or three seasons, a particularly formidable buyer often buys almost all the daily harvest without any scruples about spreading panic when thwarted (*na'ksû*), as with the case in point. This buyer, Ridha, monopolises purchases to the point of controlling price fluctuations. Every time a foreign buyer comes to buy a few kilos of flowers, Ridha always finds a way to make him leave or, one way or another, to drive him out *zulm fi zulm* (unfairly). Through his purchases, the foreign buyer obviously introduces competition and, to some extent, disrupts the 'normal' course of trade, going against Ridha's business.

Consider today's case: all that the *barrâni* had to do was to 'show up' and buy a few kilos to make the price of the *wazna* increase by 0.400 DT (Tunisian dinars, about €15) over yesterday's price. Through his purchases and his bidding, he makes the price go up which puts Ridha in an uncomfortable position. Ridha will not hesitate to use any means to permanently get rid of this 'intruder'.[5]

The simplest means which he is accustomed to using is to 'create a problem' (*yakhlaq mushkil*) and to stir up ill-feeling so that these so-called 'foreign' competitors can no longer compete with him.

This time, Ridha drove up the bidding for a bag of orange blossoms and was able to have the last word by offering 5800 DT for the *wazna,* although the price had never before exceeded 5400 DT.

This bid was strange and everyone wondered what it meant. Very quickly, however, I understood. At the time of weighing the goods, Ridha took advantage of his friendship with the *hâbat* and asked him to charge 5700 DT instead of the 5800 public bid. The price of 5700, however, was the price offered by his foreign competitor. The latter quickly condemned the unfair manoeuvre and demanded the return of the goods insofar as he was the one who had bid that price, his price...

The worst part is the argument developed by Ridha in order to make his competitor feel uncomfortable. In his defence, he used an argument based on the origin (*nisba*), *al-asl,* of the other buyer, a foreigner. Only he, as an *ould bled* (literally, a 'son of the town', a native of the village) can benefit from such an agreement and take advantage of such a favour. A foreign buyer (says Kamel, ironically) should not even be admitted in this souq, in fact, he should not even exist.

Fortunately, the so-called foreign buyer was not intimidated and stood firm in the face of Ridha's boldness, even though a simple argument turned into a fight. The story ends with this saying: *al-dînya mâ'âd yashba' mînha had* (literally, 'one is no longer satisfied with what one earns').

Exercise in analysis: the story passed in review

An argument based on the trickery of the local buyer

The Tunisians who find the outcome of this incident to be 'unfair' (or 'rather unfair') consider that Ridha was the one who behaved 'very badly' and who was unfair towards his competitor simply because he was a 'foreigner' (37).[6] To begin with, he did not respect the elementary rules of business, namely fair competition, and honesty. He preferred to cheat, trick and lie in order to deceive both his competitor and the seller, which is not acceptable in any profession. It constitutes an infringement on rights and an affront to the person of his competitor. He undoubtedly showed no respect for him.

A schoolteacher expresses himself:

> There are several 'guys' like Ridha. He is the kind of person who, thanks to his 'dirty' money, tries to have a hold on everything. They are liars [*kadhâba*], unfaithful and, most of all, thankless people. Their main goal is to win again and again without regard to the method and tricks they use...They appear right because they can buy everything, including public officials, weighmasters at the market, but they will not go very far. They will not necessarily become rich. (5)

A student says:

> It is regrettable that one lacks respect towards others whatever their background even if they are a competitor or a 'foreigner'. [She further adds that] Ridha should not have behaved in this way; he should let the other merchant buy what he wants and work under normal conditions. He should treat him as one of the town's people. He is, above all, a human being who deserves respect and consideration. (37)

Another person speaks the same way:

> Ridha should not act this way with 'foreigners' because he runs the risk of ruining his reputation and, in the world of commerce, it is necessary to know how to lose (32). Ridha should have let the 'foreigner' work with all the other competitors in the souq (49). He should accept competition from 'foreign' buyers as well as from local buyers.

Another insists that Ridha behaved selfishly and unfairly, thus forgetting that he is not alone and that he himself as a trader might some day have to buy goods somewhere else in other souqs.

A civil servant says:

> Ridha should not be selfish. He should accept the presence of other buyers for the good of the fellahs and for the good of all the village. (9)

To some, the solution appears rather simple: force Ridha to buy the product at the price that he himself offered (5800 DT) or allow the 'foreigner' to buy at the price of 5700 DT since it was 'his last price'. In this way, each one will draw a profit and the price will inevitably be the 'right price'.

Finally, one notices other considerations in those discussions relating to the attitude and the behaviour of third parties. Indeed, some are surprised to see no reaction from the public in the souq nor from local authorities, all the more so as, according to the narrator, it is a 'frequent phenomenon', not an isolated incident. Here, for example, is what a teacher says:

> In this incident, a third party should have intervened to force Ridha to behave properly towards his competitors but also towards the fellahs (18). 'Foreign' buyers must resist and organise to fight against the selfishness of the town's merchants by co-operating with fellahs to free the souq from the yoke of Ridha (21). Because (adds the teacher) it is an infringement on the person and an injustice whose first victims are fellahs (6).

Among French respondents to our questionnaire, some emphasised the necessity, in such a situation, of third-party mediation. Not only is the buyers' arrangement obviously made at the blossom pickers' expense (79), but what is more, Ridha takes advantage of the foreign buyers and alienates them in order to maintain his monopoly. It is regrettable that no one came forward to oppose Ridha's schemes and manipulations. Hence the necessity of an independent mediator or of a village wise man (73). The conflict arose from Ridha's cheating and overbidding, especially because he corrupted the weighmaster of the souq (71).

Perhaps the fellahs' interest lies in the competitive bidding process so that their product would be sold at the highest price (96). This is why one person (148) says that 'The "foreigner's" challenge to Ridha should have been supported by the fellahs instead of coming to blows. Competition would have resumed normally if Ridha had been "neutralised"'.

A foreman adds, in a rather severe tone: 'Ridha, the culprit, should have been punished for fraud and the goods should have been returned to his "foreign" competitor, no question asked' (144). It should also be said that the public weighmaster is not innocent in this incident. He should be neutral and, as such, not give in to Ridha's pressure (104). 'This is why,' a retired man says, 'the weighmaster should not agree to lower the price and Ridha should be forced to pay the high price.' It is also the solution recommended by most of the people surveyed. Since he offered to pay the price of 5800 DT, they say, Ridha should have paid that price for his purchase (100): 'As long as one accepts the principle of bidding, the one that offers the last price must honour his commitment, without prejudice to anyone else' (71). This solution only serves to address the conflict between Ridha and the foreigner, whereas the problem raised by Ridha's arrogant behaviour remains unresolved. Ridha should allow competition among buyers whether local or 'foreign' (111). One person (84) says: 'Monopoly is harmful to trade. Fair competition is best because everyone acts out of his own self-interest.' A librarian adds: '"Foreign" buyers should be able to acquire a product under the same conditions as local buyers' (107). This requires a maximum of integrity and honesty, which is to say, as a farmer notes, 'a behaviour where loyalty and respect for others are the standard' (121). 'But,' an instructor adds, 'can one be a merchant and honest at the same time?' And another respondent (116) asks, 'What could be fair in the world of commerce? It is the law of the jungle, each one [acts] in the logic of his self-interest [in which case] the "foreign" buyer's price should have prevailed.' This same retired lady concludes:

> The producers themselves [the fellahs] should set a fair price for their products in relation with the work they provided instead of subjecting themselves to the law of supply and demand which almost always operates for the benefit of 'big' traders (116).

An argument centred on the brave reaction of the 'foreign' buyer

Unlike the argument just developed, whose focus was on Ridha's cheating and dishonesty, the focus now shifts in order to show and praise the boldness and courage of the 'foreign' buyer. As one social worker says: 'one can always find someone smarter, one can always find one's master' (138). To those surveyed, the foreign competitor embodies the 'strong man' who is capable of restoring justice. What Ridha wants is to remain the master of the market by monopolising purchases. He will use any means necessary to maintain his position. This time, however, he faces a more belligerent competitor, one that is smarter than he and who has his way (76). He begins by inflating prices for the benefit of the sellers and he condemns Ridha's unfair manoeuvre. Finally, in view of the latter's partiality and arrangement with the weigh-master, the 'foreigner' manages to assert his rights. He wants his due and he gets it (134). Here is how a retired man summarises the end of the story:

> Faced with a 'foreign' buyer, Ridha pushes the bidding up (maybe with the hope of seeing him leave), then uses his influence with the weigh-master to bring the price back down to the 'foreigner's' last offer. The foreigner is not intimidated and, defending the value of his bidding, obtains restitution of the goods. (136)

A civil servant (133) says: 'One day, a "foreign" buyer will confront him (Ridha) and claim his right even if he must quarrel and get in a fight. As always, ordinary people (orange blossom pickers) are absent from the debate and subject to the law of the rich.' Says another person: 'Fortunately the "foreign" buyer did not let anyone take advantage of him. He was able to make others listen and respect his rights and his person' (110). A housewife says with relief that 'Ridha will finally understand that he is not alone in this world and that he is not the boss of the souq' (89).

As a consequence, fair competition will prevail and buyers, regardless of origin, will now find a place in this souq without Ridha's opposition or dictate. This process must inevitably lead to the solution demanded by most of the people we surveyed, for whom such a solution is necessary, namely 'to return Ridha to his role as a buyer among buyers, without (giving) threats, monopolistic pretensions or xenophobic arguments' (76).

In some ways, this solution summarises the solutions suggested by survey respondents, although each person may have focused on individual aspects. In the search for a fair outcome to this situation, three main elements are most frequently cited: First, it is necessary to give satisfaction to the foreign buyer and to restore fair competition in the marketplace, which is to say fair bidding among partners without favouritism or fraudulent practice. As one civil servant notes: 'the best offer must prevail regardless of the buyer's origins' (135). Another respondent notes: 'May the best man win, honestly and impartially in a fair and transparent sale' (108). Yet another comments that, '[what we seek is] an outcome which allows the "foreigner" to acquire goods through a bidding process which respects the amount of the bid' (65).

It will certainly result in other buyers coming to the market, and will allow a return to normal competition (62). In other words, Ridha can no longer continue to behave in this way, he can no longer resort to fraudulent practices to keep other traders from exercising their profession. He must abide by the free play of competition. He can no longer feel justified in his practices by the simple fact that he is 'from the village' and that others are not (69). As a secretary says: 'To welcome more "foreign" buyers [means that] Ridha no longer has a monopoly on purchases [and that] orange blossoms can be sold at a higher price' (74). By restoring fair competition, one restores justice insofar as all buyers, regardless of origin, receive equal treatment (123).

The second aspect of the search for a fair outcome concerns the interest of the farmers. Indeed, when this 'fair price policy' is restored, the fellahs will benefit directly from the sale of their product and from the product of their harvesting efforts. This is a way of respecting them and their work.

A retired lady's opinion is that a 'fair outcome' would be to obtain the 'best price' for the fellahs who, throughout the year, invest time and hard work in harvesting and selling orange blossoms (60). A retired man adds: 'This is why the fellahs should have rejected Ridha's manipulations and mismanagement and asked the local authorities to restore and protect a free-market economy' (136). A student says (132): 'It is necessary that the fellahs refuse to follow the path which Ridha wishes to impose and that they make no distinction between Ridha and the potential "foreign" buyers. Prices should be set according to their offer.'

The third aspect concerns the xenophobic arguments used by Ridha in order to be rid of his so-called 'foreign' competitor and to extend his pricing control. This type of argument provoked a strong reaction among respondents which, if not violent, at least expressed anger: 'Let Ridha be expelled from the souq!' a student says (110). 'Make him pay the price he had offered', a speech therapist adds (118). A civil servant expresses the opinion that the best way to deal with the problem would be to stop Ridha from buying orange blossoms for a while (70).

Many people, undoubtedly more legalistic, underscore the need to punish Ridha. As a secretary puts it: 'Ridha should have been "condemned" by the local authorities so that he can no longer repeat such behaviour' (97).

'A fair outcome,' a schoolteacher (112) says, 'would be to refer the matter to the commercial court and apply the jurisprudence governing the case'. 'Ridha,' another (115) adds, 'must be punished for his dishonesty and his cheating.' In a secretary's opinion, 'a just outcome would be that the "foreign" buyer recover the flowers at the bid price of 5700 DT and that Ridha be punished for his dishonesty and driven out of town' (117). A librarian expresses the same opinion: 'Let the "foreign" buyer recover the goods because he offered a fair price and let Ridha be condemned for dishonesty and unfair competition' (105).

Thus, to conclude this analysis of the various forms of justification put forth by the respondents, one must recognise the diversity of arguments and the wealth of axiological values to which they constantly refer. The questions raised, though not necessarily in this order, were, on the positive side, questions of loyalty, confidence, esteem, respect, consideration etc., and on the negative side, contempt, partiality, cheating, selfishness, dishonesty, disloyalty etc. Without any pretence towards the development of a global approach of these fundamental values and concepts, I have selected a few for closer study in order to outline an approach by which they may be related, in one way or another, to a sense of justice.

Respect for the person and impartiality: how those ethical-legal categories relate to the sense of justice

A quick look back to some strong evaluations

Through the eyes of Kamel, the narrator, it is possible to discern three categories or emerging visions of the collective 'we'. The first to be considered concerns the fellahs and their working conditions, about which the narrator expresses a very clear judgement. Next come the 'foreigners' and the behaviour that one should adopt towards them. Finally, there is the behaviour of a specific buyer, whose xenophobic attitude is strongly condemned.

Kamel expresses an individual or personal judgement which, in a way, reflects that of the group. In other words, he expresses a global point of view with which other people can identify. On the other hand, it is difficult to find the expression of 'I' (within Mead's meaning) within him expressing personal or intimate attitudes. In fact, his judgement is above all the expression of the social dimension of 'self'. Indeed, to understand this 'distance' assumed by the narrator, it is necessary to take into account his position within the souq.

More generally, in his judgement, the narrator promotes the idea of the need to respect the person independently of his origin or identity: whether concerning the fellahs whose 'rights' are not respected or the 'foreigner' whose person is denigrated by Ridha's contemptuous attitude and by the abusive use and manipulation of the notion of *nisba*. In the end, he blames Ridha for not respecting certain elementary rules and agreements and, most of all, for not respecting his competitor's basic rights.

Furthermore, through the judgements of the people surveyed, one can identify various levels which tie in with one another: either they condemn Ridha's *negative* behaviour or they praise his victim's *positive* behaviour. The common idea is that of the respect for the elementary rights of the person beyond any consideration of status or belonging (independent of the idea of *asl*). All opinions focus on the criticism of Ridha's attitude towards the foreigner. They condemn the lack of respect towards the person of his competitor, the arrogance with which he treated him and the absolute disregard for his rights (his right as a buyer, his right as an equal). Ridha considers himself superior because he is supposedly *ould bled.*

Behind these various 'I' who judge and condemn Ridha's inadmissible behaviour, one can also detect the expression of a more or less homogeneous 'we' (see the nuances between the judgements of the Tunisians and those of the Frenchmen). One can say that the 'we' is expressed through the individual position expressed by the 'I'. The 'we' wants all buyers to be on equal footing and wants the rights of 'foreign' buyers to be respected.

What is initially expressed among the French is their familiarity with a certain method of conflict-settlement: the role of the parties involved in the conflict, their rights and their duties as well as the institutional means of resolving the conflict by respecting the rights of all parties.

For the Tunisians and for the French, any behaviour which undermines the general standard is expressed in either of two ways: an offender who behaves badly should consequently be punished and the victim, the aggrieved party, should receive reparations. To avoid such behaviour, two conditions are suggested. The first is a respect for business law (sales and purchases). These rules must be respected in order to create a collective interest so that the partners in the souq may conclude their business and, in the case of conflict, find a compromise without infringing upon one another's rights. The second condition is the respect for certain moral principles (loyalty, honesty, impartiality, respect of others) in order to maintain and respect the conditions and the possibility of transactions and relationships between buyers and sellers. It should, however, be added that this second moral requirement is appreciated at different degrees because, for some, the world of commerce cannot be governed by moral principles.

Sense of justice and ethics of respect: marks of respect, self-respect and respect for others

Where then is the sense of justice? Such might be the first question that one could ask after exploring Kamel's story and trying to reconstruct the reactions and comments of survey respondents. In this way, one may consider that, wherever the most elementary rules and conventions are broken or violated, where marks of respect, consideration and deference are neglected and where self-respect and concern for others are denied, justice is undoubtedly subordinated. Marks of respect and satisfaction and expressions of gratitude and approval become cries of indignation and revolt, of criticism, condemnation and disapproval. Justice invariably demands signs of respect and consideration, injustice breeds contempt and humiliation. Justice is not possible without respect of the person and of human dignity. The result is a broad meaning of the sense of justice, whose principal characteristic is to call upon an inclusive theory of the fair and the unfair.[7]

As noted by Bloch, 'one believes in one's capacity to apprehend fairness. Just how variable are this word's meanings! From the beginning, it is a mix of several things.'[8] Here, then, is just the opportunity to identify these 'mixed things' or perhaps to see how they relate to a sense of justice. I have just noted that justice requires not only moral integrity, impartiality, equality, merit etc., but also respect and human dignity independent of ethnic origin, race or social status.[9] It will not be possible in these few pages to treat the full array of elements comprising a sense of justice. Rather, I shall limit the discussion to a set of such elements and, more particularly, to the relation of the idea of justice to that of respect for the person.

The notion of respect is certainly complex. As Murdoch points out, 'respect is a discreet, distant, ambiguous concept. It is related to esteem, consideration and deference.'[10] Respect refers to rights, but also to people. The issue is to recognise others as people with inalienable rights and duties.

One can find without any trouble, in any theory of justice worthy of its name, an approach to the person and a reflection on the requirement of respect. In a recent study, Forst proposes a very useful development and shows the importance of space occupied by notions of the person and identity within the various theories of justice, including liberal, communitarian, feminist etc.[11] Indeed, without tracing our thoughts back to Kant who, reasoning from the notion of autonomy, gives a fundamental meaning to the notion of respect,[12] one may find sufficient material in the works of contemporary authors to show the fundamental link between justice and respect.

The most obvious link may be found in the definition of justice proposed by Spaemann, according to whom, 'Justice means recognising that every man deserves for himself respect'.[13] One cannot find a more enlightening or suggestive definition to illustrate the matter.

In the same way, Rawls's notion of self-respect for the person occupies a central place in his theory of justice as equity.[14] From his perspective, respect is a basic condition guaranteed by the principles of justice in a well-ordered society. It is, in fact, 'self-respect' which may be considered a primary asset, perhaps one's most valuable asset. For him, 'one of the desirable features of a system of justice is that it should publicly express men's respect for one another'.[15] In his analysis, Rawls tends to confuse self-respect and self-esteem. It is important to clearly distinguish 'self-respect' from 'self-esteem', as many authors recommend.[16] For example, Forst writes that 'Self-esteem is socially constituted through something others value in me according to communal standards, but self-respect requires that I am still me in all these endeavours'.[17]

This distinction brings one easily to Ricœur's position which tends to establish a link between, on one hand, 'self esteem and the ethical context of our actions aimed at the good life' and, on the other hand, 'self-respect and the moral context of these same actions subjected to the tests for the universalisation of moral maxims'. The author adds:

> Together, self-esteem and self-respect define the moral or ethical dimension of ipseity. They define the human subject as a subject of imputation...We respect ourselves inasmuch as we are able to judge our own actions impartially. Self-esteem and self-respect relate, in every case, to a capable subject.[18]

This distinction can otherwise prove useful in order to better appreciate the attitude of the foreign buyer, who feels offended, even humiliated, by Ridha's behaviour. From this perspective, self-respect, as Le Dœuff underlines, is considered 'the act of defending one's rights, to resist everything that could deteriorate them, to refuse to be used, manipulated, exploited or degraded'.[19] When discredited or denied, self-respect encourages the refusal of any form of humiliation and causes indignation and condemnation.[20] A perfect illustration is the reaction of the 'foreign' buyer who stands firm against the false motives and the ill will of his competitor. In that sense, his attitude is unanimously approved by the people in our survey and is considered as a courageous act of indignation against injustice and, thus, a 'fair' reaction. His refusal to give up makes him, in the eyes of the respondents, a 'righteous' man who has enough self-esteem to make others respect him, because the issue is not so much the few kilos of orange blossom, but rather the offence to his person and the lack of consideration for his word and his role as a buyer. Many of the respondents, therefore, consider that he was able to come out holding his 'head high' because he refused 'to bow' his head and was able to keep his self-esteem intact. It is for these very reasons that the people surveyed consider the attitude of the local buyer morally reprehensible.

Therefore, the notion of respect turns out to be an eminently moral category, implying the existence of a moral identity and an acute sense of justice. The notion of respect is also, in a way, a legal notion.[21] I shall not, however, undertake here the study of the notion of respect, but rather focus on the strong connections which exist between the concepts of respect and of the person. These often go together, as one might speak about 'respect for the person'. The objective, then, is to examine the links between the two concepts and to see how they relate to the sense of justice.

There are, of course, multiple ways to approach that relationship. The main thing is to know what definition to give to the notions of person and justice.[22] Whatever it is, however, 'it is particularly important to keep in mind that the conception of the person is part of a conception of social and political justice'.[23] For Rawls, and in spite of the fact that since the time of Kant the notion of person has occupied a central role in moral philosophy, the notion has 'suffered from an excess of ambiguity and inaccuracy'.[24] That is why Rawls offers a clarification based on the famous 'original position', whose purpose is to establish the exact framework for finding a well-balanced agreement concerning the principles of justice. According to Rawls, the structure defined by the 'original position' undoubtedly allows an appropriate conception of the person to crystallise and, with it, the vigorous identification of the underlying character of the moral, free and equal personality.[25] Thus, he concludes that the 'original position' is not 'an axiomatical (or deductive) basis from which principles would derive, but a procedure to select the principles best adapted to the most wide-spread conception of the person'.[26] From this point, the author manages to lay the epistemological and conceptual foundations indispensable to his theory of justice as equity which takes into account the person 'as the basic unit of action and social responsibility'. It therefore cannot be denied that an elaborate concept of the person thus forms the basis for Rawls's principles of justice.

Without necessarily resorting to a formal definition of the person, it would not seem devoid of interest to begin, as Maclagan suggests, with the meaning commonly attributed by the social actors to the idea of respect for the person, 'by reference to ordinary human beings in respect of their nature as self-conscious agents'.[27] This sense of respect for the person is related to the individual moral sense and has the further advantage of leading us directly and skilfully to the question of sense of justice and injustice. One must not, however, confuse a sense of justice with a sense of respect for the person, hence our interest in approaching this study from the point of view of linkages and not in terms of identification or assimilation. In this respect, one can follow the argument developed by Maclagan, whose interest lies in clearly defining the boundaries between justice and respect, all the while recognising their interrelatedness. He writes:

> A rule to the effect that persons as such are to be respected is, plainly enough, a rule relating to the social aspect of morality. [...] It is a rule of the utmost generality; and if we ask what other concept of social morality could plausibly claim a similar width of application the answer must obviously be 'Justice'. In speaking of this as a different concept I do not mean that 'justice' necessarily refers to a different ethical fact from that to which 'respect for persons' refers. I mean merely that people who speak both of justice and of respect for persons do not always, or perhaps even commonly, treat the two expressions as interchangeable and equivalent, mere verbal variants in the way in which 'ship' and 'vessel' frequently are; and that some who use 'justice' language do not use 'respect for persons' language at all – for example, Plato and Aristotle. Whether 'justice' and 'respect for persons' do or do not refer to what is objectively the same thing is precisely one of the points that has to be determined. In any event, it would seem that, if there is any sense in talking of a principle of respect for persons at all, reflection on the concept of justice might provide some clue to what that principle means.[28]

On the whole, it appears that the study of the sense of justice and its social linkages allows us to clarify the question of what may be called the ethics of respect. Through analysis of the various argumentative registers and of the forms of justification put forth by the actors, one enters the sphere of moral values and principles that express people's sense of justice or injustice. Marks of respect, self-esteem, self-respect and respect for others, to name only a few, revolve around the person as, in Sève's words, 'a form-value equally assigned to each individual in its capacity as member of the human race'.[29] All this is essential to the constitution of the individual moral identity.

The approach which we offer is, after all, only a sketch. Consequently, it must be studied again in depth. The question of respect for the person itself deserves more substantial treatment, perhaps even a more elaborate theory such as that proposed by Cranor in a remarkable article in which he pleads for a 'theory of respect for persons'.[30] But, such was not the purpose of this study, which focuses next on certain questions of impartiality raised in our survey. Partiality can, moreover, reveal other forms of disrespect for or offence to a person.

Justice as impartiality without regard for the person: keeping a fair distance and loyalty towards another

'By justice, I understand the impartial treatment of every man [...] measured only with respect to the properties of the one who receives and by the capacity of the one who gives. Thus, his principle is [...] *to be no respecter of persons.*'[31] It is in such terms that Sève, relying on Goodwin's definition, introduces his analysis of the notion of 'regard for the person'. This expression, used with a rare technical legal meaning, perfectly summarises the idea of 'partiality' in its multiple forms. Its importance, according to Sève, 'resides in the opposition of the notions of vice and justice'.[32] As such, it expresses the opposite of 'integrity' or impartiality and the opposite of the sense of justice: to give one his due.[33]

It is in the legal and, more specifically, judicial field that this notion finds its fullest expression, indeed, its principal application. We say, for example, that a sitting judge acts with bias and out of 'regard to the person' when ruling without regard to fairness or truth. As a consequence, his judgement is marred by partiality and founded upon immediate motives or external signs that have little to do with material evidence or elements referring to the legal case of the incriminated person. As Sève writes: 'the one who acts out of a "regard for the person"', even if devoid of malice or intent, credits the apparent circumstances, which are sometimes emotional, of the citizen. More specifically, '"acting out of regard for the person" consists in taking into account qualities which are not relevant to the matter in question, for example, an individual's apparent wealth or family ties in the attribution of a function requiring well-defined competencies'.[34]

This concept of 'regard for the person' can serve as a basis for an analytical framework for the clarification of matters in 'dispute' and for explaining attitudes and justifications of the protagonists. Sève writes: 'if we extend the concept of an act of justice to acts of kindness, we may well ask whether emotional or family ties between the beneficiary and the agent would not constitute an unintentional "regard for the person" inherent in this type of relation'.[35] This question could be raised concerning the accommodating attitude of the weighmaster towards the local buyer (Ridha). The latter tries to use his privileged relationship with the weighmaster to exploit the fact that he is a native of the village and, in so doing, causes damages to be inflicted upon the person of his competitor simply because he is considered a foreigner.

Before returning to a discussion of his attitude, let us focus on the attitude of the weighmaster who, according to survey respondents, is guilty of partiality insofar as his clearly defined public function is to ensure fair invoicing and provide a standard of market weights and measures. He is the guarantor of commercial transactions. His position requires strict impartiality and he must remain neutral while on duty. There should not be, as one says, two weights and two measures.

We are well aware that what happened was, in fact, the opposite. One may, in fact, speak of favouritism.[36] The weighmaster sided with Ridha against the foreign buyer, without any regard for justice. Since he sided with a 'close relation' to the detriment of a 'distant acquaintance', one could consider that he committed an act of 'regard for the person'. It is, moreover, the opinion shared by most of the Tunisians and French in the survey. For them, the behaviour of the weighmaster is undeniably tainted with partiality. By acting against a buyer on grounds of his 'foreignness', the weighmaster demonstrated a lack of 'integrity'. In so doing, he caused offence and material damages. For that reason, his attitude was condemned for its partiality.

It would be tempting to say that the attitude of the weighmaster would, at first, not be reprehensible or condemnable insofar as it represented a 'natural' reaction aimed at 'protecting' a 'close relation' even to the detriment of a 'foreigner'. However, even when presented in this light, the argument seems in some ways distorted. To support this assertion, we can rely on Rorty's analysis of the link between justice and loyalty. Rorty suggests considering justice as extended loyalty, rather like a prism in the conception of impartiality. In Rorty's view, 'our loyalty to an extended group decreases and even disappears completely in exceptionally hard situations. [...] The more the situations are difficult, the more the links of loyalty tighten themselves among close relatives and loosen themselves towards others.'[37] Does this mean that it is necessary to oppose loyalty to justice? Certainly not, according to Rorty. On the contrary, there is less conflict between loyalty and justice than there is between degrees of loyalty, particularly as between loyalty towards small groups and loyalty towards extended groups. Thus, he arrives at the idea that the word 'justice' applies to loyalty to extended groups. From this also arises the idea that 'our moral identity is determined by the group or the groups with whom we identify – the group or the groups towards whom we can not be disloyal without losing self-esteem'.[38]

This echoes the analysis attempted in Chapter 2 concerning the relation between the 'I', the 'self', the 'we' and the category of the person. That chapter focused particularly on the centrality of the self in the dynamics of this relation and in the social building of the person and of moral identity. The bottom-line issue in the equation of distance is ultimately the 'dialectical constitution of the self'. This dialectical constitution, Ricœur notes, makes the path of effectuation of the good life go through the other one.[39] The idea of justice then takes root in this process or this dialectic and appears as the search for the 'right distance'. One can say it is a question of 'degree', 'measure' or 'size'. The search for the 'right distance' appears as the guarantee of both self-respect and respect for others and, consequently, as the guarantee of 'the recognition of the other party as foreign'. It is the condition, Ricœur adds, which 'insures the nexus among the self, the closely related and the distant'. Ricœur summarises these rather complex thoughts as follows:

> This move from close to distant or rather to the apprehension of the close relation as distant is also that of moving from friendship to justice. Friendship in private relationships stands out in the background of the public relation to justice. Before any formalisation,

> any universalisation or procedural treatment, the quest for justice is that of establishing the right distance between all human beings. The right distance is the middle ground between too little distance as characterised by many dreams of emotional fusion and an excessive distance maintained through arrogance, contempt and hatred for the 'foreigner', the unknown. I would see gladly in the virtue of hospitality the symbolic expression most approaching this culture of the right distance.[40]

The question is to know how to apprehend or fairly estimate this 'right distance' and thereby to adopt an impartial attitude. On this subject, sociological pragmatics invites one to be attentive to contexts and situations of evaluation and judgement. With regard to impartiality, it is important to take into account its context, but also its semantic content which means considering impartiality such as it is acted in ordinary life. The result is clearly a different view from that of others, especially that defended by Barry.[41] Placing himself within the tradition of the social contract and building from Rawls' theory of justice, Barry develops a conception of impartiality which one may, as Bonin does, qualify as a 'second level conception', that is a conception which 'requires impartiality only during the choice of the principles of justice and not impartiality of the principles themselves'.[42] Clearly, this perspective is not concerned with the social evolution of impartiality as a result of human situations and interactions.

That is why I propose taking the opposite view of Barry's perspective. To do so, I shall follow leads well developed by Paperman. In a recent study, she sets out to present and discuss the feminist criticism of the impartialistic theories of justice. I shall not focus on this aspect of her contribution, but instead highlight her contribution to the sociological analysis of impartiality by posing the problem of its construction and by placing it in context. Paperman starts with the possibility 'that there is no absolute criterion nor convincing philosophical definition for an essentialist type of impartiality'.[43] For her, 'the requirement for impartiality satisfies a requirement for justice. This requirement for justice, however, does not imply indifference towards the person or the situation being judged.'[44]

Such an approach makes it possible to resolve the problem of 'conflict' which might exist between the need for impartiality and personal relations or family ties. From then on, one can no longer consider these as paradoxical or incompatible; rather one must try to consider the circumstances by virtue of which one may determine the partial or impartial nature of a judgement, decision or situation. This is the guarantee and the merit of a pragmatic sociological approach. As Paperman notes, 'What is considered an illegitimate basis for favouritism or partiality in a judgement is not determined beforehand, but negotiated according to circumstances.'[45] One finds the same argument developed in Baron's assertion:

> Critics of impartiality usually acknowledge that there are circumstances in which we really should be impartial. [...] But, they emphasise, these are very special circumstances. Most of the time, especially *vis-à-vis* of friends and family, it is fine to be partial. I think this is a mistake, for two reasons. First, impartiality is often needed with regard to those close to us. We think it wrong, for instance, to heap gifts on a favourite young grandchild while giving nothing to her little brother. Second, because the demands of impartiality are so highly contextual, considerable reflection and sensitivity are needed for the agent to judge that treating so-and-so special, in this way and in this situation, is permissible. Because of this, impartiality should not be thought of as something to take into account only in special circumstances – circumstances that, in effect, come flagged as those which call for impartiality. While it is true that impartiality is only critical in certain kinds of situations, it is not always obvious which situations are those situations. We need to be sensitive to considerations that call for a perspective of impartiality, we should not regard them as most of the time morally irrelevant.[46]

Finally, it is obvious that, following the example of the problem of respect of the person, which I believe calls for more reflection, the question of impartiality and its link with justice also calls for more in-depth study. I did not come to a conclusion on this question nor did I carry out an exhaustive analysis. My first concern was to bring elements to the debate by way of a case study which, after all, was rather productive.[47]

Notes

1 Ricœur, 1995, p. 11.
2 Williams, 1994.
3 Nachi, 1998.
4 The story, as told here, was evaluated by 149 people: 55 Tunisians and 94 French. To facilitate the presentation of the arguments given by both sides and for a quick reference to their origin, we will use the following system of numbering: 1 to 55 for the Tunisians and 56 to 149 for the Frenchmen.
5 In this village, people often claim to be smarter than their neighbours and do not miss an opportunity to show it. In my study, I attempt to show the important role of cunning in people's everyday life; Nachi, forthcoming.
6 These numbers refer to the persons questioned in the survey.
7 Nachi, 1998.
8 Bloch, 1976, p. 15.
9 Boxill, 1988.
10 Murdoch, 1993, p. 10.
11 Forst, 1992.
12 Hill, 1991.
13 Spaemann, 1999, p. 73.
14 Rawls, 1987.
15 Rawls, 1987, p. 209.
16 Sachs, 1981; Darwall, 1977.
17 Forst, 1992, p. 298.
18 Ricœur, 1993, p. 98.
19 Le Dœuff, 1993, p. 51.
20 Boltanski, 1990.
21 Errera illustrates this by using examples from current French law. For him, 'respect is indeed a legal category and a legal concept vested with legal rights and obligations': 1993, p. 146. This is fundamentally about the protection of human rights; Article 9 of the Civil Code states that 'all persons are entitled to respect for their private life'. From this point of view, the notion of respect extends beyond that of self-esteem and, in a way, encompasses it. It should be noted, however, that such notions as 'respect for' and 'dignity of' the person do not always find clear legal formulation. Writing on the subject, Jorion underlines the 'difficulty of inserting a moral rule into positive law'; Jorion further notes that 'It is difficult to move from natural law to positive law in the question of one's right to dignity': 1999, p. 199.

22 For an outline of some of these definitions, please refer to the Introduction in this volume and to Chapter 2.
23 Rawls, 1993, p. 200.
24 Rawls, 1993, p. 150.
25 Ibid.
26 Rawls, 1993, p. 151.
27 Maclagan, 1960, p. 193.
28 Maclagan, 1960, pp. 193–94.
29 Sève, 1990.
30 Cranor, 1975.
31 Sève, 1990, p. 1915.
32 Ibid.
33 The term, 'acception', in the sense of 'acception of person', is translated in the *Dictionnaire économique et juridique Navarre* by 'acception', 'favouring', 'partiality'.
34 Sève, 1990, p. 1915.
35 Ibid.
36 The notion of 'favouritism' can be very enlightening to better understand this type of situation: on this subject: Cottingham, 1986.
37 Rorty, 1996, pp. 211–12. Rorty takes the example of famine: sharing food with the poor man in the street seems natural under normal circumstances, he observes, but in times of famine, we keep our food for our own family before giving to others.
38 Rorty, 1996, p. 215.
39 Ricœur, 2001, p. 72.
40 Ibid.
41 Barry, 1995.
42 Bonin, 1997, p. 138.
43 Paperman, 2000, p. 34.
44 Ibid.
45 Paperman, 2000, p. 35.
46 Baron, 1991, pp. 837–38.
47 I would like to thank Baudouin Dupret and to express gratitude for his support, his useful remarks and his insight in the reading of the various versions of this text which made its completion possible.

Bibliography

Audard, C., 'Exploitation ou exclusion? Penser l'injustice dans le contexte post-marxiste', *Critique*, 642, November 2000, pp. 976–987.

Baron, M., 'Impartiality and Friendship', *Ethics*, 101/4, 1991, pp. 836–857.

Barry, Brian, *Justice as Impartiality*, Oxford University Press, 1995.

Beignier, B., 'L'honneur', *Droits*, 19/1, 1994, pp. 97–103.

Bloch, E., *Droit et dignité humaine*, Paris, Payot, 1976.

Boltanski, L., *L'amour et la justice comme compétences*, Paris, Métailié, 1990.

Bonin, P-Y., 'La justice en tant qu'impartialité', *Revue de métaphysique et de morale*, 1, 1997, pp. 135–46.

Boxill, B.R., *Les noirs et la justice sociale aux Etats-Unis*, Nancy, Presses universitaires de Nancy, 1988.

Campbell, T.D., 'Formal justice and rule-change', *Analysis*, 33/4, 1973, pp. 113–18.

Cottingham, J., 'Partiality, favouritism and morality', *Philosophical Quarterly*, XXXVI, 144, 1986, pp. 357–73.

Cranor, C.F., 'Toward a theory of respect for persons', *American Philosophical Quarterly*, XXII, 4, 1975, pp. 309–19.

– 'On respecting human beings as persons', *The Journal of Value Inquiry*, 17, 1983, pp. 103–17.

Darwal, L.D. 'Two kinds of respect', *Ethics*, 88 (1), 1977, pp. 36–49.

Errera, R., 'Le respect, catégorie juridique', *Autrement* ('Le respect', Série Morales), 10, 1993, pp. 146–61.

Forst, R., 'How (not) to speak about identity: The concept of the person in a theory of justice', *Philosophy and Social Criticism*, 18/3-4, 1992, pp. 293–312.

Haroche, C., 'Remarques sur les incertitudes et les ambiguïtés du droit à la dignité', in C. Haroche (ed.), *Le préambule de la constitution de 1946, CURAPP* (Centre universitaire de recherches administratives et politiques de Picardie), Paris, Presses Universitaires de France, 1996.

Haroche, C. and J-C. Vatin (eds), *La considération*, Paris, Desclée de Brouwer, 1998.

Hill Jr., T., *Autonomy and Self-Respect*, Cambridge, Cambridge University Press, 1991.

Jorion, B., 'La dignité de la personne humaine ou la difficile insertion d'une règle morale dans le droit positif', *Revue du droit public*, 1, 1999, pp. 197–233.

Khatchadourian, H., 'The human right to be treated as person', *The Journal of Value Inquiry*, 19, 1985, pp. 183–95.

Le Dœuff, M., 'La question de Zazie', *Autrement* ('Le respect', Série Morales), 10, 1993, pp. 46–63.
McFall, L., 'Integrity', *Ethics*, 98/1, 1987, pp. 5–20.
Maclagan, W. G., 'Respect for persons as moral principle I', *Philosophy*, XXXV, 134, 1960, pp. 193–217.
– 'Respect for persons as moral principle II', *Philosophy*, XXXV, 135, 1960, pp. 289–305.
Mathieu, B., 'La dignité de la personne: quel droit, quel titulaire?', *Recueil Dalloz*, 2 (33e Cahier), 1996, pp. 282–86.
Melden, A.I., *Rights and Persons*, Oxford, Basil Blackwell, 1977.
Murdoch, I., 'Envoi', *Autrement* ('Le respect', Série Morales), 10, 1993, pp. 10–11.
Nachi, M., 'Le sens de la justice: Étude comparative des formes de jugement et de justification en Tunisie et en France', PhD thesis, École des Hautes Études en Sciences Sociales, 1998, v. 2.
– *L'invention de la ruse: Justesse et justification d'un moyen pour se faire rembourser une dette impayée*, forthcoming.
Paperman, P., 'La contribution des émotions à l'impartialité des décisions', *Information sur les sciences sociales*, 39/1, 2000, pp. 29–73.
Rawls, J., *Théorie de la justice*, Paris, Seuil, 1987.
– *Justice et démocratie*, Paris, Seuil, 1993.
Ricœur, P., 'Le "soi" digne d'estime et de respect', *Autrement* ('Le respect', Série Morales), 10, 1993, pp. 88–99.
– *Le juste*, Paris, Esprit, 1995.
– 'Justice et vérité', in P. Ricœur, *Le juste* 2, Paris, Esprit, 2001, pp. 69–83.
Rorty, R., 'La justice comme loyauté élargie', in R.-P. Droit (ed.), *Jusqu'où tolérer?*, Paris, Le Monde-Editions, 1996, pp. 211–19.
Sachs, D., 'How to distinguish self-respect from self-esteem', *Philosophy and Public Affairs*, 10 (4), 1981, pp. 347–60.
Sève, R., 'Personne (acception de -s)', in A. Jacob (ed.), *Encyclopédie philosophique universelle II, Les notions philosophiques*, Paris, Presses Universitaires de France, 1990, pp. 1915–16.
Spaemann, R., *Notions fondamentales de morale*, Paris, Flammarion, 1999.
Thomas, L., 'Morality and Our Self-Concept', *Journal of Value Inquiry*, 12/4, 1978, pp. 258–68.
Williams, B., 'The Idea of Equality', in J. Feinberg (ed.), *Moral Concepts*, Oxford, Oxford University Press, 1969, pp. 153–71.
– 'Personne, caractère et morale', in B. Williams, *La fortune morale*, Paris, Presses Universitaires de France, 1994, pp. 227–51.

CHAPTER 8

Intention in Action: A Pragmatic Approach to Criminal Characterisation in an Egyptian Context

Baudouin Dupret

In criminal matters, intentionality constitutes one of the central criteria in the work of legal characterisation. This research undertakes to show how magistrates and, more particularly, public prosecutors organise their activity, in practice, around the establishment of this component of the crime. After having made a few preliminary remarks concerning the recourse to a pragmatic approach in the study of law, I shall give a summary sketch of the literature in the theory of law pertaining to this question. The essentially semantic nature of these approaches will be noted as they attempt to comprehend intention as a philosophical notion independent of the institutional context, of its use. I shall then endeavour proposing a pragmatic approach in which intentionality is viewed as the result of interactions integrated in the judicial institutional context which obliges professional actors to orient themselves toward the production of a legally relevant decision. This leads me, in conclusion, to observe that lay actors adjust themselves to this constraining institutional context, influenced by inductive reasoning of professionals and by their own anticipation of the means which would enable them to obtain the most favourable or the least damaging solution for themselves from the place and the persons with whom they are confronted, or simply the solution most conforming to the routine accomplishment of their work.

Preliminary remarks: the production of legality

The pragmatic study of the legal process which leads to the sanctioning of an intentional act, an act where wrong has been done to others, requires a few preliminary remarks of an epistemological and methodological nature.

The use of ethnomethodology and conversational analysis and the reference made to them in the study of law entails an emphasis upon the difference existing between the recourse to legal material to obtain knowledge of interactional language and the analysis of legal procedure supported by an ethnomethodological and conversational process. As Rod Watson has observed,

> some of the best ethnomethodology and conversation-analysis studies of law and legal reasoning come from analysts who do not regard themselves as having any special interest in 'the law' as a sociological specialism but instead simply conceive of themselves, like Garfinkel, as doing generic ethnomethodology and conversation analysis: there is a real distinction of focus here.[1]

The following contribution is meant to instrumentalise ethnomethodology and conversation analysis to achieve a better analytical examination of the legal process. However, no longer an end in itself, conversation analysis itself no longer suffices, authorising, at the same time, the reintroduction of other analytical perspectives, provided, however, that any ironic attitude be renounced, and any impending position by which the sociologist would substitute him or herself for the interactants in the enunciation of what they do in reality. This assumes, in the sociological study of law, that neither professional nor lay knowledge, nor the sociological and positive knowledge of law are dichotomised. Succinctly stated, it could be said that in the matter of law, it would be wrong to view laypersons and professionals as 'legal dopes'.[2]

A second remark pertains to methodological differences brought about by the existence of procedural differences. The interest in legal interactions is by no means indifferent to the context of Egyptian law that can be schematically linked to the civil law family. The formal procedure is, therefore, very distinct from that which is followed in the common law system. Thus, while Paul Drew can assert that, 'in the adversarial Anglo-American criminal-judicial system, cross-examination is essentially hostile',[3] it should be noted that, in the system of civil law, the very principle of cross-examination does not really exist. This difference in procedural organisation has major consequences for the forms of verbal expression and for its utilisation.

In criminal matters, the Egyptian legal system follows the inquisitorial procedure proper to laws of Romano-Germanic tradition. This means that the occurrences of an act likely to entail penal consequences is automatically transferred to the Public Prosecutor's Office, the institution charged with conducting the inquiry and preliminary investigation of the case. In this context, the victim of the punishable act is removed from the case as party in the legal action and the public prosecutor takes the victim's place. The victim is, therefore, only called upon as a witness. The public prosecutor, after having heard the different protagonists in the case, establishes the facts and gives a first decision as to admissibility. It is thus for this person to consider the matter as closed or to hand it over to the court. In theory, the representative of the Public Prosecutor's Office (substitute for the public prosecutor) provides a *verbatim* transcript of the depositions given to him by the different protagonists whom he has summoned to investigate the case. On that basis, the public prosecutor drafts a statement (which, when handed over to the court, is entitled 'inventory of the elements of proof'). The court hears the speeches for the defence with this document as reference, submitting the matter for decision by the bench and pronouncing its judgement. According to the nature of the case, the court is composed of one or three judges. The court sessions are not transcribed. The ruling, on the other hand, is written.

The above leads to a third observation. The study of the process of the production of legality is closely dependent upon the very nature of the procedure followed before the judicial instances. In the case with which we are concerned, two particularly important points must be underscored: the essentially written nature of the legal process and the very particular organisation of the hearings conducted by the public prosecutor.

In criminal matters, the role of the advocates consists, above all, in structuring the account of the protagonist-*cum*-client so as to render it legally relevant. The low degree of interaction in this exercise should be noted. While the advocate can first be prevailed upon to ask a number of questions to the client in order to be able to construct a relevant account – which entails reflexive interaction – the advocate then, in a second instance, produces a general written and oral account, legally restructured to serve both to orient the client and to become a substitute for the client before the magistrate. It is only in a marginal way that the advocate will intervene during the interrogation of the client in order to rectify a point. It should also be noted that the sentence is not delivered in the Egyptian judicial system by a judge attended by a jury.

This difference in structure is essential in the analysis of the process of legalisation. Actually, it entails the complete adaptation of what has been established through conversation analysis such as applied in the process proper to common law. This assumes, among other things, that the study is directed towards specific materials which, until proof of the contrary, have not been considered in terms of conversationalist research and that the conclusions proper to the work on cross-examination and the jury are only quite indirectly utilised, to mention only two types of well-known research. In fact, in the Egyptian legal process, verbal interaction is, on the whole, rather minor. Sometimes a specific question is addressed to the accused, to the victim or to a witness, and sometimes there is a request for a speech by the defence lawyer – and this, itself, is generally reduced to its simplest expression on account of the extreme overload of the courts (seldom fewer than 200 cases are taken up during one and the same session, sometimes over 1000 are taken). Deliberations of courts and tribunals are generally done on the basis of a draft ruling drawn up by a magistrate and rarely discussed in detail among colleagues.

The substitute for the public prosecutor is directed by virtue of formal rules governing the organisation of the work to conduct an interrogation, the context of which is transcribed *verbatim* by the substitute's secretary. It is, however, important to note that matters generally do not proceed exactly in that manner. In most of the hearings which it was possible to attend, the interrogation took place in two stages. First of all, the substitute, after having confirmed the identities of the suspect, the victim or the witness, calls for a general account, beginning with a very broad question of the type: 'What are the details of what you admit having done?' Having heard the account in its generality and without the latter having been transcribed, the substitute takes up the account, point for point, organising it around a series of questions it is made necessary to pose by virtue of rules proper to his professional activity. The reconfiguration of the account around legally relevant questions is a fundamental element in the process of legalisation. It is to be observed that the interactive character of these hearings is greater than at the previous (lawyer) and subsequent (judge) levels in the judicial sequence. Also to be noted is the absence at this stage, as at the others, of any 'overhearing audience',[4] that is, of a silent auditor to whom the interactants address themselves beyond their direct verbal exchange.

The different protagonists of the hearing do not interact in having to address themselves simultaneously to a silent auditor, as is the case in a cross-examination which is directed at the jury. This remark can, however, be differentiated if the interaction is re-inscribed in the framework of the long sequence of the criminal proceedings. In fact, it can be assumed that the protagonists and, no doubt, the substitute for the public prosecutor more than those interrogated, address themselves indirectly to the judge who, at a subsequent stage, will be called upon to take cognisance of the facts such as revealed in the inquiry report and to make a ruling on this basis. Perhaps one should thus speak of an 'overreading audience', that is, of a silent and absent reader to whom the interactants address themselves beyond this direct verbal exchange, an auditor, in other words, for whom the hearing is deferred in time.

A fourth observation pertains to the notion of context. The context sensitivity assumed by the ethnomethodological and conversational study of the judicial sequence requires that it be resituated in the overall context of the Egyptian legal process. This implies a consideration of the extra-verbal elements in the interaction. One can illustrate this point by way of example. In the matter of drug trafficking, the police generally refer the matter to the substitutes of the public prosecutor, addressing a police report to them recording an infraction. It is widely known among members of the Public Prosecutor's Office that this police report commonly relates the facts by following a standard scenario that leads to the establishment of the crime. For the police, it is not so much a matter of describing the facts as they have occurred as of producing an account which records the crime according to the rules of the genre. Thus, it is, above all, necessary that the account be devoid of the frequent infringements of legality which, were they noted, would result in a legal flaw and in a nullification of the entire procedure.

The hyper-contextuality to which one would be circumscribed out of concern for ethnomethodological and conversational orthodoxy would risk leading to an omission of the factors proper to a larger though still-accountable context. It might be said that a contextualising context does not authorise neglect of the fact that the context is already contextualised.

One of the first consequences to be drawn from the introduction of the notion of contextualised context is to not limit the information from a given legal sequence to a single segment of this sequence, but, on the contrary, to extend it to the entire sequence in which the segment is inscribed. In other words, a punctual judicial operation must be considered as a segment in a long sequence.

From the perspective of the analysis of a single segment in the legal sequence (1 in the diagram), the interaction, in the first instance *a*, pits Q (the interrogator) against R (the respondent), the interrogator drawing up, in the second instance *b*, a report for the sake of its recipient D. If, on the other hand, one takes up the idea of the 'overreading audience' (2 in the diagram), the interaction *a* is no longer binary but becomes ternary by introducing the silent auditor (A) of the verbal interaction into the interaction itself Q-R-(A). In a second instance *b*, Q also draws up a report for the sake of its recipient D who was, in the first instance *a*, the third party in the interaction (D = (A)). The same is the case for the interaction between the policeman and

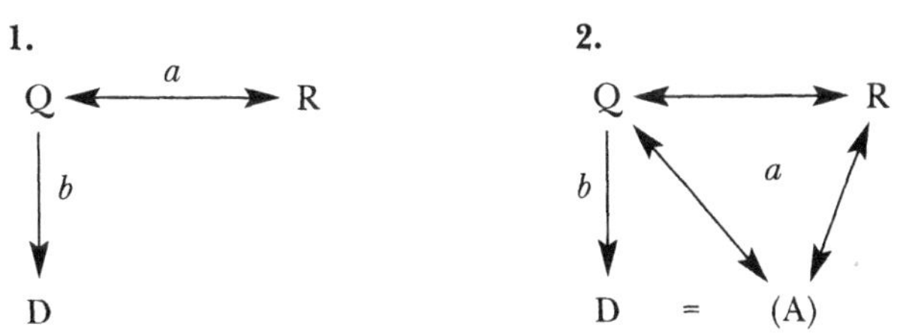

the accused. Because he must respect a certain number of rules of form, the policeman conducts his interrogation by pre-empting the objections which the substitute for the public prosecutor could make to him. In fact, the interaction with the third party of the interaction functions in the manner of the 'absent third'. Without physically participating in the interaction, the absent third closely conditions it.

This diagram would, of course, be more complex were it to relate to the legal sequence in its entirety: police interrogation, report to the substitute (discussion with the lawyer), interrogation conducted by the substitute, report to the court (pleas by the advocate) and deliberation of the court. It is, therefore, in our view, fundamental to account for all the interactants, whether physically present or not, in each segment of the long legal sequence.

A final remark concerns the utility of the notion of typification to which one turns in the study of the legal process. This notion is far from being solely the reserve of ethnomethodology and conversation analysis. Bernard Jackson, for example, proposes a model of law analysis in terms of narrative typifications.[5] Setting out from the question of the comparison of factual situations with a collective image (for example, that of 'acting like a thief'), he develops the idea of a paradigm at a distance from which are located the events that take place and that are evaluated by the different social actors. The collective image is, therefore, both the description of a typical action and the social evaluation of the performance. Comparison with the collective image in this way constitutes a transfer of modality. This is what Jackson terms a 'narrative typification of action', three characteristics of which can be distinguished. Firstly, it does not produce demonstrable judgements of what relates or not to the collective image (it is not a definition in terms of necessary and sufficient conditions), but produces judgements of relative similarity. Such a typification is not a neutral description, but comprises a form of evaluation. Lastly, certain typifications are characteristic of certain semiotic groups which are differentiated by the systems of signification (although they can, in part, be superimposed).

The narrative typifications quite evidently do not function mechanically, but, on the contrary, in a negotiated and interactionist manner.[6] The law, whether a matter of rules, decisions or other indictments and speeches for the defence makes use of narrative models in an institutional frame.[7] The legal decision to take only this, thus becomes a procedure of comparison, more evaluative than constative, of concurrent narrative units, unit(s) of fact and unit(s) of rules.

From an even more pragmatic perspective of typification, Alfred Schütz proposed his general thesis of the reciprocity of perspectives which is founded on two idealisations: the interchangeability of points of view and the conformity of the system of relevance. The reflection operates by referring to already available types, which are organised in schemas of experience and which are oriented around past experiences and consigned to the actor's stock of experience.[8] Along the lines of Schütz, ethnomethodologists have been sensitive to the social generativeness of categories. Thus, for Garfinkel, categories are both principles in the construction of reality and emerging objective realities. This is most particularly evident in his analysis of the case of Agnes, a transsexual.[9]

The realisation of categories from this perspective is oriented and constrained by a schema of naturalness and normality, that of the 'natural and normal woman' in this case. This schema provides the rules and methods of configuration of conduct, dispositions and recognisable attitudes such as realisations of the category 'natural and normal woman'. It consists of a system of conventional beliefs: persons subscribe to definitions held to be self-evident because they are legitimate; they generally take the form of background expectations of current life which they use as reference points to configure their conduct and to constitute, by interpretation, that which assumes for them the 'appearances of familiar events'. Sacks, for his part, developed a few essential insights to explore the operating value of categories in the sequential organisation of the course of action and in the construction of the observability, analysability and describability of social phenomena.

These insights can be summarised in four points: the regulated character of the selection of categories in the identification of persons, objects or events and the normative nature of the categories (collections of rights and duties); the supportive role played by the categories in the organisation and actualisation of common-sense knowledge of the social world; the sequential and temporal organisation of the courses of action (the selection of categories to define a situation makes the manner of treatment of this situation accessible just as the co-selection of categories ensures the congruence of the order of relevance necessary for the inter-comprehension and co-ordination of the action) and the capacity to make the phenomena visible and observable.[10]

Intentionality: a classic perspective

Preliminary remarks having been made, a detour must now be taken with what will be described as a classic approach to the question of intention in legal theory and philosophy so as to be in a position to put this approach in perspective with the pragmatic process, which is proposed, if not as an alternative, then at least as an indispensable complement.

The study by Mauss of the notion of the person[11] can conveniently serve as a point from which to begin such a classic description of intention in law. Mauss describes a broad evolutionary movement from a simple masquerade to the mask, from a personage to a person, a name, an individual, from the latter to a being with metaphysical and moral value, from a moral conscience to a sacred being and from that sacred being to a fundamental form of thought and action which would result in this fundamental category of contemporary understanding: the person.

It is from this perspective that a few recurrent notions of Kantian and Freudian discourse such as autonomy, liberty, will, conscience and intention are classically designated as markers of the modern conception of the person. The will, defined as the 'faculty to freely determine to act or to abstain', constitutes, along with autonomy, one of the cornerstones of modern philosophy and epistemology. According to Kantian thinking, the subject has become a causal principle of a certain force, termed 'action' or 'intentional process'.

> The subject, the Kantian 'cogito', is an autonomous instance ascribing a certain objectivity to objects in the world: objects as such, only becoming knowable in terms of the very subject which gives them a certain meaning which is never determined once and

> for all in itself, but which is always an expression of the intentionality of the subject in its actions and interactions.[12]

Liberty is also classically associated with will. 'The human being can only judge what is proper through the use of the faculty called will for the idea of will assumes the existence of other faculties through which the will can express itself.'[13] The legal principle of the autonomy of will, a veritable basis of the law of contract, probably best expresses the importance of this philosophical concept in law. Will, autonomy, liberty and intentionality thus form the very foundations of the philosophical economy of modern law, and one immediately perceives all the implications which the concept of the subject acting freely and autonomously can have in terms of responsibility, imputation, premeditation, decision or judgement – all notions which are very much seen to be present if only one looks quickly at the many codes of law.

The place occupied by responsibility in the philosophy of law originates in the Kantian philosophy of causality and imputation by virtue of which one must consider oneself as the unique and ultimate point of what happens to oneself with the notion of fault as the point of articulation. One cannot fail to observe at which point the theory of responsibility underwent a very considerable evolution in the course of the twentieth century, which not only saw it being substituted for a principle of solidarity in certain areas, but also led to its break-up in other areas (for example, with the notion of hazard in labour law), also marking the passage from a philosophy of individual fault to a philosophy of collective reparation.[14] It is nevertheless important to note that this extension in space and prolongation in time of the legal philosophy of responsibility does not occur in the sense of a de-individuation, but indeed in that of a reinforcement of the exigency of forethought and of the collectivisation of reparation. It is, in fact, not only a question of the imputation of fault, but also, anteriorly, of exigency of precaution and prudence and, posteriorly, of assumption of responsibility for the potential effects of the acts of each person.

Very interesting developments have been proposed by Herbert Hart regarding the questions of responsibility, causality and intentionality, particularly, in his *Causation in the Law* (1985) and *Punishment and Responsibility* (1968). In both works, the author closely examines legal reasoning and views it from the perspective of common sense. By briefly presenting Hart's demonstration, I believe that it is possible to identify a problem. The means that he employs to affirm the meaning assumed by certain notions in law and in common sense and the manner in which one ties up with the other do not, however, receive an entirely satisfying response. It is precisely at this level that the pragmatic perspective can cast new light on the matter.

The problem regarding intention, the only problem to concern us here, is in part subsumed, at least in the philosophy of law, under the broader question of causality and its relation to will. Intentionality is, in effect, a property of the cause of harm that is necessary to establish criminal responsibility in a number of important crimes. In other words, it is because the activation of the trigger (cause) is wilful (intention) that the death of the victim is defined as murder and sentenced as such. But again, intention is the moral quality of a physical act which has caused a certain harm. This does not mean that contemporary criminal law necessarily assumes culpable intention for all crimes. The complete theory of recklessness is there to affirm that the law demands the presence of a positive (will) or negative (lack of foresight) mental element.

Responsibility thus involves

> A minimum volitional and cognitive involvement, minimum volitional involvement being that his conduct would be an act (that is, an intentional corporeal movement and not a merely suffered movement, the effect of some physiological mechanism or of an external cause such as a physical force exerted by an other), minimal cognitive involvement being that the agent would be aware of what he does. [This involvement] is minimum in the sense that it is not necessary that one acted willingly, that one subscribed to one's act or that one had desired or intended the consequences of one's act, in order to be responsible for it. One is, therefore, responsible for acts carried out under threat because, although it is true that in such cases, one acts unwillingly, one acts despite everything intentionally and with a precise aim which is to avoid that the other carries out the harm which threatens us.[15]

Questions regarding causality appear at all levels of the law. Generally speaking, the question with which the courts are most often confronted is whether a human act or omission caused any tort. In the domain of criminal law, to which we limit ourselves here, the causal relation between the action of the accused and the specific tort which was suffered must be established, so as to establish responsibility. Hart and Honoré show how,

> as in tort, so in criminal law, courts have often limited responsibility by appealing to the causal distinctions embedded in ordinary thought with their emphasis on voluntary interventions and abnormal or coincidental events as factors negativing responsibility.[16]

It is thus the moral nature of the cause which determines the criminal responsibility and the punishment of the crime. This is again found in the utilisation of legal standards in the matter of error or ignorance as that of 'the wise and prudent man'; it is according to what one would have done in similar circumstances that one evaluates the accused conduct.

Most systems of law distinguish, in the definition of crime and its punishment, whether or not a crime is the product of a particular mental state disposing the perpetrator to the crime. In other words, intention is introduced as the determining principle of criminal responsibility and in relation to the severity of the punishment. Actually, criminal responsibility is first linked to the fact that the person has committed a crime and, second, that the person carried it out in a certain frame of mind or of will. The question of this mental state is generally raised to two levels, that of culpability and that of the evaluation of the sanction. At the level of culpability, the establishment of intention is generally sufficient, above all, for important crimes (although there are some exceptions). At the level of sanction, the character of intention which is established influences the degree of punishment.

'The concept which legal theorists speak of and define as intention diverges from its counterpart in ordinary use at certain points which are of immediate interest to the philosophy of punishment.'[17] It is first appropriate to note the existence of a rich vocabulary which, while always accounting for the concept, nevertheless provides it with nuances: 'intentionally', 'maliciously', 'wilfully' and 'recklessly' are some words used in legal English to express slightly different definitions of intention. Nevertheless, for Hart it is possible to distinguish what, in law, corresponds to intention. It is a matter of three interdependent parts which can be presented as 'intentionally doing something', 'doing something with a further intention' and 'bare intention'. In the latter case, it is the sole intention of doing something without anything being done to realise the intention in question. This hypothesis is not taken up as such in criminal law, contrary to civil law. In the second case – to do something with a further intention – one can take the example of a man who enters the house of another at night.

Here the question does not bear so much on the intention of entering the house as on the further intention of stealing something. If yes, the man would be found guilty of burglary, even though he may not have stolen anything. Numerous crimes are defined in terms of further intention, such as 'wounding with intent to kill'. Finally, in the first case – intentionally doing something – one can take the example of a man who shot at another with a firearm and wounded or killed him. To the question as to whether he intentionally wounded him, the response will be that the physical movement of the body which led the finger to press the trigger expresses, until proven otherwise, a murderous intention, proof to the contrary eventually showing that he had thought the weapon not loaded or that he had not seen his victim at the moment that he fired. Apart from the element of volition, the intervention of three other factors will be noted: a physical element (the movement of the body), the result and the circumstances.

The combination of all these elements makes it possible to observe one of the points upon which legal theory and common sense are opposed. In effect, a person will be considered guilty if the prejudicial consequences were foreseeable by him or her if he or she thought that they could result from the wilful act, even if the consequences as such were not desired. In other words:

> The law therefore does not require in such cases that the outcome should have been something intended in the sense that the accused set out to achieve it, either as a means or an end, and here the law diverges from what is ordinarily meant by expressions like 'he intentionally killed those men'.[18]

Actually, a result simply foreseen, but not intended, is generally not considered, apart from the law, as intentional. Generally, because there also exist situations where action and result are at this point connected such that it would appear absurd to say that an individual could act in a certain manner without intending that the action lead to this result (for example, someone striking a crystal vase with a hammer: even if he did it with the aim of hearing the sound of metal against crystal, common sense will consider that he broke the vase intentionally).

Following Bentham and Austin, legal philosophy has classically distinguished oblique intention, which corresponds to the foresight alone of the consequences, and direct intention, in which consequences are an end conceived to be realised. The law condemns the author of an act, the intention of which was oblique, whereas common sense will consider that the author has not acted intentionally. Hart gives the example of a man who, considering himself to be an execrable shot, shoots to kill and, contrary to his expectations, hits the target. In law, the man is guilty of murder. This is, no doubt, explained by the fact that in the two cases (direct and oblique intention), the author of the act is considered to have control over the alternatives open to him (to shoot or not to shoot). However, it will be noted that the English courts make a distinction between direct intention and oblique intention in cases of ulterior intent. In this case, it is pertinent to demonstrate that the accused considered the result of his action as an end or as the means to achieve that end. In other words, even when the bare intention is not punishable as such, jurisprudence punishes as an attempt the fact of doing something which is not itself a tort if it is carried out with the further intention of committing a crime.

In short, it should be noted that

> it is [the] principle of the autonomy of the individual which appears to be the point of convergence of our judgements as to responsibility. The fact of linking responsibility either to the wilful and cognitive involvement of the agent or to his ability, in principle, to attain a certain level of prudence and of reflection in his social interactions is explained by a fundamental decision in our system of responsibility in favour of the individual who is master of his choices, able to orient his conduct in conformity or disagreement with a system of norms.[19]

That, briefly presented, is where the philosophical and analytical study of the notion of intention results. To us, this appears to be both much and little. Much, in the sense that the different parameters of representation of intentionality are broken up and analysed in detail to reveal most of the possible scenarios. It is, however, little insofar as the common sense of intention is only constructed on the basis of hypotheses founded on the presumed ordinary use of words, whereas its legal concept is conceived only on the basis of a reading of the jurisprudence independent of any examination of the practical construction of the meaning in the different stages of the legal procedure. I should now attempt to show that the conceptions of intentionality do not correspond to an *a priori* definable semantic field outside the context of their interactional implementation. In other words, if Hart raises in this matter a number of perfectly relevant questions, he cannot give them an entirely satisfying response in his treatment of them. It is, in fact, a matter of recognising the contingent, contextual and normative nature of intention which is thoroughly constructed, utilised, reproduced and transformed by people in their daily interactions.

Intentionality: a pragmatic approach

Rather than considering that the actors find themselves subsumed in a context of action for which learned and incorporated rules are applicable and rather than analysing, consequently, the actions as if they were guided or caused by these rules, I propose adopting an approach which considers norms and rules as maxims for conduct.[20] As Hart himself underscores, when speaking of the rule of law:

> Particular fact-situations do not await us already marked off from each other, and labelled as instances of the general rule, the application of which is in question; nor can the rule itself step forward to claim its own instances. [...] Canons of 'interpretation' cannot eliminate, though they can diminish, these uncertainties; for these canons are themselves general rules for the use of language, and make use of general terms which themselves require interpretation. They cannot, any more than other rules, provide for their own interpretation.[21]

In other words,

> Legal rules cover an indefinite range of contingent, concrete possibilities. The rules must, in short, be applied, and to specific

> configurations of circumstances which may never be identical. [...] [T]he precedent having been established, there must still be a judgement as to whether the next occasion is sufficiently similar to fall within the scope of the prior judgement.[22]

This can be termed the indexical and reflexive nature of normative phenomena, that is the tendency of events to point towards the norms to which reference is made and towards the signification these same norms receive through the fact of their implementation in the course of action.

To follow a rule can be understood as a typifying practice. In Husserl, one notes the existence of a foreknowledge typical of things which operates before any predicative judgement. Expressed in sociological terms, that means that people immediately grasp things, events and persons as belonging to a species with its typical properties within 'a horizon of familiarity and pre-acquaintanceship which is, as such, just taken for granted until further notice as the unquestioned, though at any time questionable stock of knowledge at hand'.[23] This means that, 'events have "normal patterns" and "usual causes" of occurrence that can be relied upon'.[24] These schemas are certainly vague, but the actors first display their perception of the normality of events and it is only in incongruous situations that they seek explanations for the threat weighing upon normality. It is in this sense that persons are (made) morally responsible for any breach of what is perceived as the normal course of events.

Legal categories do not elude the schema of naturalness and normality. Thus, the idea of the normal person constitutes one of the points of reference for practical legal reasoning with, in consequence, the ideas of volition and cognition attached to it. As such, the conscious and intentional person, far from being an abstract and inaccessible category, is publicly constituted with the help of the methodical deployment of public, that is linguistic resources in social interaction.[25] The realisation of this category of person is, from this perspective, oriented and circumscribed by the schema of the natural and normal person, conscious and endowed with an autonomous will. This background is constantly mobilised even though it remains largely unexplained and loosely defined. That being so, to be defined as a person largely depends on the capacity of persons to present a normal appearance and to expect to be treated by others on this basis. As Harvey Sacks notes,

> In public places persons are required to use the appearances others present as grounds for treating them. Persons using public spaces are concurrently expected by others to present appearances which can be readily so used, and expect others to treat their own appearances at face value.[26]

Thus, one is not confronted with persons naturally conscious and endowed with will, but with the consciousness and will of the naturalised person in such a manner that one can evaluate the conformity and will of each occurrence and of the general type with all the rights and duties belonging to this type – which ethnomethodology terms 'membership categorisation device'.

Let us take a concrete example from the Egyptian legal context. The following excerpt is the account of a girl alleged to have been the victim of an attempted rape, redefined by the public prosecutor as breach of modesty (*hitk 'ird*).

> Question of the substitute: What took place?
> Response of the victim: I was on the street that day...when I met those two there...and they said to me come with us and they made me get into a taxi...and they went behind the Arsenal.
> Q: What was their intention in acting like that?
> R: They told me Don't worry, we are going to drink tea together.
> Q: Why did you not call for help when they took you...?
> R: I tried to scream and I rolled on the ground, but the street was empty.
> Q: What is the number of the taxi in which they took you?
> R: I don't know, this happened on the street.
> Q: Why did you not ask the taxi driver for help?
> R: The driver was afraid of them and he did what they told him to do.
> Q: What was their intention in taking you with them?
> R: I think they wanted to attempt [an attack] on my virtue, otherwise they would not have taken me to that place.
> Q: Did you know them before?
> R: No.
> Q: Do you have anything else to say?
> R: No.
>
> (Case no 5471, 1977, Mahram Bey, Alexandria)

This excerpt illustrates several interesting points as regards the question of intentionality. It will be noted that the act is always presented as having a motivation. Here, fear and trust are combined in such a way as to motivate the girl's consent to go with the two boys (Q: 'What was their intention in acting like that?' R: 'They told me Don't worry, we are going to drink tea together') and to not refuse to get into the taxi ('...and they made me get into the taxi'). On the other hand, the substitute is always seeking an individual act ('Why did you not call for help when they took you...?') which was motivated ('Why did you not ask the taxi driver for help?') and had a purpose ('What was their intention in taking you with them?'). This should be underscored insofar as it shows how the substitute constructs the interrogation with practical ends, that is, in anticipation of the different stages that have to be crossed around legally relevant questions of the type 'who did what to which purpose'.

The cases of minors and of the mentally deficient prove to be particularly interesting in the pragmatic study of the notion of intention on at least two levels. First, on the level of the intention or consent of the victim. Criminal law establishes a presumption of the absence of consent in sexual relations on the part of the minor. Consequently, the substitute's action is directed towards the establishment of minority. The first example below is taken from a case of abduction and rape of a minor, and the second from a case of attempted rape of a mentally deficient minor.

> Q: What are the distinctive features of the missing girl and what is her age?
> R: Her name is Thanâ' Husayn Qâsim, she is eight years old, she is fair-skinned and has blonde hair, she is wearing jeans and a yellow tee-shirt.
>
> (Case no 5719, 1996, Rûd al-Farag, Cairo)

> Q: What is his approximate age?
> R: He is seventeen or eighteen years old and has been mentally retarded since his birth.
>
> (Case no 7158, Sâhil, Cairo)

In both cases, however, the substitute attempts to go beyond these presumptions to discover the intention of the victim – I shall later return to the intentions of the aggressor and of the witness. In the first case, the substitute directs several questions to the parents of the girl so as to determine a background upon which to construct a plausible and legally definable scenario. The explanations given by one parent of the victim clearly reveal that the latter is aware of the inferential significance of his responses.

> Q: Does the missing girl suffer from a psychological or nervous illness?
> R: No, she is well.
> Q: Has she already disappeared before?
> R: No.
> Q: Which places does the missing girl frequent?
> R: None, she played in the street.
>
> (Case no 5719, 1996, Rûd al-Farag, Cairo)

In the second case, it is a question, even though the mental retardation of the victim does not constitute an aggravating circumstance in the case of breach of modesty, to demonstrate that there could not have been a consent by the victim as the latter is mentally deficient.

> Q: Based on the facts to which you were party, was your son in agreement with this assault or did he resist?
> R: My son is mentally retarded and he knows nothing and remained silent.
>
> (Case no 7158, 1993, Sâhil, Cairo)

The intention of the aggressor is also sought in such a manner so as to be able to define the act in accordance with the categories of law. The aggressor, whose responses are clearly oriented according to the inferential significance which he knows can be attributed to them, can adopt different attitudes. In the first case, he seems to shift the intention towards an outside agency.

> Q: What is the context of the discussion which took place between yourself and the victim?
> R: The devil sometimes rises in me and I said to myself: I should amuse myself with her in whatever way so that she comes to my place with me so that I sleep with her and I said to her...
>
> (Case no 5719, 1996, Rûd al-Farag, Cairo)

In the second case, the aggressor has recourse to a strategy to avoid detrimental inferences.

> Q: At first sight, is this a question of a person who can understand?
> R: He speaks in a jerky manner.
> Q: Is he mentally retarded?
> R: I don't know.

Q: You have known the victim since 1978 and you do not know if he is mentally retarded or not, notwithstanding the fact that it is obvious that he is mentally retarded?
R: I don't know.

(Case no 7158, 1993, Sâhil, Cairo)

The intentionality of the witness can also be questioned as the following excerpt shows.

Q: Do you suspect that her disappearance is criminal?
R: No.
Q: What is your purpose in making this deposition?
R: To take the steps necessary to find her.

(Case no 5719, 1996, Rûd al-Farag, Cairo)

This question may appear to be quite absurd. However, it reveals that the substitute does not want to neglect any hypothesis, including the possibility of the involvement of the parent who comes to make the deposition. Raising this question, he solicits a response, the possible incongruity of which would direct him to explore an alternative track. This explanation is confirmed during a later interrogation, at which time the substitute raises the question of the delay made in informing the police.

Q: What do you know about her disappearance from the house on 11 October 1996 until she was found?
R: I don't know where she was, but I heard a child from the corner say that a strange man had called her while she was playing with them and said, bring me soap from the grocer and gave her money and when she returned, he gave her twenty-five piastres and he took her into the house where we found her.
Q: When precisely were you given this information?
R: I know all that from the little boy since the day that my daughter disappeared from the house.
Q: How do you explain not having made a deposition about all that until now?
R: I told myself, those are the words of a child and we were not certain.

(Case no 5719, 1996, Rûd al-Farag, Cairo)

It indeed appears that, in the criminal process, the substitute would be seeking a legally relevant definition obtained by producing a narration of events centred around the accounts of the persons interrogated and reconstructed to the purpose of their future use in the legal process. The accounts of the persons are thus solicited to then be sifted for possible incongruities with an alternative schema in which normality would appear between the lines as implicitly suggested by the substitute.[27]

This pragmatic exploration of intentionality cannot be continued without introducing the fundamental question as to the context in which it is solicited, identified and instrumentalised for subsequent judicial ends. It clearly emerges from the preceding examples that the interactants, the members of the group of participants in the legal interaction, manifestly orient themselves to the particular context of this interaction. Generally, it can be established that statements and acts are shaped by the context which, at the same time, they renew. They are shaped by the context in the sense that statement and act must be referred to the activity immediately preceding them and to the larger environment in which this sequence takes place. They renew it in the sense that statement and act are, at the same time, results of a previous sequence and the basis of subsequent sequences.[28]

The legal context is institutional, which gives it three distinct characteristics: the discourse in this context is conditioned by its orientation towards a goal; the interaction can be subject to certain particular constraints and the discourse can be associated with inferential frames and procedures. In the first place, 'both lay and professional participants generally show an orientation to institutional tasks or functions in the design of their conduct, most obviously by the kinds of goals they pursue',[29] even though such an orientation could change according to local contingencies of interaction and locally defined status of the interactants. In the second place, the conduct is often shaped in an institutional environment by reference to goal-oriented constraints. Moreover, in view of specific contexts such as in the courtroom, it appears that 'participants shape their conduct by reference to powerful and legally enforceable constraints which impart a distinctly "formal" character to the interaction'.[30] In the third place, inferences and implications tend to be specifically developed in institutional interaction.

All these characteristics are not without consequence on the system of turns at speaking, the attitude of the interactants, the range of institutional options, the proceduralisation of interaction, the institutionalisation of the incongruity mechanism, the lexical choice, the organisation of the sequence, the standardisation of the schemas of interaction and of professional practices and the asymmetric organisation of interaction. In the legal frame, this asymmetry is particularly to be found in the configuration of exchange around the system of questions and responses and in the different strata of knowledge available to and used by laymen and professionals. In addition, the strongly routinised nature of professional action should be noted. This all means, to return to intentionality, that attention must be given to the characterisations which persons ascribe to each other in real contexts and not to the de-contextualised presumptions as to attitude and membership. The institutional frame assigns roles and types of intentions to persons belonging to it, making a number of inferences possible.

The fact that the parties are oriented towards the institutional framework and its procedural implications (the trial) means that they are aware of questions concerning personal involvement and intentions. This research intends to show that the definition of intention is inferred from concrete interactional circumstances and information and is not necessarily deduced from theoretical treatises. In the case of intention, as in other instances, representations concerning the profound nature of conscience are not at work, but rather it is the very practical and concrete orientation of persons towards a very practical and concrete result in an interactional situation inscribed in a legal frame and on the basis of discourse and accounts from which every protagonist understands to draw a certain number of inferences. The latter operate as the basis of an interplay of congruence and incongruity between the typification considered to be normal and the factual accounts. Every protagonist is involved in producing a sense of normality and an account, the facts of which are in line with or demarcate this normality. This obtains in the case of the accused as well of other protagonists: victim, witness and substitute, all of whom tend to produce an account articulating the intentional or non-intentional character of the act and the inferences which follow therefrom. Without entering into details, I give a number of typical excerpts below recapitulating a few variations of intention in action.

I have already mentioned the case of the girl who was allegedly the victim of an attempted rape.

Q: What took place?
R: I was on the street that day...when I met those two there...and they said to me come with us and they made me get into a taxi... and they went behind the Arsenal.
Q: What was their intention in acting like that?
R: They told me Don't worry, we are going to drink tea together. [...]
Q: What was their intention in taking you with them?
R: I think they wanted to attempt (an attack) on my virtue, otherwise they would not have taken me to that place. [...]
Q: Did you know them before?
R: No.
Q: Do you have anything else to say?
R: No.

(Case no 5471, 1977, Mahram Bey, Alexandria)

This excerpt clearly shows how the victim organises her words around the idea of the normal conduct which she had adopted (walking in the street). Conversely, the conduct of the accused is at odds and stands in contrast (they went behind the Arsenal), even if it did not at first appear as such – the victim thus provides the elements which make it possible to explain that she was deceived (we are going to drink tea together). The substitute participates in the production of this effect of incongruity by raising the question as to whether the girl knew her aggressors before. Had she known them, her having left with them to drink tea would not have been surprising. Had she not known them, it would, on the contrary, be clearly more surprising and it is no doubt at this level that the idea of force usefully arose (they made me get into a taxi). For the victim, her own intention is congruent with a normal schema which she constructed with her own words. Conversely, the same victim underscores the incongruity of the intention of the accused with the same normal schema. In other words, criminal intention and abnormality in terms of the schema correspond to each other.

Now, turning to the accused, I reproduce an excerpt of the interrogation conducted by the president of the criminal court in a case in which the individual accused of murder pleads the fact that he was under the sway of evil spirits at the time of the act.

Q: Why did you take Qiddisa Tumas with you on the tenth of Ramadan?

R: At the request of the victim, because there was no one who knew that she had an evil spirit and she feared that people would find out.
Q: How did you know that the victim was possessed by the devil or evil spirits?
R: She told me that she had headaches and hallucinations and I told her: You are possessed by a devil. [...]
Q: What happened to the victim when you prayed for her?
R: I felt feverish and in a terrible state of confusion and I lifted the veil she...and she did not respond and I did not know what to do.
Q: Did you undertake to move the body by yourself to the place at the bottom of the building?
R: There was no one to help me and I do not know how I lifted her.
Q: The pathologist established that the victim was in undergarments.
R: She was wearing all her clothes. [...]
Q: In what position did you place her in the hole?
R: I know nothing. [...]
Q: Was there anyone with you during the prayer for the victim?
R: No, there was no one there during the prayer and she died by herself.
Q: Was the victim wearing gold jewellery on her ears and on her breast?
R: No.
Q: The victim was wearing gold jewellery on her ears and breast.
R: She was not wearing jewellery. [...]
Q: How long did you know the victim?
R: My sister's daughter married her son.
Q: Were there other relatives?
R: No, there were no other relatives than the immediate family. [...]
Q: Have you ever prayed for anyone before and expelled evil spirits from them?
R: Yes.
Q: The daughter of the victim says that she was sane.
R: No, she never spoke with anyone else.
Q: Was there any financial compensation in exchange for that?
R: No, it was crazy.
Q: The pathologist says that you strangled her.
R: No, she died naturally.

(Criminal Court of Cairo, case no 2783, 1997)

This excerpt, somewhat long but certainly worthwhile, points out a great number of details about intention. Regarding motivation and initiative ('I took the victim at her request because she did not want anyone to know she was possessed by the devil'), it is observed that the accused attempts to show an absence of personal interest in initiating the act without, for all that, jeopardising his own credibility.[31] The question of agency is also fundamental ('I felt feverish and in a terrible state of confusion and I lifted the veil, she...and she did not respond and I did not know what to do'). The accused clearly attempts to efface his personal agency in the course of the act while not appearing to be mentally deranged and not jeopardising his credibility in the account that he gives of the action of the spirits. In other words, the accused does his utmost to minimise his active participation in the events by formulating an alternative version involving the participation of a third actor.

In doing this, he affirms common sense regarding the morality of certain matters (for example, knowing that to kill is immoral), but he also avoids the negative inferences which could be drawn on the subject of his own moral qualities. He keeps himself in the background of the scene which allows him to claim to be neither personally responsible nor mentally irresponsible.[32] The accused also attempts to give excuses for the acts committed ('There was no one to help me carry the body and I do not know how I lifted it') by invoking the action of an outside constraint effacing his personal and intentional agency. Finally, one will note the interwoven relationship of questions of personal agency and normality ('There was no one there during the prayer and she died alone, she died naturally').

Each situation is characterised by what is considered to be the normal conduct of the involved actors. In the case of death, the normal and natural character of matters is defined according to the absence of human agency in its cause. The abnormal death is that provoked by the intervention of an outside human agent. For that reason, a death which is due to the action of evil spirits cannot be considered as abnormal, as it does not result from the action of a human agent. On the other hand, suicide is abnormal because it is the result of the victim's own agency. Generally speaking, the accused is thus in the situation of having to show that he or she did not have an intention to do something, that he or she did not have the inclination to carry out what the normal typification negatively evaluates or that his intention could be explained so as to excuse him or herself. In so doing, he struggles in a net of insurmountable dilemmas. Each time, it is important to discern the complexity of the relation which the accused has with the object of the offence around which the punishable intention revolves.

The witness is also involved in the contingent production of a notion of intentionality. The latter, of course, bears on the victim and the accused, but also on the witness. By way of illustration, I shall again consider one of the cases previously mentioned and examine the testimony of the father of the victim.

> Q: For what reason did she leave the house the last time and did someone accompany her?
> R: She left to play in the building because it was her holiday and she played with the children in the building.
> Q: Did the child suffer from any psychological or nervous illness?
> R: No, she was very sane and very lively.
> Q: Was she wearing anything of value?
> R: No, we are poor, God decides.
> Q: Had signs of her womanhood appeared?
> R: No, she was a little girl but fair-skinned and with beautiful blonde hair.
> Q: Had she already disappeared from home previously?
> R: No, she was always a good girl.
> Q: What was the nature of her relationship with the family? Did she have differences with anyone?
> R: No, she was a good girl as far as we and everyone were concerned and no one ever complained about her.
> Q: Do you have differences with anyone?
> R: No, I am a peaceful man and I do not have problems with anyone. [...]
> Q: Who was this person exactly and what was your daughter's relationship to him?
> R: I do not know who it was and the girl also did not know him because the boy said he was a stranger to the quarter. [...]
> Q: Do you suspect that her death was criminal?
> R: Yes, of course.
> Q: Do you suspect someone of having perpetrated this act?
> R: God will triumph over whoever did it.
>
> (Case no 5719, 1996, Rûd al-Farag, Cairo)

The witness gives versions of intention which are closely dependent on his relation to the facts and to the main actors involved in them. This relationship is, above all, marked by exteriority. The witness is not a main protagonist and, as such, his personal agency is not, at least not directly in question. As noted by Renaud Dulong, the witness plays an auxiliary role and his or her person and affects are not of interest.[33] When he attests to the traits, characteristics, acts and gestures of a person, the witness produces a report of his conduct, his credibility and, consequently, of intentions. This is directly oriented towards a practical goal of accentuating figures and situations, of the typifications to which they are subject and, consequently, of possible qualifications of the established acts. Thus, in the example given above, the witness gives a description accentuating the normality and qualities of the child ('She was a good girl, sane and lively, still a child who wore nothing of value'). In so doing, he establishes a marked contrast between this normality and what took place, upon which background the death of his daughter necessarily appears to belong to the category of odious crimes and, by the same token, to qualify morally the presumed author. This becomes even more explicit during the testimony of the mother.

Q: Do you have anything else to say?
R: Yes, I want to say that you should have that fellow hanged.

(Case no 5719, 1996, Rûd al-Farag, Cairo)

It will also be noted that an ethical quality which is at the basis of the veracity of his or her testimony is also demanded of the witness.[34] In other words, the relationship of the witness to the subject of his or her testimony is examined so as to judge the quality of the testimony. The witness must, therefore, also orient the testimony so as to avoid detrimental moral implications which the latter could entail. Here, the witness must account for his or her own intentionality. That could consist in underscoring the typical and normal nature of the witness's situation regarding the victim by having recourse to membership categorization devices (for example, that of father or mother; see the testimony of the father) which render any intention which would be detrimental to himself incongruous.[35] Conversely, any breach of this normal schema (for example, not informing the police of new information reported by the neighbours; cf. excerpt above) must be redressed, this redress also being upheld by categorisation devices with which rights and duties are typically connected (for example, do not trust what is said by a small child).

The last category to be considered is that of the magistrate. By way of illustration, I shall return to the questions asked of the accused in a case of collective rape and the text of the inventory of the elements of proof, a document written by the substitute for the judges of the criminal court.

Minutes of the interrogation

Taking advantage of the presence of the accused, we summoned prisoners who were outside the room in which the inquiry is conducted and asked them to respond to the accusations made against them, after having informed them that the public prosecutor had opened inquiry proceedings against them. They all accepted (having taken cognisance of the matter) and then we asked if they had a representative to appear with them for the inquiry proceedings. They responded in the negative. We had all the accused, except for the first one, leave the room. A young man in his thirties, approximately 1.70 metres and of average build and dark complexion, wearing a blue garment with checks at the bottom and a blue pullover, was examined. We questioned him as to details and he responded: [...]

Q: What are the details of what you admit? [...]
Q: Did you agree to take just any woman from the street? [...]
Q: What sexual acts did you commit with the victim (woman)? [...]
Q: Was the girl willingly in this situation? [...]
Q: Did the female victim go with you of her own will to the place where the female victim was assaulted? [...]
Q: You are accused of participating with others in abduction and rape by force. What do you have to say? [...]
Q: You are also accused of participating with others in the above-mentioned theft by force. What do you have to say?
Q: You are also accused of participating with others in abduction and illegal confinement. What do you have to say? [...]
Q: Do you have a past record? [...]
Q: Do you have anything else to say? [...]

End of the statement of the accused Anwar.

Inventory of the elements of proof

Miss [...], aged 17 years [...], testifies to the fact that she [...] was in the company of her fiancé [...] and that, while they were stopped in the car [...], the accused...threatened them by exhibiting a knife (gazelle horn) and ordered her fiancé to get out of the car. [...] They forced them to get in the taxi driven by the fifth accused and they left for another place [where the first accused undertook to rape her] [...] when gunshots were heard. [They] hastened to get into the car [...], they then proceeded to an inhabited area and stopped in front of a building at the foot of which was a garage in which there was no car. The first accused got out and met the sixth accused, he then returned to the car and told the female victim to enter the garage. She obeyed the order while the sixth accused looked on. The first accused then took out a blanket and a cushion and put them in a room adjoining the garage into which the accused, with the exception of the sixth, entered. Each then removed his clothes and lay on her [...] But she made every effort to resist them and was injured on her left hand as a result of her resistance. She added that the first accused, when he led her into the room adjoining the garage, took possession of two rings she was wearing.

Observations

The first accused said [...] that he had agreed with the second, third, fourth and fifth accused to abduct just any woman whom they met and to rape her. [...] He admitted, in the minutes, at the renewal of his detention...the same thing he had said in the minutes at his arrest. The second accused said the same thing in the minutes at his arrest. [...] He admitted [...] that the first, third, fourth and fifth accused had stolen from the two victims by force, that he had stolen the watch of the male victim on the public thoroughfare by threatening to use the knife he carried and that he had kissed and seized the female victim. The third accused admitted [...] the same thing [...] and he added that he had seized the female victim by force, had lain on her and had kissed her. The fourth accused admitted the same thing as that stated by the first accused, and he added that he had grasped the female victim, seized and kissed her; he also admitted [...] having participated in the rape of the

> female victim. The fifth accused admitted [...] the same thing [...] and he added that he had grasped the female victim, had seized and kissed her; he also admitted that he had agreed with the four first accused to abduct the female victim, to rape her and to steal what she possessed by force. The sixth accused admitted [...] that he knew that the female victim had been abducted and that he had received the two rings and gold chain in return for providing the place where the accused raped the female victim.

Contrary to the victim, the accused or even the witnesses, the substitute for the public prosecutor – the figure of the magistrate in all our examples – saw no dilemma as regards morality, agency or credibility. In the accomplishment of legal work, it is essential for the substitute to produce an account fulfilling the formal conditions of the legal category (participation in the abduction and rape by force, theft by force, abduction and illegal confinement). The substitute must construct legally relevant and definable facts (agreement of the accused equals premeditation, nature of sexual acts equals rape, absence of willingness on the part of the victim equals force). In so doing, it is also indispensable for the substitute to bring to light the individual (the terms 'admit' and 'commit', but also the observations formulated by each of the accused) and the intentional (the terms 'agree', 'admit', 'know') nature of what was perpetrated. Moreover, because this takes place within the framework of routine work consisting of daily repeated procedures within familiar precincts at a time in the legal process in which the professional participants are known as well as their different functions in a controlled sequence of the production of legality, the action of the substitute is above all extremely routinised. The document evidently reproduces a stereotyped formula composed of standardised questions which assumes, in its broad lines, the *General Instructions Addressed to Public Prosecutors in Criminal Cases* as established by a circular notice of the Public Prosecutor's Office.

Conclusions

I have attempted, from a radically non-mentalistic perspective, to reintegrate the question of intention within a contextual framework. Phenomena such as motivation, purpose, intention, thought, affect etc., can be neither reified nor disconnected from the fabric of action, interaction and context through which these phenomena are publicly manifested and hence become observable and relevant.[36] Motives, purposes, reasons and intentions can, in effect, only be understood through systems of discursive exchange. In other words, the mental states and their imputation can only be understood in their linguistic publication. In this sense, we have developed a 'praxiological understanding of the "mental"'.[37]

Although the examples given in this text are 'small-scale objectives', it should nevertheless be noted, as underscored by Michael Moerman, that they are 'sufficiently actual and unimputed to merit painstaking attention from students of the strategic use of speech and of the relations between intentions and actions'.[38] They make it possible to see, case by case, how these strategies are deployed and are adapted to greater ends.

To speak of intention in law assumes that it is understood in act and in context. In so doing, we have observed the action of three factors circumscribing this configuration: the interactional nature of the verbal act, the institutional context in which it is inscribed and the distribution of positions in this context. The intention, its content and the form which it takes, upon which it has a bearing, vary from one individual to the next according to these factors. I have attempted to show that intention, in law, was not a transcendental property of volition, but a practical orientation. It is thus only in its punctual, contingent and local configurations within the constraining framework of its context at each different occasion that it can be analysed. The legal meaning of intention emerges not from pure legal logic, but from the legal environment and interactions. If the philosophy of law delineates, in the manner of Hart, the possible scenarios, on the other hand, it conceals the practical modes of the configuration. These are, however, precisely what constitute the subject of the sociology of legal action.

Notes

1 Personal communication, 18 December 1996.
2 To paraphrase a formula by Garfinkel enjoining that one not take people for 'judgemental dopes' (Garfinkel, 1967, pp. 66–75).
3 Drew, 1992, p. 470.
4 Ibid.
5 Jackson, 1995.
6 Jackson, 1995, pp. 150–151.
7 Jackson, 1988, p. 101.
8 Schütz, 1990.
9 Garfinkel, 1967.
10 Watson, 1994.
11 Mauss, 1950.
12 Stockinger, 1993, p. 48.
13 Pufendorf, quoted in Arnaud, 1993, p. 345.
14 One speaks of the crisis of responsibility 'with, as a starting point, a shift of accent formerly placed on the presumed author of the wrong but today preferably on the victim whom the wrong suffered places in a position to demand redress' (Ricœur, 1995, p. 58), with the passage 'from an individual management of fault to a socialised management of risk' (Engel, 1993). Ricœur stresses the enormous paradox of a 'society which speaks of solidarity only out of concern to electively reinforce a philosophy of risk' and 'the vindictive search for the culprit [which] is equivalent to an instillation of guilt in the identified authors of the wrong' (Ricœur, 1995, p. 59).
15 Neuberg, in Canto-Sperber, 1996: 'responsabilité'.
16 Hart and Honoré, 1985, p. 325.
17 Hart, 1968, pp. 116–17.
18 Hart, 1968, p. 120.
19 Neuberg, in Canto-Sperber, 1996: 'responsabilité'.
20 Wittgenstein, 1989, p. 202.
21 Hart, 1961, p. 123.
22 Heritage, 1984, pp. 121–22.
23 Schütz, 1990, p. 7.
24 Heritage, 1984, p. 77.
25 Watson, 1998, p. 213.
26 Sacks, 1972, p. 281.
27 Regarding this 'procedure in incongruity', cf. Matoesian, 1997; Dupret, 2003. Cf. also Moerman, 1987, p. 61: 'The defendant is accused of having killed for hire, a form of murder rather common in northern Thailand at the time of fieldwork. A usual defence in

such case is that the accused is not the kind of person who would do such a thing, that he comes from a good family, that he does not need money.'

28 Drew and Heritage, 1992, p. 18.
29 Drew and Heritage, 1992, p. 22.
30 Drew and Heritage, 1992, p. 23.
31 Cf. Komter, 1998.
32 Ibid.
33 Dulong, 1998, p. 41.
34 Dulong, 1998, p. 42.
35 Watson, 1983.
36 Watson, 1998.
37 Coulter, 1992.
38 Moerman, 1987, p. 53.

Bibliography

Arnaud, A.J., 'Liberté', in A.J. Arnaud et al. (eds), *Dictionnaire encyclopédique de théorie et de sociologie du droit*, deuxième édition corrigée et augmentée, Paris, Libraire Générale de Droit et de Jurisprudence, 1993, pp. 345–46.

Canto-Sperber, M. (ed.), *Dictionnaire d'éthique et de philosophie morale*, Paris, Presses Universitaires de France, 1996.

Coulter, J., 'Cognition in an ethnomethodological mode', in G. Button (ed.), *Ethnomethodology and the Human Sciences*, Cambridge, Cambridge University Press, 1992, pp. 176–95.

Drew, P., 'Contested evidence in courtroom cross-examination: The case of a trial for rape', in P. Drew and J. Heritage (eds), *Talk at Work: Interaction in Institutional Settings*, Cambridge, Cambridge University Press, 1992, pp. 470–520.

Drew, P. and J. Heritage (eds), *Talk at Work: Interaction in Institutional Settings*, Cambridge, Cambridge University Press, 1992.

Dulong, R., *Le Témoin Oculaire. Les conditions sociales de l'attestation personnelle*, Paris, Éd. de l'École des Hautes Études en Sciences Sociales, 1998.

Dupret, B., 'The Person in an Egyptian Judicial Context: An Ethnomethodological Analysis of Courtroom Proceedings', *International Journal for the Semiotics of Law*, 16/1, 2003, pp. 32–57.

Engel, L., 'Vers une nouvelle approche de la responsabilité. Le droit français face à la dérive américaine', *Esprit*, June 1993, pp. 13–27.

Garfinkel, H., *Studies in Ethnomethodology*, Cambridge, Polity Press, 1967.

Hart, H.L.A. and T. Honoré, *Causation in the Law*, Oxford, Clarendon Press, second edition, 1985 (first printing 1959).

Hart, H.L.A., *The Concept of Law*, Oxford, Oxford University Press, 1961.

– *Punishment and Responsibility: Essays in the Philosophy of Law*, Oxford, Clarendon Press, 1968.

Heritage, J., *Garfinkel and Ethnomethodology*, Cambridge, Polity Press, 1984.

Jackson, B.S., *Law, Fact and Narrative Coherence*, Liverpool, Deborah Charles Publications, 1988.

– *Making Sense in Law. Linguistic, Psychological and Semiotic Perspectives*, Liverpool, Deborah Charles Publications, 1995.

Komter, M., *Dilemmas in the Courtroom. A Study of Trials of Violent Crime in the Netherlands*, Mahwah NJ, Lawrence Erlbaum Associates, 1998.

Matoesian, G., '"I'm sorry we had to meet under these circumstances": Verbal Artistry (and Wizardy) in the Kennedy Smith Rape Trial', in Max Travers and John F. Manzo (eds), *Law in Action: Ethnomethodological and Conversation Analytic Approaches to Law*, Aldershot, Dartmouth/Ashgate, 1997.

Mauss, M., 'Une catégorie de l'esprit humain: la notion de personne, celle de "moi"', *Sociologie et anthropologie*, Paris, Presses Universitaires de France (extract from *Journal of the Royal Anthropological Institute*, LXVIII, 1938), 1950, pp. 333–61.

Moerman, M., *Talking Culture*, Cambridge, Cambridge University Press, 1987.

Neuberg, M., 'Responsabilité', in M. Canto-Sperber (ed.), *Dictionnaire d'éthique et de philosophie morale*, Paris, Presses Universitaires de France, 1996, pp. 1306–12.

Ricœur, P., *Le Juste*, Paris, Esprit, 1995.

Sacks, H., 'Notes on police assessment of moral character', in D. Sudnow (ed.), *Studies in Social Interaction*, New York, The Free Press, 1972, pp. 280–93.

Schütz, A., *Collected Papers 1. The Problem of Social Reality*, Dordrecht/ Boston/London, Kluwer Academic Publishers, 1990 (first printing 1962).

Stockinger, P., 'Autonomie', in A.J. Arnaud et al. (eds), *Dictionnaire encyclopédique de théorie et de sociologie du droit*, deuxième édition corrigée et augmentée, Paris, Libraire Générale de Droit et de Jurisprudence, 1993, pp. 47–49.

Watson, R., 'The presentation of victim and motive in discourse: The case of police interrogations and interviews', *Victimology: An International Journal*, 8/1–2, 1983, pp. 31–52.

– 'Catégories, séquentialité et ordre social. Un nouveau regard sur l'oeuvre de Sacks', in B. Fradin, L. Quéré and J. Widmer (eds), *L'enquête sur les catégories*, Paris, Ed. de l'École des Hautes Études en Sciences Sociales, 1994, pp. 151–84.

– 'Ethnomethodology, Consciousness and Self', *Journal of Consciousness Studies*, 5/2, 1998, pp. 202–23.

Wittgenstein, Ludwig, *Philosophische Untersuchungen* (critical edition and introduction by B. McGuinness and J. Schulte), Frankfurt, Suhrkamp, 1989.

Part Three

LEGAL FIGURES OF THE PERSON

CHAPTER 9

The Notion of 'Person' between Law and Practice: A Study of the Principles of Personal Responsibility and of the Personal Nature of Punishment in Egyptian Criminal Law

Murielle Paradelle

The concept of the 'person', in its double nature as biological and social being, presents multiple facets according to the social context in which it is placed. In this respect, the individualistic Western conception of the human being, which represents man as an autonomous subject independent of his social group (family, tribe, clan, society) is only one of several means of conceiving the person: a means which is defined in time and place and, as such, remains relative and contingent. In fact, neither the concept of the 'individual' nor even its immediate legal corollary, that of a 'subject of law', is a universal category, timeless and spaceless – at least not insofar as concerns their concrete expression or in today's widely traded idealised conceptions, which we find to be identical in all societies, whatever their structure and their mode of functioning.

The ideas of the individual and of the subject of law are the product and outcome of philosophical, political, economic, social and legal history, which has been unfolding for a long time in a specific region of the world, namely the West. For example, having been subsequently transposed into different non-Western histories – Egyptian history being one – it has not totally replaced other means of understanding man, most notably the conception of man as a collective being rather than autonomous agent:

> The notion of person, as a subject of law, is a cultural notion far from natural and one way among many of representing the human

> being as part of existing social structures as independent of the universality of the biological and psychological attributes of man.[1]

The connection between individual, society and law thus becomes evident.

Real legal and social distortions arise from this close interrelation, especially as individuation processes encounter social structures, some of which, at least, have only partially evolved. The result, then, is a concomitant visibility in terms of law and its practices: we have, on one hand, a state legal system based on the principle of the superiority of the individual as subject of law, with attendant notions, that is the recognition of the freedom of the person and of his or her capacity to distinguish between the permitted and the forbidden and, thus, to act wilfully and consciously and with the knowledge that he or she must answer for the sum of any failings and assume liability for individual penalty. On the other hand, there are social practices which present, for their part, a very different reality, a reality which is far removed from the individualistic view of man in that it is based on communitarian values. It is as a member of a group for example, a family group or a village community that an individual gains rights (protection, support, solidarity) and it is to the group that the individual owes certain duties. A man, who becomes an elder benefits as he bears the weight of the group with all that implies of the group's affirmative power and group solidarity (mostly family) and, inversely, bears responsibility for all that implies of the limitation of individual freedom to act, differing conceptions of fair and unfair and for the assertion of collective responsibility for collective action.

The Egyptian example is, in this respect, particularly representative of this duality. I have chosen within the framework of this study, to focus on these legal and social distortions that originate in abstract distortions about the accepted place and the role of man in the social group. I base my study on the analysis of two fundamental principles of Egyptian criminal law: the principle of the personal responsibility of the individual and its immediate corollary, that of the personal nature of punishment principles which, in the crucible of social practice, are sometimes neglected due to the persistence of regulatory modes arising from another view of man, of law and of justice, a view which gives rise to the personal nature of criminal responsibility and sanctions. These regulatory modes result from the perpetuation of private justice, as opposed to public justice, administered by the state, which is particularly evident through the persistence of two 'traditions': on one hand the existence and the functioning in Egypt of the *majlis 'urfi*, and on the other hand the traditional recourse to vengeance characteristic of the south of the country.

From private justice to public justice: assertion of the 'personal' nature of responsibility and sanction in Egyptian criminal law

Egyptian criminal law formulates two fundamental and closely linked principles among the general principles guiding its application: the principle of personal responsibility, by which one is criminally responsible only for one's own acts and the principle of the personality of the punishments, which dictates that one is criminally punishable only with respect to the crime committed. Two principles signify *a contrario*: that a person who is neither the author nor the accomplice of a wrongful act cannot be held criminally responsible, thus excluding the possibility of criminal responsibility for the acts of others; and that a person who has not been recognised or convicted of committing a wrongful act cannot be sanctioned, thus effectively excluding the possibility of criminal sanctions for the acts of others.

I seek then, within the framework of this first part, to answer a certain number of questions relating to the existence and the application of these two principles: How are they stated in Egyptian criminal law? In what terms? On what bases? What infringements, exceptions and other legal sentence reductions have been introduced by the legislator or by the judge? If, in fact, criminal responsibility and condemnation for the acts of others are forbidden in principle, I shall see that there are, nevertheless, statutory situations which contradict these prohibitions. How do the Egyptian courts interpret and apply such instances? What guarantees respect for their usage?

Individual responsibility and personality of the punishments: two general principles of Egyptian criminal law

Keeping in mind that criminal responsibility is personal as is the sanction to which the recognition of such a responsibility leads, Egyptian criminal law is merely affirming a principle which has been known and asserted for a very long time. Even if not new, this principle has not always prevailed.

History and evolution of the principle of the personal nature of criminal responsibility and sanctions

Originally, and this applies to Egyptian society as well as to many other mostly Western societies, criminal responsibility was of a collective nature in the sense that one did not make a distinction between the individual and the group to which he or she belonged. Implemented within a context of private revenge, the criminal process then became a group business. It became the role of the victim and, with it, the community to which the victim belonged (family, clan, tribe) to act against the offender and the offender's community which, in turn, assumed full responsibility for the act committed by one of its members. 'The internal solidarity of the clans imposed systematic retaliation,' as Botiveau says, in order to 'maintain a balance among the groups within the population.'[2] More than a punishment, counter-action consisted of reprisals.

Later on, the standards of Islam came to regulate these practices and asserted the personal nature of the responsibility and of the sanction. The principle of revenge certainly remained unchanged in its logic of retaliation, but it was no longer a question of taking on the whole group. As a rule, only culprits should answer for their acts. The very preservation of the group was at risk[3] by extended acts of revenge, in a reversal of its initial goal.

Islamic criminal law requires the discerning judgement and free will of the perpetrator as the basis for recognition of criminal responsibility and so approves the personal nature of that responsibility. It also affirms that no individual can be responsible for the acts of others which means, on the contrary, that each individual is responsible for his or her own illicit acts. The direct causal relation between the fault and responsibility recalls a more subjective conception of responsibility as asserted in several verses of the Qur'an:

Sura V, The Dinner Table, aya 105:

O you who believe!
Take care of your souls;
he who errs cannot hurt you.

Sura XVII, The Children of Israel, aya 7:

If you do good, you will do good for your own souls,
and if you do evil, it shall be for them.

Sura XVII, The Children of Israel, aya 15:

Whoever goes aright
for his own soul does he go aright;
and whoever goes astray,
to its detriment only does he go astray
nor can the bearer of a burden bear the burden of another.

Regarding the assertion of the personal and individual nature of responsibility, Islamic criminal law adds, as a corollary, the personal nature of the punishment. Whether about punishments in the category of *hudûd*,[4] those referring back to the exercise of *qisâs*[5] or those relevant to the *ta'zîr*,[6] the same basic principle applies: punishments can only be inflicted upon the author of the criminal act. There is no criminal responsibility without personal fault. There is no criminal sanction without personal responsibility. The type of justice organised by Islamic standards is a justice of retribution; each one receives a retribution according to the fault and no more than that for which he or she is responsible, no less than that for which he or she is guilty.

Sura XI, Hood, aya 111:

And your Lord will most surely pay back to all
their deeds in full;
surely He is aware of what they do.

Sura XIV, Abraham, aya 51:

That Allah may requite each soul
(according to) what it has earned;
surely Allah is swift in reckoning.

In the rule of *qisâs* (talion), one finds the idea of retribution to be exactly proportional to both the act committed and suited to the author of the act. It closely adapts the retaliation-punishment to the offence, making the culprit, and only the culprit, suffer the same damage as the one caused to the victim:

> Sura VI, The Cattle, aya 178:
>
> Whoever brings an evil deed,
> he shall be recompensed only with the like of it.
>
> Sura V, The Dinner Table, aya 45:
>
> We prescribed to them in the Tora
> that life is for life, and eye for eye, and nose for nose,
> and ear for ear, and tooth for tooth,
> and (that there is) reprisal in wounds.

One should keep in mind however, that in order effectively to administer a justice of retribution, that justice must remain at least partly private, as understood by the rules of *qisâs*. If, according to Islamic law, the victim must ask for a punishment proportionate to the injury sustained, the fact remains that the response always originates from the offended part and so is always of a private nature. However proportioned, regulated and retributive, the demand is more likely to resemble an act of vengeance than the punishment-sanction prescribed by current criminal law.

Only today, with the assumption of the judicial function by the authorities, does the transition from a private to a public system of justice come into effect, and only today do both criminal responsibility and the resulting sanctions become truly individual and personal. One thus comes to the assertion that, in terms of crime, there can be no guarantor; only the one who committed the crime must answer for that act and be punished. The consequence is the punishment of acts of revenge and the criminalisation of vindictive mechanisms by a criminal system placed under the control of a unique central authority: an authority which grants itself the power to render judgement and enforce sentences in the name of the whole of society based on the principle that the damage to the individual affects the overall public order and safety, an order and safety that the state must guarantee. The role of the victim is henceforth confined to claiming a material and moral compensation for damages suffered.

There can be no doubt that this new legal economy, in close relation with the centralisation movement affecting political structures, is also largely responsible for the emergence and development of a new conception of the person: an individual removed from his or her social group, free and answering to no one, an individual who is fully capable and fully responsible for his or her acts. Once the notions of clan or family responsibility become irrelevant, men are considered as primary agents, acting autonomously and responsible for the consequences of those acts. On the contrary, and because this responsibility is deliberately personal, it disappears when it looks as though, for certain reasons specifically recognised as exculpatory, the freedom of the agent or that person's capacity to judge were not complete at the time of the facts. 'Will', 'autonomy', 'freedom' and 'intentionality' are, henceforth, the foundation for the new perception of modern man.

As a social construct strictly dependent upon the society it is intended to regulate, the legal system can only acknowledge this shift in perception and, henceforth, consider man as a free and autonomous agent, with all that implies for imputation and responsibility, and as a 'subject of law'.

Assertion of the 'personal' nature of criminal responsibility and sanctions: personal responsibility and the personal nature of sanctions

If the Egyptian Civil Code admits civil liability for another's act, criminal law makes no such provision. Criminal law asserts that a person can be held responsible only if that person, either as principal or as accomplice, committed the alleged acts. To state that one is criminally responsible only for one's own acts amounts to an affirmation of the personal nature of criminal responsibility, with the result that the individual only has to answer for his or her own acts and the consequences that such responsibility implies. Personal responsibility is thus opposed to recognition of criminal responsibility for another's acts. A direct consequence of this principle: criminal responsibility is based on personal torts, whether intentional or not, and the burden of proof remains with the plaintiff in a criminal lawsuit. This personal fault objectifies the necessary relation between the behaviour of the agent and the tort committed. Whether an act is wilful or by simple omission, it must be personally attributable in order for the individual's responsibility to be engaged. The Egyptian jurisprudence continuously refers to this principle.

Related to the principle of personal responsibility is the constitutionally recognised principle of the personal nature of punishments. At the end of Article 66 of the Egyptian Constitution, it is stated that 'the punishment is personal' (*al-'uqûbât shakhsiyya*). To recognise the necessary existence of a personal relation of criminality between the agent and the act is to assert not only the personal character of criminal responsibility, but also the similar although separate rule of the personal nature of punishments according to which only the guilty party must support the weight of sanctions: a principle by which one person is prevented from being punished for the fault of another and which thus excludes criminal condemnation of others. Here again, Egyptian jurisprudence is consistent in its assertion.

Thus, personal responsibility and the personal nature of punishment both refer to the obligation of a person involved in the commission of a criminal act to the exclusion of anyone else, to answer for such an act and assume its penal consequences: in other words, to be the only one to suffer the punishment. Here, one is dealing with a justice which may be qualified as 'retributive': each according to his due, no more and no less; each according to his responsibility, no more and no less and each according to his fault, no more and no less.

The retributive nature of Egyptian justice may still be seen in the prescriptive remedies of the penal code for mechanisms of individualisation of the sentence.

The personal nature of punishment and the personalisation of the penalty

It is the judge who, in order to qualify an act and related sanction, must make an effort to evaluate the criminal act and its circumstances and so to determine the degree of freedom and intentions of the author of the crime and suit the punishment to the person. No more and no less than what is due; no more and no less than that for which that person may be held accountable; no more and no less than his or her guilt. In order to do so, a judge must take into account the act itself, its gravity, the material circumstances in which it was committed and any aggravating circumstances (for example, armed robbery[7] or night burglary[8]), but also the nature of the person committing the crime. Is this person an adult or a minor? First offender or a recidivist? Was this person fully aware and free at the time of the act? Indeed, certain circumstances such as madness,[9] constraint[10] and error[11] are recognised by the legislator as causes of irresponsibility.

The determination of these elements makes it possible for the judge to moderate the punishment and, therefore, 'to make it personal' in view of a fair apportionment of social responsibility for the harm that was done. Beyond merely authorising the courts to apportion blame, the Supreme Constitutional Court mandated apportionment as a judicial obligation in a 3 August 1996 ruling.[12] In ruling on an action filed to challenge the constitutionality of article 156 §2 of Agrarian law no 53/1966 as amended by law no 116/1983,[13] by which it enjoined the courts to suspend criminal fines, the Supreme Constitutional Court asserted that it was the judge's role to engage in an adequate evaluation of the sanction. To do so, the courts should consider objective elements, such as the gravity of a crime, as well as any mitigating subjective elements, including the character of the criminal, and thereby make the sentence proportional to the crime and adapted to the personality of its author. Even so, by enjoining judges to suspend fines within the meaning of Article 156 §2, the law-maker removed the ability to moderate the punishment to fit the circumstances of the case from the trial courts. As a consequence, the wording of the amendment was declared contrary to the constitutional principle of the personal nature of punishments. The sanction must be suited to the crime and not uniformly imposed regardless of personal responsibility. From this point, there may exist a difference between a legally prescribed punishment and an actual sentencing, the gap between one and the other being the measure of personal responsibility attributed to the author of the criminal act.

'Personal responsibility', 'personal fault', 'personality' and 'personalisation' of sanction are principles and notions which refer to 'a judicial tendency toward ever greater involvement with the internal states of the individual, to question his intentions, his capacities of anticipation, the expression of his will'. These are all principles and notions which refer back to recognition of the moral person which, even if it empowers one to conduct one's affairs in a legalistic manner, also obligates one to assume the consequences. From that point of view, the notion of a moral person appears closely related to other notions such as those of 'subject of law', 'freedom', 'will', 'capacity' and 'responsibility'; it appears contrary to those of 'incapacity' and 'irresponsibility'.

Egyptian criminal law requires that the author of a criminal act, at the time of the act, be fully and wholly capable of judgement, thus removing one's responsibility any time that such capacity is lacking. Thus, minors up to the age of eight may be declared irresponsible and free of criminal responsibility as well as the insane, those not in possession of their faculties (for example, by being under the influence of drugs or alcohol) and people acting under duress. Criminal intent (*animus*) is among the elements constituting a crime that must be evaluated by a judge. It presumes that a crime is committed knowingly. A crime leads to penal consequences only when the judge can link it to an agent who may be held personally accountable, i.e. a person who acted personally and freely. The legislature has established a true relation of causality between responsibility and fault, between responsibility and the penalty, and between fault and the individual's discernment. A person who is incapable of discerning the effect of his or her acts cannot legally be held responsible, since responsibility and penalty are based on personal fault, which itself consists of both material and moral elements. There follows an application of the principles concerning guarantees and exceptions.

Constitutional protection of the 'personal' nature of responsibility and criminal sanction: analysis of the jurisprudence of the Constitutional High Court

The principle of personalised punishments is recognised by the Egyptian constitution, which states in Article 66 that sentencing is personal. On the other hand, there is no similar provision made for the principle of personal responsibility, nor has the constituent assembly made any such affirmation. It is the Supreme Constitutional Court that recognised this principle by interpretation of Article 66 on the occasion of an affair implicating the criminal liability of the leader of a political party.

According to Article 15 alinea 2 of Law no 40/1977 as amended by Statutory Order no 36/1979 governing political parties, it is asserted that a newspaper's criminal liability for all material published in a party newspaper is equally shared by the author of the incriminated article and, collectively, by the editor-in-chief and the leader of the political party to which the newspaper is affiliated. However, the judges of the Supreme Constitutional Court, in a decision dated 3 July 1995, invalidated this arrangement regarding violation of the principle of individual responsibility protected within the meaning of Article 66. The court stated that

> The personal character of the sanction, as guaranteed by Article 66 of the Constitution, presupposes the personal character of criminal responsibility. Indeed, an individual cannot be declared responsible for an offence nor punishable for it if he is not considered to be the author or the co-author of the offence.[14]

On the grounds of the unconstitutionality of Article 15 of the law on the political parties, the Constitutional High Court declared that the leader of a political party was free of liability because he was not the author of the article and had committed no personal incriminating act which could justify such a sanction.

Neither the law-maker nor the judge can infer criminal liability of an individual on the basis of another's criminal liability. Thus, criminal liability for another's act is expressly rejected.

In a later ruling, on 1 February 1997, the Supreme Constitutional Court also declared unconstitutional Article 195 of the penal code. That article, in fact, held the editor-in-chief criminally liable for all material published in his newspaper regardless of any material facts for which he might have been accused. In terms of the new ruling, if there should be liability, it could only be of civil nature based on the writer's neglect; in no case could there be criminal liability.[15]

Despite all of this, as well as constitutional guarantees of personal responsibility and personalised sanctions, both principles have been compromised, whether by true exception or by sentence reductions, as prescribed by the legislator.

Exceptions and legal infringements on the 'personal' character of criminal liability and sanction

In relation to penal responsibility for others and the limitation of the principle of personal liability of the author of the offence, Egyptian legislation recognises criminal liability in cases that contradict the assertion of personal liability. It stipulates that a person may be declared personally liable for acts committed by another. In other words, it recognises the possibility of criminal liability for another's act. The offence is considered the act of another in relation to the person who will be declared responsible, even if that person is neither co-author nor accomplice and is materially removed from the incriminating facts. In this situation, the relation of material and physical participation which characterises the personal act is excluded.

Such exceptions generally refer to specific situations in which the law recognises a position of authority or control in the person considered responsible for another's act. The wrongdoings concerned are essentially fines for minor offences. Considering the gravity of the violation of the principle of individual responsibility, it would not be acceptable where serious crimes are concerned.

The following are some examples of exceptional situations expressly recognised by the legislator or the judge: The responsibility of a pharmacist for infractions of the pharmaceutical legislation committed on his or her premises by pharmacy employees;[16] the responsibility of a driving instructor for accidents caused by a student during a driving lesson; the responsibility of an employer for involuntary manslaughter in an accident caused while showing the road to his driver; the responsibility of the director and teaching staff of a school if a student hurts or kills another student within the establishment; the responsibility of the president of a university for refusing to implement a judgement of the reinstatement of a student; the responsibility of the doctor for a fault committed by a nurse.[17]

One should, however, put into perspective the impact of the exception to the principle of personal responsibility which results from these situations. Though responsibility is indirect because it originates with an act committed by a third party, it is no less personal inasmuch as one can always trace responsibility to a personal fault, whether carelessness, omission, neglect or even neglect of a legal or contractual duty. Therefore, in the 20 April 1970 ruling,[18] concerning the death of the patients given the wrong medication, if the Criminal Chamber of the Court of Cassation invalidated a Court of Appeal decision on the grounds that the nurse alone was responsible, it is because they considered that the doctor was, in fact, equally responsible for failure in his duty to supervise the work of a nurse placed under his direction. The latter had, indeed, erroneously administered a medication to patients, with fatal consequences. In the words of the court, although the fault committed was of a technical nature due in part to the nurse's error, it was also a failure of the doctor's duty of supervision. Similarly, the Court of Judicial Review condemned a pharmacist for his failure to supervise an employee in the preparation of medication on the grounds of the pharmacist's superior qualifications in the preparation of medicines.[19]

In these cases, the employer, the pharmacist, the driving instructor and the doctor each had the duty of supervision. Egyptian jurisprudence does not hold otherwise when it regularly applies the following formula to recognise this type of responsibility: *Li'an al-sâ'iq lam yakun illâ adâ fî yadd al-mâlik* ('because the driver was only an instrument in the hands of his employer'). Consequently, the employer, the pharmacist, the driving instructor and the doctor are not responsible *in lieu of* an employee, assistant, student or journalist. Responsibility, rather, is based on personal failure of responsibility, revealed in the fault committed by the person placed under their authority. The failure of a third party reveals the fault of the second party, who is charged for dereliction of duty. The responsibility of the third party is, in fact, based on his personal liability. The exception to the principle of personal liability is only apparent here. The personal act undoubtedly amounts to a failure in a duty to satisfy specific legal obligations.

The exception to the principle of personal liability, however rare, is clear in the case of the criminal liability for the failure of others.

Third-party liability: An infringement on the principle of personal punishments

Though complementary, one must be careful not to confuse the notions of third-party criminal liability and third-party condemnation. Indeed, the law makes provision for third-party condemnation even though the person condemned is not considered responsible for the offence.

Such sanctions are almost always patrimonial fines, i. e. fines chargeable to one person but payable by another. In such cases there is a transfer of responsibility for the payment of the fine. It is no longer a question of fault or negligence, but of 'guaranty' and even of 'profit'. The relation of cause to effect, of offence to condemnation no longer exists. What is more, the person accountable for the fine is not condemned for the actual offence. Consequently, this person is not required to appear before the court or answer criminal charges. In other words, he or she is not declared criminally responsible and his or her police record remains unaffected. This person is guarantor for execution of the sentence.

Egyptian legislation and jurisprudence recognise some instances of third-party condemnations. These, however, remain exceptional. An example would be the assumption of a fine due to the state by the heirs of a deceased delinquent. If an action in justice is terminated by the death of a delinquent, a sanction may be enforced once the final sentence has been pronounced. The death of the condemned person precludes the execution of corporal punishments or imprisonment. Fines, however, especially those due to the state, are considered as chargeable to the succession.[20] The heirs are held in succession to the deceased and must assume liability for the fine; here, the break with the principle of personality of the sanction is indisputable.

Also, in the case of a malpractice committed by several persons recognised as co-responsible (situation of 'co-action'), jurisprudence charges the group leader with an obligation of solidarity. Thus, this person is held responsible for common damages *in solido* with the co-defendants, who may be insolvent and thus unable to settle their debt. In this case, however, the breach to the principle of the personalisation of the sanction is less obvious than in the situation previously described, as it is not linked to criminal irresponsibility.

Sometimes third-party criminal liability can be established on the notion of profit as well as 'guaranty'. A person can be criminally liable regardless of participation in an act if it can be shown that this person profited from the misdeed. Egyptian criminal law sanctions profits earned from illicit acts as, for example, the profit on products entered illegally into the country even when the person who benefited from the transaction did not participate directly or indirectly in the act. Anyone in possession of a pornographic film fraudulently introduced by a third party is liable to six months' imprisonment and a fine of 500 Egyptian pounds.[21]

One may also find exception to the principle of the personalisation of sanctions in the closing of an establishment for a limited period of time for reprehensible behaviour on the part of its owner: such condemnation will inevitably affect all the employees, even though they have nothing to do with the misdeeds leading to the condemnation. It is, nevertheless, what the Court of Judicial Review decided in a decision pronounced on 19 December 1984, in which it rejected the ruling of the Court of Appeals that condemned a grocer for selling products at prices in excess of the maximum allowed by law, but failed to order the shop closed.[22]

These legal exceptions are not the only exceptions affecting the integrity of the principles of individual responsibility and the personalisation of sanctions. Indeed, the observation of social practices reveals, even today, that old modes of conflict resolution endure and that they originate in a rationale that is foreign to the state legal system and that is based on the rationale of the subject of law and its attributes and opposed to its fundamental principles.

From public justice to private justice: persistence of the notion of 'collective responsibility' and criminal sanctions in Egyptian society

Not all normative systems include the notion of individual. If, in the past, this ignorance was a recurring characteristic of the general system for conflict resolution, it continues to this day through the implementation of certain legal traditions based on a 'group' conception of the person. Such is the case of *majlis 'urfi* (community council) or, in an even more pronounced way, the practice of *tha'r* (revenge or vendetta): traditions which produce behaviour opposed to the state criminal system and which, moreover, violate its principles.

Between mediation and vendetta; the law affected by practices; the justice of **majlis** *'urfi; an exception to the principle of individual responsibility*

Majlis 'urfi, also called *majlis al-'arab* or *tahkîm al-'urfi*, is a means of conflict-resolution by arbitration, which is not recognised by the state. While sharply distinct from official justice, it constitutes an informal mode of settlement not reserved for minor problems. Ben Nefissa places this type of justice somewhere between the quick methods of conflict-resolution and the heavy, hierarchically organised state methods. Actually, the appointment of the members of the council, the qualification of the dispute, the opening of the debate, the organisation of the debates, the decision-making and, finally, most importantly, the method of conflict resolution are highly formal.[23]

What is striking in this type of justice is the mindset and logic behind the process, from the nomination of council members to the pronouncement of judgement. Never, and at no time during the debates, is the author of the prejudice identified as guilty or sanctioned. *Majlis 'urfi* is not a court, its decision is not a judgement, much less is it a punishment. It is not a repressive court, but a conciliatory authority. Its purpose is to restore social harmony and allow the parties to return to conditions which prevailed prior to the conflict and to restore peace of mind. Indeed, it shall be seen later that it is more a question of honour, of self-esteem and of respect than of material remedy for damages suffered. From that point on, that which characterises *majlis 'urfi* justice and which makes it so unusual and so contrary to the principle of personal responsibility is the absence of any notion of individual fault. What interests the council is not the degree of responsibility, not even the author of the offence as a person, but the nature of the act and the consequences to the group.

In fact, the personal nature and personality of the protagonist disappears[24] even to the exclusion of his or her name. A list of both parties' violations is established. The members of the council, in view of this list, make a monetary evaluation of the damages, compare the sums obtained and summon the party who appears to have committed the most damages to pay the difference to the other party. The latter generally does not accept the money and prefers to donate it to a religious or charitable organisation for the common good of the group. Indeed, if the party considered to be the most aggrieved were to accept monetary payment, it would dishonour itself by letting others think that their honour and dignity can be measured by cash. Besides, the fact that the compensation obtained is transferred back to the group clearly reflects the communitarian character of this type of justice.

Here the infringement on the principle of personal responsibility results from the fact that the culprit, never having been identified, individualised or named, is not a person who is considered responsible and liable for the payment of the 'fine' – this falls to the culprit's family or social group. The parties who appear in front of *majlis 'urfi* are not individuals, but families or groups.[25] The responsibility is a 'collective'.

One must qualify the meaning of this word, which, if used carelessly, could lead to confusion. The collective character of the responsibility that applies to the justice of *majlis 'urfi* has nothing to do with cases of collective responsibility in Egyptian criminal law, namely co-action and complicity. Co-action supposes that several persons are guilty of the same offence and had acted as equals, while complicity supposes a main author and a secondary author, i.e. an accomplice. In these two hypotheses, the infringement on the individual character of responsibility only becomes apparent because all parties are effectively implicated as having personally participated in a criminal act. As a matter of complicity, if the secondary actor (the accomplice) is considered to derive criminality from the main author, it is not a case of third-party responsibility, but a question of guilt as a personal fault.

On the subject of responsibility, the justice of *majlis 'urfi* is quite different. Though it is also collective, its nature is totally different and the exception to the principle of personal responsibility is obvious. Indeed, the group whose member caused the most costly damages is declared responsible; although the group must pay the agreed sum, it is not important to know who in the group actually committed the act. From a strictly criminal point of view, one should not speak of collective responsibility, as the author could well have acted alone and is not in a situation of co-action or complicity. To consider the responsibility involved in this case as collective, one must insist upon the fact that this responsibility does not apply to the accomplishment of the act, but to the remedy and, even more, to the restoration of social harmony. The role of the group considered to have caused the most damages to community harmony must restore the balance, rebuild what was undone and return the community to its original state through payment of a sum of money.

One should not see in this, however, an exception to the principle of the personalisation of a sanction that violates the principle of individual responsibility, because the sum of money payable by one of the parties is not at all considered a penalty. As Ben Nefissa notes, we are dealing here with a justice without culprit and, consequently, of a justice without punishment.[26]

Henceforth, we are completely outside the field and outside the logic of criminal law. The reason lies elsewhere. It is to be found, more particularly, in another conception of the person, in another motivation for conflict-resolution. The justice dispensed by *majlis 'urfi* is not retributive and the debates are not organised in the form of a trial. Negotiations and discussions are the key in this procedure, the purpose of which is to reach a consensus on the best method of restoring social unity. The fact that the party most affected refuses to accept payment is evidence of this reality, just as this sum should not be considered as a fine. Its value is more symbolic than material; it is the price to pay not in order to repair some personal damage perpetrated by one party and suffered personally by another, but to renew the social bond. The fact that it is donated to a charitable or religious organisation for the collective good is further proof that this justice wants no culprit and no victim, no repair and no penalty. Evidence of this fact may also be found in the agreement by both parties before the beginning of proceedings to abide by the decision of the council.

If the justice of *majlis 'urfi* does not really affect the principle of the personalisation of sanctions, there is, on the other hand, a social practice which abuses it openly and often in a dramatic way: that of *tha'r* or vendetta.

The practice of tha'r*: a threat to the principle of the personalisation of the sanction*

It is not my intention to engage in a sociological study of *tha'r* ('revenge by bloodshed') in Egypt. Therefore, I shall not try to analyse the cultural, political, economic and social causes of the survival of such a practice up until today, nor shall I study the personal nature of the protagonists involved in the blood feud discussed. My interest and focus here is the way *tha'r* violates the principle of the personalisation of the sanction in criminal law.

Tha'r is a method of resolution by violence of blood feuding. It is the perfect illustration of the proverb, 'violence generates violence'. Its practice follows precise and ancient customary rules made up of a chain of equal and reciprocal actions, that is actions causing equal damage. The author of a manslaughter act committed for any reason whatsoever should die by the hand of a member of the victim's family and, if the perpetrator is unreachable (notably on the run), a close relation (father, brother, uncle, cousin) should die instead so that the blood of the victim is washed and the honour of the family restored. This death will, in turn, cause another death and so on in a chain of revenge killings that can last years and affect several generations.

Where blood feud is concerned, there is no period of limitation. Time passed does not lessen the crime or absolve the author's responsibility or punishment. It matters little if the original facts go back ten, twenty, thirty years or more. A single case of manslaughter can lead to a series of similar crimes and to a lasting hatred between families, even between communities. 'The strength of the blood relationships turns the individual offence into an offence of the group.'[27] It requires, in return, that comparable damage be inflicted upon the offending group (as a rule, this damage is inflicted upon any young male member of the group and excludes women, children and elders). 'An attack against a member of the group constitutes an aggression against each member and the shame [caused by such an act] affects them all and requires collective revenge.'[28] Not responding to a family and social expectation and thus refusing to follow the tradition amounts to dishonour and to

> the loss of the role that the individual aspired to. [Even as] to aspire to a role and draw honour from it is at the centre of the process of the search for social identity. The entire range of relations concerned with the granting or the refusal of honour are means by which individuals acquire roles within the social matrix.[29]

Here, violence is a real factor of integration to local culture. It does not matter if it goes against the law of the state and it does not matter if the author of such an act risks being arrested and condemned to the extent that the exchange will allow full integration into the referent group: the family and the village social community.

Here, my interest in the study of blood feud lies entirely in its collective nature as experienced by the persons involved in the fatal chain of *tha'r*: collective resentment stemming from the first murder and collective act of response which sets the process of counter response. Moreover, there is a 'collective' author and a 'collective' victim in the sense that the perpetrator's referent group is considered responsible and the victim's group is offended. The individual is assimilated to the social group; therefore, logically, the other members are collectively responsible for any misdeeds, just as they are collectively affected by the damages that anyone suffers. In that sense, revenge by bloodshed is based on a conception of the person that is sharply different from the modern individualism forming the basis of state criminal law. Even so, the original blood crime is very often an individual act in the same way that the act of revenge perpetrated in response to the original bloodshed is also usually the act of a single person. The latter, however, never acts in his own name, but in the name of his family just as his family does not seek retribution against a specific member of the opposite family as an individual but as a member of that family. 'The vendetta is a collective act by nature, committed in the name of the family by individual performers.'[30]

The exception to the principle of the personalisation of the sanction lies in the fact that if one cannot kill the individual perpetrator of the first blood crime, the 'blood avenger' must kill any other member of the family group, even if that other member has nothing whatsoever to do with the first murder. All male and younger members of the murderer's family may, in turn, be murdered since they all assume responsibility for the acts of one another. In that sense and contrary to individual acts of revenge for personal motive, *tha'r* presents a different character as, 'it never clashes with isolated individuals but more or less important groups.'[31] Its practice hearkens back to old forms of private and collective justice, those forms that the state meant to discard by giving itself a monopoly on the dispensation of public justice recognising the individual as personally responsible, and which, when recognising collective liability (for co-action or complicity), does so, even then, on the basis of a group of individuals personally responsible.

Thus, if the persistence of acts of revenge in Egypt proves that law is never totally efficient, it speaks even more convincingly of the existence within the state of a normative pluralism inspired by social pluralism. This social pluralism is particularly obvious in a conceptual conflict between two different and opposite conceptions of the person with all that implies for the application of mechanisms for conflict resolution.

Law and practice in a pluralistic society: the notion of 'person' at the meeting point of normative orders

Between dogmatic fiction and social reality: from legal personality to communitarian personality

In fact, the continuing practices of *tha'r* and *majlis 'urfi* reinforce the effectiveness and efficiency of the family, community and village pressure on members of the group. Here one is far from the idea of the subject of law as well as from its individualism, which fully and wholly recognises the identity of the person as an individual and not as a member of such or such family, community or village. It is only

> when there is no longer anything ontologically real beyond a particular being, when the notion of 'law' refers no [longer] to a natural and social order but to a particular human being, [that] this particular human being becomes an individual in the modern sense of the word.[32]

Yet in southern Egypt, social and domestic order often go beyond the individual being upon whom it applies, just as it still associates rules to group structures and not to the sole individuality of a person seen as an entity distinct from his or her social group.

However, it would be too caricatural to see a person totally subject to the law of the group in a Sa'îdi person deprived as such of his or her identity as an individual and as a subject of law. For all their complexity with respect to their human, social, cultural and normative components, those societies are no less coherent. They do not appear as a collection of juxtaposed communities, closed to the outside world and with no contact between them and their environment. Social and legal pluralism both refer to an interactive reality, not to an impenetrable compartmentalisation of the groups that constitute this plurality. This is why, if the southern Egyptian person is effectively a subject of law and, as such, the bearer of rights and duties, the person at the same time possesses rights and duties which are granted not because he or she is an individual, but because he or she is also a member of a group, a family or clan and a village. Thus, when one hears about the capacity and the criminal liability of the Egyptian villager of Asyut, Minya or Sohag, one must keep in mind that they are certainly attributed to this person as an individual and a subject of law, but they are also determined by social membership, which dictates the whole of his or her rights and duties.

The determining process here is that of the socialisation process of the group whose membership is taken from various cultural codes, which themselves relate to different cultural spaces. The conditions and ways of life in the rural environment where these acts of revenge generally occur are not those prevailing in large city centres. The social, economic, political and cultural context is different; the traditional structure of relationships and alliances continues and further alienates the villager of Sa'îd (southern Egypt) from the moral person that the state would wish detached from family and group context. Indeed, the practice of vendetta continues to show, at least in rural areas, the power of the patriarchal family archetype. Its influence on family members is such that, at least in the practice of *tha'r*, one makes no distinction among parties.

In that sense, it constitutes the fundamental basic element of blood revenge.

The displacement and transformation of the family structure as a result of rural depopulation have noticeably changed the problem and contributed to the decline of this practice, which remains, nevertheless, solidly rooted in the culture. In rural areas, the family group represents the ultimate authority for the socialisation processes: group identity, common protection and support, and, thus, of social solidarity, commitment and community obligations of its members. This situation is different from the one prevailing in cities, where the family must compete in the socialisation process with other institutions such as schools, companies, political organisations and mass media, particularly television. In rural areas, the family represents the basic economic and social unit; it is the source and keeper of traditional values. The individual born into a family social group 'receives the accumulated cultural inheritance of the family, including the standards to which he must conform in his relations with others and particularly in his relations with other members of the family'.[33]

It should come as no surprise then, that this social being, under pressure from an all-powerful referent group, cannot see any likeness between him or herself and the legal personality imposed by modern criminal law, i.e. a free and sovereign personality whose will is the beginning and the end of everything. The practices of *majlis 'urfi* and *tha'r* are opposed or at least juxtaposed to the notion of the moral person, originating as it does in a dogmatic approach to the individual; those practices reflect another idea, that of the 'collective' person placed in a physical setting characterised by strong interdependent relationships.

In this sense, one must recognise that, according to Unsal, this rural environment makes up a 'subculture' defined as 'a distinct unifying element within national boundaries'[34] which 'constitutes, even today, a strangely efficient paradigm for the preservation of social control and reproduction from the interference of modernity.'[35] Modernity is expressed here as a state criminal code that qualifies a blood crime such as murder with premeditation and prescribes for it the sanction provided in article 230 of the Penal Code, namely capital punishment. One is indeed faced with opposing rationales, in the first case, of a blood crime which is seen as proof of virility, courage, honour and social solidarity and, in the second case, of the blood crime considered to be murder and punishable by the most severe sanction. Indeed, one is dealing with two representations of the person and two conceptions of a human being linked, as it were, biologically, without regard to social context.

Between law and practice: different visions of law

One cannot ascribe a simple act of divergence to behaviour that deviates from state law. The behaviours analysed above are normative practices, which, however different their respective contexts, obey precise rules. To be convinced, one only needs to observe the meticulous set of rules in the functioning of *majlis 'urfi* throughout the procedure, in which rules authorise a response within the context of the *tha'r*. Criminologist M. Cusson underscores the similarity between revenge and punishment: 'In both cases the normative dimension is important. One takes revenge and one punishes because a rule requires it'.[36] As for Peters, he asserts with no hesitation that

> Present day evidence from Egypt indicates that vendetta is still an accepted and wide-spread custom, especially in rural areas. Studies of the phenomenon show that the norms governing vendetta include the possibility of setting up courts of customary arbitration (*mahkama 'urfiyya ahliyya*) in order to put an end to the conflict and provide certain procedural rules to be followed by these courts. [...] In this light, I do not hesitate to apply the term law to these norms of feuding.[37]

In this way, *majlis 'urfi* and *tha'r* make reference to criteria that are claimed to be no less universal than those of state law; such criteria are even superior in that they originate in immediate normative codes considered more legitimate than state law, which, depending upon circumstance and geographic location, sometimes operates at some distance from the citizens under its jurisdiction. The legitimacy of these other codes is measured by recognition of their social validity by the referent group. There is no doubt that blood vengeance, as a mode of restoring justice, is often perceived and experienced as more relevant than the state judicial system, especially when this same judicial system shows evidence of slowness and complexity due to congestion of the courts, or renders sentences perceived as too lenient by the victims' families. Therefore, it is not rare that a murderer, tried and sentenced, should himself be murdered upon release from prison by an adversary family member dissatisfied with the court punishment. This is why revenge is to this day 'a crime strongly rooted in the conception of life and spirit of the people of this region';[38] a crime according to state law, but, according to tradition, merely another form of justice.

The longevity of such practices (*tha'r*, *majlis 'urfi*) raises a most interesting question in that it makes one realise that one cannot easily and with impunity substitute one system of justice for another or one normative code for another if the social structures and the mentality of the group have not evolved at the same time. One cannot reduce the norm to just a legal rule in the Western sense of the word; it is more than a legal rule, it is the expression of 'a duty to be justified in general terms'.[39] One must then insist, with Boëtsch and Ferrié, on the active role of 'personal morality' in acceptance of the new standard and principle of justice. In this sense, normative pluralism supposes the existence of 'a discriminatory judgement on the actual value' of available norms.[40] Boëtsch and Ferrié continue, 'the norm is more a hypothetical object relating to what is appropriate to specific people and relating to what belongs to them solely and what they can possibly hold in common [more] than an imposed rule of behaviour'[41] especially when the only reason for the rule's *imperium* is the fact that it is dictated by the state and registered in official codes.

The enduring practice of *tha'r* and operations of *majlis 'urfi*, while indicative of the persistence of different modes of organisation and the survival of traditional cultural values, are a measure of the degree of penetration of the state authority. However, and in view of the facts, one must note that the existence of 'a highly centralised legal system in which the state alone has the right to establish norms and sanction their violation' has not, in Egypt or elsewhere for that matter, succeeded in eliminating traditional means of rule-setting and conflict-settlement in favour of state institutions.[42] In that sense, the continuing practice is unmistakable proof of the failure of the will of the modern state to impose its authority and is proof of its failure to eradicate the influence of certain traditional value systems at the local cultural level.

Such failure also reveals that 'the vital force of such norms which are codified and guaranteed by a system of restraint can be upset by the value which individuals subjectively ascribe to these norms and by the interest that they may have in following them'.[43] State law, because it is self-proclaimed and imposed from the top down, is not successful in generating norms and does not succeed as the sole organiser of social behaviours. These take their inspiration from other sources, which, although not recognised as official sources of law, impose themselves from the bottom, at the level of popular practice. Such third-party means of production of norms and such third-party codes of behaviour relate to different rationales, which are themselves the product of social, cultural and thus normative pluralism at work in Egyptian society.

As underscored by Assier-Andrieu, 'the study of the systems of rules and of the process of conflict resolution does not belong only to the field of law, but to the social field in general'.[44] From this social field, then, arises the practice of *tha'r* and *majlis 'urfi*. This is in complete agreement with Cerutti, who asserts that it is necessary to anchor the analyses of law and order in social processes rather than in institutions.[45] This leads us to agree with her that law and practice 'should not be situated on different levels with various degrees of abstraction, but [that they] should be made of the same substance, made up of social relations and social practices'.[46] One should never forget, in fact, that the norm is a part of culture, society and identity.

This is why if the concept of 'person', understood as an autonomous free individual, a possessor of rights and obligations, occupies a key position within the Egyptian legal system, generally, and criminal system, in particular, and if state law does not extend to the reality of social norms of the country as a whole, it is hardly surprising that the category of 'moral person', upon which the Egyptian legal system focuses, does not represent the Egyptian as a whole nor in every role.

In fact, the individual can assume several personalities in the sense of being all in one, if not simultaneously, several persons – each a holder of privileges and duties – which vary according to the individual's social space and relational network.[47] The individual's relational constraints then shape his or her behaviour. And although one must recognise that their power is not boundless, it is also true that relational constraints limit the individual's choices, which, as a consequence, may not be available indefinitely, but which are available in a context which conditions their validity – except when the individual steps outside of the context and becomes an outlaw, something which is not easy to do, especially in a society such as Egypt.

From all of this, one may observe the existence of social relativity and its complexities which can never be reduced to a monolithic epistemological category whether legal – as in the notion of moral person – or illegal – as in the conception of the 'communitarian' man in southern Egypt. If a widespread evolutionist movement with important philosophical, political, social, economic and legal repercussions has led to the emergence, in Egyptian society and Egyptian law, of the person as an active, free and autonomous subject, it did not, however, erase that other person, tangled up in responsibilities of families and clans. This leads me to affirm, in the words of Mauss, the ultimately contingent nature of the category of 'person': a contingency of time and history, but moreover, within a given frame of time and history, that of contemporary Egypt, a contingency relating to the social space in which the 'person' category is set. From this point on, in order to understand the phenomenon fully, the observer must study the person's integration into a dynamic associating the individual, society and the state through linked social and mental structures.

One must not forget that one must deal with actors located in time and context, not with abstract figures devoid of background or relations without historical, political, social or cultural definition; hence the contrast between this conception of the person and the conception implemented by state law, whether it contradicts it, completes it or simply coexists with it.

Notes

1 Meulders-Klein, 1993, p. 437.
2 Botiveau, 1988, p. 155.
3 Botiveau,1988, p. 156.
4 Still called 'legal punishments', these punishments refer to behaviours expressly proscribed by *sharî'a* and which are, as such, considered as major religious sins. As a consequence, the judge has no latitude for evaluating whether to repress this type of wrongful act. Being held as 'God's laws', they consequently exclude any forgiveness or measure of grace. There are five *hudûd*: adultery and the slanderous imputation of adultery, theft, robbery, the crime of apostasy and the consumption of wine.
5 The *qisâs* or talion is meant to punish blood crimes by blood inasmuch as the parties cannot reach an agreement on possible compensation.
6 *Ta'zîr* refers to punishments not determined by God and therefore left to the discretion of the judge, who has the latitude to decide whether to punish certain wrongdoings not classified as *hudûd*. In the same way, the judge is free to determine the severity of the sanction, depending upon the circumstances of time and place; the safety and the integrity of society must be guaranteed in light of the fundamental principles of Islam.
7 Penal Code, Article 213/3.
8 Penal Code, Article 213/1.
9 Penal Code, Article 62.
10 Penal Code, Article 62.
11 Penal Code, Article 63, alinea 2.
12 Supreme Constitutional Court, 3 August 1996, no 37/15th judicial year, Official Gazette no 32, p. 1834.
13 This article provided that whoever should violate the dispositions of Article 152 of the Agrarian law by building on agricultural lands without having a licence would be imprisoned and fined between 10,000 to 50,000 Egyptian pounds. The detention could be suspended, but not the fine.
14 Supreme Constitutional Court, 3 July 1995, no 25/16th judicial year, v. 7, p. 86.
15 Supreme Constitutional Court, 1 February 1997, no 59/18th judicial year, Official Gazette no 7 bis, 13 February 1997, p. 58.
16 Court of Cassation, Criminal Circuit, 16 June 1979; Rec. of Court, year 30, no 148, p. 700.
17 Court of Cassation, 20 April 1970, year 20, no 148, p. 626.

18 Court of Cassation, Criminal Circuit, 20 April 1970, year 20, no 148, p. 626.
19 Court of Cassation, Criminal Circuit, 16 June 1979, Rec. of Court, year 20, no 148, p. 626.
20 Article 535 of the Code of Criminal Procedure.
21 Article 228 of the Penal Code. Egyptian law authorises the purchase of two pornographic films per person strictly for personal use. On the other hand, it prohibits its trade. If a person buys and illegally imports several of these types of films and then gives one to a third party, that third person is liable for the same sanction, although innocent of the illegal act.
22 Court of Cassation, Criminal Circuit, 19 December 1984, Rec. of Court, year 38, no 203, p. 917.
23 Ben Nefissa, 1999.
24 Ben Nefissa, 1999, p. 148.
25 Ben Nefissa, 1999, p. 149.
26 Ben Nefissa, 1999, p. 151.
27 Hindawy, 1981, p. 260.
28 Hindawy, 1981, p. 260.
29 Peristiany, as quoted by Unsal, 1990, p. 124.
30 Peristiany, as quoted by Unsal, 1990, p. 121.
31 Peristiany, as quoted by Unsal, 1990, p. 7.
32 Dumont, 1983, p. 88.
33 Hesnard, 1963, p. 55.
34 Unsal, 1990, p. 32.
35 Unsal, 1990, p. 14.
36 Cusson, 1987, p. 40.
37 Peters, 1999, p. 144.
38 Hindawy, 1981, p. 258.
39 Boëtsch and Ferrié, 1997, p. 101.
40 Boëtsch and Ferrié, 1997, p. 104.
41 Ibid.
42 Unsal, 1990, p. 153.
43 Botiveau, 1988, p. 164.
44 Assier-Andrieu, 1996, p. 187.
45 Cerutti, 1995, p. 134.
46 Ibid.
47 Rorty, 1976, p. 309.

Bibliography

Assier-Andrieu, L., *Le droit dans les sociétés humaines*, Paris, Nathan, 1996.

Ben Nefissa, S., 'The *Haqq al-'arab*: Conflict resolution and distinctive features of legal pluralism in contemporary Egypt', in B. Dupret, M. Berger and L. al-Zwaini, *Legal pluralism in the Arab world*, The Hague/London/Boston, Kluwer Law International, 1999, pp. 145–57.

Bernard-Maugiron, N., 'La Haute Cour Constitutionnelle égyptienne et la protection des droits fondamentaux', PhD dissertation, University of Nanterre, Paris X, 1999.

Boëtsch, G. and J.-N. Ferrié, 'Le sens de la justice et la force de la norme: point de vue anthropologique sur l'opposition norme/ pratique', in G. Boëtsch, B. Dupret and J.-N. Ferrié (eds), *Droits et sociétés dans le monde arabe. Perspectives socio-anthropologiques*, Aix-en-Provence, Presses Universitaires d'Aix-Marseille, 1997, pp. 101–5.

Botiveau, B., 'Faits de vengeance et concurrence de systèmes de droit', *Peuples méditerranéens*, 41–42, 1988, pp. 153–66.

Cerutti, S., 'Normes et pratiques, ou de la légitimité de leur opposition', in B. Lepetit (ed.), *Les formes de l'expérience. Une autre histoire sociale*, Paris, Albin Michel, 1995, pp. 126–49.

Cusson, M., *Pourquoi punir?* Paris, Dalloz, 1987.

Dumont, L., *Essais sur l'individualisme. Une perspective anthropologique sur l'idéologie moderne*, Paris, Ed. du Seuil, 1983.

Hesnard, A., *Psychologie du crime*, Paris, Payot, 1963.

Hindawy, N.D., 'La vendetta dans le Saïd: un aspect de la criminalité organisée en Haute-Egypte', *Bulletin du CEDEJ*, 13, 1981, pp. 257–63.

Kamel, T.M., 'Réflexions sur la justice traditionnelle islamique', *Bulletin du Cédej*, 12, 1981, pp. 41–50.

Masson, D., *Le Coran* (translation) 2 v., Paris, Gallimard, 1967.

Meulders-Klein, M.T. , 'Personne', in A.J. Arnaud et al., *Dictionnaire encyclopédique de théorie et de sociologie du droit*, Paris, LGDJ, 1993, 2nd ed., pp. 435–38.

Peters, R., 'An administrator's nightmare. Feuding families in Nineteenth century Bahriyya Oasis', in B. Dupret, B. Maurits and L. al-Zwaini, *Legal Pluralim in the Arab World*, The Hague/London/ Boston, Kluwer Law International, 1999, pp. 135–44.

Radwan, Z., 'Philosophie de la législation criminelle en droit musulman: Quelques exemples', *Bulletin du Cedej*, 12, 1980, pp. 260–77.

Ribordy, F.-X., 'Conscience juridique', in A.J. Arnaud et al., *Dictionnaire encyclopédique de théorie et de sociologie du droit*, Paris, LGDJ, 1993, 2nd ed., pp. 98–101.

Rorty, A., *The Identities of Persons*, Berkeley CA, University of California Press, 1976.

Sahlieh, S.A.A., *Étude sur le droit pénal musulman*, Lausanne, Institut suisse de Droit comparé, 1985.

Sherif, A.O., 'The Supreme Constitutional Court of Egypt and vicarious criminal liability', in E. Cotran and A.O. Sherif, *The role of the judiciary in the protection of human rights*, The Hague/London/Boston, Kluwer Law International, 1997, pp. 69–76.

Unsal, A., *Tuer pour survivre. La vendetta*, Paris, L'Harmattan, 1990.

CHAPTER 10

The Regimentation of the Subject: Madness in Islamic and Modern Arab Civil Laws

Oussama Arabi

Rufi'a al-qalam 'an al-majnûn hattâ yafîq. Legal responsibility is waived for the madman, until he awakens

a *hadîth*, saying of the Prophet[1]

The most powerful part of power is an ignorance which does not waver; he who continues in it, continues in power; he who wavers in it, wavers in power

al-Niffarî, Muslim mystic, tenth century[2]

Humanism, law and modern psychiatry

A poignant phenomenon of modernity in the West was the exclusion of the mad person from his or her natural family and community environment and incarceration in professional institutions of mental health. What might be termed the 'institutionalisation of madness' was a complex and gradual process involving the highest political instance, the modern state. The European asylum, born at the end of the eighteenth century, constituted a marked progress relative to the preceding confinement structures of the seventeenth century. As the work of Foucault shows, the seventeenth-century confining process consecrated the rule of atrocious treatment and superstition over the bodies and minds of the demented, which was commonplace in the confinement structures and which the new asylums sought to reduce by a more humane treatment aimed at reintegrating the mad person back into family and community settings. With the birth of the asylum in Europe, the state and the medical profession entered into a joint venture for the incarceration and treatment of madness, a venture which continues until our present time.

The creation of a subjective space in which the mad person was to feel responsible for his or her actions and their impact on others was the major concern of the asylums as well as the main condition for the mad person's release from the asylum. A combination of family values, religious symbols and the work ethic were the persuasion techniques used, with varying degrees of success, for this purpose. Nineteenth-century psychiatry defined the horizon of cure in terms of the immemorial symbols of the Father, God, Authority, Work, Love and Punishment.[3]

And yet the alliance between government and psychiatry in the internment of the insane and the administration of cures has recently been under attack in the West. The collusion between state authorities and mental-health professionals has been stigmatised as being unholy due to its alleged summary categorisation and inhumane treatment of the deranged; as one author put it when comparing the medieval world with the modern:

> Moreover, in the 'world we have lost', the possible causes of madness were more numerous; the criteria for insanity were less rigid; and the responses to it were more varied. This freedom of thought and action may have resulted from the almost total absence of government control of the mentally disturbed, whereas it is a conspicuous feature of modern psychiatry and the target of most of its critics.[4]

A most important insight by Foucault is that both modern lenient and humane modes of treatment and changes in the legal framework are the effects of a new 'technology of power...a transformation of the way in which the body itself is invested by power relations'.[5] The outcome is the creation and social implementation of a new notion of the human subject that is very different from the medieval theological soul:

> This (new) soul, unlike the soul represented by Christian theology, is not born in sin and subject to punishment, but is born rather out of methods of punishment, supervision and constraint...over madmen, children at home and at school, the colonised and over

> those who are stuck at a machine and supervised for the rest of their lives.[6]

The modern ideology of freedom and humanism, of the free subject and of the human soul to be freed from the shackles of authority and tradition hides the immense groundwork of coercion and subjection that underlies it, the fact that

> the man described for us, whom we are invited to free, is already the effect of a subjection much more profound...A 'soul' inhabits him and brings him to existence which is itself a factor in the mastery that power exercises over the body. The soul is the effect and instrument of a political anatomy; the soul is the prison of the body.[7]

Norbert Elias's analysis of the modern accentuation of self-constraint, the internalisation of social norms of efficiency and productivity, sheds further light on the mechanisms described by Foucault:

> Thus, the behaviour of an increasing number of persons has to be co-ordinated, interdependent acts organised with greater rigour and precision so that each single act would fulfil its social function. The individual is obliged to differentiate and to control his movements, to give them greater firmness and regularity...this is not merely a matter of conscious control. It is a characteristic trait of the modification of the psychic apparatus by civilisation, namely, that a more differentiated and predictable regulation of behaviour is inculcated in the individual since his tender childhood, a regulation which becomes a sort of automatism, of 'auto-constraint', from which he is incapable of liberating himself, even were he to consciously formulate the wish.[8]

In the present chapter, I employ Foucault's and Elias's perspectives on modernity in order to understand changes in the legal status of the insane in modern Arab laws as compared to their status in medieval Islamic law, namely that modern psychiatry and law 'both derive from a single process of epistemologico-juridical formation [which] makes the technology of power the very principle both of the humanisation of the penal system and of the knowledge of man'.[9] The legal procedure of the double examination of the mad person's soul by medical and judicial authorities, implemented by modern Arab states and derived from modern Europe, has no precedent in classical Islamic law and legal culture. In the latter, madness was unproblematic and required no expertise – judicial, medical or otherwise – for its determination; the Arab states' borrowed procedure belongs rather to what Foucault terms: 'the entry of the soul onto the scene of penal justice, and with it the insertion in legal practice of a whole corpus of "scientific" knowledge'.[10]

Again, Elias complements Foucault by insisting on the political nature and function of this knowledge, a science of the mind at the service of political control and its multiple instances, the centralised institutions of the modern state: 'The specific stability of the mechanisms of psychical self-constraint that constitutes the typical behaviour of 'civilised' man is closely linked to the monopolisation of physical force and the intensified power of the central social organs'.[11] Thus, Arab legal culture has come to be cast in the moulds of modernity and, therefore, some word of demystification of the gains is in order. To be sure, some gains have been made, but so too have some losses.

Islamic law's perspective on the insane is of interest in this regard as it belongs to a different political and cultural constellation from that of the modern European scene, especially concerning the relation between the law, medical knowledge and the state. Islamic legal categorisation and provisions for the insane predate the modern collusion between power, knowledge and the law. *Sharî'a* does not call for the segregation of the non-violent deranged subject under the control of the medical profession and the supervision of central state authorities. In the eyes of Muslim jurists, the *locus* of power over the insane resides in the family authority; the nearest male relatives are to assume guardianship, protection and legal representation in all acts relating to monetary transaction and marriage of the insane (see below). Thus *sharî'a*'s interest in the insane is of more of a protective nature, rather then expressing a political desire for control, as may be suggested by its specific provisions for the insane person's marriage; its aim is the integration rather than his or her exclusion, of the lunatic into the wider community. The present-day Arab legal and state attitude towards the insane resembles that of modern Europe: it is that of medical expertise, judicial verdict, incarceration and exclusion. This contrasts with the pre-modern Islamic legal care for the mad individual, male or female, which was more accommodating, communally oriented and integrative.[12] This conclusion is in line with the results of the most comprehensive work to date by Dols on Muslim medieval attitudes towards the insane: 'What becomes evident is that [Islamic] society permitted a much wider latitude to the interpretation of unusual behaviour than does modern Western society and much greater freedom to the disturbed, non-violent individual'.[13]

In what follows, I discuss one aspect of the modern institutionalisation of madness as revealed in an imperceptible change in the legal status of the mad person in contemporary Egyptian (and other Arab) civil law when compared with their status in classical Islamic jurisprudence. As a representative of the latter, I expose the relation of madness in its legal capacity in the treatises of the medieval period, culminating in the Ottoman civil law, the Majalla of 1877. To be sure, the Majalla may not uncritically be considered as classical Islamic law as it belongs to a centralised and codified judicial system implemented by the Ottoman state in the nineteenth century in a bid to modernise state administration and strengthen state power and control over the body politic. Although some steps towards centralisation were already apparent in the eighteenth century and earlier through the privileged status accorded to Hanafi law by the Ottoman state, the absence of a unified formal code and the presence on the benches of Ottoman courts of judges belonging to the Shafi'i, Maliki and Hanbali *madhhabs*[14] testify that premodern Islamic adjudication was part of a constellation of political and judicial practices that is markedly different from the modern context of the Majalla.

In one important respect, however, that of substantive law, the Majalla still carries the classical Islamic wisdom on the subject; its provisions contain a critical notion of the legal person in relation to madness, whereby the possibility of recovery from madness is explicitly given a legal effect. The following analysis shows that a radical transformation in the notion of legal capacity of the mad person took place with the consolidation of the modern state in the Muslim Middle East.

I have taken the two poles of the transformation to lie between the Hanafi Ottoman Majalla of 1877 and the New Egyptian Civil Code of 1949. This periodisation is not totally exact as the Majalla is better viewed as belonging to the modern period, although its provisions on madness still face in the direction of pre-modern times. No adequate analysis could limit itself to formal provisions of the law without investigating the institutional and procedural mechanisms of their implementation. In the last quarter of the nineteenth century, Ottoman and Egyptian states were decidedly plunged in the institutional-conceptual mimesis of contemporary European institutions, first as regards military arts and technology but then also in the administrative, judiciary and scientific realms. These mutations in the power-knowledge institutions could not fail to affect the implementation of Islamic law, in terms of codification, procedure and legal evidence.

Thus, the Majalla carries the historical memory if not exactly the reality of Islamic medieval legal practices; it is a double-headed judicial structure with one head facing towards modern Europe and the other towards the Orient. Although the Ottoman Majalla was not implemented in Egypt, it was until 1926 the dominant civil code in the societies of the Middle East covering Ottoman Turkey, Iraq, Syria, Palestine and Lebanon. The juxtaposition of its provisions on the mad person's legal capacity with those contained in more recent Arab legislation is significant in its own right: it indicates what the present-day Arab state tolerates and does not tolerate in the psychological make-up of its citizens, and what the highest political instance considers as legally admissible against the legally inadmissible act to be interdicted. The legal provisions also disclose the mechanisms that the state sees fit to deploy for determining the acceptable legal standard of mental health. There is good reason to believe that the level of tolerance of psychic disorder by modern Arab states, as reflected in their European inspired laws, fares poorly when compared with the more permissive attitude of classical Muslim jurists.

The Egyptian 1875 Muhammad Qadrî Pâshâ's Code of Personal Status could be considered representative of the Hanafî family law of Egypt. As early as 1835, the Ottoman governor of Egypt, Mehmed Ali, issued a decree prohibiting all legal and judicial rulings that were other than Hanafî in doctrine. Although not officially promulgated, Qadrî's codification came to be the *de facto* practical legal manual of personal-status courts and lawyers since its appearance. Containing, as it did, provisions very similar to those of the Majalla regarding the legal capacity of the mad person, Qadrî's code could be regarded as the nineteenth century expression of juridical Egypt's endorsement of Islamic law on the interdiction of the insane. Here again, caution is a must, for the same caveat of double nature applies to the implementation of Qadrî's code provisions by the modern state judiciary as to the Majalla.

In the wake of the creation in 1880 of the state-controlled 'Abbasiyya Lunatic Asylum and the institutional association between the nascent Egyptian psychiatry and state authorities, European knowledge and power structures invaded the Islamic legal doctrine on insanity, thus transforming the judicial and medical context of its application. In particular, with the British occupation of Egypt, modern Egyptian psychiatry came into existence with the establishment of the 'Abbasiyya mental hospital:

> 'Abbasiyya proved very influential in the diffusion of Western norms on mental health ... F.M. Sandwith, as director of the Egyptian health service, was responsible for overseeing the running of the mental hospital. Sandwith hired a young French-trained Egyptian doctor as director of 'Abbasiyya ... In 1889, the facility held some 300 patients and a staff of two medical men, four officials, two chief attendants and 32 attendants.[15]

'Abbasiyya was the first and largest state mental hospital in the Arab Middle East: Khanka Hospital, founded in 1912, was Egypt's second largest mental health institution and, like 'Abbasiyya, came under the control of the Mental Health Division at the Ministry of Public Health. Institutional and conceptual changes borrowed from Europe affected the nature of Islamic contract law just as much as they influenced the judicial assessment of mental derangement. The change in the legal status of the insane came with the political recognition accorded to Western-trained psychiatrists by the Egyptian state in the late nineteenth century. As experts in mental health, they acquired a determining role in the judicial definition of madness and, hence, in the implementation of legal provisions on the state's subjects.

Finally, and in a paradoxical comeback, the rulings of classical *fiqh* on the insane resurface in the New Iraqi Civil Law of 1951: An authentic return of *sharî'a* or a mere retrograde appearance? This way of putting the question does not reveal itself to be fruitful, as the Ottoman and Egyptian experiences in modernising Islamic law in the nineteenth and twentieth centuries clearly indicate. The ongoing borrowing of centralised European state administrative and judicial structures has changed the very meaning of the implementation of *sharî'a* in matters of evidence and procedure, not to mention the basic meaning of legal obligation itself. The subjects of modern Arab states, whatever the sources of the substantive content of their codes, are held legally accountable before the state central authorities, a concept not altogether absent from the implementation of Islamic law in historical times that was overshadowed by the religious underpinnings of legal obligation in the medieval world of classical Islam. Moreover, the institutional weights accorded to modern procedure, evidence and psychiatric knowledge by the judicial structure of the modern state are methods that constitute mandatory rationalities that inescapably intervene in the court's operation and its assessment of the litigation cases brought before it, whatever the source of its substantive provisions, whether French civil law, as found in Egypt and Syria, or classical Islamic law, as found in Iraq.

Judicial versus *de facto* interdiction of the mad: a new interpretation of the law of the land

A striking difference between the Ottoman Majalla and the Egyptian Civil Code of 1949 regards the role of state authorities in the legal determination of madness.

In the last quarter of the nineteenth century, the state, in Muslim lands, did not legislate for the judicial interdiction of the mad person. But, the Ottoman Majalla, following the Hanafî (also Shafi'i and Hanbali) position, provided for the *de facto* interdiction of the insane without any ruling of the judge: 'Article 957. The madman...is *de facto* interdicted [*al-majnûn mahjûr aslan*].'[16] In Egypt, at the same period, Qadrî's Code of Personal Status assigned the same category of *de facto* interdiction to both the insane and the minor: 'Article 482. The minor and the lunatic are interdicted [*yuhjar 'alâ al-saghîr wa'l-majnûn*].'[17] Both the state of madness and the concomitant loss of legal capacity required neither a judicial verdict nor a medical verification. The determination of madness was taken to be unproblematic and the legal nullity of the mad person's transactions was considered as a matter of course that required no intervention from the judge.

By contrast, in mid-twentieth-century Egypt, the state, via the judicial function, became the only party authorised to interdict the insane from legal acts and transactions. Under the New Egyptian Civil Code of 1949, matters of legal capacity and interdiction have come to fall under the joint jurisdiction of both the Civil Code and the Islamic laws of personal status. Thus, Article 113 of the New Egyptian Code stipulates that interdiction (*al-hajr*) is exclusively a prerogative of the courts: 'The madman...is interdicted by the court; the lifting of interdiction is by the court [*al-majnûn tahjur 'alay(h) al-mahkama, wa-tarfa' al-hajr 'anh*].'[18]

The Egyptian Civil Code here is reproducing Article 42 of the preceding Law no 99 (1947) of *al-majnûn tahjur 'alay(h) al-mahkama, wa-tarfa' al-hajr 'anh* (the name given to the *sharî'a* courts of personal status in Egypt at the time): 'The adult who suffers from insanity...is judicially interdicted; the lifting of the interdiction is exclusively judicial [*yuhkam bi'l hajr 'alâ al-bâligh li'l-junûn...wa-lâ yurfa' al-hajr illâ bi-hukm*]'.[19] Interdiction by the court might be detrimental to the material interest of the demented, for although the mad person's transactions after the proclamation of interdiction are invalid, his or her transactions prior to interdiction are legally valid: Article 114 [of the civil code, second clause].

> If the transaction of the insane took place before the proclamation of the verdict of interdiction, it is not invalid, unless his state of lunacy was common knowledge at the time of contracting, or the other party was aware of it.[20]

Medical expertise is a correlative to the judicial function, a correlative that should also be seen as a consolidation of the state's role of ultimate and exclusive arbiter of mental health. By 1950, the introduction by Mehmed Ali, governor of Egypt (1805–48) and builder of the modern Egyptian state, of a European medical infrastructure such as medical education in Egypt (Qasr al-'Aynî Medical School, founded in 1827) was well developed. During this time, the Egyptian medical establishment developed intimate connections with the legal and administrative structures of the state.[21] It is no great surprise, therefore, that the same Law no 99 (1947) by *al-majnûn tahjur 'alay(h) al-mahkama, wa-tarfa' al-hajr 'anh* states that medical doctors and hospitals are the privileged authority in judging mental health:

> Article 64: The attending physicians and directors of hospitals and asylums should, as the case may be, inform the Attorney General of the cases of loss of legal capacity due to mental disease [*hâlât fiqd al-ahliyya al-nâshi'a 'an 'âha 'aqliyyiyya*] as soon as they establish it.[22]

To be sure, medical practitioners had no such authority in classical Islamic jurisprudence (see below), and medical opinion was only to be sought in the circumscribed case of the mad-woman whose condition might get better through marriage. Thus, Article 64 is a sheer novelty in Muslim personal-status law and could be viewed as an instance of the complex interactions between *siyâsa* (modern-state law) and *sharî'a* (Islamic law) in Egypt's moving towards modernity.

In Law no 99, Egyptian legislators employ the Muslim juridical term *hisbiyya*, to designate the courts of personal status matters in the mid-twentieth century; their use of this term points to both continuity and innovation in the legal status of the mad. Deriving from *al-hisba*, a legal structure of classical Islamic law whose function was to supervise the general good of the community,[23] the use of the term indicates a sense of approval or, at least, non-opposition by the orthodox jurists to the intrusion of medical opinion in the determination of madness and legal capacity. The modern extension of the legal power of medicine to cover insanity *in toto* could be justified on the basis of historically sedimented guiding principles of Islamic jurisprudence.

One such principle could be the *hisba* principle of furthering the public good; alternatively, the general Islamic legal maxim of: 'No harm is permitted by the law' (*lâ darar*)[24] could be appealed to in this context. Though at variance with specific rulings of classical *fiqh*, such an extension of medical power could still be integrated into the large margin of legal interpretation provided for by the universal principles of *sharî'a*. Thus Fahmy, discussing '*siyâsa* and *sharî'a*', describes the *modus vivendi* between forensic medicine and Islamic law in the latter half of the nineteenth century:

> The central position of legal medicine in the Egyptian legal system should be obvious by now. Far from signalling its demise, the introduction of these novel methods of establishing legal proof was meant to bolster the shar'. At no time were any of these new methods, including autopsy, considered contrary to *sharî'a*. Rather like the old qânûn legislation of the Ottoman sultans, the use of

> medicine was meant to complement sharî'a in areas where the stringent fiqh principles made it difficult to convict the defendant or in defining as illegal acts that had not been criminalised by sharî'a.[25]

The purists could always object that classical *sharî'a* is no longer the applied law in these modern interpretations of general welfare and legal evidence, for what is Islamic law, it may be interjected, if not the specific content of its juridical rulings, which the modernists are literally abandoning through their tendentious appeal to the more general principles of *fiqh*? A fruitful way out of this dilemma is to underline the fact that classical Islamic law rulings belonged to a different social and political setting than modern society and that present-day Muslim jurists need not be bound by these rulings. This seems to be what has actually happened regarding the rules of evidence and the legal status of the insane and, more recently, in the new Law no 1 passed in 2000 on *khul'* divorce in Egypt.[26] The body of *sharî'a* is better viewed in the way that Muslim jurists, legislators, judges and theologians take to be Islamic rulings and provisions in a particular historical and social setting, rather than an *a priori* constituted corpus that is conserved in one school or one jurist's legal manual. Viewed from this perspective, Islamic law is much more a living law – flexible and receptive to novel practices and new conditions that constantly affect human existence in real history.

Between interdiction (*hajr*) and care (*nazar*): madness and the subject in classical Islamic law

Perhaps the most serious transformation in the legal status of the mad in modern Arab civil legislation came with the disappearance of a crucial distinction between two types of madness, a distinction explicitly recognised in the provisions of the Ottoman Majalla and Qadri's code. Classical Muslim jurists worked with a two-tiered category of the mad, distinguishing between total madness, *junûn mutbiq*, and partial madness, *junûn ghayr mutbiq*, with direct consequences on the legal rights of the deranged subject. This distinction was their way of doing justice to that fact that madness admits degrees and that some types of madness are characterised by intermittent periods of lucidity. They were aided in this by the communal orientation of Islamic law in its provisions for mad persons, a juridical attitude in which the patriarchal family was the *locus* of both the knowledge and treatment of the insane. In contradistinction to modern European and Arab law, Muslim jurists did not believe that medical expertise, although possibly helpful with cures, was required for the determination of cases of mental illness. They left the assessment of mental health to the family and local community of the individual. Furthermore, they developed a legal mechanism for the social integration of the deranged subjects through marrying them to healthy partners.

Thus, we could situate the *sharî'a* treatment of madness within a number of crucial parameters which are at variance with the modern social and juridical culture surrounding mental illness: the marriage ethic, which considers marriage and procreation as a religious value to be encouraged; the sexual ethic, which puts the satisfaction of male and female sexual desire of the deranged person, rather than his or her explicit consent, as a sufficient condition for valid marriage; the long-term protection and care for the (non-violent) mad through marriage and the extended family, rather then through their internment in professional facilities.

Islamic legal thought of the classical era (fourth century AH/ tenth century CE) was not obsessed by a hypothetical unity of the subject and consequently accorded the partially mad subject under recovery (*ifâqa*) the freedom to act and live as a semi-normal person, buying and selling, concluding contracts and establishing a family.[27] The capacity to formulate intentions and recognition of their sexual desire were not denied to those men and women who suffered from temporary insanity, as long as these transactions took place under recovery.

The state, in the person of the judge, had no business in determining either madness or the return of sanity, because 'were we to leave the determination of the sanity of human behaviour to the judge, the majority of people would be interdicted [*law waqafnâ tasarruf al-nâss 'alâ al-hâkim kâna akthar al-nâss mahjûran "alayh*"]'.[28] In the *fiqh* of the four *madhhabs*, a mad person could therefore enjoy full legal capacity during states of lucidity and suffer interdiction when in the state of dementia.[29] Except for the Maliki school in which some jurists require that the lifting of interdiction be judicial, both the interdiction and its lifting are *de facto* as seen in Ibn Qudâma's explanation: 'As the interdiction of the insane is not the effect of a decision of the judge, its lifting also does not require a decision of the judge'.[30]

Islamic law recognises that, in his or her own interest, the mad person should not be accorded full legal autonomy, i.e. that a mad person is not a full legal subject, *mukallaf*: 'For us, he is not a subject of legal obligation (*ghayr mukallaf*)'.[31] Crucial consequences follow that affect the basic rights of the insane and their legal capacity, of which the most important are the denial of all personal capacity to the mad person via interdiction (*hajr*) and the legal denial of the capacity of the mad person to contract and dispose freely of his or her assets and wealth. Legal capacity (*ahliyya*) is a function of reason and adult discretion, both of which are lacking in the mad person. Thus, the Hanafî jurist, al-Kâsânî (d. 1189), expresses:

> All the transactions of the insane are legally invalid: his divorcing, manumitting, depositions, contracting, buying and selling, all have no legal effect; it is not legally admissible for one to accept the mad person's donation, alms or his testament. This is so because capacity is the condition for the validity of the act legal [*al-ahliyya shart jawâz al-tasarruf wa in'iqâdihi*] and there is no capacity in the absence of reason [*wa-lâ ahliyya bi-dûn al-'aql*].[32]

In a fundamental respect, the insane is thus considered less than a fully human subject if one follows the Hanafî jurists' definition of humanness (*âdamiyya* – substantive of Adam, the first human] in terms of the ability to perform recognised legal acts in the human world of commerce and kinship: exchange, contract, marriage by choice, donation. According to the Hanafî legists al-Sarakhsî (died 1090) and al-Mirghinânî (died 1196), who elaborated this juridical assessment, it was the *madhhab*'s founder, Abu Hanifa himself, who raised his voice in protest against the exclusion of the adult spendthrift (*al-safîh al-mubadhdhir*) from the domain of transactions.[33] This, he said, would amount to a fundamental disregard for his essential human character:

> For Abu Hanifa, the adult squanderer may not be interdicted because the denial of his legal autonomy constitutes a loss of his humanity [*âdamiyya*]...To deny the legal effect of his acts and words is tantamount to equating the squanderer with beasts and madmen

> [*al-majânîn*]... for the human being [*al-âdamiyyu*] is distinguished from the rest of the animal world by the legal recognition of his acts.[34]

The mad person loses part of his or her humanity by virtue of the incapacity to exercise reason and autonomy in relation with the rest of the social world.

Notwithstanding the deprivation of the insane from the capacity to effect autonomous legal acts, so essential a mark of the fully human individual, Muslim jurists insist on safeguarding their basic rights and interests. The juridical notion employed to that effect is *al-nazar lahu*, 'the Law's care for the subject's interest', a generic legal principle of classical Islamic jurisprudence especially relevant to the categories of interdicted persons: the minor, insane, spendthrift and bankrupt debtor. In connection with the interdicted lunatic, *nazar* represents the law's concern for the material, biological and psychological interests of the mad person, mainly a concern for his or her survival, wealth, protection and sexual desire. The same Hanafî legist who describes the insane person as lacking in basic human character due to the inability to be an autonomous agent in the human world of exchange and kinship relations recognises, nevertheless, the objective interests of the mad subject, interests to which the law must cater for 'The mad person [*al-majnûn*] who is denuded of all reason as well as the imbecile [*ma'tûh*] who is deficient in reason are to be interdicted from all transactions; this, because of the Law's care for their interest [*nazaran min al-shar' lahumâ*].'[35] These interests in Islamic law are legally objective, i.e. they stem from what the Divine Law itself considers to be the essential elements in human life, irrespective of whether the particular subject involved is aware of them or not.

Thus, physical survival, wealth, care and sexual needs of the insane individual, whenever these interests are applicable, are provided for by *sharî'a*. Being a weak person in the welter of competitive human claims and incapable of defending his material and moral interests independently, the deranged subject is placed under the custody of a guardian (*walî*), the nearest male relative. If madness intervenes before puberty and continues thereafter, then the guardian is the father; if it intervenes in adult age, then the priority order of guardians is the son, father and grandfather. The *wilâya* or guardianship covers two domains:

the person of the mad individual, *al-wilâya 'alâ al-nafs* and the supervision of that person's assets, *al-wilâya 'alâ al-mâl*. Guardianship over the person comprises three domains: *hifz*, the physical security and protection of the ward; *nafaqa*, guaranteeing his or her subsistence; and *zawâj*, arranging his or her marriage when marriage is necessary for his or her protection or for the satisfaction of his or her sexual needs. Guardianship over the wealth of the mad person covers all transactions whereby his or her assets and property could be sold, bought etc., at the discretion of the guardian and in the interest of the ward.

The legal recognition of the mad subject's sexual desire cuts across the juridical differences in the four Sunni *madhhabs*: there is consensus that, whether male or female, the mad person may be allowed to contract marriage through the guardian if the former evinces symptoms of sexual activity.[36] The *madhhabs* of Islamic law only disagree on the necessary conditions of marrying the mad person, with Malik granting an unrestricted authority to the custodian to contract a wife or husband for him or her; by contrast, al-Shafi'i allows it only when the mad subject manifests desire for the other sex:

> With regard to the [male] person who completely lacks reason [*al-zâ'il al-'aql bi-junûn mutbiq*], no one except his father or custodian may marry him: this is the ruling of Malik...In the opinion of al-Shafi'i, he may be contracted for marriage by his guardian only if he shows signs of sexual desire through pursuing women [*yajûz tazwîjuhu idhâ zaharat minhu amarât al-shahwah bi-ittibâ' al-nisâ'*] for in marrying him without his need for it, harm is done to him by assigning him obligations that are contrary to his interest.[37]

In the last statement, al-Shafi'i has in mind the two financial obligations of a Muslim husband, namely, the dower (*mahr*) and material support (*nafaqa*), which he believes would be quite unnecessary to bear by the sexually inactive mad person. The Hanbalis support Malik: 'Regarding the insane adult, the ruling of Ahmad [b. Hanbal] and al-Khirâqî is that his father may contract him for marriage whether sexual desire is present or not.'[38] As for the mad woman, Abu Hanifa, al-Shafi'i and the Hanbalis are in agreement that her guardian may allow her to marry in two cases: either

> if she evinces a desire for men [*idhâ zaharat minhâ shahwat al-rijâl*] as both her interest and need are met in getting married [*fî tazwîjihâ*

> *maslahatuhâ wa-daf'u hâjatihâ*] or in the case that medical diagnosis predicts positive effects of marriage on her mental condition [*idhâ qâla ahl al-tibb anna 'illatahâ tazûl bi-tazawwûjihâ*].[39]

Despite the jurists' statement that marriage be allowed if medical expertise predicts amelioration in the mental condition of the sick, common opinion seems to have put expediency and hope in recovery as top priorities, arranging forced marriages for the demented. Certain modern practices of forced marriages continue to reflect the popular expedient belief that marriage may help the mentally sick to get better. Although this expectation might be true of particular types of mental illness, the dangers of generalising this practice are ample. In a recent study, two Egyptian psychiatrists

> compared the incidence of marriage and degree of fertility in three mentally ill out-patient groups at Qasr al-'Aynî Hospital in Cairo. There were no significant differences in marriage and fertility between the manic-depressives and the controls. Schizophrenics on the other hand, had a lower incidence of marriage and produced fewer children than the other two groups. This trend was particularly manifest after the onset of their psychosis. As might be expected, forced marriage failed as a treatment for the illness, and indeed there was a higher incidence of divorce among schizophrenics than in the other two groups.[40]

The Ottoman Majalla and Qadrî's code still reflect the wisdom of Islamic jurisprudence on the subject of madness and his rights. The first article on the subject of the lunatic in the Majalla explicitly states:

> Article 944. The madman is of two kinds [*'alâ qismayn*]. The first is the totally mad person [*al-majnûn al-mutbaq*]: he is the one whose madness occupies all his time. The second is the partially mad person [*al-majnûn ghayr al-mutbaq*]: he is the one who is demented in some periods and is awake [*yafîq*] in other periods.[41]

Interpreting the general statement of interdiction (*de facto*) of the insane in Article 957 of the Majalla, the Ottoman authority, 'Ali Haydar, reverts to the distinction between the two kinds of madness underlined in the preceding provision 944. He explains: 'The madman is interdicted because, if his madness is total, he is devoid of reason...While if he is awake and has recovered, his interdiction is *de facto* removed and his transactions are legally valid.'[42] In other words, the Ottoman jurists' basic legal category is not madness as such or the generic notion of madness, but the critical distinction between the two types of madness.

The rationale of the interdiction *de facto* of the insane, provided for in Article 957 (see above), is understood to be the lack of discernment in his or her acts, a fact which puts him or her in the company of the undiscerning minor: 'Article 979: The totally mad person is considered legally as the undiscerning minor [*al-majnûn al-mutbaq huwa fî hukm al-saghîr ghayr al-mumayyiz*]'.[43] When the person reaches the age of reason (*al-rushd*), they are no longer under the tutelage of his guardian (*walî*) and enjoy full legal capacity. The same ruling applies to the partial mad person who regains reason: during periods of lucidity, he or she comes to enjoy legal autonomy and acts at this time do not require the authorisation of the guardian: 'Article 980: The transactions of the partially mad person when in the state of awakening are legally like those of the sane person [*tasarrufât al-majnûn ghayr al-mutbaq fî hâl ifâqatihi ka-tasarrufât al-'âqil*]'.[44]

At the same period in Egypt, Qadrî's Hanafî Code of Personal Status worked, just as with the Ottoman Majalla, using Islamic law's basic distinction between the totally mad and the intermittently demented person: 'Article 483: All the transactions of the mad person who never recovers [*al-majnûn al-mutbaq al-ladhî lâ yafîq bi hâl*] are null and void; but those of the one who is intermittently mad and awake [*yajin wa yafîq*] are, when in the state of awakening, legally like those of the sane person'.[45]

Modern Arab legislation: state control of the subject of madness

With the increasing involvement of the state in the determination of madness, Egyptian jurisprudence, culminating in the mid-twentieth century civil law, has come to operate with an undifferentiated category of madness. The age-old distinction honoured in Islamic law between *majnûn mutbaq*, a totally mad person, and *majnûn ghayr mutbaq*, a partially mad person, has altogether disappeared from the text of the law, leaving behind a universal concept of the mad subject, *al-majnûn*. Following the European way[46] under the generic concept of insanity, the mad person is deprived of civil rights and obligations: 'Article 45: He who lacks discernment due to underage, idiocy or madness, is unfit for the exercise of his civil rights [*lâ yakûnu ahlan li-mubâsharat huqûqihi al-madaniyyah man kâna fâqid al-tamyîz li-sighar fi'l-sinn aw 'uth aw junûn*]'.[47] Such universality seems to accord well with the immersion of the state in the legal definition of madness. The very mechanism of judicial interdiction requires a single yes/no verdict to the question: Is the subject mad or not? The privilege of answering 'not totally mad' or 'partially mad' is no longer possible as it could not be translated into judicial procedure. The fluidity of classical *fiqh* allowing *de facto* interdiction during relapse and *de facto* autonomy during recovery had to give way to the rigid state institution.[48]

Modern Egyptian legislation on the legal status of the lunatic copies French civil law where the interdiction of the mad person is always judicial. In this regard, French jurists have distinguished between three cases: the interdicted mad person, *l'aliéné interdit*; the non-interdicted mad person, *l'aliéné non interdit* and the interned mad person, *l'aliéné interné*. The judicially interdicted mad person has no legal capacity whatsoever during interdiction, so that even in periods of lucidity his or her acts have no legal effect (*nul de droit*). However, French jurisprudence has found that the nullity of such transactions is not absolute (*nul de plein droit*), and that it requires a ruling of nullification by the court at the request of the mad person after the interdiction is lifted or at his or her heirs' request. On the other hand, the second party to the transaction may not request a validation of the transaction on the grounds that it was done during recovery as judicial interdiction is sufficient legal proof of the persistence of madness.[49]

The non-interdicted mad person may not be considered as lacking in legal capacity, but his or her transactions are susceptible to nullification on general legal grounds. In such cases, the person requesting nullification must prove to the court that the subject was in a state of dementia when concluding the transaction in question. Yet it is not enough to demonstrate that the subject was in a habitual state of lunacy (*état habituel de démence*), as this does not prove that his or her will was absent when the transaction was concluded. The category of the non-interdicted mad person in French civil law seems to allow, in practice, what the *fiqh* concept of partial madness permits for the insane to perform when in a state of recovery. The contested legal acts are nullified only when it is demonstrated to the satisfaction of the court that the subject lacks, in fact, the capacity for reason at the moment that the act was effected. Thus, though operating with a different set of juridical notions from that of Islamic law, the French system is sufficiently flexible to reflect the complexities of legal acts when performed by mentally disturbed individuals.

The third category in French civil law concerns the non-interdicted mad person who has been assigned to a mental health institution by the next of kin. As mental hospitals are authorised by the state, their admission of that person is sufficient proof of his or her *de facto* loss of legal capacity. Consequently, his or her transactions are subject to nullification by the court. What distinguishes this case from that of the interdicted mad person is that presence in a mental institution is not as clear a verdict of madness as a decision of interdiction by the judge.[50] The meaning that French jurists give to the assignment of the insane person to a mental-health facility resembles the structure of *de facto* interdiction of Islamic law, with the important difference being that this assignment is not recognised as a legally valid interdiction by French law. In the latter, the final verdict on the subject's sanity is neither that of the next of kin, nor that of psychiatrists; it is in the hands of the court.

The Iraqi comeback: a chapter in modern Arab civil law

In modern Arab civil legislation on madness, the New Iraqi Civil Code of 1951 distinguishes itself by its wholesale adoption of the provisions of Islamic law. As in other areas of the code, a choice was expressly made in favour of the classical Islamic provisions rather than their European counterparts that prevailed in Egypt's and Syria's new civil laws of the same period. A somewhat paradoxical feature of this comeback of classical Islamic law lies in the fact that it was intimately connected with the person of 'Abd al-Razzâq al-Sanhûrî Pâshâ, the same jurist appointed in charge of civil codification by the Egyptian and Syrian governments. Thus, identical rulings of Western inspiration on the judicial interdiction of the mad person in both the

Egyptian and Syrian mid-twentieth century civil laws are no coincidence. And yet Sanhûrî and the Iraqi jurists chose to strengthen Islamic substantive civil and contract law in Iraq rather than following the provisions of French law adopted in Egypt and Syria.

There is an irony of sorts in the comeback of *fiqh*'s provisions on madness on the Arab juridical scene after 1950. If anything, Iraq's extant legal structure was not very different from that of Syria, where civil capacity and transactions were still regulated by the Hanafî Ottoman Majalla. The historical configuration of the Majalla as an already codified and enforced state code shows that, despite the Iraqi adoption of the substantive rulings of classical *sharî'a*, the larger political and judicial structure remains similar to that of Egypt and Syria, i.e. decisively different from the cultural and political setting of pre-modern Islamic law. Was it the intent of Sanhûrî and the Iraqi Committee of Codification to preserve the substantive rulings of *fiqh* in the new judicial and legal structures of the Iraqi nation-state? This certainly seems to be the case as explicitly stated in the Explanatory Memorandum of the draft proposal of the New Iraqi Civil Code: 'The provisions contained in this proposal were taken from the Egyptian draft proposal...and from the present Iraqi laws, in particular the *Majalla*...and from Islamic law. *The overriding majority of these provisions derive from Islamic law.*'[51]

Article 94 of the New Iraqi Code does away with the judicial interdiction of the mad *person*, reverting to the Islamic ruling of *de facto* interdiction: 'Article 94:...the lunatic is *de facto* interdicted [*al-majnûn mahjûr li-dhâtihi*]'.[52] In Article 108, the distinction between total madness and partial madness is given legal effect: The totally mad person is considered legally as the undiscerning minor (*al-majnûn al-mutbaq huwa fi hukm al-saghîr ghayr al-mumayyiz*). As for the partially mad person, his or her transactions, when in the state of lucidity, are legally like those of the sane person (*ammâ al-majnûn ghayr al-mutbaq fa-tasarrufâtuhu fî hâl ifâqatihi ka-tasarrufât al-'âqil*).[53]

Does the Iraqi change augur well for the insane in terms of the protection of their rights and interests? As weak subjects, the law should cater to their protection via its special provisions on the legal status of mad persons. The Iraqi solution adopts classical *fiqh*'s solutions on the legal status of the mad person. In the eyes of the Muslim jurists, madness and reason are taken to be transparent phenomena, requiring no special powers for their detection. The setting is that of the neighbourhood or small community, in which a consensus is bound to emerge quickly about the behaviour of its members. In such a community, neither the wisdom of the judiciary nor the expertise of the medical profession are needed to determine what is already open and clear to everybody. In the concise statement of the Hanbali Ibn Qudâma, madness is salient: 'Madness does not demand an effort of interpretation and it is not an object of disagreement [*al-junûn lâ yaftaqir ilâ al-ijtihâd wa-lâ khilâfa fîhi*].'[54]

The Prophet's legal capacity is waived for the mad person until he awakens (*hadîth: rufi'a al-qalam 'an al-majnûn hattâ yafîq*: see endnote 1) rules that legal autonomy is denied to the mad subject until recovered from madness. At the basis of classical Islamic jurisprudence on madness lies therefore a flexible notion of the human personality, allowing the possibility of cyclical states of relapse and recovery (*ifâqa*) and adapting the law to the complexities of subjectivity. For it is well known that many conditions of madness, especially those of split personality or schizophrenia, involve longer or shorter periods of normal behaviour and, consequently, the question of the legal capacity of the mad person may not have a single answer for both states of relapse and awakening. The main danger in such a context lies in the notion of *ifâqa* or recovery: how could the community ascertain such a state in which the awakened mad person is to repossess the right to marry, contract and transact on his or her own? Are the neighbourhood and the family sufficiently neutral, free of prejudice against madness and preconceived ideas about it that they could formulate such a judgement of recovery?

With regard to the differing assessments between *fiqh* and modern civil law, no simple answer can be given, as the modern institutionalisation of madness involves both a judicial and a medical aspect. A vacillation of sorts occurs in the *locus* of the power to judge mental illness as we move from medieval Muslim legal culture into the modern period. In the former, the subject's parents and close kin are invested with the authority to interdict him or her. By contrast, French civil law has accorded a privileged position to the judge in the determination of loss of legal capacity, since a judge is the only authority fit to issue such a verdict, after considering the available evidence, including the opinion of mental experts. The intent of modern civil law is double: to determine the presence of lunacy and, when confirmed, to protect the mad person's interests from abuse and exploitation. Medical expertise comes to the help of the judge in the first process. In addition to testimony by relatives and acquaintances, professional opinion is determinant, since it is supposed to provide objective and expert information on the mental condition of the subject. This information is highly valued in contemporary legislation because it has greater chances of escaping the influence of bias and vested interests that might attach to the testimony of family and friends.

Put in this manner, the distance between *fiqh* and civil law appears rather vast, which it is, in light of the wide gap in the social and political environment separating the medieval from modern times. But what happens when substantive Islamic provisions on madness are enforced in a modern setting as in the Iraqi context? In what concrete sense would the procedures of a present-day Iraqi court be different from those of an Egyptian court when the legal acts of a person are contested in court? More specifically, suppose a plaintiff claims that, by virtue of its Islamic provisions, the subject is *de facto* interdicted by Iraqi law due to insanity and that, consequently, his or her acts have no legal effect, whereas the defendant claims that the transaction occurred with the valid consent and normal behaviour of the subject and hence the transaction is perfectly lawful.

If such a litigation arises before an Iraqi court, the judge would proceed in a way which would be very similar to that of an Egyptian or French judge. The judge would not take the claims of the alleged mad person's family of *de facto* interdiction at their face value, but he would seek to establish the general mental condition of the subject from all possible sources: the family, neighbours, personal history. He would interrogate the subject in court and would certainly seek psychiatric evaluation whenever there is doubt about one aspect or another of the subject's behaviour. These *de jure* structures of procedure and evidence are indispensable when it comes to litigation cases in which the acts of an alleged mad person are contested in court. Whether under the Egyptian or Iraqi models, in this context it is the judge who, in both systems, has to determine the veracity of the allegations regarding the mental health of the subject and, consequently, the validity of the legal acts in question. In these cases, the judge has to establish legal capacity *de jure*, using the modern methods of judicial procedure and evidence.

Conclusion

To speak of a 'modern Islamic law', a product of the necessary ever-increasing impact of *siyâsa* (state administration) on *sharî'a* in modern times, is another way of recognising that the implementation of the provisions of Islamic law on madness by the judicial apparatus of the nation-state has brought it very close to modern civil law. The above analysis shows essential changes in the very meaning of *fiqh* provisions on the legal capacity of the insane due to their inclusion in the nation-state's power structures. Confirming Foucault's analysis, modern administrative and judicial structures comprise a specific epistemic material, a knowledge dimension which inevitably infiltrates the substantive content of the articles due to the institutional authority that this knowledge enjoys. Thus, when it comes to actual application to litigation, the articles of the Iraqi civil code are much closer to those of Egypt's and Syria's French-inspired articles than it first appears.

Madness is a highly complex phenomenon in both structure and degree and its varieties defy any unique or unqualified solution to the problem of the mad person's legal acts. The differences in its treatment between Islamic and modern civil law testify to its intractable character. Broadly speaking, the modern treatment of madness exemplifies a universal trend of European modernity in its attitude *vis-à-vis* the dark aspects of human existence: death, madness, disaster and indigence. Greater state administrative and scientific control of these sombre dimensions of human life has created the modern illusion of their mastery by human power. This has come about mainly via their exclusion from the open view of lay men and women through sanitary and medical measures of isolating the dead, the mad and the destitute: 'out of sight, out of mind'. Concomitantly, the waning of traditional religious discourse breaks down the role of the constant reminder of human frailty that this discourse used to perform in pre-modern societies. If the advance in human knowledge has increased human mastery over inner and outer environments, it has also contributed towards weakening the hold of the religious universe, a universe marked by the millenary call for modesty and recognition of limitations. A valuable part of human wisdom was lost in the process as modern society's scientific and bureaucratic organisation shunned away the other scene: the ingression of weakness in power, death in life, and unreason in reason.[55]

Thus is seen the mixed blessing of increased organisational efficiency, technological mastery and medical progress. Playing on the self-aggrandisement of the modern ego, these advances are marshalled in a self-deceptive distortion of the fundamental truth of human frailty. It could be argued that modernity has provided its own reminders of the horrible side of life, namely the revolution in the means of information, radically bolstered by the electronic-media industry in the course of the twentieth century. Radio and television have brought live news inside the intimate walls of households, with its haunting images of innumerable tragedies, brutalities and disasters that continue to wreck human existence. The issue, however, is not with the media coverage, but with the receiving end, the modern ego of technological civilisation, which persists in its ignorance of essential human weakness, a persistence which is the price of the illusion of mastery. For, in the mystical disclosure of al-Niffarî, 'the most powerful part of power is an ignorance which does not waver; he who continues in it, continues in power; he who wavers in it, wavers in power'.[56]

The twentieth century shift to state control of madness in Middle Eastern societies was effected through the double mechanism of judicial function and medical definition. This shift marks a radical break with the Islamic juridical ideology of the classical period. For the latter, madness was transparent and, consequently, required no special expertise for its disclosure. In particular, the judge had no business in issuing interdiction orders on grounds of madness, as intervention was seen as restricting human behaviour to preconceived norms of rationality. In *fiqh*, the margins of normal behaviour were conceived of as being very wide, so much so that if mental abnormality were detected, it had to be of extreme salience. Thus was legally sanctioned a rich subjective world allowing for a variety of states on the normality/abnormality scale. A subject was to be interdicted only if his or her divisions and incoherence had become so prominent as to produce an unproblematic case of madness.

In the wake of nineteenth-century state centralisation in Muslim lands and the concomitant introduction of medical expertise in the domain of mental life, a new type of power over the soul of the individual came into being. At the risk of oversimplification, someone could now report someone to the authorities for lack of rational behaviour and the judge could invoke professionally sanctioned medical criteria in justification of a decision of interdiction. The intrusion of mental health experts into the vagaries of subjectivity and its regimentation into classifiable categories went hand-in-hand with the growing regimentation and control of its citizens by the state. To be sure, the rationales behind state and medical power are distinct: a desire for greater control of the social body in the first case, and furthering the reaches of human knowledge in the second. Yet, there could be no doubt that their collusion was profitable to both, putting the interior of human subjects under their shameless gaze with its promiscuous effects. The subjects of madness in twentieth century Arab civil laws have thus joined their counterparts across the globe on the path to modernity.

Notes

Author's Note: I would like to thank Dr Baudouin Dupret (CNRS), Dr Nathalie Bernard-Maugiron and the CEDEJ, Cairo, for their cordial invitation to present this study at the CEDEJ-ESF Workshop on 'Legal Personality in Modern Arab Laws', Cairo, 7–9 November 1999. Baudouin Dupret has provided critical and valuable remarks that helped bring the study to its present shape.

1 A *hadîth* from the Prophet that served as the backbone of the *fiqh*'s characteristic ruling on the legal capacity of the mad person. The prophetic saying occurs in similar wording in Ahmad b. Hanbal, *al-Musnad*, 6 v., Cairo, al-Maymâniyyah Press, 1896, v. 1, p. 154, v. 6, p. 100; see also Abû Dawûd, *al-Sunan*, 4 v., Cairo, Mustafâ Muhammad Press, n.d., no 4401, 4403; al-Nasâ'î, *al-Sunan*, 8 v., Cairo, al-Misriyya Press, 1930, v. 6, p. 156.

2 Muhammad b. 'Abd al-Jabbâr al-Niffarî (tenth century CE) was a Sufi, a practitioner of Islamic mysticism. The quoted excerpt is from

the chapter 'Stand on power', in his *Book of Stands* (*Kitâb al-Mawâqif*), 1935, p. 118.

3 Foucault, 1972. Foucault draws attention to the symbolically charged depiction for modern psychiatry of the oft-invoked confrontation between ignorant power's attitude towards the mad (represented by the convention member, Couthon) and the enlightened philanthropist and administrator of Bicêtre Hospital in Paris, Pinel: 'As for the liberation of the insane at Bicêtre, the story is famous: the decision [by Pinel] to remove the chains from the prisoners in the dungeons; Couthon visiting the hospital to find out whether any suspects were hidden...Pinel immediately leading him to the section for the deranged. He asked to interrogate all the patients. From most [of them], he received only insults and obscene apostrophes. It was useless to prolong the interview. Turning to Pinel, [Couthon]: Now, citizen, are you mad yourself to seek to unchain such beasts? Pinel replied calmly: Citizen, I am convinced that these madmen are so intractable only because they have been deprived of air and liberty.' Foucault, 1984, pp. 141–42.

4 Dols, 1992, p. 6.

5 Foucault, 1984, p. 171.

6 Foucault, 1984, p. 177.

7 Ibid.

8 Elias, 1975, pp. 185–86. Elias's position is discussed by Baudouin Dupret in the first chapter of the present volume.

9 Foucault, 1984, p. 171.

10 Ibid.

11 Elias, 1975, p. 188.

12 Classical Islamic culture's integrative posture regarding the insane was intermingled with medical treatment. Historically, the Islamic hospital (*mâristân*) was notorious for its inclusion of a special ward for the insane, so much so that the meaning of the word *mâristân* among Muslim populations has come to specifically denote a mental health facility: Dols, 1984.

13 Dols, 1992, p. 4.

14 El-Nahal, 1979.

15 Rogan, 2002, pp. 111–12.

16 Haydar, 1929, v. 9, p. 17.

17 Qadrî, 1917, p. 81.

18 Al-'Utayfî, 1949, p. 215. For a verbatim reproduction of the Egyptian provision in the Syrian Civil Code of 1949, see Article 114 of the latter, providing for the judicial interdiction of the insane: *al-Qânûn al-Madanî*, 1949, p. 45.

19 Munîb, 1951, p. 74.
20 Al-'Utayfî, 1949, p. 215. See Code Civil Français, Article 503.
21 On the relationship between the rising Egyptian state's military, administrative and judicial structures and the establishment of modern medical education in 19th century Egypt, see Fahmy, 1998.
22 Munîb, 1951, p. 80.
23 The traditional juridical meaning of *hisba* is 'the enforcement of the good and the prohibition of the bad' (*al-amr bi'l ma 'ruf wa'l nahy 'an al-munkar*, The Qur'an 3:109). The *muhtasib* was an administrative-legal function in the medieval Muslim world which functioned well into the nineteenth century. The *muhtasib* was in charge of market prices, measures and weights, as well as public morality. The most notorious comeback of this judicial structure took place in Egypt in the summer of 1996, when a *hisba* ruling of the Court ordered the separation of Professor Abû Zayd from his wife on grounds of the husband's apostasy from Islam. As a consequence of this case, Egyptian legislators passed a new law drastically limiting the function of *hisba*. For a detailed review, see Thielmann, 1998.
24 Al-Suyûti (d. 1505), 1936, pp. 59–60.
25 Fahmy, 1998, p. 40.
26 See Arabi, 2001.
27 In this regard, it is worth noting that the Ottoman Law of Family Rights of 1917 (Article 9) abandoned the Hanafî position which allowed the marriage of the insane man or woman and ruled that such marriages are invalid.
28 Ibn Qudâma, 1348 AH, v. 4, p. 525.
29 For the classical Hanafî position, see al-Sarakhsî, 1324 AH, v. 24, pp. 156–57; for the Shafi'i, see al-Shâfi'î, 1961, *Bâb al-hajr 'alâ al-bâlighîn* (Chapter on the interdiction of adults), v. 3: p. 218; for the Hanbalis, see Ibn Qudâma, 1348 AH, v. 4, p. 525.
30 Ibn Qudâma, 1348 AH, v. 4, p. 525.
31 Ibn Qudâma, 1348 AH, v. 7, p. 393.
32 Al-Kâsânî, 1327–48, v. 7, p. 171.
33 On the historic controversy about the rights of the squanderer in Islamic law see Arabi, 2000.
34 Al-Mirghinânî, 1996, v. 4, p. 391; al-Sarakhsî, 1324, v. 24, p. 160.
35 Al-Sarakhsî, 1324 AH, v. 24, p. 156.
36 Procreation, being a fundamental legal end (*qasd*) of Muslim marriage, the licence to marry accorded to the mad of both sexes raises the question of the well-being and rights of their offspring. In the pre-modern kinship structures of extended families and

clans, it was presumed that the children of the mad subjects' union were to be raised and protected by the extended family.

37 Ibn Qudâma, 1348 AH, v. 7, p. 393.

38 Ibid.

39 Ibn Qudâma, 1348 AH, v. 7, p. 390.

40 Racy, 1970, p. 121. The above summarises the research results of Islam and Deeb, 1968.

41 Haydar, 1929, v. 9, p. 6. Article 944 occurs in the introduction to Book IX: On Legal Terms Regarding Interdiction...(*Fî al-Istilahât al-Fiqhiyya al-Muta 'alliqa bi'l-Hajr...*).

42 Haydar, 1929, v. 9, p. 18.

43 Haydar, 1929, v. 9, p. 50.

44 Ibid.

45 Qadrî, 1917, pp. 81–82.

46 Code Civil Suisse, Article 17: 'Les personnes incapables de discernment, les mineurs et les interdits n'ont pas l'exercise des droits civils'.

47 Al-'Utayfî, 1949, p. 109. Article 47 of the Syrian Code (1949) is a replica of the Egyptian Article 45: *al-Qânûn al-Madanî*, 1949, p. 27.

48 To be sure, in practice, French jurists allow greater freedom in judicial judgement than the formal textual dichotomy of the civil law would seem to grant; in particular, this appears in the juridical category of the non-interdicted mad person (*l'aliéné non-interdit*) by virtue of which French civil law jurists recognise the possibility of states of recovery and valid consent for the mad; see the succeeding discussion in main text.

49 Josserand, 1933, v. 1, p. 300; Colin and Capitant, 1923–1925, v. 1, pp. 579–581.

50 Colin and Capitant, 1923–25, v. 1, p. 572.

51 *al-Qânûn al-Madanî*, 1951, p. 4; emphasis added.

52 *al-Qânûn al-Madanî*, 1951, p. 32.

53 *al-Qânûn al-Madanî*, 1951, p. 34.

54 Ibn Qudâma, 1348 AH, v. 4, p. 525.

55 Over and above the inherent frailty and eventual surrender of the human body to the elements, Freud's work on the death drive as integral to the human psyche, as well as his location of the irrational as part of normal behaviour, give us serious reason to question the delusive protective posture of 'scientific' discourse.

56 Al-Niffarî, 1935, p. 118.

Bibliography

Arabi, O., 'The interdiction of the spendthrift (*al-safîh*): A human rights debate in classical *fiqh*', *Islamic Law and Society*, 7/3, 2000, pp. 300–24.

– 'The dawning of the 3rd millennium on *sharî'a*: Egypt's law no 1 of the year 2001, or women may divorce at will', *Arab Law Quarterly*, 3, 2001, pp. 2–21.

Colin, M. and H. Capitant, *Cours élémentaire de droit civil français*, 3 v., Paris, 1923–25.

Dols, M., 'Insanity in Byzantine and Islamic Medicine', *Dumbarton Oaks Papers*, 38, 1984, pp. 135–48.

– *Majnun: The Madman in Medieval Islamic Society*, Oxford, Clarendon Press, 1992.

Elias, N., *La dynamique de l'Occident*, Paris, Calmann-Levy, 1975.

El-Nahal, J., *The Judicial Administration of Ottoman Egypt in the Seventeenth Century*, Minneapolis MN, Bibliotheca Islamica, 1979.

Fahmy, K., 'Law, medicine and society in nineteenth-century Egypt', *Egypte/Monde arabe*, 34, 1998, pp. 17–51.

Foucault, M., *Histoire de la folie à l'age classique*, Paris, Gallimard, 1972.

Foucault, M., 'Madness and civilization', in P. Rabinow (ed.), *The Foucault Reader*, trans. by R. Howard, New York, Pantheon Books, 1984, pp. 140–77.

Haydar, A., *Durar al-hukkâm sharh Majallat al-ahkâm*, trans. F. al-Husaynî, Ghazza Press, 1929.

Ibn Qudâma, M.D., *al-Mughnî*, 12 v., Cairo, al-Manâr Press, 1341–1348 AH.

Islam, M. and H. Deeb, 'Marriage and fertility of psychotics. A study at an Arab psychiatric clinic', *Journal of Social Psychiatry*, 1968.

Josserand, L., *Cours de droit civile positif français*, 2 v., Paris, 1933.

Kâsânî, A.B. al-, *Badâ'i' al-sanâ'i' fî tartîb al-sharâ'i'*, 7 v., Cairo, 1327–1348 AH.

Mirghinânî, B.D. al-, '*al-Hidâya*', in J.D. al-Zay'alî (ed.), *Nasb al-râya takhrîj ahâdîth al-hidâya*, 5 v., Beirut, Dâr al-Kutub al-'Ilmiyya, 1996.

Munîb, M.K. (ed.), *Qawânîn al-ahwâl al-shakhsiyya*, Cairo, Dâr al-Fikr al-'Arabî, 1951.

Niffarî, Muhammad b. 'Abd al-Jabbâr al-, *Book of Stands (Kitâb al-Mawâqif)*, trans. A.J. Arberry, Cambridge University Press, 1935.

Qadrî, M., *Kitâb al-ahkâm al-shar'iyya fî'l-ahwâl al-shakhsiyya*, Cairo, al-Hindiyya Press, 6th edition, 1917.

Qânûn al-Madani, al-, Iraq, Baghdad, al-'Anî Press, 1951.

Qânûn al-Madani, al-, Syrian Republic: Ministry of Justice, Damascus, 1949.

Racy, J., *Psychiatry in the Arab East*, Copenhagen, Munksgaard, 1970.

Rogan, E., 'Madness and marginality: The advent of the psychiatric asylum in Egypt and Lebanon', in Eugene Rogan (ed.), *Outside In: On the Margins of the Modern Middle East*, London, I. B. Tauris, 2002, pp. 104–25.

Sarakhsî, S.D. al-, *al-Mabsût*, 30 v., Cairo, al-Sa'âda Press, 1324 AH.

Shâfi'i, al-, *al-Umm*, 8 v., ed. Muhammad Zuhrî al-Najjâr, Cairo, al-Kulliyyât al-Azhariyya Press, 1961.

Suyûti, J.D., al-, *al-Asbâh wa'l-nazâ'ir*, Cairo, Mustafâ Muhammad Press, 1936.

Thielmann, J., 'La jurisprudence égyptienne sur la requête en hisba', *Egypte/Monde arabe*, 34, 1998, pp. 81–97.

'Utayfî, J.D. al- (ed.), *al-Taqnîn al-madanî al-misrî*, Cairo, Dâr al-Nashr li'l-Jami'ât al-Misriyya, 1949.

CHAPTER 11

The Person and His Body: Medical Ethics and Egyptian Law

Baudouin Dupret

The judicial realm is a *locus* where debates on public morality and its definition evolve and are temporarily settled. The mere fact that issues pertaining to this field are brought before the courts points to a growing trend towards the 'juridicisation' of privacy (or intimacy), otherwise known as the 'publicising' of the private realm, that is the intrusion of public and legal regulation in the realm supposedly kept for the individual. In this sense, the analysis of legal debates on morality allows one to analyse modes of construction of the public sphere by focusing on the place kept for the individual within this sphere and, inversely, on the place that the individual keeps for him or her self within it. Such an analysis brings to the light a number of tensions between the normativity of individual choice and that of public morality. This stands out clearly in the case of the field of medical ethics, in which all the stakes involved in the relationship are found between the individual and his or her body in the autonomy of individual will, in individual responsibility and in the freedom to dispose of oneself. A case in point is the dispute over the notion of 'therapeutic purpose' that regularly arises on the Egyptian judicial scene.

I present my argument by using this dispute as a starting point. In the first part of this contribution, I attempt to outline the parameters of the legal and judicial debate in Egypt. Following a few comments on a number of axiomatic legal principles, their role and their transfer from one legal system to another, I examine the nature of existing legal provisions and those pertaining to jurisprudence by focusing on the example provided by the notion of 'therapeutic purpose'. I then extend the discussion to include the main principles of medical ethics and, more particularly, the assumption of the autonomy of the patient's will and its legal corollary, the requirement of consent. This leads me to distinguish two types of constraints that may restrain the use of this autonomy of will: autonomous constraints, that is those pertaining to the current legal order, and heteronomous constraints, i.e. those stemming from an alien normative order.

In the second part of this work, following a comment on the paths followed simultaneously by individualisation and moral restraint, I seek to argue that the spread of the assertion of an autonomous 'self' takes place together with the shrinking of the realm where autonomous 'intimacy' is free from any legal intrusion. The paradox inherent to this growing assertion of a 'pure self' and to the expansion of law into the realm of privacy is that it leads to the notion of an inalienable 'inner-self' that is given no public voice. I show that privacy, when it is subjected to the legal system, becomes the object of a moral judgement in the eyes of a 'virtual public opinion'. By way of conclusion, I comment on the role of morality in the shaping of public space.

The framework of the legal and judiciary debate

Introductory note

This contribution begins with several comments on the axiomatic principles of law and their possible transfer from one legal order to another. Whether regarding interpretative principles (for example, the rationality of the ruler), legal standards (for example, the good family man) or legal axioms (for example, the personality of the criminal sanctions), one is constantly faced with fundamental elements on which rests the whole economy of a legal system and its judicial interpretation. For example, it is manifest that 'the anthropology underlying the legal philosophy of the Enlightenment asserts the principle of the irreducible singularity of human nature found mainly in the freedom allowing the individual to have control over and to be the primary agent of his own body's movements'.[1] Hence the importance, with regard to medical matters, of the concepts of therapeutic purpose, consent, responsibility and aim. Thus, French law has a rule according to which 'no harm can be made to the integrity of the human body unless it is a therapeutic necessity for the individual' and 'the consent of the individual in question must be obtained beforehand except in the case when his state of health requires therapeutic treatment to which he is unable to consent'.[2]

As seen further on in this discussion, quite similar axiomatic principles prevail in Egyptian law. This similarity is due to processes of legal transfers on a more or less significant scale. For example, it is well known that French law has had a great influence on the shaping of Egyptian law. In this particular case, one can really talk about the migration of concepts and legal principles. But this migration should not be seen simply in terms of legal exogeneity or cultural assimilation, for that would suppose conceiving of legal systems only in a very static and autarkical manner. It would also suppose being able to determine the tangible content of the notion of legal culture, a problematical task. Finally, it would neglect the whole issue of why, from an endogenous perspective, have recourse to a foreign legal model.

In a previous publication,[3] I tried to show that the 'instrumentalisation' of the Western legal model should not be confused with its 'Egyptianisation', that is with the idea of a re-injection in this model of the basic features of the local legal 'culture'. In other words, the fact that an Egyptian elite has recourse to the Western legal model does not mean that the model has been the object of a re-introduction of the characteristics particular to Egyptian 'legal culture', but simply that it was used for a specific aim. One should not overestimate the adaptation to the Egyptian context of a legal code inspired by the West: indeed, there has been a transfer that is historically testifiable and empirically verifiable. However, this transfer took root and so one must now consider it as a fact. Generally speaking, this does not create a problem for anyone. Whatever its inspiration, Egyptian law is practised by Egyptian lawyers and by those who are subject to law and serve within the Egyptian judicial realm and with the support of Egyptian referential texts. If the issue of exogeneity is raised, it is for neither legal nor judicial reasons, but rather for political ones.

The legal and case-law provisions: the case of 'therapeutic purpose'

As a first example of Egyptian legal and case-law provisions in matters of medical ethics, I take the notion of 'therapeutic purpose'.

Egyptian law defines a medical act (*'amal tibbî*) as 'any act necessary or desirable for use by a doctor of his right to practise medicine'. The following conditions must be filled for an act to be considered as medical: that the individual performing the act be fully authorised to treat patients (*tarkhîs qânûnî bi-muzâwalat al-'ilâj*), obtaining, beforehand, the patient's consent (*ridâ' al-marîd*); that there be a therapeutic purpose (*qasd al-'ilâj*). This third requirement is justified by the fact that the aim is to cure the patient, on which rests the doctors' right to practise medicine and surgery. Therapeutic purposes require good faith (*husn al-niyya*). Since integrity of the body (*salâmat al-jism*) is a public matter, the therapeutic purpose makes up an essential condition. When there is no such purpose, the doctor moves outside the realm of legality even though the acts may have had the patient's consent (this point is important in order to understand one of the controversies that I will discuss further on in this chapter). The principle of therapeutic purpose is summarised in Article 14 of Decree number 224–1974 by the Ministry of Health, which includes ethical rules and the professional oath of medicine: 'the doctor has to do everything possible for his patients, he must strive to reduce suffering and he must treat them in a sensitive and humane manner'.

If one compares this position of the Egyptian legal doctrine regarding the therapeutic purpose with Article 16–3 of the French Civil Code, one can clearly see the close relationship between both. This is a first example of common legal roots or what we may call legal 'kinship' that stems from transfer processes. In this respect, the ruling of the State Council that reflected the doctrine mentioned previously actually copies the corresponding French terminology. Moreover, this foreign origin does not seem to bother the actors involved in the definition of law or in a legal dispute. That may be possible because there is always the option of finding provisions holding a similar view on the notion of purpose in the tradition of *fiqh*.

But it is most probably the result of a total and non-conflictual integration of provisions and principles that are foreign in origin, but that are applied in the local way. Following Bernard Lepetit, according to whom the origin of history should be sought in the present,[4] I would like to suggest the idea that if one is to look for the foundations of law, he or she should start the inquiry by focusing on current medical practice. This practice clearly puts, at the centre of its whole economy, the modern notion of the individual, as conceived by Norbert Elias,[5] as 'this ideal of the self that wants to exist on its own'. One must then accept the consequences. More particularly, one notes the heavier weight of notions such as 'responsibility'. Therefore, criminal law links responsibility, on which the sanction is based, with the notion of intentionality or of predictability. In other words, criminal law makes the conscious and willing individual to be the basic unit of its economy.

Basic principles of medical ethics

> Different values (reliability, serving the patient whatever his origins may be, keeping the medical secret, discretion) and principles ('especially to not harm', forbidding abortion and euthanasia: not destroy a human life) have shaped the medical profession. These values and principles have been expressed by corporate bodies (associations, academies) either in the nearly legal form of a professional code of ethics or through an ethical code [...].[6]

Law 415–1953 in Egypt pertaining to medical practice (*muzâwala mihnat al-tibb*) states, in its first article, that 'medical practice and doing surgery are authorised to any Egyptian whose name is registered on the doctors' cause-list at the Ministry of Health and on the register of the Doctors Syndicate'. This practice to perform a medical act is, thus, limited only to licensed doctors so far as the act in question is justified by its aim to serve the general interest. Under this condition, there is no limitation to the right of doctors to practise their profession, which is organised by a law that authorises performing all types of surgical operations necessary to save a human life or to reduce the ill that threatens it, save for exceptional cases provided for by the law. But, the practice of this profession is closely linked to this end, outside of which the fact of inflicting injury on someone else's bodily integrity is sanctioned by the Criminal Code. To put it differently, saving a human life or reducing a life-threatening illness are included in the permissive clauses (Criminal Code, Articles 7 and 60) that allow one to avoid the sanction normally provided for inflicting injury on someone else's physical integrity (Criminal Code, Article 240). The principle is the same in France, where 'the doctor's action is justified if he purposefully inflicts injury on the patient's bodily integrity because law authorises it as long as he is pursuing a therapeutic aim'.[7]

Thus, the basic principle is the right to body integrity (*haqq al-insân fî salâmat al-jism*). All parts of the body, whether visible (*zâhira*) or hidden (*bâtina*), are concerned. Furthermore, it is the material nature of the prejudice (*jasâmat al-'udwân*) that is sanctioned and not the higher value of one organ compared to another (*qîmat al-'udû*). Three elements are taken into consideration: first, preserving the natural functioning of the organs (any act reducing the level of bodily, mental or psychological health of the victim constitutes an injury to body integrity); second, preserving the overall integrity of the organs of the body and, finally, relieving the body from physical and psychological suffering (any act exposing the victim to further suffering thus constitutes an injury to body integrity).

To sum up, obtaining legal authorisation to perform a medical act (*ibâha tibbiyya*) on the patient's body, which constitutes a departure from the right to body integrity, comes under three conditions: being legally authorised to treat patients, intervening with a therapeutic purpose and obtaining the patient's consent. The first two conditions have already been discussed. I now turn to the third condition.

Autonomy of the will and the patient's consent

The centring of medical ethics on the individual finds no better example than in the requirement of the patient's consent.[8] This requirement is totally linked to the right to physical integrity and its corollary, the right of non-interference. If the principle is that of physical integrity, no harm can be done to the latter without the patient's consent, which is the only factor legitimising that person's treatment. Of course, the question has been raised concerning the conditions for consent: consensus was reached on the requirement to inform the patient. But there are different views on the nature of this information and they are expressed by two main contending trends.

The first, of a more traditionalist brand, seems to be promoting a kind of medical paternalism that would allow the doctor to conceal from the patient what he or she thinks should remain unknown to the patient. The other trend, rather anti-paternalistic, requires complete information for the patient. For the supporters of a moderate anti-paternalism, this information must respect the criterion of the cautious individual. But for the advocates of a radical anti-paternalism who reject any claim to a therapeutic privilege, it is rather the notion of full information that prevails (criterion of 'the consent that the patient would give were he fully informed of all the facts pertaining to his personal case'). All of these trends are reflected in the courts: for example, the ruling of 7 July 1964 of the Court of Appeal that defined consent to a medical act in French law,[9] the different cases of British case-law reflecting the traditionalist point of view[10] and the American case-law supporting the view of informed consent.[11]

As seen earlier, Egyptian law also imposes the condition of the patient's consent (*ridâ' al-marîd*). This consent must be obtained beforehand (*sâbiq li'l-'amal al-tibbî*), freely given (*hurr*), conscious (*mutabassir*) and given by an individual who has legal authority (*sâdir min dhî ahliyya*). Moreover, and this shows the Egyptian law's anti-paternalistic stance, consent must stem from conditions of full knowledge of the nature, type and dangers of the possible consequences of the medical act requiring such a consent, this being so that the patient be able to express acceptance or refusal. In cases of incapacity (*'adîm al-ahliyya*, that is, for children under seven years of age) or of reduced capacity (*nâqis al-ahliyya*, i.e. being not yet of adult age), consent must be obtained from the individual who legally represents the patient.

All of these provisions clearly highlight the primacy of the autonomy of will within the economy of the legal system. Not only is it the individual who is referred to by these rights, but an individual who 'asserts himself by the capacity given to everyone to create on his own initiative a new state of affairs according to Kant's definition of free-will'.[12] The idea is really that of the individual as a central unit capable of choice and action. In other words, the individual comes to be identified with the person, i.e. with the unit who holds the legal or theological responsibility.

> As Locke had already said, the term 'person' is one pertaining to the courts [forensic]; this means that treating an individual as a person is to consider him responsible for his deeds before the courts, in the literal or metaphorical sense, of law or of morality – or even, for some, before the courts of divine judgment.[13]

Here lies the origin of the above-mentioned penal principle of 'individuality of the sanctions'. By making the individual 'en-soi' a subject of the law, the legal system ran into a paradoxical situation where the generalisation and abstraction of rights and duties take place at the same time as their personalisation.

The limits to the autonomous use of will

This marked 'individualisation' of law-making draws criticism based on the autonomous normativity of the current system of positive law as well as on the heteronomous normativity of religion. Here, one enters into the vicious circle discussed by Norbert Elias[14] that perpetually opposes the supporters of the individualist conception (individuals without a society) to those advocating a holistic view (a society without individuals). Both trends give a metaphysical dimension to their basic unit, the ineffable 'self' of the inner-self and the 'community' with higher interests.

The use of an autonomous limitation: a case of transsexuality

In 1982, Sayyid 'Abd Allah, a medical student from al-Azhar University, consulted a psychologist, claiming to suffer from deep depression. The psychologist examined him and concluded that the young man's sexual identity was disturbed. After three years of treatment, she decided to refer him to a surgeon so that he could undergo a sex-change operation, which eventually took place on 29 January 1988. This type of operation involved many consequences of an administrative and legal order. The first was the refusal by the dean of the Faculty of Medicine of al-Azhar University to allow Sayyid to write her examinations while also refusing to transfer her to the Faculty of Medicine for women. In order to obtain this transfer, Sayyid made a request for a name change at the Administration Office for Civil Status. The University of al-Azhar maintained that Sayyid, who in the meantime had changed his name to Sally, had committed a crime. Indeed, according to the university, the doctor who had done the operation had not changed his sex, but had mutilated him and this simply to allow Sally to have legitimate homosexual relations.

Meanwhile, the representative of the Doctors' Syndicate of Giza summoned the two doctors who had performed the operation before a medical board, which ruled that they had made a serious professional mistake by failing to prove the existence of a pathology before operating. On 14 May 1988, the Doctors' Syndicate sent a letter to the Mufti of the Republic, Sayyid Tantawi, asking him to issue a *fatwâ* on the matter. This arrived on 8 June 1988, concluding that if the doctor showed that it was the only cure for the ill, this treatment was authorised. However, this treatment cannot solely result from the individual desire to change sex, but must be the therapeutic result of a pathology decided by the proper authorities.[15] This *fatwâ* is not clear on whether the 'psychological hermaphroditism' from which Sayyid suffered was an admissible medical reason or not. Thus, everyone claimed that the text supported their own view on the matter.

On 12 June 1988, al-Azhar University brought the matter before the courts, holding that the surgeon must be condemned in compliance with Article 240 of the penal code for having inflicted permanent injury to his patient. The Attorney General and his deputy public prosecutor then decided to examine the case. They referred it to a medical expert. The latter concluded that, while from a strictly physical point of view, Sayyid was a man, psychologically he was not so. Thus, ultimately the diagnosis of psychological hermaphroditism was relevant and surgery was, in fact, the proper treatment. According to the report, the surgeon had only followed the rules of his profession since he had consulted the proper specialists, had carried out the operation correctly and had not inflicted permanent physical disability on the patient.[16] The latter could thus be considered a woman. On 29 December 1988 the Attorney General decided not to follow up the charge. The final report confirms that the operation was carried out according to the rules. Let us note that the case in question is not explicitly set in the realm of Islamic law even though what underlies the core of the dispute are diverging views on morals based on Islam.[17]

The use of a heteronomous limitation: a case of excision

In July 1996, excision was the object of a decree by the Egyptian Minister of Health (ruling 261–1996) claiming, in its first article, that 'the excision of girls is forbidden whether it be in public or private hospitals or clinics, except in pathological cases declared such by the head of the Department of Gynaecology and Obstetrics and following the doctor's suggestion'. In its second article, the decree states that 'the performance of such an operation by someone who is not a doctor is a crime punishable according to the rules and regulations'. This decree, which forbids the practice of excision in hospitals, is only one in a long series of unfruitful campaigns against this practice.

The new decree created quite a stir in a society where excision is still widely practised. A group of people led by Sheikh Yusif al-Badri petitioned the administrative court of Cairo, requesting that the decree of the minister be suspended and quashed. To justify their request, they presented a number of arguments: the decree's contravention of Article 2 of the constitution that makes the principles of Islamic *sharî'a* to be the main source of law; the consensus among Muslim legal scholars (*fuqahâ'*) on the legitimacy of excision as a Prophetic tradition, of which they only discuss the mandatory or recommended aspect and the impossibility for the government to modify a clause of the Qur'an or a rule deemed mandatory or recommended in Islamic law. In its ruling on 24 June 1996, the administrative court decided in favour of the claiming party, considering that the single fact of being a licensed doctor is enough to be allowed to practise medicine and surgery freely. The Minister of Health appealed against the decision to the high administrative court that ruled on the matter on 28 December 1997.

This ruling touches upon three issues: the claimants' authority to act when their personal interest is not directly involved; the scope of the legislator's (here the minister) power to sanction customs justified by referring to *sharî'a*, and the right to physical integrity and its legal limits.[18] Regarding the first question, the court considers that the personal interest of the claimant is presumed regarding administrative matters for anybody enjoying a legal status. As for the second issue, the court distinguishes between a principle of absolute relation and interpretation and principles, leaving room for reasoning and, thus, for the legislator's intervention. Since excision does not enjoy the consensus of the legal scholars, it cannot be an absolute rule and, from this point of view, the intervention of the legislator is totally legitimate. As for the third question, the court considers that Law 415–1954 does not authorise doctors and surgeons to perform excision insofar as a surgical operation is only authorised in case of illness and must be performed with the intention to cure. The court adds that following the Islamic saying, 'neither prejudice nor counter-prejudice', excision is forbidden by *sharî'a* as well as by positive law.

Privacy in the eyes of its judges

Using the results of my study on medical law and ethics, in this chapter, I will analyse the relations between morality, public space and privacy. In a perspective drawing mainly from the works of Norbert Elias, I will seek to show how the strengthening of a discourse on the individual and on his or her rights and duties stems from a transformation of society and of human relations that constitute it towards the moral 'euphemisation' of power struggles.

Introductory note: the individual and moral (self-)restraint

It is important to frame this study within the wider dynamics of space, social groups and also within the Egyptian state since the time of Mehmed 'Ali. Indeed, it is impossible to understand the phenomenon of the centring of Egyptian law on the individual without taking note of the growing trend towards political and legal centralisation that shaped the country's structuring process. I do not intend to give a historical account of this phenomenon, but simply to highlight the fact that the building of an army of conscripts as well as legal and judicial standardisation, to take only these two examples, are fully part of the phenomenon of monopolisation (synonymous with centralisation) that marks the rise of the modern state. On the scale of Egypt's land and population, such a monopolisation process can only come with a gradual differentiation of functions. Thus arose specialised legal professions or, as Fahmy shows,[19] the totally new field of legal medicine began to grow. But the differentiation of functions brought with it an increasing level of interdependence. To use a military analogy, let us recall that increasing the length of a chain of command leads to the increase in mutual dependence between the different links. For those who prefer an analogy with a fishing net, let us note that every mesh is influenced by both its neighbour and by the overall tension of the net. If even only one of them breaks, then, it is the overall equilibrium that is jeopardised.

One of the main achievements of Elias, from whom I borrow this pattern of social evolution, is to have established a link between interdependence and self-restraint, the demonstration of the significance, in a dynamic process of relations constrained by a framework of complex interaction, of the trend towards the establishment of codes of behaviour, their rise as distinctive signs, their gradual spread and common use, and, finally, their assimilation during the process of socialisation that all the individuals undergo in society. These codes of behaviour, these moral codes are, thus, the product of a growing self-restraint that, for its part, reflects a marked individuation. Individuality, interdependence and self-restraint are in a relationship of mutual conditionality rather than of apparent opposition: 'the separation and differentiation of the psychological functions of a human being or what we understand by the term "individuality" can only take place when the individual grows up within a group of individuals, in a society'.[20]

Individualisation, the strong assertion of individual consciousness and the control of emotional reactions that stems from it, in short, all attitudes towards oneself and others that seem obvious and natural reflect 'a very particular historical imprint of the individual'. The 'individualised' individual, that of the hypertrophy of self-awareness, is the individual who, through the formation of society, is forced to adopt 'a very high degree of reserve', to control his or her instincts and to impose a moral code upon him or her self.

> In a word, this self-awareness corresponds to a structure of interiority that appears during very particular phases of the process of civilisation. On one hand, it features a high degree of differentiation and a strong tension between the imperatives and prohibitions of society, assimilated and transformed into internal constraints, and, on the other hand, the instincts and learnings specific to the individual which are not surmounted but restrained.[21]

Expansion of the self and contraction of intimacy

The realm of medical ethics fully reflects this paradoxical and simultaneous trend of the hypertrophy of the individual and contraction of his or her area of sole competence (the individual's privacy). A brief overview of the development of Egyptian case-law will show that the legal restriction of the individual's right to autonomous action takes place at the same time as the assertion of the individual enjoying an autonomous will.

As early as 1891, the medical profession in Egypt became legally codified; illegal medical practice was sanctioned and barbers and other non-licensed practitioners were barred from medical practice. As for the patient's consent to performing a medical act on his or her body, in 1897 it was the object of a ruling by the Court of Appeal which found innocent an individual who was not a doctor but who had operated on someone, claiming to having done so with the latter's consent, upon his request and with the intention of curing him.[22] In a second phase, while remaining mandatory by legal doctrine and case-law in order to perform a medical act, the patient's consent lost its status as a clause, exempting from criminal responsibility the one who performs the act without being legally entitled to do so. Thus, the Court of Appeal sanctioned a barber who had operated on a customer for pilosity on his eyelid and injured him because he was not allowed to perform such an operation and so was liable to unintentional injury.[23] Later on, the Court of Appeal further refined its position by claiming that it is the will and knowledge of the person who performs the operation concerning the fact that this operation inflicts injury on the body integrity of the victim which makes up the condition of this injury.[24]

Thus, on the one hand there is the principle of autonomy of the individual, the meeting point of our judgements of responsibility.

> The fact of linking responsibility, either to the voluntary and cognitive involvement of the agent or to his legal capacity to reach a certain level of caution and reflection in his social interactions derives from a fundamental choice regarding our system of responsibility in favour of the individual who has control of his choices, capable of behaving in compliance or at odds with a system of norms.[25]

On the other hand the constant expansion of law into the realms (that seemed reserved) of the autonomy of the will, realms of the free will that law endeavours to restrain in order to ratify a claim for the moral regulation of individual behaviour 'for the sake of ethical imperatives aiming to bend habits that are "bad" because they are "politically incorrect" (smoking, alcoholism, sexual harassment, etc.)'.[26]

One is witnessing here what Ferrié calls the 'publicising of the private [realm]'. In a symmetrical fashion, one can also speak of a 'contraction of privacy'. If one takes privacy or intimacy in the sense of sexuality, one can observe, for example, that 'the "putting into discourse of sex", far from undergoing a process of restriction, on the contrary, has been subjected to a mechanism of increasing incitement'.[27] The publicising of the private comes down to the fact that the possession of what supposedly belongs exclusively to the domain of the inner-self or of privacy can only be claimed in public terms.

In other words, claiming the right to the autonomy of the private presupposes the establishment of a 'public culture of private life' and, thus, also its constantly-heavier regulation. On the subject of sexuality, I follow Foucault who argues that one must then consider it like something that

> one had to speak of as a thing to be not simply condemned or tolerated but managed, inserted into systems of utility, regulated for the greater good of all, made to function according to an optimum.

> Sex was not something that one simply judged; it was a thing that one administered. It was in the nature of a public potential, it called for management procedures, it had to be taken charge of by analytical discourses.[28]

Hence the growing intrusion of the will to regulate that law, more than any other institution, has shown. Thus law finds itself at the heart of the growing will individually to master the natural environment. It represents a favoured tool for the open and never-ending task particular to modernity:

> The refusal to make do with what nature has given us in terms of strength, sex or face, the concern for mastering its mystery and functions and the effort to maximise its powers and resources. Understand, control, increase. Beauty, performances or pleasures, a mobilisation aiming to fit more appropriately and more intensely into the given thing par excellence that is one's own body.[29]

This publicising of the private gives meaning to a number of claims regarding the legalisation of medical practices involving the body: plastic surgery, sex change operations, abortion. As Ferrié, Boëtsch and Ouafik note, the legalisation of abortion, for example, is the product of a claim for the acknowledgement of the individual right to have control over one's own body.[30] As such, it is a public procedure in the same way as the procedure which aims to forbid it. In this case, the whole initiative seeks not so much to determine the boundaries of life or the rights of the unborn child – otherwise, a fundamental problem – as to impose its 'will to moralise sexual relations'.[31]

What comes out of this discussion is the close relationship between the relations of the individual and his or her privacy, and the publicising of the latter. If one agrees with Isaac Joseph[32] that a public space is an 'area of knowledge', then one's privacy, at least, in its modern guise, can also be considered as such. Everything is set up so as to make it into an object that is both visible and made visible as well as an object of knowledge. It must then be treated as such, that is not to consider it as a private, internal and inaccessible phenomenon, but rather as a transparent and social one that is part of the public realm.[33] Then, law is no longer to be seen as a tool to straighten private behaviours that become public interest because they are deviant, nor is it to be considered as a means publicly to sanction public will as the sum of individual wills. Rather, it constitutes one of the procedural means available to the actors to ensure the visibility and mastery through knowledge of the public phenomenon of privacy. In this sense, contraction of privacy does not mean that the boundary between the public and the private is moving at the expense of the second, but rather that the legal autonomy of the intimate is gradually being chipped away.

Restrained individuality: the inner-self and public muteness

While the requirement of consent for performing a medical act reflects the strengthening of the process of centring on the individual, the fact that it is only a necessary but not a sufficient condition to perform this act shows the constraints that are put on the autonomy of one's will. The patient's consent does not suffice since he or she does not exercise free will over his or her body. The concept of 'physical integrity' is, indeed, considered as belonging to the public realm, and the preservation of this integrity is a matter of public interest.[34] The only justification for interfering with this principle of general interest is the pursuit of a higher general interest, i.e. the therapeutic aim. And so one can see the simultaneous development of a process of centring on the individual and of a strong assertion of the public order, the latter being able ultimately to spread to integral intimacy except for what is presented as its irreducible minimum: the 'inner-self'.

The rise of this irreducible minimum is well accounted for in Norbert Elias's chapter (in his work *The Society of Individuals*) on self-awareness and on the view on man under the title of the second part: 'The Reflecting Statues'. Today, our shared perspective on man and on self-awareness is felt to be the only normal one and thus naturally as not requiring any explanation, even though this view is historically determined. The intensification of man's reflective activity, the repression of urges and the detachment that follows, the concrete expression given to the idea of a conscious subject that exists regardless of the world that subject knows, and the conception of man as a closed system are all trends that are becoming mainstream today. This process of intensive, diversified and pervasive regulation has led to the creation of self-repressive mechanisms and the related assertion of the personal experience of the individual 'drawing the limits of his "interiority" with regard to the world that is "external" to him, to other objects and to other beings'.[35]

The public–private dichotomy rests on historically determined premises, whether with regard to the Western or the Eastern setting. What matters here is to note that, whatever their learnings are, theories are always based on the sharp distinction between 'me' and the 'rest', 'I' and the 'others'. They acknowledge the existence of an autonomous 'me', although perhaps while trying, at the same time, to restrain it as much as possible. This has never been clearer than in the Abû Zayd case. The principle of the petition for *hisba*, itself, which made instituting proceedings possible is that of an action to protect the public order. This thus implies that the principle of the existence of a distinction between the particular and the common and, therefore, between the private and the public, is founded. The claim to restrain what belongs to the inner-self of an individual (freedom of conscience) leads to the acknowledgement of the existence of this inner-self. By attacking the right to express one's convictions freely, in short, by making apostasy into a legal concept, it is paradoxically the right to the free expression of one's convictions that is asserted even if one tries to define its jurisdictional realm in a restrictive way.

Therefore, the court asserts the existence of a distinction between apostasy and conviction:

> Apostasy necessarily belongs to material acts having an external existence. These facts must necessarily manifest themselves clearly [*labs*] [...]. One cannot declare a Muslim ungodly as long as there is evidence ruling out his excommunication. As for conviction, it is what man confidentially holds within himself, that of which his heart is deeply convinced and that he wills.
>
> This is clearly different from apostasy which represents a crime that is materially founded and that is presented before the courts so that, consequently, its occurrence may be concluded. This is part of what the courts can examine or of what must be judged and what pertains to it. Conviction is, on the contrary, located in the human soul and enclosed in its inner-self. This is a matter which is inaccessible to the courts. People must not inquire about it.[36]

Naturally, the jurisdictional realm (the self) of free conviction is defined in a restrictive manner. This court of the conscience that is the inner-self is only competent in the realm of privacy of conviction: any publicity would be regarded as an abuse of power. The distinction between conviction and apostasy thus springs from a narrow definition of the realm particular to privacy and from confining its status to the secrecy of the conscience. However, one only has to recall the courts of the Inquisition to realise that the idea of an inner-self out of the reach of public intervention is not a biological fact, but rather a social and historical construct.

Privacy and public judgement

In the name of which principle can the autonomy of the will be restrained? As seen earlier with regard to medical ethics, Egyptian law justifies this limitation by invoking public order, a notion generally understood as the set of fundamental standards and values of a society that one is not allowed to go against.[37] Without getting into the issue of the identification of these standards and values, let us simply note that they refer to a conception of intimacy or of the private realm that is publicly acceptable, to a definition of public morals. When plaintiffs question the ruling of the Minister of Health that forbids excision in public hospitals, they clearly seek to make a matter of conviction and of religious practice into one involving the interests of the whole community. The whole technical aspect of the *hisba* and of the personal interest involved highlights the problem of determining what, on matters of a private order, concerns or does not concern society.

To follow along the lines of Norbert Elias's argument, one notes this paradoxical requirement of an individual who is constantly more individualised, independent and in control, but who is also in compliance with public opinion, normal in the statistical, hygienic and social sense of the term and integrated into the standard. The law of medical ethics perfectly reflects this centring on the individual coupled with a wide-ranging conception of the public order. As always, the judicial power, when facing this type of loosely defined category, enjoys considerable power regarding assessment, interpretation and determination. When a text's level of formality is particularly low, the judge reproduces the letter of a legal statement of which it is up to the judge to determine the meaning, by a linguistic operation whose guaranties of accuracy and justice are, at the least, difficult to assess. The real constraint is having to justify a ruling in the public eye, that is, to give an interpretation a meaning that the judge will consider shared by most people. In order to be protected from criticisms of subjectivity or arbitrariness, the judge refers to supposedly objective standards such as morals or social consensus.[38]

Thus, the whole question revolves around these standards, their elaboration and their performance. It is the judge's task to make the morality that is trying to be established appear as common evidence, as normality itself. We talk of naturality when the judge emphasises the normality of the biological or transcendental order of things, and of communality when the stress is on the normality of the sociological order. In the first case, that of conformity to the things of nature, the judge claims to model behaviour on 'previously set' rules of nature, whether immanent or transcendental. As for the second case, that of communality, on the contrary, the judge will claim to bow to 'public opinion', thereby forcing the rule to conform to the social will. In practice, the judge's attitude will oscillate between the two ends of the spectrum of normality, sometimes invoking a principle of an external order and sometimes of an order that is specific to the society. It is very tempting for the judge to refer to an external principle, whether it be morals or religion.

The arguments put forward do not generally well conceal the private philosophical or religious views,[39] that is supposing they are trying to conceal them at all. Indeed, the advantage of a principle with an external order is that it is located radically outside what may be put into question, thus asserting its inviolability. In this situation, disagreeing publicly is particularly difficult, a fact which explains the existence of an apparent unanimity unable to find the means to protest; this is what Ferrié calls 'negative solidarity'.[40] We have here one of the most efficient mechanisms for imposing a collective morality by individuals who do not necessarily support these prescriptions but who are unable (in fact or supposedly) publicly to oppose them for fear of being sanctioned by the community to which, as virtual as it may be, is attributed a set of specific intentions and desires.

The Biblical narrative of a paradise where the first representatives of mankind were unaware of their nudity before touching the forbidden fruit of knowledge offers a perfect metaphor of this concomitance of individuation, that is of becoming self-aware and of the rules of self-restraint that it carries with it, as well as the imposition of a collective morality. This imposition most often functions on the mode of individual summons (or of the acceptance of such a summons) to subscribe to a moral code shared by society and by all of its members. But what is important to note here is the simultaneous development of individual self-awareness and of the formation of a moral conscience.

Conclusion: privacy, morality and the public realm

To conclude, I would like to suggest an avenue of research allowing one to link privacy, morality and the configurations of the public realm.

With the help of Norbert Elias, and by taking the example of the law pertaining to medical ethics, we are able to locate the process going from monopolisation to individualisation and interdependence within the Egyptian setting. This phenomenon carries with it the necessity to control emotions, feelings and affects. All moral codes revolve around this control. But at the same time morality, which is the product of this individualisation, tends to restrain the rights of the individual. Or more to the point, the only way for an individual to request that his or her rights be respected is to do so in the name of prevailing morals with which compliance is shown. Of course, this prevailing morality is not the product of the aggregation of individual wills, but rather the attribution of a will to a silent majority by politically-driven actors. If we are right to say that moral rules are set by political actors, by moral entrepreneurs, then we must admit the fact that morality is both a public and a political issue. Public, obviously, since morality is strengthened through a process creating modern society. Political, also, insofar as imposing the moral rule becomes a means of participating in the power game. It is, then, probably possible to view morality as the political 'euphemisation' of power struggles.

Notes

1 Cayla, 1996.
2 Civil Code, Article 16–3, Law no 94–653, 29 July 1994, Article 3: *Journal Officiel*, 30 July 1994.
3 Dupret, 1997.
4 Lepetit, 1995.
5 Elias, 1991.
6 Parizeau, 1996.
7 Penneau, 1996, p. 3.
8 Botros, 1996.
9 French Court of Cassation, Cass. civ., 29 May 1951, D.1952.53; Cass. civ., 7 July 1964, D.1964.625.
10 Bolam vs Friern Hospital Management Committee (1957) 2A11 FR 18; Chatterton vs Gerson (1981) 3WLR 1003; Sidaway vs Brd. of Governors of Bethlem Royal Hospital (1985) 2WCR 480.
11 Salgo vs Leland Stanford Jr. University Board of Trustees (1957); Canterbury vs Spence (1972).
12 Bouretz, 1996.
13 Montefiore, 1996.
14 Elias, 1991.
15 Skovgaard-Petersen, 1997, pp. 319–34.
16 Niyâba, 1991.
17 The case did not end with this ruling. In September 1999, the Cairo Administrative Court issued another ruling which recognised that Sally had taken all the necessary legal measures to register at al-Azhar University. The Court therefore ordered the university to admit her to the Faculty of Medicine for Women (*al-Hayat*, 30 September 1999; Court of Administrative Justice, case no 4019/50, 1st circuit, 28 September 1999). On 14 November 1999, al-Azhar filed an appeal against the Administrative Court decision, charging that Sally did not meet its moral and ethical standards in view of the fact that 'she performs as a belly dancer in night clubs and has been arrested several times on vice charges' (*Middle East Times*, 18–24 November 1999). The same Administrative Court issued a ruling, on 20 June 2000, suspending the implementation of the September 1999 ruling, on the ground that new evidence had been produced (interviews with newspapers, including photographs of Sally dressed as a belly dancer) which contradicted the conduct required of a woman belonging to this Faculty. Accordingly, the Court transferred the case to the State Litigation Office for further inquiry (Court of Administrative Justice, case no 1487/54, 20 June 2000).

18 Bälz, 1998.
19 Fahmy, 1998.
20 Elias, 1991, p. 59.
21 Elias, 1991, p. 65.
22 Court of Appeal, 2 April 1897.
23 Court of Appeal, 4 January 1937.
24 Court of Cassation, 28 March 1983, Majmû'a al-qawâ'id al-qânûniyya, C4, no 188, p. 184.
25 Neuberg,1996.
26 Cayla, 1996.
27 Foucault, 1990, p. 12.
28 Foucault, 1990, pp. 34–35.
29 Gauchet, 1985, p. 130.
30 Ferrié, Boëtsch and Ouafik, 1994, p. 682.
31 Ferrié, Boëtsch and Ouafik, 1994, p. 686.
32 Joseph, 1991.
33 Watson, 1998, p. 211.
34 Council of State (Majlis al-dawla), 28 December 1997.
35 Elias, 1991, p. 164.
36 Court of Appeal, Cairo, 14 June 1995.
37 Carty, Carzo and Jori, 1993.
38 Ost and van de Kerchove, 1993.
39 Ibid.
40 Ferrié, 1997, pp. 80–82.

Bibliography

Bälz, K., 'Human rights, the rule of law, and the construction of tradition: The Egyptian supreme administrative court and female circumcision (appeal no 5257/43, 28 December 1997)', *Egypte/Monde arabe*, 34, 1998, pp. 141–53.

Botros, S., 'Consentement', in M. Canto-Sperber (ed.), *Dictionnaire d'éthique et de philosophie morale*, Paris, Presses Universitaires de France, 1996, pp. 310–13.

Bouretz, P., 'Identité morale', in M. Canto-Sperber (ed.), *Dictionnaire d'éthique et de philosophie morale*, Paris, Presses Universitaires de France, 1996, pp. 446–52.

Carty, J.A., D. Carzo and M. Jori, 'Ordre', in A.J. Arnaud et al., (eds), *Dictionnaire encyclopédique de théorie et de sociologie du droit*, 2nd ed., Paris, Librairie Générale de Droit et de Jurisprudence, 1993, pp. 415–17.

Cayla, O., 'Droit', in M. Canto-Sperber (ed.), *Dictionnaire d'éthique et de philosophie morale*, Paris, Presses Universitaires de France, 1996, pp. 439–46.

Dupret, B., '"Vent d'est, vent d'ouest": l'Occident du droit égyptien', *Egypte/Monde arabe*, 30–31, 1997, pp. 93–112.

Elias, N., *La civilisation des mœurs*, Paris, Calmann-Lévy, 1973.

– *La société des individus*, Paris, Fayard, 1991.

Fahmy, K., 'Law, medicine and society in nineteenth-century Egypt', *Egypte/Monde arabe*, 34, 1998 (2), pp. 17–51.

Ferrié, J.-N., 'Enonciation et visibilité des morales au Maghreb et au Machrek', 'Sociétés et cultures musulmanes d'hier et d'aujourd'hui', Paris, Association Française d'Études sur le Monde Arabe et Musulman, 1996 (unpublished paper).

– 'Solidarité islamique sans consensus en Egypte: un cadre d'analyse', *Les Annales de l'Autre Islam*, 4, 1997, pp. 73–83.

Ferrié, J.-N., G. Boëtsch and A. Ouafik, '"Vécu juridique", norme et sens de la justice: à propos de l'avortement au Maroc', *Droit et Société*, 28, 1994, pp. 677–90.

Foucault, M., *History of Sexuality I*, trans. R. Hurely, London and New York, Penguin Books, 1990.

Gauchet, M., *Le Désenchantement du monde. Une histoire politique de la religion*, Paris, Gallimard, 1985.

Joseph, I., 'Voir, exposer, observer', in I. Joseph (ed.), *L'espace du public*, Paris, Plan urbain, 1991.

Lepetit, B., 'Le présent de l'histoire', in B. Lepetit (ed.), *Les formes de l'expérience. Une autre histoire sociale*, Paris, Albin Michel, 1995.

Montefiore, A., 'Identité morale', in M. Canto-Sperber (ed.), *Dictionnaire d'éthique et de philosophie morale*, Paris, Presses Universitaires de France, 1996, pp. 691–97.

Neuberg, M., 'Responsabilité', in M. Canto-Sperber (ed.), *Dictionnaire d'éthique et de philosophie morale*, Paris, Presses Universitaires de France, 1996, pp. 1306–12.

– *Bonnes moeurs, discours pénal et rationalité juridique. Essai d'analyse critique*, Bruxelles, Publications des Facultés universitaires Saint-Louis, 1981.

Niyâba, 'General Prosecution's Memorandum in Case no 21 of the Year 1988' (Mudhakkirat al-niyâba al-'âmma fî al-qadiyya raqam 21 li-sana 1988), *Majalla hay'a qadâyâ al-dawla*, 35/4, 1991, pp. 159–69.

Ost, F. and M. van de Kerchove, 'Moeurs (Bonnes)', in A.J. Arnaud et al., (eds), *Dictionnaire encyclopédique de théorie et de sociologie du droit*, 2nd ed., Paris, Librairie Générale de Droit et de Jurisprudence, 1993, pp. 380–83.

Parizeau, M.-H., 'Bioéthique', in M. Canto-Sperber (ed.), *Dictionnaire d'éthique et de philosophie morale*, Paris, Presses Universitaires de France, 1996, pp. 155–60.

Penneau, J., 'Médecine', *Jurisclasseur Pénal*, Fascicule 40, 1996.

Qâyid, 'U.'A., *Physicians' Criminal Liability: Comparative Study Islamic sharî'a – Positive Law (al-Mas'ûliyya al-jinâ'iyya li'l-atibbâ': Dirâsa muqârana fî'l-sharî'a al-islâmiyya wa'l-qânûn al-wad'î)*, Cairo, 1987.

Skovgaard-Petersen, J., *Defining Islam for the Egyptian State: Muftis and Fatwas of the Dâr al-Iftâ*, Leiden-New York-Köln, Leiden, 1997.

Watson, R., 'Ethnomethodology, Consciousness and Self', *Journal of Consciousness Studies*, 5/2, 1998, pp. 202–23.

CHAPTER 12

Can *Hisba* be 'Modernised'? The Individual and the Protection of the General Interest before Egyptian Courts

Nathalie Bernard-Maugiron

Prompted by recent discussions centred on *hisba* in Egypt, the present research endeavours to re-situate this procedural technique in the broader question of the role of the individual in defence of the general interest, summoning a few legal principles and tracing their recent evolution. The research is mainly based on Egyptian law, but also refers to developments known in other countries, above all in France and, secondarily, in the US.

Legal personality can be defined, in law, as the capacity to become a holder of rights and liable to obligations. Among the rights that legal personality confers are the possibility of access to justice and, its corollary, the capacity to be summoned before the courts. This capacity to take action is represented in a particular act: to bring a claim before the court. The nature of the rule of law is, in effect, sanctionable by the public authority and legal action is the means to request its implementation.

The judge may not examine litigation *ex officio*; a matter must be laid before him by one of the concerned parties. Egyptian procedural law, like French law,[1] requires of the individual a direct and personal interest in order that his legal action be deemed admissible. In the contrary case, the case is declared inadmissible without its substance being examined by the judge.

Interest is a vague notion and one which the combined efforts of academics and the judge have not always succeeded in defining or circumscribing.

> Jurisdictional rulings which usually orient academics [the doctrine] do not appear to give legal force to a single and precise conception of interest such that uncertainties of precedents are added to doctrinal differences and further obscure an already complex notion.[2]

It is also a multifaceted notion, the criteria of which vary according to jurisdictional orders (civil, administrative, constitutional) and which may even vary within a single jurisdictional order (administrative).

Interest is generally defined as an advantage of a material (payment of a sum of money) or a moral nature (compensation for an infringement upon honour, name or the intimacy of private life) which would result from a ruling, assuming that the claim is recognised as well-founded: 'To say of a person that he has an interest in taking action is to say that the claim that he presented is likely to modify his legal condition by improving it'.[3] The applicant must prove that he or she will derive a personal advantage from the outcome of the trial. This is underscored by the adages: 'no interest, no action', restated in Egyptian law as *haythu lâ maslaha fa-lâ da'wâ,* and 'interest is the measure of the action': *al-maslaha manât al-da'wâ.* As for the direct character of interest, it is 'less a condition related to the tort than to the chain of causality between the tort and the act of the person from which the tort ensues'.[4] Academics see the requirement of interest as intended to 'sparingly use the time of the judges, state funds and to prevent the creation of pointless and vexatious disputes'.[5] It is thus essentially a question of filtering claims so as to avoid encumbering the courts.

There is, however, in Egyptian as in French law, a litigation called 'objective', in which legal action is not aimed at defending a personal interest, but seeks the redress of transgressions against the general interest of society. The action, therefore, does not aim at redressing the violation of a subjective right or of a liberty, but the violation of the principle of legality according to which laws shall be respected. General interest is, itself, also a flexible imprecise notion, 'both indefinable and irreplaceable'.[6] It is a question of the interest which is effectively or potentially common to members of a community, a common good which exceeds and transcends the sum of particular interests. It is thus a contingent notion, dependent on the philosophy and the system of values upon which the society is based, the content of which varies according to government. Its defence is confided in the state which is charged to protect and promote the interest of the entire collectivity.

The question, of course, arises as to whether private individuals can be empowered to act in defence of the general interest, if popular actions (*actio popularis*) can be deemed admissible. Why not conceive that any individual, without having to prove a direct or personal interest, would be authorised to seek punishment for the violation of a norm in defence of the general interest threatened by the illegality of a norm or of a behaviour? As regards criminal matters, popular action would correspond to popular accusation, 'a process by which any citizen has the right, in behalf of society, to seek the punishment of the guilty'.[7] This procedure would allow private individuals, other than the direct victims, to be parties concerned in proceedings against crimes and offences in order to protect the social order. If the acceptance of this type of action in criminal matters would run the risk of leading to denouncement and other types of abuse, why not envision authorising it in other litigation, in particular, administrative and constitutional, so that each citizen might be party concerned in the defence of the public order?

Alongside personal interest and the general interest, a new category of interest has recently appeared in other countries such as France: collective interest shared by a group of individuals who find themselves in a similar situation. These collective interests, which are sometimes aimed at defending a 'cause', such as that of believers or, more prosaically, economic interests, are raised not by the public prosecutor but by associations or even by ordinary individuals, who are led to act as a 'private public prosecutor'. The private person, individual or group is induced towards taking action in a community interest. In any case, his or her action is intended to have a significance surpassing the parties in the case and extends, in power, to all members of a more-or-less definite collectivity.

This contemporary evolution of procedural law in a large number of 'modern' legal systems thus entails a waning of the individualist conception of legal action and of the law. How not to be tempted to compare this contemporary evolution, which some link to 'post-modernism', to the 'renaissance' of the procedure of *hisba* in Egypt in the last few years? A procedure with disputed origins, it has frequently been used as a way of referral to courts for the defence of essential values under the jurisdiction of Islamic public order and has recently been expressly incorporated into the Egyptian corpus of positive law. This resurgence of a known institution of Muslim law has often been analysed as the incorporation of a traditional institution, laden with its entire past, into contemporary law. The present research, rejecting this hypothesis, attempts, on the contrary, to deny *hisba* its singularity and its Arab-Muslim specificity and to relocate it in the more general and paradoxical contemporary phenomenon of the collectivisation of the legal process and of the strengthening of individualism.

I shall thus briefly review the different types of litigation known in Egyptian law and shall examine the place accorded or refused by each of them to the protection of the general interest by individuals. I shall then make a detour so as to broaden the discussion, evoking an evolution recently encountered in other countries before returning to Egyptian law and the *hisba* petition.

Egyptian jurisdictions and the protection of general interest

Each order of jurisdiction has fixed its own criteria for the admissibility of claims according to the type of litigation which is brought before it. A direct and personal interest is required for the majority of actions in civil matters, because they guarantee the respect for individual prerogatives. The same holds for full judicial administrative actions or for civil actions taken by victims of punishable offences. The action for abrogation of an administrative act (petition for action *ultra vires*), which comes under the heading of objective litigation, is certainly accessible to ordinary private individuals, but the latter must prove a direct and personal interest. In criminal matters, the public prosecutor has a near monopoly on the defence of the general interest, exercising public action so as to ensure the prosecution of offences. Constitutional litigation also merits examination for its intent is the protection of the fundamental norm upon which the entire organisation of public powers rests.

Civil litigation

Civil litigation, in principle, opposes individuals who seek to protect personal interests, subjective rights or civil liberties. Article 3 of the Egyptian Code of Civil and Commercial Procedure of 1968, as amended by Law no 81 of 1996, requires of all applicants that they present a direct and personal interest (*maslaha shakhsiyya wa-mubâshira*). As in France, Egyptian academics and judges have interpreted this requirement as residing, in principle, in a right which has been violated or for which an imminent risk of violation exists. Consequently, only the holder of the right or his representative, to the exclusion of all other individuals, can institute proceedings. It is exceptional for the public prosecutor to intervene to protect the interests of society.

Criminal litigation

Criminal law rests on the idea that the individual who has contravened the law, committed a misdemeanour or a felony has thereby infringed upon the interests of society and that society ought to defend itself. It does this through a state institution created especially to this purpose: the public prosecutor (*al-niyâba*), who will decide on the advisability of legal proceedings. The public prosecutor alone can initiate action, to the exclusion of individuals. Criminal trials do not require a personal and direct interest on the part of the applicant, as the public prosecutor seeks only to enforce respect for the law and to punish infringements on the social order. However, when the offence is the source of damage or injury, the victim can institute proceedings before the criminal courts at the same time as the prosecution or, independently, before civil jurisdictions.

Prosecution and compensation thus come together in the same proceedings even if the underlying interests are distinct:

> the interest in prosecution which the victim of an offence can have – which is essentially a 'moral' interest – does not appear to necessarily coincide with the interest which society can derive from the application of punishment (deterrent, neutralising or re-socialisation actions), but to reside often in the satisfaction of a personal interest, that is, the exercise of 'revenge' which is not public but private.[8]

In Egypt, as in France, general interest and individual interest are thus clearly separated and the opening of criminal proceedings is reserved for the public prosecutor alone who can institute legal proceedings even if the victim decides not to lodge a complaint. This principle is based on the idea that society has an interest in seeing that its offenders are punished.

Administrative litigation

Administrative acts, statutory or individual, are liable to infringe upon individual liberties or on private property. Two hypotheses can be distinguished, according to whether the administrative act constitutes a direct cause of grounds for individual complaint or not. In the former case, it is a question of a full judicial action (*da'wâ al-qadâ' al-kâmil*), which is accessible to the person whose rights have been infringed upon. The conditions which the interest must fulfil are thus similar to those required in civil matters where the applicant seeks to protect a personal right. In the latter case (action for abrogation or petition for action *ultra vires, da'wâ al-ilghâ'*), the applicant seeks the annulment of an administrative decision by reason of its illegality. Therefore, a subjective right is not exercised, but an invocation of the general protection of the laws, seeking to expose an abuse of power. One would imagine that this recourse would be accessible to all. In fact, a public interest is undeniably at stake: the legality of an administrative act. Moreover, the objective is to have the administrative judge undertake examining the conformity of an act to other norms. This is not, however, the conception which has been adopted. The applicant must have a personal interest, must have been affected by the administrative act and be included among its potential addressees.

Thus, in conformity with Article 12 of the law of 1972 on the Council of State: 'claims presented by persons having no personal interest are inadmissible'. Of course, differing from civil actions or from full judicial actions, an infringement upon the rights of the applicant is not required, as a simple personal interest suffices for the action to be deemed admissible. In addition, the Egyptian administrative judge is seen to be flexible in the judgement of this situation and lessens rigour by requiring only that the applicant be 'in a particular legal situation [*fî hâla qânûniyya khâssa*]' *vis-à-vis* this administrative act.[9] Nevertheless, the individual cannot invoke the protection of the interests of Egyptian society or respect for the law which would have been violated by the adoption of an illegal administrative act. The public prosecutor cannot intervene to protect the general interest in distinction with criminal litigation, having always been considered as too closely linked to the executive to be in a position to oppose abuses perpetrated by political or administrative organs.

Constitutional litigation

The Egyptian Supreme Constitutional Court is charged with the review of the constitutionality of laws and administrative regulations, that is, it observes that all the laws voted by the parliament and all the administrative regulations adopted by the executive power are in conformity with the provisions of the 1971 constitution. This jurisdiction, therefore, defends the fundamental principles listed in the constitution, that is the basic values of the Egyptian State (organisation of public powers and protection of fundamental rights).

There exists an action to protect the general interest. The ordinary judge before whom a litigation is in progress can decide, on his own initiative, to contest the constitutionality of the law which should be applied and transfer the case to the Supreme Constitutional Court. In this case, the judge has no direct and personal interest to see the law declared unconstitutional, but seeks only to protect the Egyptian legal order. The judge acts, however, as a public authority and not as an ordinary individual.

In addition to this referral to court by the judge dealing with the merits of the case, there is another way of referral which is used more in practice: that which is left to the initiative of the parties. The law on the Supreme Constitutional Court foresees that a case can be referred to it by one of the parties in dispute before the judge on merits. This law refers in all procedural matters to the Code of Civil and Commercial Procedure. And, as seen, the latter requires, in its Article 3, that the applicant, in order to be admitted before the civil or commercial courts, have a direct and personal interest. As the legislator has not been more explicit regarding the characteristics required of the interest, it is for the Supreme Constitutional Court to determine them.

The court has decided that, since only indirect review was allowed – that is a litigation needs to be pending before a judge dealing with the merits of the case for a plea of unconstitutionality to be raised – it is necessary that the author of the plea of unconstitutionality bring proof that there exists for this person a bond (*irtibât*) between the interest in the action on the merits of the case and the interest in the action on unconstitutionality. Since the early 1990s, the Supreme Constitutional Court not only requires that the judgement on the plea of unconstitutionality 'would have effects [*yu'aththir*]' on the action dealing with the merits of the litigation, but that it would also be 'indispensable to resolve [*lâzim li-l-fasl*] the claim which is connected to it and which is pending before the judge on merits'. Thus, the outcome of the legal proceedings must depend on the validity of the norm. Should the response which it gives to the question placed before it by the judge on merits not affect the attitude of the latter in the main trial, the court will refuse to give a ruling.

One could imagine that this type of litigation would be more widely accessible and that the individual interest of each person see that the fundamental norms of the state are respected and would fit in with 'the general interest of the public collectivity wanting to further exist'.[10] The general interest in the framework of constitutional review would be to see that the hierarchy of norms and the rule of law are respected. The requirement of a direct and personal interest in constitutional litigation is, however, not specific to Egypt, but exists at most of the other constitutional courts that recognise the same type of referral. What is paradoxical in Egyptian litigation is that the state would always be the defendant in the constitutional proceedings. The state, opposing the individual who claims that the constitution has been violated, will defend the law and not the constitution. One could have thought that, since the defence of the general interest traditionally falls to the state and since respect for the principle of legality is in the general interest, it would have to defend the constitution and not the law.

Towards a recognition of new forms of interests

The notion of interest in Egyptian law has, in very large measure, restated the analogous concepts of French law. In France, the criteria of legal proceedings were elaborated in the nineteenth century within a liberal and individualist perspective, centred on the valorisation of man as subject. The prevailing idea was that modern society must perceive man as subject in order to distinguish itself from non-modern societies in which the group is perceived as an entity. Individuals defend their personal interests and the state is charged to ensure the well-being of all, going beyond particular interests:

> Torn by the sterile and insoluble confrontation of antagonistic interests, irreparably divided over itself, civil society only accedes to unity by way of the mediating intervention of the state which prescribes, assembles, incorporates and ensures social integration.[11]

The general interest also makes it possible to legitimate the state and its activity, it alone being able to stand as guarantor for the well-being of all.

The distinction between private interest and general interest tends to be blurred. Individualism in legal action is in the process of waning in Western law. It is being rediscovered there that society is not made up only of isolated individuals, but that the collectivity which groups them together also has its own reality with specific objectives. The distinction between the public and the private spheres also tends to diminish, with the intervention in the public space of individuals who are in competition with power holders to impose other systems of reference. This phenomenon also gives rise to the 'negotiated law' in which even administrative decisions are increasingly more often worked out in collaboration with their addressees.

General interest, for its part, formerly represented by the public prosecutor alone, is breaking up into a sum of collective interests. Judiciary law thus attempts to modernise itself in order to adapt to social phenomena and to the conflicts of its times. Given the lack of precision or the silence of the texts, this adaptation will be effectuated mainly by the judge, to whom it falls to open more or less wide the doors of the court, determining and weighing the interests as they appear. The judge has therefore accepted to recognise appeals based on a new type of interest, the collective interest, to defend the great causes or the simple egoistic interests of a group of individuals. In Egypt, the judge has even gone to the extent of declaring admissible individual actions in defence of the general interest.

Defence of the collective interest by groups: the 'great causes'

Beside individual interest and general interest, a new form of interest has appeared: collective interest. One speaks of collective interest when a group of persons takes legal action in the interest of the social category that it claims to represent (for example, the collective interests of a profession). Collective interest is thus distinct from both the personal interest of the group (for example, the protection of its existence, of its property, of the conditions of its functioning) and from the individual interest of its members. It makes it possible for groups[12] that are not personally aggrieved to be recognised as having the capacity to take action – on the condition, however, that they are judged to be representatives of a distinctly identifiable collectivity and that the interest of this collectivity would be clearly distinct from the general interest:

> Contemporary case-law, marked by a progressive and constant relaxing of conditions placed on the admissibility of groups to take legal action translates the existence of interests, other than individual and subjective, at the same time as their adaptation to an evolving economic and social environment.[13]

These groups will be able to take action without being dissuaded by the complexity and the cost of the legal proceedings, as is the case for ordinary individuals.

The courts, by granting them the right to take legal action, reinforced the legal recognition of these groups. The idea prevailed for a long time in France that intermediary bodies were pointless or even harmful and that they threatened to compromise individual freedom. This aversion entailed an exclusion of collective action and the construction of a highly centralised state charged with embodying the general interest. Civil society therefore intervened only marginally in the creation and protection of the law. This reticence was even stronger as regards associations, their disinterested objectives having always inspired defiance by the public powers. Even in France, this hostility towards and distrust of groups tends to lessen. Jurisdiction has accepted plaints introduced by private institutions with the aim of defending a group interest. The legislator has followed and has gradually become oriented towards a broadening of the rights of groups to take legal action.

The French orders of jurisdiction do not all have the same attitude regarding collective appeals introduced by groups. The administrative courts began very early to recognise actions for abrogation introduced by unions or even by associations. In criminal matters, subsequent to lively controversies, the Court of Cassation ultimately authorised unions to claim damages in respect of facts causing direct or indirect harm to the collective interest of the profession which they represent.[14] This solution was ratified by the legislature[15] and extended by the judge to union actions in civil matters, even in the absence of criminal offence.

Associations, which were for a long time held at a distance from the courts, were authorised by the legislator to claim damages for the defence of collective interests relevant to their social purpose (for example, associations to fight against racism, consumer protection, anti-alcohol leagues, associations having the protection of the environment as their aim). Thus, special authorisation enabled these associations to take over from the public prosecutor without, however, substituting themselves for him or obstructing the courts. In the absence of a special text, however, criminal courts refuse to recognise such plaints. In civil matters, that is in the absence of a punishable criminal offence, courts are still very divided; the Court of Cassation[16] continues to deem inadmissible plaints introduced by unauthorised associations, while civil courts dealing with the merits of the case are more liberal.

If the recognition of the notion of group interest is, in large part, resultant of changes in economic legislation,[17] other domains have also been affected. The cause of believers is included among the 'great causes' that the judges dealing with the merits of the case have authorised associations to defend.

Cases have been submitted on several occasions to the French courts concerning expeditious litigation (*juge des référés*) demanding the banning of films which they viewed as attacking the Catholic faith. The first instance was the film *Ave Maria*, the banning of which was requested by the Saint Pious X Association on the grounds that it constituted 'a particularly violent outrage to the essential values and realities of French Catholics'. Its complaint was judged admissible and it obtained that advertisements of the film depicting a cross upon which was tied a woman with naked breasts, which, according to the judge, constituted 'a manifestly illicit disturbance',[18] would be removed from all public places. It was then the turn of the film, *Je vous salue Marie*, Jean-Luc Godard's, to be summoned to appear before a court of expeditious litigation by the General Alliance against Racism and for the Respect of French and Christian Identity (AGRIF) and the National Confederation of Associations of Catholic Families. The admissibility of the action was not questioned even though their claim was rejected in substance,[19] just as the judge deemed admissible the action introduced by the same AGRIF in the instance of Martin Scorsese's *La dernière tentation du Christ.*[20]

Although no legislative text authorises these associations to make this type of complaint, the court nevertheless deemed their actions to be admissible. In the case of *Ave Maria*, the Court of First Instance in Paris held that the associations were entitled to take action:

> seeing that, whether by their statutes or by their personal right founded on an individual belief that they intend to defend through the recourse to legal proceedings, the principles and the norms constituting the Catholic religion and morals and invoke, in order to do this, a moral interest held as legitimate by the rules of French social life.[21]

The appeal judge confirmed this ruling of the judge of First Instance, stating that:

> with good reason, the first judges, on grounds adopted by them in this regard and which the court adopts, declared the Saint Pious X Association and the intervening parties on the side of this association admissible in their action and interventions since the former, by its statutes, and the latter, by their statutes or personal rights founded on an individual belief which could, in no way, be placed in doubt, act to defend, through the recourse to legal proceedings, the principles and dogmas of the Catholic religion and morals, invoking a legitimate moral interest.[22]

In the case of *Je vous salue Marie*, admissibility was granted on the grounds 'that, according to the terms of their statutes, they [the associations] intend to defend, by sole legal means, the fundamental principles and dogmas constituting the Catholic religion and morals'.

In all of these cases, the judge invoked the statutes of the association to establish its right to take legal action, thus referring to the collective interest of the said association and not to the individual interests of its members (their right to the respect of their beliefs). Nevertheless, the aim of these associations was broad, even in a secular state such as France, namely to protect principles and fundamental dogmas constituting the Catholic religion and morals. Many academics were thus astonished that the complaint had been judged admissible by the judge.[23] The question is, in fact, to know where to draw the line between collective interest and general interest. If private law groups are authorised to defend collective interests and if public law moral persons continue to call upon the general interest, the demarcation between the two types of interest is likely at times to be difficult to determine. Is the general interest characterised by the number of persons involved? By the types of interest in question? Is the collective interest not but an aspect, a part, of the general interest? 'These new collective interests are only divisions of the general interest detached from the latter for reasons of commodity or of efficacy in prosecution.'[24] Until the present time, the judge has hidden himself behind the purpose of the association to form an opinion as to its interest in taking action.

The recognition of the interests of groups carries the risk, moreover, of infringing upon the prerogatives of the state and of undermining its legitimacy.

> By admitting the access of individuals to the criminal trial, above all, when it is a matter of groups which act more and more overtly in the name of general interests and with the aim of prosecution, making the 'criminal couple' to be a 'ménage à trois', there is no doubt that the traditional role of the state has been weakened or, indeed, partially put in question.[25]

There is also the risk that only the most powerful associations or the most popular of them succeed in having their legal actions declared admissible.

> In the end, these decisions in favour of the admissibility of 'associational' actions instituted with a view to the defence of objectively considered collective interests, those of 'great causes', are still confined to a few domains in which pressure groups are strong and know all the better to make themselves heard by the law as the causes that they defend meet with a favourable echo in the population and are massively relayed by the media.[26]

Along with collective actions in defence of great causes, other actions have appeared in the defence of the egoistic collective interests of a group of individuals.

The defence of egoistic collective interests by individuals

Industrial society has engendered a new type of legal relations entailing more and more often entire categories of individuals – and not isolated individuals – in which damages are simultaneously likely to affect a large number of persons. For the purpose of enabling injured parties who are unaware of their rights or who fear high legal costs to defend themselves, a new type of collective protection has appeared.

The US, although known for its individualism, has what is termed class action, 'an action introduced by a representative on behalf of an entire class of persons with identical or similar rights which leads to the pronouncement of a judgement having the force of *res judicata* towards all the members of the class'.[27] In this system, 'the representative does not act to defend a great cause but rather egoistic interests of individuals'.[28] This mechanism, which exists on the federal level as well as on the level of states, makes it possible to concentrate litigation before a single jurisdiction.

The action is instituted by an individual who represents an unorganised group of persons who find themselves in the same legal situation, that is who are confronted with similar questions of law or fact. It enables the victims to unite and reduce their costs and enables the defenders to regulate, for once and for all, a question which would have given place to numerous and interminable litigation. A victim can, however, request his exclusion from the group in order to retain the right of individual action. The court controls the representivity of the initiator of the action;

it will ensure that the plaintiff is, in fact, a member of the 'class' of persons whose interest has been brought before the court and that he or she acts in the interest of this same class. The representative, approved by the court, takes responsibility for all the costs of the proceedings. The ruling will have the force of *res judicata* towards all the members of the group, and eventual damages obtained by the representative will be distributed among them.[29] This traditional institution of equity has undergone significant development in the last decades to face the new needs engendered by economic and social changes.

This procedure has been introduced in other areas, including Quebec, that belongs to the family of Civil Law.[30] A 'collective complaint' based on class action was introduced there in 1978, but clashed with the reticence of judges, who interpreted the conditions of admissibility in a restrictive manner so as to limit its use.[31] As for France, there was an attempt in the 1990s to introduce an 'action by joint representation' inspired by class action, but this was a failure. The legislator authorised consumer associations to take legal action in order to obtain compensation for individual injury or loss suffered by several consumers. In distinction to class action, this action cannot be taken by individuals, but only by consumer associations approved at the national level. In addition, the action reposes explicitly on a mandate bestowed by members of the group on the association which represents them. The attempt was repeated with approved associations for the protection of the environment, but it met with the same failure. And the failure was such that 'the action by joint representation, far from representing a first step towards group action, constituted an elegant means of burying it'.[32]

Another procedure has also appeared in the United States: the '*qui tam* actions' from the Latin, '*qui tam pro domino rege quam pro se ispo in hac part sequitur*', meaning 'he who as much for the king as for himself sues in this matter'. By means of this *qui tam* action, individuals lodge complaints on behalf of the sovereign and then share with the state the eventual damages obtained. This action is not based on a personal damage, but on a damage suffered by the power as such. It thus makes it possible to associate private initiatives and public controls in the protection of collective interests.[33]

The recognition of action for the protection of collective interests infringes upon a certain number of classic principles of judiciary law as, for example, the principle of hearing the full argument of both parties. The consequences of the judge's ruling are not limited to only the parties at trial, but extend to all members of the represented community even when not present at the trial. As for the responsibility of the defendant, it is the damage suffered by the whole of the collectivity and not only by the party present at the legal proceedings that must be considered. Thus, in place of the sole compensation for damage suffered there is now the compensation for the full damage produced.[34]

A new category of rights can be recognised in collective action, but the individual is still nevertheless faced, as in general interest, with a choice which he or she does not entirely master. He or she must, in fact, submit to the choice made by his or her representatives. How is one to avoid that only the most powerful succeed in making themselves heard?

> The fear is to see, somewhat following the example of the United States, the establishment as general interest of the particular interests of the strongest groups to the detriment of the less powerful which, only because they cannot make themselves heard, are relegated to the role of bearers of individual interests.[35]

To recover his autonomy, the individual will, therefore, be inclined to take action alone.

The defence of the general interest in Egypt by individuals: the hisba *petition*

Although, as seen, Egyptian law requires that the applicant have a direct and personal interest, some courts have consented to examine actions based on a *hisba* petition. It is a question of an institution in Muslim law which enables individuals to act in the name of the defence of Islamic public order. Its origin is found in the Qur'anic obligation incumbent on every Muslim to command goodness and condemn misdeeds (*amr bi-l-mâ 'rûf wa-nahî 'an al-munkar*)[36] and has been used as a way of referral to the courts on behalf of the protection of religious values common to the Islamic community. Attempts to put this procedure back into force have recently occurred before various Egyptian courts with greater or lesser success. A double motive is generally invoked by the applicants in support of their petition: as Muslims, they have a direct and personal interest in combating all that which could represent a transgression of Islam; in addition, the general interest of society is also in question: Islamic principles, the laws of God and belonging to the Egyptian public order.

This procedure was first brought before the civil courts, most particularly the courts of personal status, during the affair of Nasr Hamîd Abû Zayd, a professor of Arab literature accused of apostasy by reason of his writings and sentenced to separate from his wife.[37] It was also put forward in the case of Youssef Chahine's film, *The Immigrant* (*al-Muhâjir*), in which the applicants requested the banning of the film for having represented and debased the prophet Joseph.[38] In both cases, the judges dealing with the merits of the case were divided as to the admissibility of this type of action. The Court of Cassation, finally approached with the first case, concluded by ruling, in August 1996, that the *hisba* petition was admissible, by basing itself on a text from 1931 and the regulations of *shar'î* religious courts (*lâ'ihât tartîb al-mahâkîm al-shar'iyya*). Article 280 thereof indirectly authorised the *hisba* petition, as it authorised the judge to refer to the main texts of the Hanafite school of Islamic law which included *hisba*.[39]

The law, however, lacked clarity for, at that time, Article 3 of the Code of Civil and Commercial Procedure required only that the applicant have a 'born' (*qâ'im*) interest, even if the courts always required a direct and personal interest. The Code of Civil Procedure was amended subsequently to this case in 1996, and since then requires that proof be given of the applicant's direct and personal interest, stating, in addition, that this requirement holds for any action based on the Code of Civil and Commercial Procedure or on any other law.

One can scarcely avoid comparing the Abû Zayd and *al-Muhâjir* cases with the plaints introduced in France against films by Catholic associations. In both instances, the applicants sought to protect religious values, Muslim, on one hand, Catholic, on the other. In Egypt, of course, the complaint was not introduced by an association but by an individual. However, in the Abû Zayd case, a group petition was not far removed as the recourse had been taken by a collective of lawyers. In addition, it will be noted that in the case of the film *Ave Maria*, abbots for example, intervened individually along with the Saint Pious X Association and the judge deemed their intervention admissible on the basis of 'individual belief'.

Egyptian administrative jurisdictions have also been drawn to examine the question of the admissibility of *hisba* petitions, which they always refused to examine. In 1981, for example, an applicant invoked *hisba* before the Court of Administrative Justice of the Council of State so as to obtain the abrogation of a presidential decree which had awarded a high decoration on a vice-president of the Council of State. The applicant held that this distinction was contrary to the principle of the independence of the judiciary, as this judge would have to rule in the future on the legality of presidential decrees. The applicant invoked the protection of public order (*al-nizâm al-'âmm*). The administrative judge rejected this argument, stating that Egyptian administrative law requires at least a personal interest in actions for abrogation and that the mere quality of 'citizen' seeking to defend the public order was insufficient. In the contrary case, added the court, 'this would mean allowing the admissibility of *hisba* petitions'. The Supreme Administrative Court, before which the case had been appealed, confirmed the dismissal of *hisba* petitions, but held that, as an advocate, the applicant had a direct and personal interest in the abrogation of the decree.[40]

However, the court rejected the appeal in substance. When the Court of Administrative Justice and then the Supreme Administrative Court were approached, in 1996 and 1997 respectively, with an action for abrogation against a decree from the Ministry of Health forbidding hospitals to practise excision, the applicants made a point of invoking a direct and personal interest,[41] introducing an action based on Article 12 of the law on the Council of State and not a *hisba* petition. In its judgement of 28 December 1997, the Supreme Administrative Court stated that

> the extensive interpretation of the condition of personal interest respective of actions for abrogation does not entail confusion with the notion of the hisba petition because the admissibility of the petition for action ultra vires [action for abrogation] is always subordinate to the presence of a personal interest on the part of the applicant.[42]

This unvarying position of the administrative judge in the rejection of *hisba* petitions can be explained by the flexibility of his interpretation of the notion of direct and personal interest and by the fact that no text pertaining to administrative matters exists, similar to that of 1931 on personal status, which could serve as a basis for the recognition of *hisba*.

The question of the admissibility of *hisba* petitions has also been referred to the Egyptian Supreme Constitutional Court which held that the requirement of a direct and personal interest on the part of the plaintiff excludes popular actions brought before the courts to defend the general interest and that, consequently, the *hisba* petitions based on the defence of public order are inadmissible. Thus, an applicant sought to have a press law from 1995 declared unconstitutional, a law that had hardened the penalties incurred in the case of publication crimes. Although not party to any litigation before a judge dealing with the merits of the case, the applicant based his action on a *hisba* petition and held that he had the right to take action 'for the protection of freedom'. The Supreme Court rejected his petition, holding that he had no direct and personal interest.[43]

Subsequent to the Abû Zayd case, the *hisba* procedure was monitored in the matter of personal status by giving the public prosecutor a fundamental role in endorsing or not endorsing private initiatives. Law no 3 of 29 January 1996 foresaw that any person wishing to introduce a *hisba* petition as regards personal status must approach the Public Prosecutor's Office with a substantiated petition. The office of the public prosecutor, then, has discretionary power to deal with this petition either by approaching the courts itself or by considering the case closed. As in criminal matters, the public prosecutor takes the place of the applicant; the individual who submits a case to the public prosecutor sees all rights he or she has relating to the petition being removed. This law, while integrating *hisba* into Egyptian positive law in the matter of personal status has, at the same time, significantly reduced its scope, enabling the state to assume control for the protection of the general interest.

Thus, an analysis of case-law clearly shows that *hisba* has often been invoked by applicants not to defend strictly religious values, but to defend the public order in a more general manner. This impression is further confirmed by a reading of works of academics. *Hisba* does, indeed, belong to contemporary Egyptian positive law, and the majority of jurists describe it as an institution enabling one to approach the courts to ensure the protection of the principle of legality. In a work devoted to the notion of interest before the Supreme Constitutional Court, one author first reviews the interpretation given to the notion of interest by other orders of Egyptian jurisdiction. Describing the administrative action for abrogation, he emphasises the fact that Egyptian courts require a personal interest on the part of the applicant 'which excludes *hisba* petitions that authorise an individual to submit such a petition to ensure the protection of the principle of legality [*mabda' al-mashrû'iyya*]'. In a footnote, the author then states: 'as to actions for abrogation and *hisba* petitions in France, see André Delaubadère, *Traité de droit administratif*, and Georges Vedel, *Droit administratif*'.[44] Both are classic works which, on the pages indicated, treat the principle of legality. As for the Supreme Constitutional Court, it assimilates the *hisba* petition with the direct review of constitutionality of laws, a procedure not available in Egypt which would allow individuals to raise a case directly before the Court without having to go through the judge on the merits.

The Abû Zayd case has shown the type of abuse to which *hisba* could lead in the matter of personal status, entailing an intervention of the legislator to regulate its use strictly by substituting the public prosecutor for the author of the petition. But why not envisage making this procedure accessible in the frame of administrative and constitutional litigation with the objective of protecting legality? It will be noted, in fact, that the *hisba* petition has not always been invoked for the defence of fixed religious values, but that it can also be called upon for the defence of public liberties. This was so in the case brought before the Supreme Constitutional Court in which the applicant invoked the protection of the freedom of expression to challenge the new press law, as in the case before the Council of State in which the applicant invoked the guarantee of the independence of the judiciary.

Contemporary values could be found among the standards and fundamental values of Islam that *hisba* seeks to preserve. In a country such as Egypt, which reserves only an insignificant place for intermediary groups such as unions, associations and NGOs, and associates them only infrequently with management of public affairs, could *hisba* not become the means for the individual to participate in power; could it not be a way to give the individual access to the public sphere? In particular, in constitutional litigation, this would amount to recognising the right of direct review by the constitutional judge as already exists in other countries. In order to prevent discrimination between individuals, this recourse would be open without distinction to Muslims and non-Muslims.[45] The risks of drift would be limited by the fact that it is the state, through its laws and its regulations, which would be summoned before the courts and not an individual.

The splitting up of the notion of interest draws forth, at the other end, the 'redeployment' of the judiciary process of the concept of responsibility. Paul Ricœur has shown how the appearance of responsibility without fault has entailed a loss of the sense of responsibility for an action, the concepts of solidarity, security and risk tending to replace the idea of individual fault. This phenomenon of de-individualisation, of collectivisation, of transition from 'an individual management of the fault to a socialised management of the risk',[46] the perverse effect of which will be the increasingly insistent search for someone responsible and the growing difficulty to identify the responsible[47] person, will lead to the questioning of the principle of individuation of punishments.[48] Thus, the collectivisation of interest and the loosening of the requirement of individual and personal interest would correspond to the collectivisation of responsibility through the socialisation of risks, at the cost of the concept of imputation of individual fault. As regards the protection of the environment, for instance, the requirement of personal interest at the start of a legal action and of a fault at the other end would vanish. To the 'mass violations'[49] would correspond a 'mass responsibility'.[50]

At the risk of being provocative, could the 'resurgence' of *hisba* not be perceived, rather than as a return to so-called traditional society, on the contrary, as a manifestation of the modernity of Egypt or even of its 'post-modernity' located in the contemporary and paradoxical phenomenon of 'self-absolutisation' and the 'exaltation of differences',[51] the phenomenon of individuation and interdependence underscored by Elias. *Hisba* is also inscribed in the present crisis in the representation of the individual where the individual again begins to carry out missions formerly confided to representatives. It would also be inscribed in another contemporary phenomenon, characterised by a growing individual intervention in the public sphere, which entails a *rapprochement* of public and private spheres earlier separated by a 'deep abyss'.[52]

In the same manner as American class action, a traditional institution of equity which has undergone significant development in the last years, *hisba* could be used to respond to new needs. The individual, indeed, is inscribed in a social, political and historical configuration and it is this dynamics of individual/society/power that will determine individual and collective behaviour and the application of the law to the social sphere in the rhythm of its reconfigurations. *Hisba* would then be but one example of recovery through the needs arising in one of the phases in the 'process of civilisation' of a traditional institution relating to an old normative system.

Notes

1 Egyptian law has adopted the basic concepts of French law in the matter, and Egyptian academics refer amply to French authors in their treatises and handbooks.
2 Laligant, 1971, p. 45.
3 Cadiet, 1992, p. 369.
4 Cadiet, 1992, p. 374.
5 Morel, *Traité élémentaire de procédure civile*, 2nd ed., 1949, Sirey, no 27, quoted by Bussy, 1997, p. 12.
6 Vedel, 1986, p. 3.
7 Van de Kerchove, 1990, p. 87.
8 Van de Kerchove, 1990, p. 94.
9 For a particularly flexible judgement of this condition, see the decision of the Council of State of 28 December 1997 on excision in which the Egyptian Supreme Administrative Court considered that the quality of Muslim citizen sufficed to represent a direct and personal interest for the applicant: Bälz, 1998, pp. 144–45.
10 Rigaux, 1990, p. 182.
11 Chevallier, 1990, p. 141.
12 For examples in comparative law for the defence of collective interest by specialised public organs (and not private groups) and the magnitude assumed by this phenomenon, see Cappelletti, 1975, pp. 581–83.
13 Hecquard-Theron, 1986, p. 68.
14 Court of Cassation, combined chambers, 5 April 1913.

15 Article L. 411.11 of the Labour Code, restating a law of 12 March 1920: 'They [the unions] have the right to go to court; they can, before all jurisdiction, exercise all the rights reserved for the civil party relating to acts directly or indirectly prejudicial to the collective interest of the profession which they represent'.

16 Court of Cassation, combined chambers, 15 June 1923.

17 At which point one could speak of the 'decadence' of the notion of general interest in this domain. See Guinchard, 1981.

18 'The representation of the symbol of the cross in blatant conditions of publicity and at places of inevitable public passage constitutes an act of aggressive and gratuitous intrusion in the intimate depths of the beliefs of those who, moving freely along public ways and seeking no contact or individual colloquy with a specific work or performance, see themselves – beyond any manifestation of will on their part – necessarily and brutally confronted with an expression of commercial publicity which is questionable and misleading and which, in any case, is constitutive of a manifestly illicit disturbance.' 'Tribunal de grande instance' TGI, Paris, 23 October 1984, Recueil Dalloz, Paris, 1985, p. 32.

19 'Whereas if the freedom of conscience and the right of each that his beliefs be respected must be ensured and protected against any act of aggressive intrusion and illegitimate provocation, the exercise of this liberty must be compatible with that – equally fundamental – of the freedom of artistic or literary expression.' TGI, Paris, 28 January 1985, Recueil Dalloz, Paris, 1985, p. 130. Also see *Gazette du Palais*, Paris, 1985, *chronique* Bertin, pp. 92–93.

20 TGI, Paris, 22 September 1988 and Paris, 27 September 1988, *Gazette du Palais*, 1988, pp. 735–39, note Bertin.

21 TGI Paris, 23 October 1984, Dalloz, 1985, p. 32.

22 Paris, 26 October 1984, *Gazette du Palais*, 1984, p. 729.

23 *Juris-classeur périodique*, 1985, II, 20452, note Hassler and *Revue trimestrielle de droit civil*, 1985, p. 767, obs. J. Normand.

24 Guinchard, 1981, p. 148.

25 Van de Kerchove, 1990, p. 113.

26 Guinchard, 1990, p. 626.

27 Boré, 1997, p. 359.

28 Boré, 1997, p. 396.

29 For a description of the functioning of this procedure, see Boré, 1997, pp. 359–79.

30 For examples of private initiatives for the protection of collective interests in Germany, Sweden and Italy see Cappelletti, 1975, pp. 585–86.

31 Boré, 1997, pp. 380–94.
32 Boré, 1997, p. 435.
33 See Khalil, 1997. For other examples of the combination of private initiatives and controls by public organs see Cappelletti, 1975, pp. 583–84.
34 Cappelletti, 1975, p. 597.
35 Zeghbib, 1998, p. 501.
36 Qur'an, sura 104.
37 In January 1994, the Court of First Instance deemed the petition inadmissible for lack of direct and personal interest on the part of the applicants, but its ruling was overturned in June 1995 by the Court of Appeal, which deemed the petition admissible as a *hisba* petition. For an analysis of this case see Dupret, 1996; Dupret and Ferrié, 1997a; Dupret and Ferrié, 1997b; Bälz, 1997; 'Jurisprudence Abû Zayd', 1998.
38 The first judge accepted, in December 1994, to examine the *hisba* petition, but his decision was set aside on appeal in March 1995 for lack of direct and personal interest on the part of the applicant. For an analysis of the case, see Bernard-Maugiron, 1997; Bernard-Maugiron, 1999.
39 These regulations were explicitly abrogated by Article 4 of the law promulgating Law no 1 in the year 2000, organising a number of procedural aspects in the matter of personal status.
40 See *Markaz al-musâ'ada al-qânûniyya li-huqûq al-insân,* al-hisba *bayna al-dawla al-madaniyya wa'l-dawla al-dîniyya* (*The* hisba *between secular and religious state*), Cairo, January 1996, pp. 7–10.
41 Bälz, 1998, pp. 144–45.
42 It is true that, in the case in point, the Council of State rendered a particularly extensive interpretation of the notion of direct and personal interest, declaring admissible the action of the applicants on the basis of their quality as 'Muslim citizens'.
43 Supreme Constitutional Court (SCC), 4 May 1996, no 40/17e, Digest of Rulings of the Supreme Constitutional Court, v. 7, pp. 615ff.
44 'Ali, 1996, p. 34, note no 2.
45 For the Copts' use of the *hisba* procedure, see, for example, 'Copts learn to use courts like hesba sheikhs', *Middle East Times*, 24 August 1997.
46 Engel, quoted by Ricœur, 1995, p. 58.
47 Ricœur, 1995, p. 59.
48 Ricœur, 1995, p. 60.
49 Cappelletti, 1975, p. 572.

50 Frogneux, 1999, p. 75.
51 Chevallier, 1998, p. 663.
52 Cappelletti, 1975, p. 575.

Bibliography

'Ali, I.M., *al-Maslaha fî al-da'wâ al-dustûriyya* (*The Interest in the Constitutional Action*), Cairo, Dâr al-nahda al-'arabiyya, 1996.

Bälz, K., 'Submitting faith to judicial scrutiny through the family trial: The "Abû Zayd case"', *Die Welt des Islams*, 37, 1997, pp. 135–55.

Bälz, K., 'Human rights, the rule of law, and the construction of tradition', *Egypte/Monde arabe*, 34, 1998, pp. 141–53.

Berger, M. and B. Dupret, 'Jurisprudence Abû Zayd', *Egypte/Monde arabe*, 34, 1998, pp. 169–201.

Bernard-Maugiron, N., 'Anatomie sociologique d'une affaire égyptienne. Le procès de 'l'Emigré', de Youssef Chahine', in G. Boëtsch, B. Dupret and J.-N. Ferrié (eds), *Droits et sociétés dans le monde arabe et musulman: perspectives socio-anthropologiques*, Aix-en-Provence, Presses universitaires d'Aix-Marseille, 1997, pp. 167–92.

– 'Legal pluralism and the closure of the legal field: The al-Muhajir case', in B. Dupret, M. Berger and L. al-Zwaini (eds), *Legal Pluralism in the Arab World*, The Hague, Kluwer Law International, 1999, pp. 173–89.

Boré, L., *La défense des intérêts collectifs par les associations devant les juridictions administratives et judiciaires*, Paris, Librairie générale de droit et de jurisprudence, series 'Bibliothèque de droit privé', 1997.

Bussy, F., 'Action', *Dalloz procédure civile*, March 1997, pp. 1–32.

Cadiet, L., *Droit judiciaire privé*, Paris, Litec, 1992.

Caillé, A., 'La sociologie de l'intérêt est-elle intéressante?', in A. Caillé, *Splendeurs et misères des sciences sociales*, Genève, Droz, 1986.

Cappelletti, M., 'La protection d'intérêts collectifs et de groupe dans le procès civil', *Revue internationale de droit comparé*, 1975, pp. 571–97.

Chevallier, J., 'Le concept d'intérêt en science administrative', in *Droit et intérêt*, Bruxelles, Publications des Facultés universitaires St Louis, 1990, 1, pp. 135–63.

– 'Vers un droit post-moderne? Les transformations de la régulation juridique', *Revue de droit public et de science politique en France et à l'étranger*, 3, 1998, pp. 659–90.

Debbasch, C. and J.-C. Ricci, *Contentieux administratif*, Paris, Précis Dalloz, 5th ed., 1990.

Deswarte, M.P., 'Intérêt général, intérêt commun', *Revue de droit public et de science politique en France et à l'étranger*, 5, 1988, pp. 1289–313.

Druet, F.-X. and E. Ganty (eds), *Rendre justice au droit. En lisant Le juste de Paul Ricœur*, Namur, Presses universitaires de Namur, 1999.

Dupret, B., 'L'affaire Abû Zayd, universitaire poursuivi pour apostasie', *Maghreb-Machrek*, 151, January–March 1996, pp. 18–22.

Dupret, B. and J.N. Ferrié , 'For intérieur et ordre public. Ou comment la problématique de l'Aufklärung peut permettre de décrire un débat égyptien', in G. Boëtsch, B. Dupret and J.-N. Ferrié, (eds), *Droits et sociétés dans le monde arabe et musulman: perspectives socio-anthropologiques*, Aix-en-Provence, Presses universitaires d'Aix-Marseille, 1997a, pp. 193–215.

– 'Participer au pouvoir, c'est édicter la norme: sur l'affaire Abu Zayd (Egypte: 1992–1996)', *Revue française de science politique*, 47/6, 1997b, pp. 762–75.

Frogneux, N., 'De nouvelles composantes du concept de responsabilité', in F. -X. Druet and E. Ganty (eds), *Rendre justice au droit. En lisant Le juste de Paul Ricœur*, Namur, Presses universitaires de Namur, 1999, pp. 75–88.

Gérard, P., F. Ost and M. van de Kerchove (eds), *Droit et intérêt*, Bruxelles, Publications des Facultés universitaires St Louis, 1990, 3 volumes.

Guinchard, S., 'Grandeur et décadence de la notion d'intérêt général: la nouvelle recevabilité des actions civiles en cas d'infraction à la législation économique', *Mélanges Vincent*, Paris, Dalloz, 1981, pp. 137–54.

– 'L'action de groupe en procédure civile française', *Revue internationale de droit comparé*, 2, 1990, pp. 599–635.

Hecquard-Theron, M., 'De l'intérêt collectif', *L'actualité juridique-Droit administratif*, 1986, pp. 65–74.

Ismâ'îl, K.S., *Qadâ' majlis al-dawla wa ijrâ'ât wa-siyâgh al-da'wâ al-idâriyya [Decisions of the State Council and Procedure in Administrative Action]*, Cairo, Dâr al-taba'a al-hadîtha, 3d ed., 1993.

'Jurisprudence Abû Zayd', *Egypte/Monde arabe*, 34, 1998, pp. 169–201 (special dossier on the Abû Zayd case).

Khalil, A.A., 'The right of private individuals and groups to enforce laws through privatization of administrative authority', in E. Cotran and A.O. Sherif (eds), *The Role of the Judiciary in the Protection of Human Rights*, The Hague, Kluwer Law International, CIMEL Book Series, no 5, 1997, pp. 335–46.

Laligant, M., 'La notion d'intérêt pour agir et le juge administratif', *Revue de droit public et de science politique en France et à l'étranger*, 1971, pp. 43–82.

Lascoumes, P., 'Intérêt et rationalisation de l'action humaine: la notion d'intérêt en sociologie. Pesanteurs et redéfinition de l'utilitarisme', in P. Gérard, F. Ost, and M. Van de Kerchove (eds), *Droit et intérêt*, Bruxelles, Publications des Facultés universitaires St Louis, 1990, 1, pp. 103–18.

Markaz al-musâ'ada al-qânûniyya li-huqûq al-insân (Center for Human Rights Legal Aid), *al-Hisba bayna al-dawla al-madaniyya wa'l-dawla al-dîniyya* (Hisba: *is Egypt a Civil or Religious State*?), Cairo, January 1996.

Pacteau, B., *Contentieux administratif*, 4th ed., Paris, Presses Universitaires de France, 1997.

Rangeon, F., *L'idéologie de l'intérêt général*, Paris, Economica, 1986.

Ricœur, P., 'Le concept de responsabilité. Essai d'analyse sémantique', in P. Ricœur, *Le Juste*, Paris, Esprit, 1995, pp. 41–70.

Rigaux, M.-F., 'Intérêt particulier et intérêt général devant la cour d'arbitrage', in P. Gérard, F. Ost and M. Van de Kerchove (eds), *Droit et intérêt*, Bruxelles, Publications des Facultés universitaires St Louis, 1990, 3, pp. 153–83.

Sâwî, A.S., *al-Wasît fî sharh qânûn al-murâfa'ât al-madaniyya wa-l-tijâriyya* (*al-Wasit on the Explanation of the Code of Civil and Commercial Procedure*), Cairo, 1994.

Starck, B., *Introduction au droit*, 3rd ed., Paris, Litec, 1991.

Thielmann, J., 'La jurisprudence égyptienne sur la requête en *hisba*', *Egypte/Monde arabe*, 34, 1998, pp. 81–97.

Van de Kerchove, M., 'L'intérêt à la répression et l'intérêt à la réparation dans le procès pénal', in P. Gérard, F. Ost and M. Van de Kerchove (eds), *Droit et intérêt*, Bruxelles, Publications des Facultés universitaires St Louis, 1990, v. 3, pp. 83–113.

Vedel, G., 'Preface', in F. Rangeon, *L'idéologie de l'intérêt général*, Paris, Economica, 1986, pp. 1–5.

Zeghbib, H., 'Principe du contradictoire et procédure administrative non contentieuse', *Revue de droit public et de science politique en France et à l'étranger*, 2, 1998, pp. 467–503.

CHAPTER 13

Regulating Tolerance: Protecting Egypt's Minorities[1]

Maurits Berger

Throughout Islamic history, non-Muslim communities under Muslim sovereignty have been granted a degree of autonomy to administer their own religious and family law affairs. The subsequent situation of separate courts and laws for Muslims and non-Muslims, the legal system of a 'plurality of religious family laws',[2] has been maintained in contemporary Egypt, albeit in an adapted form.

In this research, I examine the status of non-Muslim communities within the framework of Egyptian plurality of religious family laws in the second half of the twentieth century by addressing the preliminary question of this book: have there been any changes in the legal status of the individual Egyptian in the course of the twentieth century, and can these changes be attributed to European influences? While Egypt's religious family laws, like most – if not all – contemporary Egyptian laws, have been influenced by European legal thought in both substance and doctrine, I will argue that Egypt's system of plurality of religious laws has remained, in essence, truthful to its Islamic legal roots. This especially shows in the treatment of the individual: even though the introduction of conceptions such as citizenship might have given rise to an individualisation of the Egyptian legal subject, in matters of family law, the individual Egyptian is still considered to be a member of a collective, that is his or her religious community.

In this study, I discuss some elements of this collective approach. First of all, the legal structure of the Egyptian plurality of religious laws upholds that the applicable family law is determined by one's religion. Changing religion is equal to becoming a member of another community, including its family law. More important, however, is that the Egyptian non-Muslim communities are, indeed, treated as collectives when it comes to family law. This appears from two sets of court cases which explicitly deal with this issue, one dating from the 1950s and the other from the 1980s, in which the courts express a concern for the preservation of the identity and cohesion of these minorities. This concern is given voice by means of the legal concept of 'public policy', which is also examined in this chapter. The third element of the collective approach is its legal-political framework of religious tolerance. Based on these considerations, I intend to demonstrate that one of the main characteristics of Egypt's system of plurality of religious laws is the protection of the collective identity of the non-Muslims.

Legal structure: attempts at unification[3]

Dhimmî and citizen

In order to understand the origin of contemporary Egyptian plurality of religious laws, a short detour must be made regarding Islamic law as described in *fiqh* literature. Islamic law distinguishes between persons residing within Islamic territory (*dâr al-islâm*) and those outside this territory (*dâr al-harb*). Within Islamic territory, a further distinction is made between Muslim and non-Muslim residents, the *dhimmîs. Dhimmîs* are legal subjects under Islamic sovereignty, with the explicit understanding that it is the duty of the Muslim sovereign to protect the *dhimmîs.* The relationship between Muslim and *dhimmî* communities was modelled as an 'indefinitely renewed contract through which the Muslim community accords [the *dhimmîs*] hospitality and protection [...] on condition of their acknowledging the domination of Islam'.[4]

Dhimmîs were granted religious freedom, which, in legal terms, translated into a certain degree of judicial and legislative autonomy with regard to their religious and family law (the latter being considered an intrinsic part of religion). In all other matters, Islamic courts were competent to pass judgement and Islamic law was applicable. The ensuing coexistence of Muslim and non-Muslim family-law systems is what has been named a plurality of religious laws.[5] It meant, in effect, the existence of separate courts and family laws for Muslims and non-Muslims. While Muslim courts and laws were part of the Islamic state, the non-Muslim communities could administer their religious and family-law affairs in a relatively autonomous manner.

It should be borne in mind that, in addition to the relative autonomy in the field of religion and family law, *dhimmî* status also marked a separate status in many respects in the legal, political and social spheres. Since the 1950s, many Western and non-Muslim authors have written on the nature of this status, mostly depicting it as derogatory and inferior. What concerns me in this research, however, is the particular issue of family law which, in my opinion, is of an entirely different nature.

Dhimmî-status was a collective, not an individual status: it was determined by virtue of membership of a non-Muslim religious community and not by being a non-Muslim subject of the state.[6] This changed by the end of the nineteenth century by the Ottomans with the introduction of the concepts of nationality and citizenship. The Ottoman Empire (of which Egypt was an autonomous province from 1517 until 1914) officially abrogated the separate legal *dhimmî*-status for its non-Muslim subjects in 1856 and declared all subjects equal before the law, therewith introducing the concept of Ottoman citizenship. However, Muslim and non-Muslim citizens still maintained a separate legal status in the field of personal-status law. This new status of non-Muslim subjects, being Ottoman citizens on one hand, and enjoying a separate status in family matters on the other, was continued by Egypt when it was detached from the Ottoman Empire and became a British Protectorate in 1914.[7]

With its independence in 1922, Egypt came under the growing influence of the ideology of nationalism, which emphasised the unity of the republic and its citizens and was also one of the reasons for unification of the legal system.

Contemporary Egyptian plurality of religious laws

This movement for unification led to two radical changes in Egyptian plurality of religious laws. First, the legislative autonomy, which in the nineteenth century encompassed what would nowadays be called personal status law, was limited in the course of the twentieth century to matters of marriage and divorce. All other issues such as inheritance, guardianship and capacity were codified in laws largely based on Islamic law, but applied to all Egyptians regardless of their religion, hence becoming Egypt's common law in matters of personal status. Second, the judicial autonomy was abolished in 1956 with the abrogation of Muslim, Christian and Jewish family courts and the integration of their activities into a single national court system.

The unification of the court system was seen as a first step towards unification of personal status laws.[8] This final and most radical step in the process of unification was never put into effect, however. Committees had been appointed as early as 1936 to look into this matter and proposals have been submitted – and rejected – ever since, but all these initiatives concentrated on the unification of non-Muslims laws, never on the unification of Muslim and non-Muslim laws.[9] This is one of the most telling demonstrations of Egypt's plurality of religious laws persevering in its communal structure. It means that, although the semi-autonomy of non-Muslim communities has been narrowed down considerably during the first half of the twentieth century, the origins of this legal system have still been maintained in two respects. First, religious freedom granted to non-Muslims is still upheld in legal matters which are essential, namely, marriage and divorce.[10] This, in turn, means that Egyptians still derive their legal status in these matters from their religion or, rather, their belonging to a certain religious community.

Second, the fact that non-Muslims have lost the authority to administer their family-law affairs to the national courts, which are predominantly staffed by Muslim judges,[11] seems to be largely compensated by the sensitivity of the Egyptian judiciary to the preservation of these communities and their identities within the context of their respective religious laws, as will be demonstrated when discussing the court cases below. The means to express this sensitivity is the use of the notion of 'public policy' (*al-nizâm al-'âmm*). It is a legal concept of European origin that was introduced into Egyptian legal doctrine in the late nineteenth century. Public policy denotes the norms and rules considered essential to the legal order of a society. Its interpretation is left to the courts and its discussion will therefore be left to the following paragraphs. As a preliminary remark, however, it may be observed that the preservation of the identity of religious minority communities appears to be essential to Egypt's legal order.

First case: protecting the Italian and Greek communities in Alexandria (1953–54)

Historical background

Since Ptolemaic times, Alexandria has had a mixed community of Egyptians, Greeks and Jews. During the nineteenth century, the city of Alexandria had also become a safe haven for many Mediterranean peoples who fled wars and famine at home: Greeks, Armenians, Italians, Lebanese. Their settlement in Egypt was encouraged by the Egyptian ruler Mehmet Ali (1805–48), who had ambitious plans for modernising his country. Alexandria grew from a sleepy town of 13,000 inhabitants in 1821 to a thriving city with ca. 100,000 inhabitants in 1840, doubling to ca. 200,000 in 1872 and again tripling to ca. 600,000 in 1937.[12] By then, Alexandria had become a commercial centre with Egypt's only stock market and major banks and trade houses.

The Greeks and Italians, who are the focus of the discussion below, constituted the largest non-Egyptian communities in Alexandria during the first half of the twentieth century. In the census of 1937, Alexandria had almost 600,000 inhabitants, with more than 88,000 foreigners, 36,822 of whom were Greek and 14,030 Italians.[13] According to the Alexandrian court ruling that will be examined below, the two communities together had almost doubled to 90,000 people in 1954.[14] During the 1960s, however, foreign communities had dwindled to negligible numbers. Their exodus started with the Suez Crisis in 1956, which prompted the Egyptian state to expel most of the Jews, British and French from the country and to nationalise foreign assets. The following waves of nationalisation strangled private enterprise and drove off many of the remaining foreigners.[15]

Legal background

In most matters of personal status law, the Egyptian Civil Code of 1949 allows foreigners residing in Egypt to have their national personal status laws applied to them. This was also the case with foreigners who had been living in Egypt for generations, but were still considered legal aliens since residence or birth in Egypt did not entitle them to Egyptian citizenship. The choice by the Egyptian legislature to apply the law of nationality rather than the law of domicile appears to have been made out of consideration for foreigners residing in Egypt: applying the law of their domicile would have meant the application of Egyptian (Muslim) personal-status law, which was considered 'unfair' to them.[16]

For cases involving more than one nationality, the so-called 'conflicts rules' of the Egyptian Civil Code, the guidelines on how to determine which law is applicable, provide solutions. For instance, the national law of the husband applies to divorce and the national law of the deceased applies to inheritance. In the following court cases, Articles 12 and 28 of the Egyptian Civil Code are of relevance. Article 12 stipulates that the national laws of *both* spouses are to be taken into account with regard to 'the substantive conditions of a marriage', i.e. the (in)validity of a marriage. Article 28 stipulates that foreign law will not be applied if it violates public policy.

The court cases

In the 1950s, a specific issue repeatedly arose before the courts of Alexandria. It concerned the situation of the marriage between a Catholic Italian and a Greek-Orthodox Greek which was concluded in the Catholic church. It was argued that such a marriage was void because the Greek Civil Code deems a marriage involving a Greek-Orthodox only valid if concluded by a Greek-Orthodox priest. This argument was based on Article 12 of the Egyptian Civil Code which demands that the marriage should be valid according to *both* Italian and Greek law.[17] The Alexandrian courts, in several instances, concurred with this argument.[18]

Given the fact that both Italian and Greek laws at that time made divorce virtually impossible, these rulings of the Alexandrian courts served as an alternative way for dissolving these kinds of marriage. Apparently, the number of petitions applying for nullity of Italian-Greek marriages came as a shock to the Alexandrian judiciary, because the Court of First Instance found it necessary to put a halt to it. Initially, the court repealed its previous rulings with the following argument:

> Considering that in the large city of Alexandria, Greeks and Italians have lived side by side for many centuries, are linked by bonds of matrimony and have multiplied on a large scale to the extent that their number nowadays reaches 40,000 to 50,000 people, the annulment of a marriage based on the ground that the religious ceremony has been performed by one priest rather than another is a serious threat which will shake the foundations of this mixed community [...] and will ruin conjugal life without plausible reason. Moreover, the Catholic and Orthodox rites as well as the Protestant rite share the same faith; their doctrines are very much alike, especially with regard to marriage which they all consider to be a sacrament. Therefore, this court considers that a woman of the Orthodox rite who accepts celebrating her marriage in a Catholic church and to receive the blessing of a Catholic priest, has implicitly converted to the other (i.e. Catholic) rite. Not only because her husband – whom she has chosen and has accepted to live with under the same roof and carrying his name – is Catholic, but because the two rites are virtually identical with regard to their substantial principles and their doctrines. Matters relating to the form of marriage are excepted, but these have no influence whatsoever on the foundation of the Christian faith.[19]

The court tried to save the mixed marriage with the feeble ground of the 'implicit conversion'. Indeed, the annotator to the published ruling exposed the weakness of this argument by remarking that the Catholic Church itself does not accept conversion to Catholicism by mere consent to marriage in its church.[20]

A year later, an identical case was raised before the same court, which seized the opportunity to make some corrections to its previous ruling. First, the 'many centuries' of intermarriage between the Greek and Italian communities was changed into 'many generations' and their number was doubled to 90,000. More important, however, is the way that the court modified its argument not to accept the nullity of these marriages. It recognised the shortcomings of its argument of 'implicit conversion' and turned to the concept of public policy to reach the same result:

> In the city of Alexandria only, the number of Greeks and Italians has reached 90,000 people, united by bonds of marriage for many generations. Due to these mixed unions, a special environment has been created which differs profoundly from those in Greece and Italy. Therefore, Egyptian public policy demands the protection of this situation, now and in the future, in order to safeguard the family against religious quarrels, quarrels which in no respect touch the foundations of these religions themselves.[21]

Comments on the ruling

The courts' primary concern wavers between, on one hand, the harmony between the Greek and Italian communities and, on the other hand, the bond of matrimony. On closer inspection, however, the latter consideration seems not to have been of great importance for the courts. In both court cases, the claimant had demanded nullity of the marriage on two grounds: the omission of a Greek-Orthodox celebration (nullity under Greek law) and impotence of the husband (nullity under Italian law). Whereas the court had great difficulty with the first plea, it easily accepted the second, and in both court cases declared the marriage void.

Apparently, the court was concerned with the bond of matrimony only insofar as it reflected the integrity of each of the two communities. The court made the following causal connections: the two communities are united by means of marriage; marriage is a religious union; in order to establish this union, a choice must be made for the religion of one of the spouses which is also the religion of his or her community. The court at first concurred with a strict application of the Egyptian conflicts rules and ruled that a marriage validly concluded in accordance with one religion (Catholicism) was void because it was not validly concluded in accordance with another (Greek-Orthodoxy). Later, however, the court became apprehensive for reasons which are not entirely clear, but the court mentions 'religious quarrels'. These could possibly be inspired by previous rulings which, in effect, said that the Greek (Orthodox) law untied what had been united by Italian (Catholic) law.

The crucial point of the latter ruling is that the court deems the prevention of communal disorder within the city of Alexandria to be of greater importance than the strict application of the law. The court does so by means of the doctrine of public policy. Based on Article 28 of the Civil Code, the application of foreign laws as stipulated by that code is precluded due to their violation of Egyptian public policy. In the opinion of the court, disharmony and possible disintegration of these Alexandrian communities constituted such a violation. While one could argue that the city's social or economic peace might be at the heart of the court's reasoning, the ruling does not make any mention of such considerations. It appears, therefore, that indeed the integrity and stability of religious-ethnic communities themselves are considered to pertain to public policy, that is they are considered essential for the Egyptian national legal order. What is intriguing is that the foreignness of both the communities and their respective laws is not the issue; the fact that, in the reasoning of the court, these communities have deep-rooted social and economical ties to Alexandria is apparently enough to make them a integral part of the Egyptian legal order.

But what exactly was the status and identity of the Greek and Italian communities of Alexandria? As seen, very few of them carried Egyptian nationality and, as a matter of law, the court considered them to be legal aliens and applied their national laws. At the same time, however, the court pointed out that most of these foreigners were born and raised in Alexandria, often descending from families who had lived in Alexandria for generations. The court indicated explicitly that the members of these communities consider themselves Alexandrian, rather than Italian or Greek, having more affinity with Egypt than with their national countries. Thus, although they were legal aliens from a legal perspective, they were considered an intrinsic part of Egyptian society.

The comparison with the communities of non-Muslim Egyptians comes to mind, but fails for two reasons. First, the Italian and Greek communities in Alexandria were essentially ethnic rather than religious communities. The Italian community, for instance, consisted of both Catholics and Jews. Also, as opposed to Egyptian non-Muslims, the applicable law of the foreigners was connected with their nationality, not their religion.

An Egyptian Copt converting to Catholicism, would change from Coptic to Catholic family law, while Italian family law would apply to an Italian, regardless of his or her religion. Whatever the definitions of the identity of the Italian and Greek communities in Alexandria (the court did not give any[22]), the court felt that it had sufficient reason to disregard the foreign national law in order to protect their integrity and identity.

Second case: protecting the essential values of the Christians (1979 and 1984)

As in the previous case, the following conflicts that were decided by the Egyptian Court of Cassation were related to religiously mixed marriages. In the present case, the parties involved were not foreigners, however, but non-Muslim Egyptians.[23]

Legal background

Egypt has recognised a number of religious communities which are entitled to application of their own family laws. These communities are categorised as follows. First, distinction is made between religions (*dîn*), of which usually only Christianity, Judaism and Islam are mentioned. A religion can be divided into 'rites' (*milla* or *madhhab*) which are defined as ways of practising that particular religion. Each rite can be subdivided into 'sects' (*tâ'ifa*), which the Court of Cassation has defined as 'groups of people [...] who share a common ethnic origin, language or customs'.[24]

The Muslims, who constitute the majority of the Egyptian population, are governed by Egyptian Muslim family law. The largest minority are Christians,[25] consisting of three rites which are subdivided into a total of twelve sects[26] which share a total of six personal-status laws.[27] The Jewish community of Egypt, which consisted of two sects, each with its own law,[28] has become almost non-existent.[29]

In case of mixed religious marriages, Egyptian Muslim family law always applies if one of the spouses is Muslim. Relevant for the case in question is the rule that Egyptian Muslim family law also applies to a Christian couple if the spouses do not share the same rite and sect.[30] (Note that this rule does not apply to foreign couples, as illustrated by the previous case, except if one of the spouses had Egyptian nationality.) Egyptian Muslim family law will hence be applied in case of a marriage between, for instance, a Christian and a Jew, a Catholic and an Orthodox, or an Armenian-Catholic and a Roman-Catholic. Consequently, Christian family law only applies to those Christian couples who share the same rite and sect.

The court cases

In one Egyptian Christian couple, husband and wife belonged to different Christian sects. Because Egyptian Muslim family law was applicable to their marriage, the husband had drawn the conclusion that he was entitled to enter into a second polygamous marriage. His wife claimed the nullity of this second marriage, arguing that such marriage might be valid according to the law, but was a violation of public policy. This case was brought before the Court of Cassation, which issued an elaborate ruling.[31]

The court started with the consideration that the husband was right from a purely legal point of view. Egyptian Muslim family law applied to his marriage; hence, the Christian husband enjoyed the same rights as a Muslim husband. In principle, therefore, he was entitled to enter into a second polygamous marriage. The court then continued to make an exception to this rule. Egyptian Muslim family law is not applicable, it argued, when its rules

> are in conflict with any of the principles of the essence of the Christian faith [al-mabâdi' al-muttassila bi-jawhar al-'aqîda al-masîhiyya] and which, if violated by the Christian, will render him an apostate of his own religion, corrupting his doctrine and infringing on his Christianity.

The court concluded that polygamy is indeed against the essence of the Christian faith, based on the following consideration:

> The unity in Christian marriage is considered to be one of the principles of Christianity [...] and one of the characteristics of a Christian marriage is its single relationship which can only be

> founded by one man and one woman. [...] The prohibition of polygamy for men and women has been one of the principles that has been predominant in Christianity for the past twenty centuries and never has been subject of dispute, not even when the church split up into a European and an Eastern [church] and in Catholic, Orthodox and Protestant rites [...]. This [prohibition of polygamy] has been considered one of its essential principles, regardless of the church, rite or sect [...]. Due to this principle, a second marriage concluded during the existence of the first marriage is considered null and void, even if both spouses agreed to it.

Moreover, the court argued, polygamy is a right which God has endowed specifically to Muslim men:

> It is clear that polygamy is allowed by Islamic *sharî'a* [...]. It is also obvious that this divine message is directed only to Muslims. The largest part of it [i.e. the message] is religious to the extent that it would be hard to claim that this purely religious principle is applicable to someone who does not originally believe in the doctrine to which the permission of polygamy is related. [...] Therefore, permitting a Christian to enter into a polygamous marriage, despite the fact that this contradicts the most basic tenet of his religious faith, constitutes a violation of the law.

In short, the prohibition of polygamy is considered to be such an essential rule of the Christian faith that a Christian husband may never enter into a second marriage even if the applicable Egyptian Muslim family law grants him the right to do so.

Could it be argued, as the wife had done, that the polygamous marriage of her husband was against public policy? The court rejected this argument, stating that public policy in matters of law related to religious doctrine, that is personal status law, is governed by principles of Islamic law, being the religion of the majority of Egyptians. It would therefore be inconceivable that the Islamic concept of polygamy in itself is a violation of public policy. The court argued that the non-application of Islamic law, in this particular instance, was based on the spirit of the law:

> The Explanatory Memorandum of Law 462 of 1955 reads: 'Respect is to be ensured for the sovereignty of the law that is to be applied so that no right of any group of Egyptians, Muslim or non-Muslim, will be infringed when their law is applied.' This is a clear indication that the legislature has demanded respect for all laws, general as well as special [i.e. the non-Muslim family laws]. Therefore, the

violation of basic principles connected with the core of the doctrine and the essence of the religion constitutes a circumvention of its [i.e. the legislature's] spirit and a transgression of its intentions.

Five years later, however, the court made a slight modification to this consideration in two other cases of mixed Christian marriages. Although the subject-matter of these cases was quite different from the one of 1979, the line of reasoning is similar. The question laid before the court was whether the Catholic spouses of different rites could use their rights of divorce as stipulated under Egyptian Muslim family law, even though this law itself specifically prohibited divorce for Catholics.[32] The court went on to explain that the Catholic prohibition of divorce was codified by the Egyptian legislator in deference to Catholic law: '[This rule] is for the benefit of this particular sect [i.e. the Catholics] in order to protect their religious faith and is not for the benefit of the person of the claimant. As such, this rule pertains to public policy'.[33]

While in the case of polygamy, it was said that essential rules of a non-Muslim faith should not be violated, the Court has now gone a step further by stating that the protection of a non-Muslim faith in itself is a matter of public policy.

Comments on the rulings

The 1979 and 1984 rulings are key rulings in matters of Egyptian plurality of religious laws. They are important for two reasons. First, because they define the core issues which make up the legal personality of Christian communities. It answers the question of Ricœur, albeit related to a collective rather than a person: what are the characteristics of a person to deserve respect which, in turn, entitles that person to become a legal subject?[34] In the words of the court, the identity of the Christian communities is based on 'the principles of the essence of the Christian faith which, if violated by the Christian, will render him an apostate of his own religion, corrupting his doctrine and infringing his Christianity'. This is the identity on which the existence of these communities as legal entities is based, separate from the other Egyptian citizens.

This gives rise to the second issue: the conflict between communal and national interests. It is in the interest of the communities to apply their own family laws, as it is in the interest of the state to apply its national laws. Egyptian Muslim family law applies as common law to mixed Christian marriages. The question to be answered by the Court of Cassation was what to do when this common law infringed upon essential rules of the particular Christian communities to which the spouses belonged. The issue is a principal one: if Egyptian common law recognises the freedom of religion for non-Muslim minorities and creates autonomous frameworks within which these communities can administer their own religious affairs, what will this common law do if it, itself, is the cause of infringement of these rights? In both cases – polygamy and Catholic divorce – the court ruled that 'a rule of Islamic law' is not to be applied when it constitutes a violation of the 'essence of Christian faith'. National interests had to give way to communal interests, albeit interests that are 'essential' to their faith.

In the polygamy ruling, the court based this consideration on the spirit of the law and the intentions of the legislature. In the Catholic divorce rulings, however, it argued that the protection of the faiths of the non-Muslim communities in Egypt is a rule of public policy. This protection rule of non-Muslim minorities is reminiscent of the aforementioned collective *dhimmî* status under Islamic law. Thus, this solves the paradox that had arisen earlier: the polygamous marriage by a Christian can in itself not be considered a violation of public policy, but such a marriage can be prevented by invoking public policy on the grounds that the integrity and identity of the Christian community must be protected.

Tolerance

The 'collective approach' which is so typical of the Egyptian plurality of religious laws cannot be explained by the mere fact that specific laws are being applied to specific groups of people. The application of law is, indeed, often based on a communal quality of the person involved: his nationality, religion, function or place of residence. In the two case studies mentioned above, these qualities are, respectively, nationality and religion. What is distinctive of these cases, however, is the assumption of communal cohesiveness and shared identity of the communities involved. Specific laws also apply, for example, to the Greeks of Alexandria or the state employees of Egypt, but they cannot be considered 'sufficiently homogeneous communities of a corporate type'[35] who are allowed to maintain their community laws. One may be a Greek national, but, according to the Egyptian court, being a Greek national belonging to the Greek community of Alexandria makes quite a difference. One may be a Greek Orthodox or Italian Catholic, but being an *Egyptian* Orthodox or Catholic calls for special consideration for respective religious identities.

It goes beyond the scope of this chapter to point out the historical, social, political and other reasons for this distinctive communal nature of the non-Muslim (both foreign and local) communities in Egypt – and in the Middle East in general, for that matter – but, it may suffice here to remark that native non-Muslim communities in this region have always been more or less homogeneous and exclusive since the arrival of Islam,[36] not only because of their semi-autonomous status, but also because they often lived apart from Muslims.[37] The situation of the Greek and Italian communities in Alexandria in the 1950s had different and less deep historical roots, but they were nevertheless treated by the courts in a fashion similar to Egyptian non-Muslim communities. In both cases, these communities behaved and were tolerated as separate communities within Egyptian society[38] and, in both cases, there was a 'collective approach', i.e. identities and interests of the communities received different attention by the Egyptian judicial and legislative authorities.

In order to understand the relations and interactions between the Egyptian state and its ethnic and religious minorities, I suggest examining the legal-political tenet on which its system of plurality of religious laws is based, namely religious tolerance. In the following, I argue that the system of Egyptian plurality of religious laws could perhaps be best understood in terms of 'us' and 'them', i.e. Muslims and non-Muslims, rather than Norbert Elias's 'I' and 'we', which is also the underlying premise used by the theories and studies mentioned in the introduction to this book.[39]

'Protecting the rights of religious minorities'

Religious tolerance is an issue with which every religious community in the world is confronted. The historical, political and social circumstances are, of course, different for every one of them. The main historical difference between religious tolerance practised in Europe and the Arab-Muslim world,[40] for instance, is that large non-Muslim communities have been – and still are – living within the latter region ever since the sovereignty of Islam, while non-Christian minorities in Europe have until recently been very limited in number. Also, many non-Muslim communities under Islamic rule were granted legal status as *dhimmîs* from the moment of Islamic conquest. Although their treatment as *dhimmîs* differed from region to region within the Arab-Muslim world[41] and often went hand-in-hand with discriminatory measures by Muslim rulers, the shared basis of this status was the tolerance professed by Islam for non-Muslim monotheistic religions which resulted in unhindered freedom and virtual autonomy in matters of religion and family law.

In Europe, on the other hand, the issue of religious tolerance was not raised until the twelfth century and was primarily concerned with Christian heretics and schismatics. It was not until the sixteenth century that religious tolerance was actually practised in order to settle the violent strife between Catholics and Protestants. As far as non-Christians were concerned, they were tolerated, but just barely, often suffering various forms of persecution.[42] Tolerance of non-Christian minority communities in Europe again became the subject of debate in the second half of the twentieth century with the large numbers of mostly Muslim immigrants.

The concept of tolerance: a comparison

Historically, tolerance has not been an issue in the Arab-Muslim world in the way that it was in the West. While religious tolerance may *de facto* have been practised by means of the *dhimmî*-status, Islamic political and legal thought has never made reference to, or developed a concept of tolerance. The reasons for the absence of such a concept can only be speculated on and are beyond the scope of this chapter. One of the main reasons might be sought in the fact that different schools of thought as well as the largest movement that separated from Islamic Sunni orthodoxy, the Shi'ites, were considered part of the Muslim community and, therefore, needed not to be 'tolerated'. Tolerance exercised towards non-Muslim communities has been coined by the Hanafite[43] doctrine of Islamic law with the phrase 'Leave them and what they believe',[44] meaning that Muslim authorities will not interfere in non-Muslim religious affairs, including their family law.

The Islamic legal literature never developed a theoretical framework for this legal principle, but has limited itself to deliberations on what was to be considered within or without the boundaries of legal autonomy to which the non-Muslims were entitled.[45] Egypt, by the same token, also has not developed a political-legal doctrine of tolerance in relation to its religious minorities. In order to discuss concepts of tolerance, I therefore resort to vocabulary used in Western discourse.

Contemporary Western literature defines tolerance as 'a deliberate choice not to interfere with the conduct of which one disapproves'.[46] This definition has two aspects. First, tolerance is exercised by someone who has the power to *not* also tolerate the conduct of which he or she disapproves, but nevertheless chooses to be tolerant. When certain behaviour is tolerated or rights are granted, the tolerator merely indulges him or herself. Second, tolerance is exercised in matters involving firmly held beliefs. It implies that the tolerator strongly objects to a certain behaviour or opinion, but nevertheless decides to accept it.

These characteristics are shared by the religious tolerance as exercised in the Arab-Muslim world of the past as well as contemporary Egypt: the dominant Muslim majority has the power not to accept non-Muslim beliefs, which, in cases such as the consumption of wine and pork and the belief in Christ as the son of God are indeed abhorrent to a Muslim believer, but the choice had been made to 'leave them and what they believe'. It is very well possible that this choice was made on practical rather than moral grounds, for instance, because the Muslim conquerors were initially outnumbered by their non-Muslim subjects,[47] but that does not change the practice of tolerance itself.

However, the practice of religious tolerance in the Arab-Muslim world differed completely from any Western concept of tolerance. Both concepts initially dealt with religious-minority communities to which certain rights and autonomies were attributed. During the Catholic-Protestant strife of the sixteenth and seventeenth centuries, however, Western religious tolerance acquired an individual approach. The inter-Christian conflicts were resolved, 'not by granting special rights to particular religious minorities, but by separating church and state, and entrenching each individual freedom of religion. Religious minorities are protected indirectly, by guaranteeing individual freedom of worship.'[48] Moreover, minorities, tribes, kin groups and other communities that Elias names as 'pre-state units' disappeared altogether under 'the dominant pressure urging people towards state integration', being left with only three alternatives for survival: preservation of their identity 'as a kind of museum piece', renouncing a part of their identity or 'the encapsulation of an older, pre-state society within a larger state society which is so powerful and self-confident that it can tolerate such encapsulated earlier societies in its midst'.[49] The latter seems an apt description of the non-Muslim communities in Egypt.

Western tolerance, as it is today, developed from the freedom of religion of the individual into the larger concept of liberalism with its strong emphasis on individual freedoms and rights. Religious tolerance in contemporary Egypt, on the other hand, has maintained the freedom of religion which under Islamic law was attributed to non-Muslim communities.[50] The resulting collective approach towards non-Muslim minorities in the Egyptian plurality of religious laws has, as a main characteristic, the prevention of any direct interaction between state and individual. Non-Muslim communities may enjoy protection against persecution and may even be allowed to manage their own religious and family-law affairs, but this protection does not extend to individual members of these communities. The communities are free to act against deviant individual members. Western literature, when referring to this particular exercise of tolerance in the Ottoman Empire, has labelled it an 'imperial regime of tolerance' because tolerance was exercised by an imperial power in order to maintain peace and to collect taxes, regardless of intolerance among the subjects of the minority communities;[51] it has also been called a 'federation of communities'[52] or a 'federation of theocracies'.[53]

This communal approach is essentially still in place within the Egyptian system of plurality of religious laws, which has created separate legal realms, each for one of the religious communities. The separation allows them to coexist with each other and with the larger Muslim community while maintaining their differences on essential issues. Rules of Christian law may be incompatible with those of Egyptian Muslim family law (such as polygamy, for instance), but each community can live according to its rules within the confines of its legal boundaries. The Coptic Pope is free to issue decrees making divorce among Copts even more difficult, while such limitations are considered against the Islamic concept of freedom of divorce. Heresy is only taken to the courts when it is directed against Islam; theological dissent among Christians is a matter for the relevant Christian community authorities.

Another difference with the Western concept is the individual's freedom of choice. The religious communities in the Egyptian system of plurality of religious laws are not voluntary associations. Membership is predetermined by religion. The individual who wants to step out of his or her community has no choice other than to change community by conversion (although this is not allowed for members of the Muslim community). One's religion determines one's social and, definitely, one's legal identity. A Copt is subject to Coptic family law whether he likes it or not. In this respect, tolerance could be defined as allowing an individual to belong to a community and to have the community's rules applied, rather than allowing him to choose a community.

Conclusion

Egypt's non-Muslim communities

As mentioned above, the theories and studies mentioned in the introduction to this book are not to much avail for our understanding of the system of Egyptian plurality of religious laws. The basic premise of this system should be seen in the dichotomy of 'us' and 'them', i.e. Muslims and non-Muslims, rather than 'I' and 'we', as is common in the approach in Western thought towards religious tolerance. While Egyptian society has undergone tremendous changes in the past century in making the non-Muslims part of 'us', they have retained a separate status in matters of family law that, in that respect, sets them apart as 'them'. This attitude also shows in the Egyptian legal literature on the subject of non-Muslim family law.[54]

The comparative approach to religious tolerance which I present here is of course rather superficial, but serves the purpose of illustrating that one of the main characteristics of Egypt's system of plurality of family law, i.e. the separate and semi-autonomous status of religious communities, has no relation whatsoever with European political and legal thought. This is interesting since Egypt has gone to great lengths in the first half of the twentieth century to discontinue the separate status of the religious family laws in Egypt. Nevertheless, the system of the plurality of religious laws has, in essence, been preserved. Moreover, it is telling that, against a background of an increasing tendency to abrogate ethnic and religious differences, Egyptian courts did the exact opposite by championing the preservation of the identity of non-Muslim minority communities. For this purpose, they used the (originally European) concept of public policy, hence indicating that protecting the integrity and identity of non-Muslim communities is essential to the Egyptian legal order.

The approach to the non-Muslim communities in Egypt in matters of family law can most clearly be seen through two aspects: the structure of the Egyptian legal system and the way in which these communities are dealt with by the system. First of all, the relations between state, communities and individuals are made up of a two-tier system: the state allows a certain measure of autonomy to non-Muslim communities – again, only in the field of family law. The legislature and judiciary make an effort to protect the religious identities of these communities while the relation between communities and individual members is left to the communities themselves as part of their autonomy; this relation is not touched by the state. Communities may hold on to their privileges based on the rights acquired as far back as the early years of Islam, and thereafter repeatedly reiterated, but it is the Egyptian state authorities that uphold and maintain the system. The role of communities in defining and developing their own rules and identities is directed inwards towards the religious minority communities themselves, and seems of little consequence in relation to their identity and position within the larger social and legal framework of the Egyptian state.

Second, it is the Egyptian authorities that decide what is in the best interest of the religious minorities as collectives. The recent (Western) developments in the interaction between state and individual have apparently not been able to encroach upon this situation. Even the initiative to defend and protect their identity is not taken by the communities themselves, but by state authorities such as the legislature and the judiciary. This protection of minority rights is therefore more a duty for the authorities rather than a right to be exercised by the communities. The care with which the Egyptian judiciary concerns itself with the rights of the religious-minority communities in Egypt is illustrative. The courts could have made it easy upon themselves by merely implementing the laws regardless of the consequences, but there was an unwritten obligation to pay heed to the identities of the communities involved.

It could, therefore, be argued that the manner in which Islamic legal tradition had granted protection for religious minorities under Islamic rule has continued in the contemporary Egyptian system of plurality of religious laws, regardless of the steady influence of (European) concepts such as citizenship, nationality and legal unity. Moreover, it is especially the benevolent but patronising attitude of Egypt's legislature and judiciary that seems to be an indication that non-Muslims in Egypt still enjoy – although restricted to the realm of family law – a status akin to their former status under Islamic law as 'protected people', the *dhimmîs*. This has become a pejorative term, due to discriminatory measures that were connected to it such as the special poll tax, dress code, denial of political positions and a separate legal status with regard to the law of evidence in the Muslim courts. These measures have long been abrogated, but the non-Muslim communities nevertheless seem still 'protected' within the field of personal-status law. I would therefore argue that this particular feature of *dhimmî* status, i.e. a protective and patronising attitude by a Muslim state, has been preserved in contemporary Egyptian plurality of religious laws.

Notes

1 This study was part of my doctoral thesis on public policy and Egyptian personal status law. I am grateful for the elaborate comments made by B. Dupret, CNRS-CEDEJ, and those of my supervisors R. Peters and Th. M. de Boer (University of Amsterdam).

2 This is a direct translation of the Egyptian term *ta'addud al-sharâ'i'*. In European literature, the term 'interreligious law' is more common.

3 This paragraph is mostly based on Berger, 2001. This article contains extensive bibliographical references.

4 Cahen, 1991; see also Fattal, 1958, pp. 72ff.

5 This legal system is also called a 'personal legal system', indicating the rules of a religiously or ethnically homogeneous community without territorial bonds: cf. Arminjon, 1949, pp. 83–84; Vitta, 1970, pp. 188–89.

6 Cf. Mahmassânî, 1972, p. 102.

7 Egypt confirmed the continuation of this system by Law 8 of 1915.

8 Cf. Explanatory Memorandum to Law 462 of 1955; Salâmah, 1960, p. 310.

9 See Abu Sahlieh, 1979, pp. 116–17; Barsum, 1981.

10 It has been argued that marriage and divorce were originally the fields of law for which Islamic law had intended a degree of autonomy. The extension of this autonomy into other matters of personal-status law occurred during the Ottoman period: cf. Boghdadi, 1937, pp. 87, 343ff; Elgeddawy, 1971, pp. 18–19, 29–30.

11 Abu Sahlieh, 1979, p. 119; Brown, 1997, p. 68.

12 These figures and most of the following historical information is based on Ilbert and Yannakakis, 1997.

13 Figures mentioned in Courbage and Fargues, 1998, p. 189, note 61.

14 In 1960, Linant de Bellefonds spoke of 120,000 Greek nationals in all of Egypt: Linant de Bellefonds, 1960, p. 835.

15 The 1986 census counted 10,834 foreigners out of almost 3 million inhabitants, 64 of which were Jews. See Courbage and Fargues, 1998.

16 Abdalla, 1970, p. 166.

17 Apparently, the conclusion of a marriage by a priest was considered to be a substantive rather than a formal condition for the validity of the marriage.

18 Cf. Court of Appeal, 9 April 1950 (*Revue Egyptienne de Droit International*, 6, 1950); Court of First Instance, 25 December 1951 (*Revue Egyptienne de Droit International*, 9, 1953).

19 Court of First Instance, 23 June 1953 (*Revue Egyptienne de Droit International*, 9, 1953, p. 158). This is also briefly mentioned in Linant de Bellefonds, 1960, p. 835.
20 Court of First Instance, 23 June 1953 (*Revue Egyptienne de Droit International*, 9, 1953, p. 158). This is also briefly mentioned in Linant de Bellefonds, 1960, p. 835.
21 Court of First Instance, 23 February 1954 (*Revue Egyptienne de Droit International*, 10, 1954, p. 151). This is also briefly mentioned in Linant de Bellefonds, 1960, p. 835.
22 Ilbert and Yannakakis, (1997, pp. 25, 66), use the term 'colonies' for the Greeks and Italians of Alexandria, arguing that this refers to a common ethnicity or nationality, rather than the term 'community', which historically refers to a common religion.
23 This paragraph is an elaboration of one of the cases discussed in Berger, 2001.
24 Case no 23, year 46, 26 April 1978 (Majmû'a al-Ahkâm li-Mahkama al-Naqd, 1980).
25 Estimates of the number of Christians in Egypt vary from 3 to 15 million out of a total population of more than 60 million. The official figure of 5.7 percent (ca. 3.5 million), albeit vehemently opposed by Egyptian Christian authorities, seems to be a correct indicator (see, for the same figure, Courbage and Fargues, 1998, p. 209).
26 These are the Orthodox rite, divided into Coptic, Greek, Armenian and Syrian sects; the Catholic rite, divided into Armenian, Syrian, Coptic (all three seceded from the Orthodox church), Latin (Greek-Catholic from Lebanon), Maronite (from Lebanon), Chaldean (from Iraq), and Roman sects and the Protestant rite (mistakenly recognised as a sect by governmental decree of 1850 and, hence, still retaining the official status of a single sect, regardless of its subdivisions).
27 These are the personal-status laws of the Coptic-Orthodox (1938), Greek-Orthodox (1927), Syrian-Orthodox (1929), Armenian-Orthodox (1940), Catholic (1949) and Protestant (1902). As with Muslim law, a large part of the Christian laws – as laid down, for instance, in the New and Old Testament, ordinances from patriarchs and bishops, customary law and case law – are not codified.
28 These are the Rabbinic and the Karaite sects, each with their own personal-status law: the law compiled by Ben Schomu'im in 1912 for the Rabbinites and the law compiled by Eliyahu Bischias in 1912 for the Karaites.
29 According to the Ahram Center for Political and Strategic Studies, fewer than 100 Jews lived in Egypt in 1997: (1998, p. 108).

30 Article 6 of Law 462 of 1955. This is not a rule of Islamic law, but is based on the practice of Christian courts in Egypt which refer mixed Christian couples to *sharî'a* courts which were only allowed to apply Islamic law. This is an exclusively Egyptian solution which does not exist in the plurality of religious laws in, for instance, Syria, Lebanon and Jordan.

31 Case nos 16 and 26, 17 January 1979 (Majmû'a al-Ahkâm li-Mahkama al-Naqd, 1980).

32 Article 99/7 of the Decree on the Organisation of the *sharî'a* Courts.

33 Case no 1392, 5 February 1984 (Majmû'a al-Ahkâm li-Mahkama al-Naqd, 1988); no 31, 10 April 1984 (Majmû'a al-Ahkâm li-Mahkama al-Naqd, 1984).

34 Ricœur, 1995, p. 34.

35 This is a characteristic of a 'personal legal system' (see note 5 in this chapter) as defined by Vitta, 1970, p. 188.

36 Cf. Jambu-Merlin, 1958, p. 8; Vitta, 1970, p. 188.

37 This was especially the case in the cities where inhabitants organised themselves in quarters in accordance with their religion and social status: cf. Chabry, 1984, pp. 40–41; Hodgson, 1974, v. 2, pp. 109–10. These religious alignments can still be found in most Egyptian cities and villages today.

38 Historically, 'integration' of non-Muslims into Muslim society was never an issue – neither requested by Muslims nor asked for by non-Muslims. This can be interpreted as a form of tolerance, but it has also been argued that Muslims opposed integration to prevent the Islamic system from being compromised by mixing with non-Muslim systems: Jambu-Merlin, 1958, p. 8. or, in the opinion of Chabry, 1984, p. 26, however, to preclude equality between Muslims and non-Muslims. Others argue that there was, indeed, no integration, but also never a full segregation nor a divided society: cf. Courbage and Fargues, 1998, p. xii. As a side remark, it should be noted that segregation is not necessarily the same as inequality, an issue which is still a subject of heated debate among modern scholars of the status of *dhimmîs* and non-Muslims.

39 Elias, 1991, pp. 206–7.

40 I use this term to refer to the geographical area from Morocco to Iraq, including the Middle East, but excluding the Gulf countries where, with the exception of Yemen, most non-Muslims were expelled. This used to be, by and large, the territory of the Muslim Empires of the first centuries of Islam, later to be incorporated into the Ottoman Empire.

41 See, e.g., Courbage and Fargues, 1998.

42 The Jews in Europe were not forced to convert, but their religious freedom and practices were limited to what the Christians believed to be the correct interpretation of the Old Testament, the pope being the ultimate judge of what constituted correct Jewish doctrine: cf. Muldoon, 1979, pp. 30–31. The other group of non-Christians in Europe were the *mudéjars*, the indigenous Muslims of territories that were conquered as part of the *reconquista* of Muslim Spain during the thirteenth, fourteenth and fifteenth centuries. Their situation was not much better than the Jews in Europe, being treated 'with a mixture of toleration and prosecution', but they ceased to be a matter of concern after 1499, when they were given the choice between conversion or emigration: cf. Fletcher, 1992, pp. 135–44.

43 This is the doctrine to which Egypt adheres insofar as Islamic personal-status law applies (Article 280 of the Decree of 1931 on Organisation of the *sharî'a* Courts).

44 Natruka-um wa-mâ yadînûnâ: cf. the Hanafî scholar Kûsûnî (d. 587/1191), 1986, v. 2, pp. 311–12.

45 Cf. other Hanafî scholars such as Ibn 'Âbidîn, v. 2, p. 386, v. 3, p. 229; Sarakhsî, v. 5, pp. 38–41. For contemporary Egyptian authors referring to this issue, cf. 'Abd al-Wahhâb, 1959, pp. 256–57; 'Abd al-Rahmân, 1969, pp. 46–53; 'Abd Allâh, 1954, pp. 69–73; Abû Sa'ûd, 1986, pp. 433–37; Salâmah, 1960, pp. 309–46.

46 Horton, 1993, p. 3. See also Kymlicka, 1995; King, 1976; Raz, 1994.

47 Cf. Courbage and Fargues, 1998, p. x. It has even been argued by some that Muslim authorities opposed the conversion of their non-Muslim subjects to Islam because that would entail the loss of income from taxes specially imposed on non-Muslims: cf. Dennet, 1950; Courbage and Fargues, 1998, pp. 22–23. Of course, it could also be argued that Islamic tolerance for non-Muslim religions was a purely moral one, based on the Qur'anic prohibition of coerced conversion to Islam.

48 Kymlicka, 1995, p. 3.

49 Elias, 1991, pp. 214–15.

50 Coincidentally, this collective approach has also become fashionable in the West after World War II, albeit in terms of minority rights and the aforementioned multicultural societies; the question as to how these rights should be recognised is still a matter of debate: cf. Kymlicka, 1995, pp. 2–4.

51 Walzer, 1997, pp. 14, 17–18.

52 Modood, 1997, pp. 21–23.

53 Kymlicka, 1995, p. 157.

54 See Berger, 2001, pp. 105, 123.

Bibliography

Abdalla, E., 'La philosophie du législateur égyptien en matière de conflit des lois', *L'Egypte Contemporaine*, 340, April 1970.

'Abd Allâh, 'I.D., *al-Qânûn al-Duwalî al-Khâss al-Masrî*, Cairo, Dâr al-Nahda al-'Arabiyya, 1954.

'Abd al-Rahmân, J.J., *Tanâzu' al-Qawânîn*, Cairo, Dâr al-Nahda al-'Arabiyya, 1969.

'Abd al-Wahhâb, S.D., *Mudawwana al-Ahwâl al-Shakhsiyya li-ghayr al-Muslimîn al-Misriyîn w'al-Ajânib*, Cairo, Maktabat al-Nahda al-Misriyya, 1959.

Abû Sa'ûd, R., *Wasit fî Sharh al-Ahwâl al-Shakhsiya li-ghayr al-Muslimîn*, Alexandria, Dâr al-Jâmi'iyya, 1986.

Abu Sahlieh, S.A.A., *L'impact de la religion sur l'ordre juridique, Cas de l'Egypte, Non-Musulmans en pays d'Islam*, Fribourg, 1979.

Ahram Center for Political and Strategic Studies, *al-Hâla al-Dîniyya fî Misr*, Cairo, Ahram Press, 1998.

Arminjon, P., 'Les sytèmes juridiques complexes et les conflits de lois et de juridiction auxquels ils donnent lieu', *Recueil des Cours de l'Académie de Droit International de La Haye*, 1, 1949.

Barsum, G., 'Vers une loi unifiée du statut personnel en Egypte', *Bulletin du CEDEJ*, 13, 1981, Cairo.

Berger, M., 'Public policy and Islamic law: The modern *dhimmî* in contemporary Egyptian family law', *Islamic Law and Society*, 8/1, 2001.

Boghdadi, H., 'Origine et technique de la distinction des statuts personnel et réel en Egypte', thesis, University of Cairo, 1937.

Brown, N.J., *The rule of law in the Arab world. Courts in Egypt and the Gulf*, Cambridge, Cambridge University Press, 1997.

Cahen, C., 'Dhimma', *The Encyclopaedia of Islam*, Leiden, Brill, 1991.

Chabry, L. and A., *Politique et minorités en Proche-Orient*, Paris, Maisonneuve & Larose, 1984.

Courbage, Y. and P. Fargues, *Christians and Jews under Islam*, London/New York, I.B. Tauris, 1998.

Dennet, D.C., *Conversion and the Poll Tax in Early Islam*, Cambridge MA, 1950.

Elgeddawy, K., *Relations entre systèmes confessionnels et laïque en droit international privé*, Paris, Dalloz, 1971.

Elias, N., 'Changes in the We-I balance (1987)', in N. Elias, *The Society of Individuals*, Cambridge MA, Basil Blackwell, 1991.

Fattal, Antoine, *Le statut légal des non-musulmans en pays d'islam, Imprimerie Catholique*, Beruit, 1958.

Fletcher, R., *Moorish Spain*, London, Phoenix, 1992.

Hodgson, M., *The Venture of Islam*, Chicago IL and London, The University of Chicago Press, 1974, v. 2: The expansion of Islam in the Middle Periods.
Horton, J. (ed.), *Liberalism, Multiculturalism and Tolerance*, New York, St. Martin's Press, 1993.
Horton, J. and S. Mendus (eds), *Aspects of Tolerance. Philosophical Studies*, London and New York, Methuen, 1985.
Hussain, S., 'Status of Non-Muslims in Islamic State', *Hamdard Islamicus*, 16/1, 1985.
Ibn 'Âbidîn, *Radd al-Mukhtâr 'alâ al-Darr al-Mukhtâr*, Beirut, 1987.
Ilbert, R. and Illios Yannakakis (eds), *Alexandria 1860–1960. The brief life of a cosmopolitan city*, Alexandria, Harpocrates Publishing, 1997.
Jambu-Merlin, R., 'Essai sur l'histoire des conflicts de lois au Levant et en Afrique du Nord', *Revue critique de droit international privé*, 1958.
King, P., *Tolerance*, London, George Allen & Unwin Ltd, 1976.
Kûsûnî, 'A. D. al-, *Badâ'i' al-Sanâ'i' fî Tartîb Sharâ'i'*, Beirut, Dâr al-Kutub al-'Ilmiyya, 1986.
Kymlicka, W., *A Liberal Theory of Minority Rights*, Oxford, Clarendon Press, 1995.
Linant de Bellefonds, Y., 'La jurisprudence égyptienne et les conflits de lois en matière de statut personnel', *Journal de Droit International*, 3, 1960.
Mahmassânî, S., *al-Qânûn wa-l-'alâqât al-dawliyya fî-l-islâm*, Beirut, Dâr al-'ilm li-l-malâyîn, 1972.
Modood, T. (ed.), *The Politics of Multiculturalism in the New Europe: Racism, Identity and Community*, London and New York, Zed Books, 1997.
Muldoon, J., *Popes, Lawyers and Infidels*, Liverpool, Liverpool University Press, 1979.
Raz, J., *Ethics in the Public Domain. Essays in the Morality of Law and Politics*, Oxford, Clarendon Press, 1994.
Ricœur, P., *Le Juste*, Paris, Esprit, 1995.
Salâmah, A., 'al-Maqsûd bi-Ahkâm al-*sharî'a* al-Islâmiyya allatî tantabiqû fî Masâ'il al-Ahwâl al-Shakhsiyya li-ghayr al-Muslimîn', *al-'Ulûm al-Qânûniyya wa'l-Iqtisâdiyya*, Cairo, 1960.
Sarakhsî, *Kitâb al-Mabsût*, Cairo, 1906.
Vitta, E., 'The conflict of personal laws', *Israel Law Review*, 5/2–3, 1970.
Walzer, M., *On Tolerance*, New Haven CT and London, Yale University Press, 1997.

Index

Aarnio, A. 25, 34, 35
Abâza, Alî 98
Abâza, Khamîs 98
'Abbas Pasha 106
'Abbasiyya (lunatic asylum) 270
'Abd Allâh, 'I.D. 369, 370
'Abd Allah, Sayyid/Sally 301, 302
'Abd al-Rahmân, J.J. 369, 370
'Abd al-Wahhâb, S.D. 369, 370
Abdalla, E. 366, 370
'Abduh, Muhammad 130–32, 138
Abraham(ic) 118, 237
Abû Sa'ûd, R. 369, 370
actiones see personae, res and actiones 10, 55
âdâb 122, 125
Adam 148, 276
âdamiyya 276
'adhâb 96, 99, 111
Afghani, al- 132
'afrît 152
Agnes (case of _, a transsexual) 80, 203
Agrama, Hussein 136
Agrarian law (Egypt), Article 156 §2 241, 260
ahliyya 115, 256, 273, 276, 300
Ahram Center for Political and Strategic Studies 367, 370
akrasis 75, 79
Aladdin 167
al-Ahrâm 143, 166, 168
al-asl 174
Al-Azhar University 301, 302, 314
Alexandria(n) 98, 114, 212, 218, 349–54, 359, 367, 370, 371
al-hajr 272, 274, 276, 290, 291
'Ali, I.M. 342
aliéné interdit 281
aliéné interné 281
aliéné non interdit 281, 291
Alleaume, Ghislaine 5
al-majnûn 264, 271, 272, 277, 279, 280, 283, 284
al-mîrî 106
al-nazar lahu 277
al-sirât a-mustaqîm 147–48
Althusser 25
al-Manâr 132
al-Urwa al-wuthqa' 132
Amenhotep 153
American University in Cairo vii, viii, 168
amina 58
amrâd rûhâniyya 144
anâ 58, 59
anâ mazûr 145
'andu wâhid 145
'âqil 149
'âql 147, 149, 151, 276, 278
Arendt, H. 41, 61, 63
Aristotle, Aristotelian 10, 44, 118, 186
Arkoun, M. 57, 60, 63
Arminjon, P. 366, 370
Arnaldez, R. 58, 59, 63
Arnaud, A.J. 32, 34, 35, 38, 227–29, 262, 263, 315, 316
Article 15 (Egyptian Constitution) 243
Article 66 (Egyptian Constitution) 240, 242, 243
Asad, Talal 89, 90, 111, 113, 135, 137
Ash'arism 57
ashâb al-rutab 103
Ashmûn, town of 97
Assier-Andrieu, L. 258, 261, 262
asyâd see also zâr 152
Asyut 254
attâr 156
Aubry, C. 24, 34, 35
Audard, C. 175
Augustinian 119
Austin 209

Ave Maria (film) 329, 334
Avicenna 58, 59

Badri, Sheikh Yusif al- 303
Baer, Gabriel 110, 113
Balandier, G. 46, 61, 63
Bälz, K. 315, 339, 341, 342
Baqlî, Muhammad Qandîl al- 111, 113
Baron, M. 191, 193, 194
barrâni, barrânia 173
Barry, B. 190, 193, 194
Barsum, G. 370
Beccaria 88–90
Beignier, B. 194
Ben Achour, Y. 63
Ben Nefissa, S. 248, 250, 251, 262
Benslama, F. 59, 60, 63, 64
Bentham 20
Berger, Maurits vi–viii, 4, 262, 342, ch. 13
Berger, P. 33
Bernard-Maugiron, N. vii, viii, 4, 262, 288, ch. 12
bi'l-qadâ' wa'l-qadar 92
Bicêtre Hospital (Paris) 289
Bideiwî, Alî 98
Bideiwî, Dissoûkî 98
Bideiwî, Muhammad 98
Bischias, Eliyahu 367
Bloch, E. 183, 192, 194
Boèce 62
Boëtsch G. 257, 261, 262, 308, 315, 316, 342, 343
Boghdadi, H. 366, 370
Bolam vs Friern 314
Boltanski, L. 35, 79, 81, 192, 194
Bonin, P-Y. 190, 193, 194
Boré, L. 340–42
Botiveau, B. 236, 260–62
Botros, S. 314, 315
Bounfour, A. 168
Bouretz, P. 314, 315
Boxill, B.R. 192, 194
Brague, R. 58, 59, 63, 64
Brinton, Jasper 110, 114
Brown, Nathan J. 110, 114, 366, 370
Buddhism 14
Burguière, A. 18, 33, 35
Burke, Kenneth 136
Bussy, F. 339, 342

Cadiet, L. 339, 342
Cahen, C. 366, 370
Caillé, A. 342
Cairo University vii, ix
Campbell, T.D. 194
Cannon, Byron 110, 114
Canterbury vs Spence 314
Cap Bon 172
Capitant, H. 291, 292
Cappelletti, M. 339–42
Carrithers, M. 10–12, 14, 32, 35–38, 61, 64
Carty, J.A. 315
Carzo, D. 315
Case no 2783 (Criminal Court of Cairo) 219
Case no 5471 (Mahram Bey, Alexandria) 212, 218
Case no 5719 (Rûd al-Farag, Cairo) 213–15, 221, 222
Case no 7158 (Sâhil, Cairo) 213–15
Catholic University of Leuven vii, viii
Catholic(s), Catholic Church, catholicism 328–30, 334, 350–60, 362, 367
Cayla, O. 316
CEDEJ (Centre d'Études et de Documentation Économique, Juridique et Sociale) viii, ix, 5, 61, 139, 262, 288, 366, 370
Cerutti, S. 258, 261, 262
Chabry, L. and A. 368, 370
Chahine, Youssef 334, 342
Chartier, R. 35
Chatterton vs Gerson 314
Chazel, F. 35, 37
Chevallier, J. 339, 342

Christian, Christians, Christianity 10, 14, 40, 56, 58, 97, 118, 148, 150, 159, 167, 265, 329, 348, 351, 354–58, 360, 362, 363, 367–70, 372
Civil Code (Egypt) 128, 239, 268, 269, 271, 272, 350, 353
Civil Code (France) 192, 297, 314
Civil Code (Iraq) 282, 283, 286
Civil Code (Switzerland) 291
Civil Code (Syria) 289
CNRS (National Center for Scientific Research) viii, ix, 4, 288, 366
Code of Civil and Commercial Procedure (Egypt) 322, 324, 334, 344
Code of Personal Status (Muhammad Qadrî Pâshâ's) 269, 271, 280
Code of Selected Enactments *see also* Qânûn al-Muntakhabât 104
Colin, M. 291, 292
Collins, S. 10, 32, 35–38, 61, 64
Colliot-Thélène, C. 32, 36
Committee of Codifications (Iraq) 283
Copt(s), Coptic 79, 82, 143, 158, 166, 167, 341, 354, 363, 367
Cottingham, J. 193, 194
Coulter, J. 31, 34–36, 79, 82, 228
Courbage, Y. 366–70
Court of Appeal (Egypt) 245, 247, 300, 306, 307, 315, 341, 366
Court of Cassation (Egypt) 245, 260, 261, 315, 334, 339, 340, 354, 355, 358
Court of Judicial Review (Egypt) 245, 247
Courty, G. 33, 36
Couthon 289
Cranor, C., F. 187, 193, 194
Cromer, Lord 86, 88, 110, 114
Cusson, M. 256, 261, 262
da'wâ al-ilghâ' 323
da'wâ al-qadâ' al-kâmil 323
dâr al-harb 346
dâr al-islâm 346
Daressy, G. 167, 168
Darwall 192
Daval, R. 51, 52, 61, 62, 64
De Benoist, A. 42, 61, 64
Deguilhem, Randi ii, 4
Debbasch, C. 342
Declaration of the Rights of Man 28
Decree of Replacing Flogging by Imprisonment *see also Lâ'ihat tabdîl al-darb bi'l-habs* 87, 88
Defrance, J. 33, 36
Delaubadère, André 337
Dennet, D.C. 369, 370
Descartes 56, 58
Descombes, V. 53, 62, 64, 79–81
Deswarte, M.P. 343
dhât 57
dhimmî(s) vii, 346, 347, 358, 360, 365, 368, 370
Dijon, X. 34, 36
disciplina 122
diyya 92, 94, 95, 97
djinn(s) viii, 143–46, 148–54, 160, 164–67
Doctors' Syndicate (Giza) 298, 302
Dodier, N. 80, 81
Dols, M. 266, 292
Drew, Paul 198, 227, 228
Druet, F.-X. 37, 38, 343
Duerr, H.P. 18, 33, 35, 36
Dulong, R. 222, 228
Dumont, A. 18
Dumont, Louis 22, 33, 34, 36, 261, 262
Dupret, Baudouin ii, v, vi, viii, Introduction, ch. 1, 63, 118, 119, 134, 136, 137, 139, 162, 167, 168, 193, ch. 8, 258, 262, 288, 289, ch. 11, 341, 343, 366
Durkheim, E. 11, 32, 35–37, 50

École des Hautes Études en Science Sociale (EHESS), Paris, ix, 64
Egyptian National Archives 87, 98, 110
Eisenstadt, S.N. 135, 137
Ejchenrand, J. 167, 168
Elgeddawy, K. 366, 370
Elias, Norbert, Eliasian 4, 16–21, 30, 32, 35–37, 63, 119, 120, 122, 123, 125, 135, 138, 266, 267, 289, 292, 298, 301, 304, 305, 309, 311, 313–16, 338, 359, 362, 368, 370
El-Nahal, J. 289, 292
Engel, L. 34, 36, 227, 228, 341
Enlightenment 88–91, 109, 128, 295
Errera, R. 192, 194
ESF (European Science Foundation) iv, 4, 288
Espéronnier, M. 112, 114
Etzioni, A. 40, 45, 61, 64
eudaimonia 119
European University Institute (Florence) x, 138

Fahmy, Khaled viii, 2, ch.4, 273, 290, 292, 305, 315, 316
falâsifa 57
fallâhîn 121
falsafa 57
Farag, I. 135, 136, 138
Fargues, P. 366–70
fasîkh 159
Fattal, Antoine 366, 370
fatwâs 121, 130–32, 137, 139, 302
Ferrié, J.N. v, ix, 2, 32, 37, ch.3, 136, 137, 257, 261, 262, 307, 312, 315, 316, 341–43
Fichte 11
fiqh (literature, manuals, doctrines, principles, concepts, provisions, tradition) 34, 92, 93, 117, 125–27, 136, 270, 273–76, 281, 283–88, 292, 297, 346
Fletcher, R. 369, 370
Forst, R. 183, 184, 192, 194
Foucault, M., Foucauldian 14, 25, 34, 37, 90, 100, 104, 108, 112–14, 122, 125, 264–67, 286, 289, 292, 307, 315, 316
Freud(ian) 15, 204, 291
Frogneux, N. 342, 343
fuqahâ 57, 303

Ganty, E. 37, 38, 343
Garfinkel, H. 80–82, 197, 203, 227–29
Garrigou, A. 32, 35–37
Gasper, M. 135, 136, 138
Gauchet, M. 315, 316
General Alliance against Racism and for the Respect of French and Christian Identity (AGRIF) 329
General Instructions Addressed to Public Prosecutors in Criminal Cases 225
Gérard, P. 343, 344
Gharbiyya, province of 98
Ghazali 58
Gibbard, A. 78, 80–82
Gizeh 143, 149
Godard, Jean-Luc 329
Goodwin 187
Gounot, E. 16, 28, 32, 34, 37
Gueth, Anton 12
Guinchard, S. 340, 343
Gumplowicz 20

hâbat 172, 174
Habermas(ian) 4
hadîth(s) 137, 264, 288
Hallaq, W.B. 136, 138
Hamadsha 168
Hamzah, Dyala 136
Hanafî, Hanafite: doctrine, law, legist 93, 94, 268, 269, 271, 276, 277, 280, 283, 290, 334, 361, 369
Hanafi, Muhammad 97

Hanbal Ahmad b. 94, 278, 288
Hanbali(s) 268, 271, 278, 284, 290
Hanîfa, Abu 94
haqq 60, 128, 262, 299
harami 85
Haroche, C. 194
Hart, Herbert L.A. 205–7, 209, 210, 226, 227, 229
hasad 158
Hassan, Muhammad b. al- 94
Haydar, A. 279, 289, 291, 292
Hecquard-Theron, M. 339, 343
Hegel 24, 56
Heidegger, Heideggerian 48, 79
Henry, C. 33, 37
Herder 33
Heritage, J. 81, 82, 227–29
hermeneutique du self, hermeneutic(s) 53, 62, 71, 79, 80
Hesnard, A. 261, 262
Heyd, Uriel 112, 114
hifz 278
Hill, T. Jr. 192, 194
Hindawy, N.D. 261, 262
hisba, hisbiyya vi, 4, 129, 130–32, 136, 273, 290, 293, 310, 311, 318–21, 323, 325, 327, 329, 331, 333–39, 341, 343, 344
hitk 'ird 212
Hobbes 20
Hodgson, M. 368, 371
Höfert, A. 138, 139
Honoré 207, 227, 229
Horton, G. 369, 371
Hoyle, Mark S.W. 110, 114
hudûd 101, 111, 237, 260
Humboldt University (Berlin) x
huqûq 60, 128, 129, 281, 341, 344
Husserl 211

Iblîs 148, 167
Ibn 'Âbidîn 369, 371
Ibn Qudâma 276, 284, 290–92
Ibrâhîm, Khawâja 97
ifâqa 275, 280, 283, 284
iftâ' 129–34, 137, 317
ihtisâb 129–33
ijtihâd 129–34, 136, 138
Ilbert, Robert ii, 5, 366, 367, 371
Ilhâmî Pasha 106
Imbâba (Cairo) 142, 151, 166, 167, 169
Institut d'Études Politiques d'Aix en Provence ix
Institut d'Études Politiques de Paris viii
Institut Français du Proche-Orient vii, viii
iqrâr 92
IREMAM (Institut de Recherche et d'Études sur le Monde Arabe et Musulman) 4
irshâd 121
Isambert, F.A. 37
islâh 120, 124, 126, 130, 132, 133
Ismâ'îl, K.S. 343

Jabartî, 'Abd al-Rahmân al- 100, 112, 114
Jackson B.S. 37, 202, 227, 229
Jackson, S. 137, 138
Jacob, A. 62, 64, 65, 195
Jacques the Fatalist 78
Jallâd, Fîlîb 112–14
Jam'iyya al-Haqqâniyya, al- 92
Jambu-Merlin, R. 368, 371
Je vous salue Marie (film) 329, 330
Jew(s), Jewish, Judaism 100, 112, 118, 148, 167, 348, 349, 353–55, 366, 367, 369, 370,
Johansen, B. 136, 138
Jori, M. 315
Jorion, B. 192, 194
Joseph (the prophet) 334
Joseph, Isaac 308, 315, 316
Josserand, L. 291, 292
junûn ghayr mutbiq, al-majnûn ghayr al-mutbaq 274, 278, 279, 280, 283

junûn mutbiq, al-majnûn al-mutbaq 274, 279, 280, 283

kadhâba 175
Kamel 172–74, 182
Kamel, T.M. 262
Kant, Kantian 13, 15, 21, 28, 29, 39, 42, 44, 56, 58, 65, 183, 185, 204, 205, 301
Karaite 367
karâma, al-karâma fûq kul shay' 162, 163
Kâsânî, A.B. al- 276, 290, 292
Kelsen, Hans 25, 34, 37
Kennedy, J. 166, 168
Kennedy–Smith Rape Trial 82, 229
Khalil 341, 343
khammas 158
Khanka Hospital 270
Khankî, Azîz 86, 110, 115
Khatchadourian, H. 194
Khirâqî, al- 278
Khnum 153
khul' 274
King, P. 369, 371
kirbâç see also kurbâj 100
Kishk 132
Kitab al-nafs 59
Komter, M. 80, 82, 228, 229
Kûmî, 'A. al- 135, 138
kunâfa 100, 112
kurbâj see also kirbâç 100
Kûsûnî, 'A.D. al- 369, 371
Kymlicka, W. 369, 371

lâ darar 273
La dernière tentation du Christ (film) 329
La Fontaine, J.S. 13, 14, 32, 37
Lâ'ihat tabdîl al-darb bi'l-habs see also Decree of Replacing Flogging by Imprisonment 2, 87–91, 108–10
labs 146, 150, 310
Lacroix, B. 32, 35–37
Ladrière, P. 54, 56, 62–64
Laligant, M. 339, 343
lams al-shaytân 145
lamsa 'ardiyya 145
Langbein, John 90, 111, 115
Lascoumes, P. 344
Layish, A. 136, 138
Le Dœuff, M. 184, 192, 195
Lebensform 40
Leithy, el- 112, 114
Lenoble, J. 27, 34, 37
Lévi-Strauss, C. 81, 82
Lewis, Bernard 110, 115, 139
Linant de Bellefonds, Y. 366, 367, 371
Locke, J. 20, 22, 34, 37, 88, 127, 301
Luckmann, T. 33
Ludwig-Mayerhofer, W. 135, 138
Luhmann 30
Lukes, S. 10, 13, 14, 32, 35–38, 61, 64
Luther 119
Luxor, Louxor 152, 168

ma'tûh 277
Macdonald, D.B. 167, 168
Maclagan, W.G. 185, 186, 193, 195
madhhabs 268, 275, 276, 278, 354
mahâkim 92, 115
Mahkâmat al-Qadya 89
Mahkâmat Tanta 98
Mahmassânî, S. 366, 371
Maison Méditerranéenne des Sciences de l'Homme 5
majâlis, majâlis siyâsiyya 87, 92, 98, 100
Majalla (of 1877), Ottoman civil law 268
majlis 'urfî 235, 248–50, 253, 255–58
Majlis al-Ahkâm 92–94, 98, 106, 111–13
Majlis al-dawla 315, 343
Majlis Tanta 99
makhâwî 152
Mâlik 94, 278

Maliki 268, 275
Margalit, A. 81, 82
maslaha 132, 319, 322, 342
maslaha al-âmma 132
mass al-shaytân 143
Masson, D. 262
Masud, K.M. 136, 139
Mathieu, B. 195
Matoesian, G. 80, 82, 227, 229
Mauss, M. 10–14, 30, 32, 36, 37, 55–57, 62, 64, 167, 204, 227, 229, 259
McFall, L. 195
MacIntyre, A. 135, 136, 138
Mead, G.H. 34, 35, 38, 39, 48, 50, 52, 61, 62, 64, 181
Mehmed, Ali viii, 85, 89, 91, 100–2, 104, 109, 110, 113–15, 269, 272, 312
Melden, A.I. 195
Messick, B. 136, 139
Meulders-Klein, Marie-Thérèse 9, 21, 32, 33, 38, 260, 262
Michot, J. 63, 64
Minûfiyya, al-, province of 95, 111
Minya 254
Mirghinânî, B.D. al- 276, 290, 292
Mixed Courts, the 86, 87, 110, 114
Modood, T. 369, 371
Moerman, M. 31, 34, 38, 226–29
Mona 155
Montefiore, A. 38, 314, 316
Montesquieu 88
Morel 339
Morsy, S.A. 166, 168
Moureau-Bondy, C. 79, 82
mudîriyya 95, 111
mufti(s) 92, 94, 130–32, 139, 302, 317
muhtasib 100, 290
mujtahid 130
mukallaf 276
Muldoon, J. 369, 371
Munîb, M.K. 290, 292
Murdoch, I. 183, 192, 195
Musa, Abu 94
mush sâba 173
Musil 15
mustaftî 121, 131, 132, 137
Mu'tazilism 57
mutakallimûn 57

na'ksû 173
nabbût 93, 94, 98
Nachi, M. v, vi, ix, 2, 3, ch. 2, 167, ch. 7
nafaqa 278
nafs 57–59, 147, 148, 278
Nassîm, Rahmîn 100
National Confederation of Associations of Catholic Families 329
nâzir 106
nefesh 58
Neuberg, M. 227, 229, 315, 316
New York University viii
Niffarî, Muhammad b. 'Abd al-Jabbâr, al- 264, 288, 291, 292
nisba 173, 174, 181
Niyâba 314, 316, 322
nuqta 156, 167

Ockham, William of 22, 119
Ogien, R. 79, 81, 82
Orthodox 201, 273, 350–52, 356, 359, 361, 367
Ost, F. 27, 34, 37, 315, 316, 343, 344
Ouafik 308, 315, 316
ould bled 173, 174, 181
Oxford University viii

Pacteau, B. 344
paideia 122
Paperman, Patricia 80–82, 190, 191, 193, 195
Parizeau, M.H. 314, 317
Paton, A. 85–87, 110, 115
Peers, Douglas 111–13, 115
Penal Code (Egypt) 95, 113, 240, 243, 255, 260, 261, 302
Penneau, J. 314, 317
Peristiany 261

personae, res and actiones 10, 55
Peters, R. 34, 38, 89, 102, 103, 111–13, 115, 256, 261, 262, 366
Petit, J.-L. 45, 64
Pinel 289
Pinès, S. 63, 65
Plato(nic) 118, 186
Powers, D. 136
Princeton University viii
'principle of difference' 43, 44
'principle of equal freedom' 43
prosopari 58
Protestant 125, 351, 356, 360, 362, 367
psukhe 58
Pufendorf 32, 227
Putnam, H. 80, 82

qâdî 92–95, 97, 99, 111
Qadrî Pâshâ, Muhammad 269–71, 279, 280, 289, 291, 292
qalb 147
Qânûn 124, 126, 273, 297, 315, 317, 324, 341, 344, 370, 371
Qânûn al-Filâha 100
Qânûn al-Madani 289, 291, 292
Qânûn al-Muntakhabât *see also* Code of Selected Enactments 104
Qânûn al-Sultânî 95, 99, 100, 101, 103, 104, 112
Qaradawi al- 132
qarîn 152–54
Qasr al-'Aynî Medical School 272, 279
qatl 92
qatl 'amd 92
qawâ'id 128, 315
qisâs 92, 94, 95, 237, 238, 260

Rabbinite, Rabbinic 367
Racy, J. 291, 292
Radi, S. 79, 82
Radwan, Z. 262
Rafi'î, Abd al-Rahmân al- 86, 110, 115
Rangeon, F. 344
Rao, Anupama 111, 115
Rau, C. 24, 34,35
Rawls, J. 39, 41–45, 61, 65, 183–85, 190, 192, 193, 195
Raz, J. 369, 371
Razi, Fakhr al-Din al- 58
res see personae, res and actiones 10, 55
Ribordy, F.-X. 263
Ricci, J.C. 342
Ricœur, P. 23, 24, 26, 29,34, 36–39, 48, 50, 52, 53, 61, 62, 65, 184, 189, 192, 193, 195, 227, 229, 338, 341, 343, 344, 357, 368, 371
Rîda', Rashid 130, 131, 136, 139
Ridha 172–81, 184, 188
Rigaux, F. 34, 38, 339, 344
Rogan, E. ii, viii, 289, 293
Roman(s) 10, 14, 55, 355
Roman Empire 12, 54, 57, 90, 92, 108, 118, 198, 367
Rommel, G. 24–26, 34, 38
Rorty, A. 21, 22, 33, 38, 189, 193, 195, 261, 263
rûh, arwâh 57, 143, 147–49, 161, 166
Rukush (little girl) 158, 159
rushd, al- 280

Sa'id Pasha 105–7, 111
Sacks, H. 81, 82, 203, 211, 227, 229, 230
sâdât kirâm 103
sâhib al-haqq 128
Sahlieh, Abu S.A.A. 263, 366, 370
Saint Bonaventura 119
Saint Pious X Association 329, 334
Saint-Joseph University (Beirut) ix
Sakaranaho, T. 136, 139
Sakaya 154
Salâmah, A. 366, 369, 371
Salgo vs Leland 314
Sâlim, Latîfa 86, 110, 111, 115
Salvatore, A. v, x, 2, ch. 5

Sandel, M. 42–45, 61, 65
Sandwith, F.M. 270
Sanhûrî Pâshâ, 'Abd al-Razzâq al- 283
Santoro, E. 135, 136, 139
Sarakhsî, S.D. al- 276, 290, 293, 369, 371
Saunders, L.W. 166, 168
Savatier, R. 34, 38
Sâwî, A.S. 344
Sayyeda Aisha 159
Sayyeda Zeinab 159
Schapp, W. 39, 46–49, 61, 65
Schomu'im, Ben 367
Schrader, Abby 112, 113, 115
Schrader, G. 48, 61, 65
Schütz, A. 33, 203, 227, 229
Scorsese, Martin 329
Searle, J.R. 38
Sève, Lucien 62, 65, 186–88, 193, 195
Sha'rawi, al- 132
Shâfi'î, al- 94, 268, 271, 278, 290, 293
shakhs, *shakhsiyya* 58, 60, 240, 292, 322, 370
sharî'a V, 2, 38, 91–96, 98, 99, 101, 103, 108, 111, 115–17, 119–21, 124–29, 131–37, 139, 260, 267, 270–75, 277, 283, 286, 292, 303, 304, 317, 358, 368, 369, 371
Sharrock, W. 79, 82
Shaykhzâda 112, 115
shaytân, al- 148, 150, 173
Sheikha Nadia 145, 167
Sherif, A.O. 263, 343
Shifa 59
Sidaway vs Board of Governors Bethlem Royal Hospital 314
Sirhank, Ismâ'îl 112, 115
Sitz im Leben 26, 27
siyâsa 91–96, 98, 99, 109, 273, 286
Skovgaard-Petersen, J. 130, 136, 139, 314, 317
Smith, W.C. 135, 139
Sohag 254
Soheir 151, 156
Sorbonne University vii
Sosoe, L. 61, 65
Spaemann, R. 183, 192, 195
St Thomas (Aquinas), Thomist 56, 57, 118, 119
Stockinger, P. 32, 38, 227, 229
Stoic(s), Stoicism 14, 55, 118, 119
Strauss, A.L. 35, 38
Suchman, L. 80, 82
Suez crisis (1956) 349
sulh 156, 157
Sultan ('Umar Bey's slave) 106, 107
Supreme Constitutional Court (Egypt) 134, 241, 243, 260, 263, 324, 325, 336, 337, 341
Sura V: the Dinner table 237, 238
Sura VI: The Cattle 238
Sura XI: Hood 237
Sura XIV: Abraham 237
Sura XVII: The Children of Israel 237
Suyûti, J.D. al- 290, 293

ta'zîr 99, 101, 102, 237
tahdhib 121
tahkîm al-'urfî 248
Talal, Asad 89, 113
tamaddun 121, 122, 128
Tantawi, Sayyid 302
Tanzimat 88, 91, 113
Taylor, C. 13, 32, 38, 51, 58, 62, 65
telos 41, 122
Testament, New 367
Testament, Old 367, 369
Teubner, G. 25, 34, 38
tha'r 248, 251–58
Thai (cultural context)
Thailand 31, 227
The Immigrant (*al-Muhâjir*) (film) 334
Thévenot, L. 35, 79, 81
Thielmann, Jörn 136, 290, 293, 344
'three Cs' (*corvée*, corruption and *courbash*) 86

'ulamâ' 103
'Umar Bey Wasfî 106, 107
umma 126
University of Amsterdam vii, 366
University of Liège (Belgium) ix
University of Montreal (Canada) ix
University of Sfax (Tunisia) ix
Unsal, A. 255, 261, 263
'Utayfî, J.D. al- 289–91, 293

van de Kerchove, M. 315, 316, 339, 343, 344
Vatin, J.C. 194
Vedel, Georges 337, 339, 344
Vergesellschaftung 119, 123
Veyne, P. 38, 65
Vitta, E. 366, 368, 371
Voltaire 89, 90

Waardenburg, J. 63, 65
walî 277, 280
Waline, M. 28, 34, 38
Walzer, M. 41, 61, 65, 369, 371
Watson, R. 31, 34, 35, 38, 81, 82, 197, 227–29, 315, 317
wazna, waznât 173, 174
Weber, M. 20, 33, 36, 38
wilâya 277, 278
Williams, B. 62, 65, 79, 80, 82, 192, 195
Wittgenstein, L. vii, 40, 227, 230
wujûh al-nâss 103

yafiq 264, 279, 280, 284
Yannakakis, Illios 366, 367, 371

zabtiyya 95
zafâra 156, 157, 158
Zaghlûl, Ahmad Fathî 86, 88, 110–13, 115
zahir 173
zâr see also asyâd 151, 152, 156–58, 164, 167, 168
zawâj 278
Zayd, Professor Abû Nasr Hamîd 334, 336, 337, 341–43
Zeghbib, H. 341, 344
Ziadeh, Farhat 88, 111, 115

www.ingramcontent.com/pod-product-compliance
Ingram Content Group UK Ltd.
Pitfield, Milton Keynes, MK11 3LW, UK
UKHW021816051026
15470UKWH00025B/8